Tax Indemnities and Warranties

Second Edition

Tax Indemnities and Warranties

A guide to the commercial and taxation considerations on the sale of a company

by
Tim Sanders LLB (Hons), Solicitor
of Theodore Goddard
Philip Ridgway BA LLM ATII, Barrister
of Deloitte & Touche

Tolley Publishing Company Limited
A member of the Reed Elsevier plc group

Published by
Tolley Publishing Company Limited
Tolley House
2 Addiscombe Road
Croydon
Surrey
CR9 5AF
0181 686 9141

Typeset by
Kerrypress Ltd, Luton
Bedfordshire

Printed and bound in Great Britain
by Redwood Books, Trowbridge, Wiltshire

ISBN 1 86012 336 8

Preface

The years since the first edition in 1992 have seen some of the longest Finance Acts on record, and some of the most fundamental changes to corporation tax since the introduction of the imputation system in 1972. Consequently, the warranties given on the sale of private companies have multiplied and the form of tax deeds altered considerably.

This book is intended for those who do not deal with tax warranties on a daily basis, although it is hoped that those who do will find it a useful reference work.

Since the last edition, the Inland Revenue have published their internal guidance manuals. Unfortunately, although they shed light on the Inland Revenue's thinking, there is litle statutory authority given to substantiate some of the points they make. Indemnities are still taxed by law and untaxed by concession. A regrettable situation for a document that forms part of nearly every private share sale.

We have taken the opportunity in updating the book to add new chapters on due diligence, deferred tax, statutory indemnities and the tax clauses and assumptions in finance leases.

We would like to take the opportunity to thank the army of people who helped in the production of this book. First, those who typed (and retyped and retyped) the manuscript: Yvonne King, Sarah Bush, Lisa White and Dawn Neill. Second, our colleagues at Theodore Goddard and Deloitte & Touche who provided many helpful comments, especially Alex Thomas who helped with proof reading and Bob Doye who provided the drinks; and thirdly, the staff at Butterworths, especially Val Akers and Jennifer Wilson, who both managed to keep smiling in the face of adversity. Notwithstanding their input, any errors remain ours.

Finally, as we said in the first edition, we would like to dedicate this book to our wives and children who have again put up with much, although the late night visits to the pub have tended to be fewer this time. So it is to Debra, Alexander and Sebastian, and to Kate, James and Alice that we dedicate this book, knowing that their interest in it was only an interest in getting it finished and that they will read no further than this.

Tim Sanders 27 November 1998
Theodore Goddard
150 Aldersgate Street
London EC1A 4EJ

Philip Ridgway
Deloitte & Touche
Hill House
1 Little New Street
London EC4A 3TR

Contents

Table of Cases

Table of Statutes

Table of Statutory Instruments

1973/334	**Income Tax (Employment) Regulations**	
	Reg 26	12.5.4
	Reg 29	12.5.4
	Reg 42(2)	12.5.4
1979/591	**Social Security (Contributions) Regulations**	
	1 Sch 3(3)	12.5.3
	6(2)	12.5.3
	12(2A)	12.5.3
1986/1711	**Stamp Duty Reserve Tax Regulations**	7.17.2
1992/3218	**Banking Co-ordination (Second Council Directive) Regulations**	12.2.6
1993/774	**Income Tax (Employment) Regulations**	
	Reg 42(2)–(3)	12.8.2
	Reg 80	12.8.2
1994/1995	**Foreign Companies (Execution of Documents) Regulations**	5.7
1994/3226	**Exchange Gains and Losses (Transitional Provisions) Regulations**	7.8.16
1994/3227	**Exchange Gains and Losses (Alternative Method of Calculation of Gain or Loss) Regulations**	7.8.16
1994/3230	**Local Currency Elections Regulations**	7.8.16
1995/2518	**Value Added Tax Regulations**	7.18.8, 7.18.9, 12.8.6
1995/1268	**VAT (Special Provisions) Order**	12.7.2
	Art 5	12.6.3
	(1)	7.18.7
	(2)	12.7.2
1995/1537	**Public Offers of Securities Regulations**	11.2.1
	Reg 9	11.2.3
1996/1349	**Exchange Gains and Losses (Transitional Provisions)(Amendment) Regulations**	7.8.16

European Union

EC Council Directive No 88/361 (25 June 1988)		
	Art 1	7.16.1

Chapter 1

The Tax Due Diligence Process

Introduction

1.1 The purchase of the shares in a private company is a complex and often time consuming process. It has been described as an area where the maxim *caveat emptor* is at its most rampant. A purchaser must therefore use all the means of protection available: due diligence investigations, warranties, indemnities, retentions from the purchase price, guarantees and earn outs. Although the investigation of the target and the negotiation of the tax warranties and tax deed are often looked at separately, they are part of an integrated process and during the period of negotiation there should be a constant flow of information between the purchaser's various advisers.

It is usual for the purchaser's solicitors to produce a standard form set of warranties; ideally the warranties should be tailored to meet the specific concerns of the purchaser before being sent to the seller. These concerns will be prompted by both the purchaser's actual knowledge of the industry in which the target operates and the investigating accountants' due diligence report. This chapter looks first at the purpose of the due diligence process and then looks at the tax section of a typical due diligence report.

Purpose of the due diligence process

1.2 The primary purpose of the due diligence process is to identify areas where there is a potential exposure to a tax liability in order to protect against that exposure by any or all of the following:

(a) a reduction in the price;

(b) a retention from the price;

(c) seeking the appropriate warranties and indemnities; and/or

(d) excluding or rejecting certain disclosures.

As a final resort, the most drastic course of action is to abort the acquisition.

Notwithstanding that the primary purpose of the investigation is to identify areas of potential tax exposure, there are a number of secondary objectives which should be borne in mind when carrying out the tax investigation.

Tax profile

1.2.1 The tax investigation can be used to build up a tax profile of the target. How has the target handled its tax affairs? Does it have an in house tax function? Does that in house function deal with complex matters or does it habitually seek outside advice? When seeking advice does it 'opinion shop' or does it readily accept advice which may be against the target's interests or wishes? What is the target's relationship with the Inland Revenue, Customs and Excise and foreign tax authorities? Has the target traditionally taken an aggressive stance on tax planning? Does it use 'tax products' or does it manage its tax charge within the confines of its daily operations?

The answers to these questions will help both with understanding the various revenue authorities' attitudes towards the target and also with the practical task of integrating the target into the acquiring group.

Post acquisition planning

1.2.2 The target will need to be integrated into the acquiring group in the most tax efficient way. The investigation can be used to identify which company in the acquiring group is the best company to acquire the target. If it is intended to dispose of some of the target's assets, which may include subsidiaries, the investigation can be used to identify either tax saving opportunities or identify inherent liabilities which could be triggered on a reorganisation of the target or a disposal of assets.

Tax planning for the seller

1.2.3 Another, and perhaps unexpected, use of the tax due diligence exercise is to identify tax saving opportunities for the seller. Where the target is an owner managed business, the identification of tax saving opportunities for the seller may smooth the acquisition and make the seller more prepared to accept a reduction in the price in the event that contingent liabilities are identified. It may persuade a reticent seller to sell thus preventing the target from being acquired by a competitor at a later date. Of course, where the purchaser does suggest tax planning opportunities to the seller, the seller should take independent advice. It is not the purchaser's job to underwrite the seller's tax charge.

Interaction between due diligence, the tax warranties and the tax deed

1.3 It should be remembered that the tax investigation does not form any sort of guarantee about the status of the target and is no substitute for full warranties in the purchase and sale agreement and a tax deed. Nevertheless, the fact that full warranties and an indemnity are to be given does not mean that the tax investigation should not be undertaken diligently. The information obtained will help the purchaser decide whether and at what price to proceed with the purchase.

The tax investigation

1.4 The tax issues to be investigated are generally the same as those covered by a full set of tax warranties, these are dealt with in Chapter 7; in this section we look at other types of information which may have a bearing upon the tax investigation.

General information

1.4.1 Before beginning any in-depth tax investigation, it is worth having an overall view of the target or target group. What type of business is being acquired? Which industry sector does it operate in? Has it grown organically or through acquisition? Is it an owner managed company or is it part of a large group? Is the company being sold as the result of a divestment programme or because the seller received an offer which was too good to refuse? Are there any specific tax risks associated with the business? Is the target an investment company and if so has this been accepted by the Inland Revenue? Finally, and perhaps more importantly, what are the issues which are important to the client?

The company's governing documents

1.4.2 Although the legal due diligence process will usually deal with compliance with the target's memorandum and articles of association, it is worth reviewing them from a tax perspective to see what types of shares have been issued and what sort of rights attach to them. The rights attaching to the shares will be important for ascertaining whether the shares are ordinary share capital or whether they give rise to issues under *Sch 18* to *ICTA 1988*.

Share register and share history

1.4.2.1 The share register will show who are the registered shareholders of the target: this may not be the beneficial owner of the shares and it will be important to ascertain who is actually selling the shares for the purposes of giving warranty and indemnity protection. Are they solvent?

Would they be able to meet any liabilities arising if a claim were made? Would the purchaser actually be able to find the seller in the event that it is necessary to make a claim?

The share register will show whether the target stands in a direct group relationship with its owner (indirect group relationships will be more difficult to ascertain and will require searches to be made against shareholders on the register and so on until ultimate ownership can be ascertained). It will also show whether any of the shareholders are non-resident, in which case it will be necessary to consider how easy it will be to recover the purchase price in the event of a breach of warranty or a claim under the tax deed. Should there be a retention from the price or an amount held in escrow? If so, how long should it be held?

It might be possible to ascertain whether the company is close, ie under the control of five or fewer participators, or under the control of its directors.

What the register will not reveal is whether any shareholder on the register as acting as nominee.

By going through the share register it should be possible to construct the shareholding history of the target. To assist in the tax investigation, it will be necessary to obtain details of all bonus issues, rights issues, conversions of shares, warrants and securities, any repayment of share capital, any redemptions of share capital and any purchases by the target of its own shares. When compiling the share history it will be necessary to take a view on whether to obtain details going back to incorporation for tax planning purposes. For example, *ICTA 1988 s 210* applies in certain circumstances so as to treat a bonus issue following a repayment of share capital as a distribution: it will therefore be necessary to ascertain whether there have been any such repayments of share capital.

Shareholders' agreements

1.4.2.2 It is increasingly commonplace to have shareholders' agreements in place which govern the control of the target. These should be reviewed to see whether, for example, they affect the group structure (see *Steele v EVC International NV (formerly European Vinyls Corporation (Holdings) BV)* [1996] BTC 425) or whether they require payment for group or consortium relief.

Group structure

1.4.2.3 Where the target group is complete, it is always wise to obtain or draw up a group structure chart and to confirm that this ties in with the seller's own opinion of the group structure. It is not unknown for the seller's company secretary, treasury and tax department all to have a different group structure chart.

The due diligence report — taxation section

1.5 The accountants' due diligence report will usually cover many issues and although the tax section will normally be drafted at the same time as the rest of the report, it will usually be necessary for the tax adviser to read the entire draft report before signing off on the taxation section to ensure that there are no other matters which have come to light during the rest of the investigation which could have a bearing on the tax liabilities of the target.

Introduction

1.5.1 The introductory section will usually set out the scope of the investigation and the sources of information relied upon. It is important for the adviser and the client to ensure that this is consistent with the terms of engagement.

Scope of the work

1.5.1.1 Before beginning the due diligence investigation it is preferable for the investigating accountants to discuss and agree in writing the scope of the investigation. This will include:

(a) the level of materiality; ie when should a tax issue be reported to the purchaser? Much will depend upon the size of the acquisition and the concerns of the purchaser;

(b) the companies to be investigated; where the target is being bought out of a group should other companies in the group be investigated? This is an increasingly common issue because the Inland Revenue have the power in certain circumstances to collect tax from a company which has been in the same group as a defaulting company;

(c) the period covered by the review; generally the Inland Revenue can assess for up to six years unless there is fraudulent or negligent conduct in which case they can go back 20 years. Depending upon time constraints, it is usual to review the last three years and then to take a decision on earlier years; obviously, if there are still open years before these, these should be investigated;

(d) areas of tax to be covered; much will depend upon the industry in which the target company operates as to whether specialist advice needs to be sought eg petroleum revenue tax;

(e) areas which are of importance to the purchaser;

(f) areas of specific risk identified by the purchaser;

(g) issues specific to the target's business or industry;

(h) staffing of the investigation;

(i) the timetable;

(j) the budget; and

(k) access to the target; the ability to investigate the target will be dependant upon whether key personnel are available to be interviewed and upon the availability of the target's tax files (see *ADT Ltd v BDO Binder Hamlyn* [1996] BCC 808 in which the investigating accountants had no access to the seller's personnel).

It is usual to include a paragraph which sets out the more material aspects of the scope of the investigation carried out.

Names of advisers and management who were consulted

1.5.1.2 It is usual to include the names of the advisers eg. auditors, tax advisers and corporate finance advisers, who were consulted and the documents and papers which were used. It is also usual to give the names of the management who were consulted and more importantly those who were not and the reasons why they were not. Where an adviser or member of management was not consulted, it is important to state why they were not consulted. Was access denied or were they simply not available whilst the investigation was being carried out?

Details of the companies excluded from the review

1.5.1.3 Because of time and budgetary constraints, it may be impossible to review all of the companies in the target group. The question of which ones to review may be answered by the question of materiality. Where only part of a group is being acquired, a decision will need to be taken whether any of the companies which are not being acquired need to be investigated. The status of other group companies is becoming increasingly important as tax legislation imposes secondary liabilities on other group members. For example, *ICTA 1988 s 767A* introduced by *FA 1994* and *ICTA 1988 s 767AA* introduced by *FA 1998* allows the Inland Revenue to collect unpaid corporation tax from the target if the target's previous owners or other members of the target's former group default in certain circumstances. Notwithstanding that the Inland Revenue have confirmed that they will originally seek to collect the tax from the former owners (see IR Tax Bulletin, October 1994 p 168), the risk still remains.

Obviously, the extent to which other group companies can be investigated will depend upon the degree of access given and the seller will understandably be reticent about giving access to what might be very sensitive information.

Tax computations

1.5.2 The introductory paragraph will usually include a statement to the effect that the target is resident for tax purposes in the United Kingdom either because of its place of incorporation or because of the place of management and control. Sometimes there is a negative statement to the effect that the target is not resident in any other jurisdiction. If the target is dual resident this should be stated.

In reviewing the target's tax returns the investigating accountant will in effect be 'marking' the former accountant's papers. In making those returns the former accountant will have taken a view on a number of items and this view will nearly always be more aggressive than the view taken by the investigating accountants. It is important to remember, therefore, that a different or more aggressive view is not necessarily a wrong view. There may be a potential exposure; however, it will be necessary to test this against the materiality criteria.

Status of tax computations

1.5.2.1 It is first necessary to identify the accounting periods under review and whether any of them are short as this may impact upon payment dates and filing dates under Pay and File. There should be a statement as to the status of the tax returns which should have been submitted during the period under review. Where the period under review is short, it may be necessary to go back before that period.

Major issues raised by the Inland Revenue

1.5.2.2 There should be a statement as to the major issues raised by the Inland Revenue. This should examine whether these were one off or whether they are likely to recur, and whether any special agreements were reached. If they were, it will be necessary to consider whether these will continue once the target has been acquired.

Foreign companies

1.5.2.3 Where the target group includes foreign companies, there should be a statement as to the status and outcome of tax audits carried out by foreign tax authorities. Where appropriate, foreign legal and tax advice should be taken. If local advice is to be taken, this should be factored into the timetable.

Claims and elections

1.5.2.4 There should be a statement to the effect that all claims and elections have been made within the statutory time limits. Where a claim or election is joint or requires the consent of another company it is necessary to confirm that the consent has been given and also that the claim, election or consent cannot be withdrawn after the agreement has been entered into. The agreement may need to provide for joint elections to be made after the date of the agreement, for example, where there is a claim to group relief, and possibly a contractual undertaking that where joint elections have been made they cannot be withdrawn without the purchaser's consent.

Taxation provision in the accounts

1.5.3 The most visible tax information is the tax charge provided in the accounts as this is available for public inspection. Many larger companies try to manage their tax charge so as to keep it within a certain range. Smaller companies, however, usually seek to minimise the charge on a year by year basis which means the actual tax charge can be quite erratic.

Balance sheet tax liabilities

1.5.3.1 There is usually a statement as to the balance sheet taxation creditor and debtor provision in respect of:

(a) corporation tax;

(b) advance corporation tax;

(c) tax withheld at source;

(d) overseas taxes;

(e) PAYE and NICs;

(f) VAT;

(g) stamp duty; and

(h) Interest and penalties.

There should also be a statement as to whether it is considered that these provisions are adequate. It is necessary to check that the tax computations are consistent with the provisions in the statutory accounts. This will ensure that there are no significant unprovided for tax liabilities.

Where there are differences between the accounting and taxation treatment of items in the accounts, an analysis needs to be carried out to see which are permanent differences and which timing differences.

Deferred tax

1.5.3.2 There should be a statement as to the adequacy of any deferred tax provision. If deferred tax is not accounted for, there should be a statement as to why this is, for example, losses carried forward or surplus ACT which is likely to be recoverable.

The treatment of deferred tax in the tax deed is dealt with in Chapter 10.

A calculation should be done to confirm that there would be no liability to corporation tax if the target disposed of all its capital assets for their book value.

Profit and loss charge for the last two years and reconciliation of tax charge

1.5.3.3 It is usual to provide a reconciliation of the tax charge. If the current rate of corporation tax is applied to the profits shown in the accounts, the figure arrived at will be different from the actual charge to corporation tax. The reconciliation of the tax charge shows how this difference arises. Where timing differences are not permanent, for example where the mismatch arises because of the difference between depreciation in the accounts and the rate of capital allowances for tax purposes, this will have already been accounted for in the deferred tax charge. Where timing differences are permanent, for example where expenses are disallowable for tax purposes ie business entertaining expenses or where an asset which is depreciated does not qualify for capital allowances, these will need to be added back for the purposes of taxation.

The company's auditors will have already done this exercise and usually it is a matter of checking their reconciliation.

Reliefs

1.5.4 The reliefs which may be available within the target are carried forward losses, ACT, capital losses and loan relationship debits. The extent to which these should be investigated depends mainly upon whether the purchaser is paying for them; if not, they will be a bonus. If they are to be paid for, the purchaser will have to ensure that nothing is done which will cause them to be disallowed. It is usual for the purchaser to pay for any reliefs only once they have been agreed and the target's tax liability reduced accordingly. If they are not being paid for, the seller should not be asked to warrant their availability.

Trading losses

1.5.4.1 There should be a statement as to the amount of trading losses being carried forward. Trading losses can be carried forward indefinitely and be set against the profits of the same trade. The losses are disallowed if in the three years either side of a change of ownership of the target there is a major change in the nature or conduct of the target's trade (*ICTA 1988 s 768*). This provision was specifically introduced to prevent companies trading in losses.

Advance Corporation Tax

1.5.4.2 There should be a statement as to the amount of ACT being carried forward. ACT can be carried forward indefinitely and set against the target's mainstream corporation tax liability. ACT will be disallowed if, in the three years either side of a change of ownership of the target there is a major change in the nature or conduct of the target's trade (*ICTA 1988 s 245*).

ACT is to be abolished from 6 April 1999; however, companies with surplus ACT at that time will continue to carry the surplus forward under a system of shadow ACT (unless they elect otherwise). The company will continue to calculate the ACT which would have been paid on a distribution (shadow ACT) and this will be set against the corporation tax charge and, to the extent that there is a difference between the shadow ACT and the amount of ACT which would have been set off against mainstream corporation tax under the current regime, carried forward surplus ACT will be able to be used to reduce the corporation tax payable against it. Under the new regime there will need to be a statement of surplus ACT carried forward and the likelihood of the target being able to use it.

Capital losses

1.5.4.3 During the 1980s, there was a large trade in capital losses. The Inland Revenue tested the efficiency of these sales in *Shepherd v Lyntress* [1989] STC 687. Following their defeat, the Inland Revenue introduced a new *Sch 7A* to the *TCGA 1992* (introduced in *FA 1993 s 88* and *Sch 8*). The effect of *Sch 7A* is to 'ring fence' losses within the group in which they were incurred. However, although the legislation prevented the use of bought in capital losses, it did not prevent a company with capital losses buying in a capital gain. Such schemes were stopped by *FA 1998 s 137* inserting a new *Sch 7AA* into *TCGA 1992*.

It is therefore necessary to ascertain what effect *TCGA 1992 Sch 7A* and *7AA* would have on the gains and losses of the target group.

It is necessary to ascertain whether any of the capital losses have arisen as a result of connected party transactions and therefore are only capable of being set off against gains with the same connected party under *TCGA 1992 s 18(3)*.

Presale dividends

1.5.4.4 If the target company has cash, it will normally be tax efficient for the seller to extract the cash by way of presale dividend before the sale otherwise the seller may be liable to tax on the cash assets of the target company. If the seller is a company, excess cash can be taken out by way of dividend provided the target has sufficient distributable reserves. Prior to April 1999 (no ACT should arise provided a group income election is in force). This can be done even if the target has insufficient cash resources by borrowing from the parent (keeping the dividend outstanding on inter-company loan account) and the purchaser putting funds into the target at completion and procuring that the target repays the inter-company debt at completion. The contract needs to be carefully drafted for both stamp duty purposes (to avoid the application of *s 57, SA 1891*) and capital gains tax purposes; (see *Spectros International plc (in voluntary liquidation) v Madden* [1997] STC 114). If the seller is an individual, the funds can be extracted by way of stock dividend which can reduce the capital gains tax liability on the sale (see Taxation Magazine 1996 Vol 138 (3579) pp 126–129 and (3580) pp 158–161).

Provided the presale dividend is paid within 14 days of the change of ownership, *Sch 7* to *FA 1997* will not apply (see *para 6* of *FA 1997 Sch 7*) and if paid more than 14 days before the change of ownership, the Inland Revenue have indicated that it is unlikely that *Sch 7* to *FA 1997* will apply (see Inland Revenue Bulletin No 29 (30 June 97) item 3).

Loan relationship debits and deficits

1.5.4.5 *Finance Act 1986* introduced a whole new regime for the taxation of the gains and losses and interest paid and received on loan relationships.

There should be a statement as to the losses, represented by debits and deficits which are capable of being carried forward and used in subsequent accounting periods. Again, anti-avoidance provisions apply to prevent a purchaser buying a company solely to gain the benefit of these losses.

Sale of business assets/subsidiary companies

1.5.5 It is necessary to ascertain the target company's history with regard to any assets or subsidiaries that it has sold.

Where assets have been sold, any gains made at the time may have been rolled over into other assets of the target or of the selling group. Where the gains have been rolled into assets of the target, the base cost of the target's assets will be correspondingly reduced and any subsequent disposal will give rise to a larger gain then might otherwise have been anticipated. Where the gain on an asset were held over into wasting assets, the purchaser will be concerned, inter alia, to ensure that any such gain is not material and likely to crystallise in the immediate future, for example, due to the expiration of the ten year period since the hold over (*TCGA 1992 s 154*).

Group reorganisation

1.5.6 Where the target has been involved in a group reorganisation, it is necessary to ascertain what role the target played. Where the target was moved around the group, it will probably be irrelevant to the purchaser; it will affect the cost of the target to the seller and the seller's capital gains tax computation. However, where the target has been involved by having received or disposed of other assets in the group, there may be latent gains within the target.

Details of any reorganisation

1.5.6.1 The steps in any reorganisation should be set out in some detail. This helps the purchaser to understand the target company or group and also the purchaser's advisers to focus on what has happened and more clearly ascertain the tax consequences. It is not unknown for the seller to be unsure as to the exact steps in a previous reorganisation or even for different people to provide different versions of what has happened. Obviously, where this occurs, the purchaser should be more careful about the warranties and indemnities obtained in this area.

Details of tax clearances obtained

1.5.6.2 Certain transactions can be cleared with the Inland Revenue in advance; notably transactions under *TCGA 1992 ss 135, 136, 139* and *140A* under *TCGA 1992 s 138*, transactions under *ICTA 1988 s 703* under *ICTA 1988 s 707* and transactions under *ICTA 1988 s 213* under *ICTA 1988 s 125.* Where such clearances were obtained, they should be examined to ensure that the transaction described is the one which was actually carried out. Where there are discrepancies these should be noted and the potential tax consequences examined. Where clearance was not sought and the transactions were within the ambit of a section for which clearance could be granted, this should be stated, and enquiries made as to why the clearance was not sought.

Financing

1.5.7 The proposed financing structure should be set out together with any suggested alternatives. The tax consequences of each should be stated.

International matters

1.5.8 It is increasingly common to have to involve advisers in other jurisdictions. Where this happens it is necessary to keep the client appraised of what is being done and how much it is costing. It is also necessary to project manage the due diligence process so that the information is received within the requisite time scale, is of the right quality and is co-ordinated.

Overseas reviews

1.5.8.1 Where the target group includes overseas companies or branches it will be necessary to employ foreign advisers. When doing this it is necessary to explain exactly what is required and by when. It is necessary to alter the documentation so as to deal with foreign law. Although this point is obvious, it is surprising how many tax deeds refer to six or seven year periods when the foreign jurisdiction has no concept of these time periods and rely on a final audit by the relevant authorities.

Transfer pricing

1.5.8.2 Transfer pricing is becoming increasingly important. It is necessary to ascertain the target company's exposure to transfer pricing adjustments and any likely tax liabilities. It is therefore necessary to examine the transfer pricing policy of the group of which the target is a member. Even if there is an acceptable policy, it is necessary to examine whether and how that policy has been implemented across the group. For accounting periods beginning on or after 2 July 1998 there are penalty provisions where the transfer pricing agreements of which the target is a party are not sufficiently documented. A statement given as to their adequacy of the transfer pricing documentation and any potential exposure.

Thin capitalisation

1.5.8.3 There should be an analysis of payments made to non-resident group companies and whether such payments could be treated as distributions under *ICTA 1988 s 209*. Where the payments are made to an overseas company which is controlled by a UK company it is often the case that any applicable double tax treaty will not override the UK legislation (for example, the UK/US double tax treaty).

Residence and CFC issues

1.5.8.4 Where the target has overseas subsidiaries it is necessary to address the question of whether any of them are controlled foreign companies ('CFCs'). The law in this area has been amended by *FA 1998* to take account of self-assessment. For accounting periods ending on or after 1 July 1999 the company making the return will have to assess whether a subsidiary is a CFC and make a return accordingly. Consequently, it will be necessary to review any overseas subsidiaries to ensure that they have been returned correctly.

PAYE and NIC's

1.5.9 There should be a statement as to the status of the completion and submission of all year end returns ie forms P9D, P11D, P14 and P35. Similarly, there should be a statement as to whether the monthly PAYE and NIC remittances have been made on a timely basis and if not whether adequate provision has been made for any interest and penalties. Other matters to consider are: whether all benefits provided to directors and 'higher paid employees' have been correctly accounted for on form P11D; whether the company pays premiums for directors' liability insurance; whether PAYE and NIC has been applied to all directors' remuneration.

Systems including dispensations

1.5.9.1 Details should be given of all dispensations which have been granted by the Inland Revenue and of any special agreements which have been reached. These should be compared with those negotiated by the purchaser and an analysis done of the effect of the acquisition.

Outcome of PAYE and NIC audits

1.5.9.2 Details should be given of any enquiries raised by the PAYE audit office, investigation section, special office and the DSS. Details should be given of any settlement that was reached and also whether the enquiry has ended or is still ongoing. It is also necessary to analyse whether the issues involved will affect future periods and whether it is likely that the company will be investigated again.

Summary of approved and unapproved share schemes

1.5.9.3 There should be a summary of any share schemes and profit related pay schemes. These are:

(a) approved employee share schemes (*Sch 9* to *ICTA 1988*);

(b) unapproved share schemes (*ICTA 1988 ss 136* and *139*);

(c) ESOTs (*FA 1989 s 68*);

(d) profit sharing schemes (*ICTA 1988 s 186*); and

(e) profit related pay schemes (*ICTA 1988 s 180*).

For each scheme the rules should be examined together with the formal approval by the Inland Revenue. There should be a statement as to whether the returns have been submitted within the prescribed time limits. There should also be an analysis of how the purchase will affect the various schemes.

Subcontractors in the construction industry

1.5.9.4 Where the business includes construction operations it is necessary to ascertain whether the construction industry tax deduction scheme has been applied. Basically, the scheme applies where the target company spends, on average, more than £250,000 a year on construction operations (this will increase to £1,000,000 in August 1999). It will apply to banks, building societies, insurance companies and large corporates.

Where the target company is itself a sub-contractor it is necessary to ascertain whether the company has complied with the regulations.

In both cases it will be necessary to examine the target's in house procedures to ensure that the regulations have been complied with. There is now potential for large tax exposures in this area.

VAT

1.5.10 The due diligence process will probably require a specialist team to investigate the VAT affairs of the target. At the most basic level, the report should state whether the target is registered for VAT; if it isn't it should state whether the registration thresholds have been exceeded during the previous 12 months or whether they are likely to be exceeded in the next 30 days? Is it advantageous to apply for voluntary registration? Allied with the question of registration is the question of penalties for late registration; whether any penalties have been provided for; and, what actions are being taken to rectify the position if the target has not been registered.

Summary of VAT position

1.5.10.1 There should be a general summary of the VAT position of the target. It should be stated whether the target is, or has been a member of VAT group, the name of the representative member, the names of the other companies in the VAT group and whether there are any outstanding VAT liabilities. As a member of a VAT group is jointly and severally liable for other liabilities of group members, consideration should be given to obtaining an indemnity for any outstanding VAT liabilities.

The VAT returns for the last two years should be examined to ensure that VAT has been correctly accounted for. In particular, it is necessary to ensure that VAT has not been reclaimed on excluded expenditure, that invoices necessary to support input tax recovery have been retained, that VAT returns have been filed within the correct time limits, that any tax has been paid within the requisite time limits and to the extent that there are interest and penalties that these have been adequately provided for.

There should be a statement as to any likely disputes with Customs & Excise. Issues to look at include any transfers of a going concern, land and property transactions, the capital goods scheme, any agency agreements the company has entered into and whether the company's accounting systems are adequate.

Outcome of control visits

1.5.10.2 The report should state when the last control visit was made and what the outcome was. Were there errors identified? It should state whether these have been corrected and whether there are any outstanding disputes.

Summary of penalties

1.5.10.3 The VAT regime includes numerous penalty provisions and it is unlikely that the target will have escaped without any of them applying. There should be a statement as to the current position and any penalties incurred within the previous two years.

Customs

1.5.11 Customs duties are becoming increasingly important. The report should consider whether all duties payable have been paid or accounted for and whether adequate provision has been made for unpaid duties and any interest and penalties.

It should state whether there have been any disputes and whether these have been resolved and also if similar issues are likely to arise in the future or if the issues are likely to affect future periods.

Details of duties payable on importation of goods

1.5.11.1 Where customs duties are payable, details should be given of the amounts and the goods on which they are payable.

Warranties and indemnities

1.5.12 After the various tax issues have been addressed it is usual to include suggestions as to which specific issues should be addressed under the warranties and tax deed so as to offer the most protection. These should be considered in conjunction with the *de minimus* limit in the agreement. If necessary, the limit should be excluded where it is apparent that a major liability will arise.

Details of warranties and indemnities given on acquisitions

1.5.12.1 Where the target company has acquired shares and the tax liabilities identified relate to those acquisitions or the companies acquired, it is necessary to examine any of the warranties or indemnities given to the target company at the time of the acquisition to see whether a claim can be made and what can be done to protect the position.

Impact of the proposed transaction

1.5.13 There will usually be an analysis of how the proposed transaction will affect the group structure and any liabilities that will arise on any subsequent reorganisation. Where it is proposed to sell off some of the assets of the companies acquired it will be necessary to examine whether any liabilities under *TCGA 1992 s 179* will arise if the assets are hived down into a new company for the purposes of the sale.

Similarly, if the past acquisition planning involves the amalgamation or rationalisation of trades it will be necessary to examine whether *ICTA 1988 ss 245* and *768* will apply to disallow carried forward ACT and losses.

Profit and cash flow projections

1.5.14 It is becoming increasingly common for the accountants to produce a computer model of the expected cash flows and projected profit and to compute the expected tax charge. This will give the purchaser an idea of how the acquisition finance can be serviced and the expected future returns. The assumptions on which the model is based should be stated and any anticipated deviations should be highlighted.

Following on from modelling the cash flows will be a computation of the expected tax charge and an analysis of the ability of the combined group to mitigate the charge. It is usual to include a summary of the timing of the expected tax charge.

Planning opportunities

1.5.15 Finally, it is usual to include any planning opportunities. Unless specifically requested these are likely to be the more obvious planning opportunities arising out of the due diligence report based upon future plans of the purchaser which have been explained to the investigating accountants rather than a specific analysis of the opportunities available.

Amongst the issues to be considered are:

(a) will the purchaser's post acquisition actions cause a disallowance of ACT and losses carried forwards or backwards?

(b) can capital allowances be disclaimed to reduce losses carried forwards where *ICTA 1988 s 768* could apply and what does the sale and purchase agreement say can be done?

(c) can the base costs in subsidiaries be increased by share reorganisations if there is an intention to dispose of them?

(d) can rollover relief claims be made?

(e) should foreign subsidiaries be transferred to another company in the group, for example a Dutch mixer?

(f) is there scope for rationalisation and the liquidation of subsidiaries to create capital losses?

(g) how do the accounting policies of the acquired company compare with those of the acquirer and will a change create a tax liability?

(h) an amended group income election should be submitted;

(i) what effect will a change in accounting reference date have?

(j) do any upstream loans give rise to distribution problems under *ICTA 1988 s 209*?

(k) can withholding taxes be saved by re-routing payments through the new group?

(l) how do the dispensations for PAYE and NIC compare and should they be updated?

(m) should the company become part of the acquirer's VAT group?

Obviously, there are far more issues to be considered; however, the basic rule is to do the housekeeping first and then to consider any reorganisations.

Chapter 2

Indemnities given on the Sale of Shares in a Private Company

Introduction

2.1 This chapter and the next three consider the taxation and drafting issues connected with the typical tax deed given by the seller on the sale of a private company. The sale of a private company usually takes one of two forms: either, the purchaser is approached by the proprietors of the target company who wish to realise the capital value locked in the target company or a larger, often public company, which sees the potential in a private company, approaches the target's shareholders. In either case, the purchaser will make detailed enquiries into the workings of the business to ascertain the price it must pay for the target company. It is, however, fair to say that the purchaser can never be fully confident that it has found out everything that there is to know about the target company. Furthermore, there is always the possibility that the seller has manipulated the affairs of the target company to make it look more attractive than is actually the case. In these circumstances, it is reasonable for the purchaser to require some protection against unforeseen and unprovided for tax liabilities. Because a tax claim is usually for a quantified sum, an indemnity provides the purchaser with a quicker route to recompense than the tax warranties which require the purchaser to establish breach, damage and quantum (see Chapter 6 below).

Indemnities are not, as a general rule, given where there is a bid for a public company; it would be absurd for a hostile bidder to suggest that the seller-shareholders should indemnify the bidder in the event that their calculations are wrong. Furthermore, the shareholders and management are usually quite distinct: the shareholders would object to being responsible for matters in which they weren't involved. Where an offer is made for a public limited company's shares, the requirement to publish annual reports and accounts means that there is a wealth of information in the public domain that makes it possible to learn far more about the company than would be the case in a private company sale. Where the company is also listed on the Stock Exchange, information is available because of the requirement to publicise certain transactions under the Stock Exchange's Admission of Securities to Listing (the *Yellow Book*). To a lesser degree this is also true of companies whose shares are dealt in on AIM. Listed companies and to some degree AIM companies tend to appoint public relations companies to publicise their activities and to give presentations to both shareholders and the press about the target company's activities. Where someone makes a hostile bid for a public company it is expected that they will take the risk of any unforeseen liabilities in the company. On the other hand, it is very rare for there to be a hostile bid for a private company (the authors know of only one).

A note on terminology

2.2 The terms 'tax deed', 'tax indemnity', 'tax deed of covenant' and 'covenant to pay' are often used to describe the document which protects the purchaser from unexpected tax liabilities in the target company. The terms are often used interchangeably and this can create some confusion. In the chapters that follow, the term 'tax deed' is used to describe the document regardless of its form. Where the form of the document is important the terms 'target indemnity', 'purchaser indemnity', 'covenant to pay' and 'hybrid covenant' are used to identify the different types of tax deed. These terms are explained in paragraphs 2.5.1–2.5.5 following.

What is a tax indemnity?

2.3 Typically, in agreeing to sell the shares in a private company, the seller will agree to give 'the usual tax indemnity.' In fact, although it is usual to give an indemnity, the form that it takes is by no means standard and will depend upon amongst other things the bargaining power of the parties, the perceived tax risks and the extent and findings of the due diligence exercise.

Commercial rationale

2.3.1 Commercially, the tax deed is no more than an agreement which allocates risk between the seller and the purchaser. At its simplest, it draws a line between two periods of time, typically either the periods pre and post completion or the periods pre and post the date of the last audited accounts, and then seeks to allocate the risk of a tax charge arising in the target between the seller and the purchaser. Having allocated the risk, it then seeks to carve out exceptions in certain specified circumstances. When drafting a tax deed the question to ask in the event of a hypothetical tax charge arising is: whose risk should it be? Shorn of all the legal verbiage that is all a tax indemnity seeks to do. The rest of the tax deed provides the mechanics for making a claim.

Legal definition

2.3.2 Legally, an indemnity is a separate, enforceable contract to hold someone harmless against loss. An indemnity can be contrasted with a contract of guarantee, which is only enforceable, unless the contrary intention is stated, if there is a primary obligation. If, for any reason, there is no primary liability, the contract of guarantee will fail.

The distinction between an indemnity and a guarantee was explained by Holroyd-Pearce LJ in the case of *Yeoman Credit Ltd v Latter* [1961] 2 All ER 281 at 295.

> 'An indemnity is a contract by one party to keep the other harmless against loss, but a contract of guarantee is a contract to answer for the debt, default or miscarriage of another who is to be primarily liable on the promises.'

Thus, in the case of *Coutts & Co v Browne-Lecky* [1947] KB 104 Oliver J held that the guarantor of a minor's overdraft could not be sued on the guarantee because under the *Infants' Relief Act 1874* the minor himself was not liable for the loan. Had the contact been one of indemnity, the fact of the minor's contractual incapacity would have been irrelevant because there would have been a separate contractual obligation. The actual decision in the *Coutts & Co* case is no longer valid after 9 June 1987 because of the *Minors' Contracts Act 1987*; however, the general principle remains '. . . and has raised many hair-splitting distinctions of exactly that kind which brings the law into hatred, ridicule and contempt by the public' (per Harman, J *Yeoman Credit Ltd v Latter* [1961] 2 All ER 281 at 298).

The approach now adopted by the courts is to try and discern the intention of the parties, and where one of the parties is under a disability, the courts will infer that the parties must have intended the contract to be one of indemnity. Moreover, it is now common to include in a guarantee a clause to the effect that the guarantee shall remain effective notwithstanding the disability of one of the parties. What then is the difference between an indemnity and a guarantee which provides that the guarantor will remain liable? The answer appears to be in the measure of damages. An indemnity holds that third party harmless against loss whereas a guarantee makes good a deficiency. The two may be very different. The modern tax deed is usually a hybrid in that it is enforceable as an indemnity and yet it usually provides for the indemnifying party to pay an amount equal to the tax suffered.

The difference between indemnities and warranties

2.3.3 A warranty is a contractual term, a breach of which gives rise to a right to damages. An indemnity is an enforceable contractual right which gives rise to a debt claim. In *Webb v Stenton* (1883) 11 QBD 158 at 527 Lindley LJ described a debt as '. . . a sum of money which is payable or will become payable in the future by reason of a present obligation'. Until there is a quantified amount, there cannot be a debt claim. There is a common law obligation to mitigate damage under a warranty claim; there is no such common law obligation under an indemnity because the indemnity gives rise to a right to payment for a certain sum (*White*

& Carter (Councils) Ltd v McGregor [1962] AC 413). The tax deed may include a mitigation clause but this will state that certain sums must be set off, eg losses which the purchaser did not pay for, before the amount of the debt is ascertained. The tax deed therefore gives the purchaser a more direct claim for recompense for pre-completion tax liabilities than would a claim under the warranties.

Why give an indemnity for tax liabilities?

2.4 It is unusual to find tax indemnities in transactions carried out outside the UK. The United States, Canada and Australia tend to have much shorter and more generally drafted clauses covering tax liabilities. Civil Law countries tend to use warranties to cover tax liabilities. Why then has the UK (and Ireland) developed the use of the tax indemnity? There appear to be three reasons:

(a) history;

(b) market practice; and

(c) *caveat emptor.*

The first two are not really satisfactory from a legal point of view.

History

2.4.1 The pre-completion tax liabilities of a target company were once covered, together with all other matters, by way of comprehensive warranties. The tax liabilities covered by the warranties included liabilities to income tax and surtax. However, there were some circumstances in which the target company had a secondary liability for which there was no statutory right of reimbursement. In such circumstances the primary liability fell upon the sellers. If a liability devolved on to the target company, it was recognised that the target company was entitled to seek an indemnity for the liability from the seller: for, in effect, the target was paying a tax liability for which the seller had had the benefit and was rightly liable: from this the practice evolved of seeking an indemnity from the seller to cover not only the secondary liabilities but also the primary liabilities of the target company. Once this had become acceptable in the market place, it was only a matter of time before the purchaser, seeking ever greater protection, became included as a party to the indemnity. These blanket indemnities in favour of both target company and purchaser continued to be used for a number of years and indeed a number are still in use today. However, the case of *Zim Properties Ltd v Proctor* [1985] STC 90 (see 2.6.12 below) and subsequent Inland Revenue practice meant that the use of such indemnities in favour of the target company could result in a potential tax charge on the target company upon receipt of the amount paid under the indemnity. The seller would then have to gross up the payment to take account of this extra tax charge.

Consequently, it has become the practice for the seller to agree to give an indemnity in favour of the purchaser alone or, where the purchaser insists that any payment be made to the target company, that such payment be made to the target company at the direction of the purchaser (see 3.6 below). The original reason for which an indemnity was given has been lost sight of, namely the protection from secondary liabilities, other reasons have therefore had to be found.

Market practice

2.4.2 If a seller were to argue in favour of a return to an indemnity for secondary liabilities only, it is probable that the purchaser and target company would respond with the second answer to the question, why give a tax indemnity ie that it is now accepted market practice. It is almost impossible to sell a private company's shares without giving a tax indemnity; it does occasionally happen, but only in exceptional cases.

Caveat emptor

2.4.3 The third answer to the question why have a tax deed and the one which probably holds most sway, but which is also to some extent a product of lawyers' attempts to rationalise and give legal foundation to the argument that indemnities ought to be given because it is market practice, is that there is a recognition that the maxim *caveat emptor* (let the buyer beware) should be relaxed a little in the case of private company sales.

Form of the tax deed

2.5 Having said that a tax deed is merely a means of allocating risk, the ways in which this can be done are various. However, there are four basic forms in use:

(a) an indemnity from the seller to the target company ('target indemnity');

(b) an indemnity from the seller to the purchaser ('purchaser indemnity');

(c) a covenant by the seller to the purchaser to pay a defined amount ('covenant to pay'); and

(d) a covenant to pay the purchaser an amount equal to the amount that would have been paid had an indemnity been given to the company ('hybrid covenant').

Target indemnity

2.5.1 The target indemnity was the form most commonly in use before 1985. A typical indemnity clause would be as follows:

> 'The [Covenantor[s]/Seller[s] [jointly and severally covenant[s]] with the Company (for itself and as trustee for each Group Company) to indemnify each Group Company against:'

The reason for this type of indemnity is historical (see 2.4.1 above); however, following the case of *Zim Properties Ltd v Proctor* [1985] STC 90 the target indemnity became very inefficient for tax purposes (see 2.4). Target indemnities are still found occasionally but the trend is more towards the covenant to pay described in 2.5.3 below.

Notwithstanding the tax inefficiencies of the target indemnity, there is also a legal objection to its use. The target company in a share sale is a passive third party, that is, it is the object of the sale and not a party to it. The purchaser buys an asset (the target company) and if that asset is worth less than the purchaser thought, it is the purchaser that has suffered the loss and the party which should be recompensed. Simply because in law the target company is a legal person and is capable of entering into contracts and of being involved in the sale and purchase transaction by giving undertakings etc does not make it logical that it should be included as a party to the contract.

An indemnity can be given by the shareholders to the target company for any secondary liability which the target company may incur as a result of non-payment of tax liabilities by the shareholders. For example, a loan creditor of the target company could require the shareholders to indemnify the target company against any tax liability of the shareholders which it pays on their behalf so that the company does not finance the shareholders at the expense of the loan creditor. In these circumstances, the target company needs to be a party to that indemnity but this is because it is a contract between the shareholders and the company. Such an indemnity could be given in the above example regardless of whether the target company is being sold. Where the target company is being sold, the sale contract does not involve the target company. The sale of a second-hand car may be used as an analogy. In the event that something is wrong with the car the natural inclination of the purchaser would be to seek recompense from the seller because the car is not as valuable as was first thought. If the seller reimburses the purchaser, it is for the purchaser to decide whether to remedy the defect or use the money in some other way. In the case of the sale and purchase of shares in a private company the situation ought to be the same. In our view logic dictates an agreement between the seller and the purchaser.

Purchaser indemnity

2.5.2 A purchaser indemnity may take one of two forms:

'The [Covenantor[s]/Seller[s]] [jointly and severally covenant[s]] with the Purchaser to indemnify the Purchaser against any loss resulting from a Claim for Tax made against any Group Company'.

or:

'The [Covenantor[s]/Seller[s]] [jointly ad severally covenant[s]] with the Purchaser to indemnify the Purchaser against any Claim for Tax made against any Group Company.'

It is thought that neither of these is effective for the following reasons.

Indemnity for loss suffered in consequence of a diminution of the value of target

2.5.2.1 If the indemnity is drafted so as to indemnify the purchaser for any loss suffered by the purchaser as a result of a tax claim made against the target company ie an indemnity for the diminution in the value of the target company's shares, it is arguable that technically the purchaser has suffered no loss. Although the target company is reduced in value because of a tax claim arising out of events prior to completion, this was an inherent liability of the company when purchased and the purchaser made a bad bargain paying more than the company was worth. The loss was therefore suffered at the time the offer was accepted. It may be that such an argument would not succeed following the case of *Eurocopy plc v Teesdale and Others* [1992] BCLC 1067 (see 8.4.2.3). However, as there are ways of dealing with the problem that avoid having to deal with the issue it is considered that this type of indemnity should be avoided.

Indemnity to the purchaser for a loss suffered by the target

2.5.2.2 If an indemnity is a separately enforceable contract to hold a person harmless against loss, it is impossible to see how a person can be held harmless for a loss suffered by a third party: what is the damage suffered by the person held harmless? Again, it is considered that this type of indemnity should be avoided.

Covenant to pay

2.5.3 A covenant to pay is an agreement whereby the seller promises to pay to the purchaser an amount equal to any tax paid by the target company. A typical covenant to pay clause is as follows:

'The Seller[s] covenant[s] [jointly and severally] with the Purchaser that, subject to the following provisions of this deed, the Seller[s] will, [as directed by the Purchaser,] pay to the Purchaser [or the Company] whether or not the Company is or may be entitled to claim reimbursement of the payment from any person or a company an amount equal to:'

The purchaser is paid an amount equal to the tax claim which is assumed to be the decrease in the value of the shares (on a net assets basis). The purchaser is placed in the same position as it was prior to the claim and can opt whether to put the money into the company by way of loan, subscription for shares or capital contribution or to keep the cash. Alternatively, the purchaser can direct the seller to pay the amount to the target; this is equivalent to the purchaser loaning the sum to the target and in these circumstances it would be usual for the purchaser and target to set up an inter company loan account. However, the covenant to pay is not an indemnity in the strict sense as the tax claim is not against the purchaser but against the company. The tax analysis for the covenant to pay is dealt with in 2.5.5.

Hybrid covenant

2.5.4 The hybrid covenant attempts to be true to the original rationale of having a target indemnity and yet seeks to have the tax advantages of a covenant to pay. A typical hybrid indemnity clause is as follows.

> 'The Seller[s] covenant[s] [jointly and severally] with the Purchaser to pay from time to time to the Purchaser such sums as would if paid to the Target Group indemnify and keep indemnified the Target Group against each and every Claim for Tax where the Claim for Tax in question arises whether in whole or in point from:'

Effectively, it is a promise to pay an amount measured by reference to the amount that would have been payable had an indemnity been given to the target. The problem with this type of clause is that if the target had been indemnified, it would have been liable to tax on the receipt and a gross up clause would have been included; however, as the clause seeks to gain the benefits of a covenant to pay the purchaser is not liable to tax. There is therefore a potential windfall to the purchaser which is usually dealt with by an exclusion.

Such an exclusion would be included in the general exclusions from liability and might read:

> 'In computing the amount to be paid by the Covenantor[s] under this deed in respect of any Claim for Tax no account shall be taken of any Tax which the Target Group would have been liable in respect of such amount had it in fact been paid to the Target Group.'

The tax aspects of the hybrid covenant are dealt with in 2.7.3 et seq.

Difference between covenant to pay and hybrid covenant

2.5.5 Under a covenant to pay the seller promises to pay the purchaser an amount equal to a tax claim in respect of unprovided for tax liabilities which arise prior to completion. Under a hybrid covenant the seller promises to pay the purchaser an amount equal to the amount which would have been payable had the seller indemnified the target. The hybrid covenant recognises the historical origins of the tax indemnity. There may be little difference in the amount payable under a hybrid indemnity and a covenant to pay, and in practice the amount payable will, in any event, be defined under the indemnity. Arguably, without such definition there would be no need to include a separate clause covering any costs in a hybrid covenant as such costs would be part of the loss suffered as a result of the tax claim. A covenant to pay would need to include, as part of the definition of tax claim, a clause providing for the tax claim to include costs and expenses of dealing with the claim.

If the hybrid covenant is used, it is necessary to exclude any gross up that would have been included in a target indemnity.

Example A

Seller A covenants to pay to purchaser B an amount equal to any tax suffered by target company C.

C receives a tax demand for £100.

A pays B £100. A's disposal proceeds are retrospectively reduced by £100 under *TCGA 1992 s 49(1)(c)* and ESC D33. If A made a gain on the original disposal then the tax referable to the £100 will be refunded. If A made a loss, the loss will be increased by £100. B has a reduced base cost under *TCGA 1992 s 38*. There is no tax liability in C.

Seller X covenants to pay purchaser Y an amount equal to the amount which X would have paid target company Z had Y indemnified Z. Assume corporation tax is payable at 50%.

Z receives a tax demand for £100.

X pays Y £100. However, if Y had paid Z, Z would have been taxable at 50% on the receipt. In order to put Z in the position it would have been, X would have to pay Z £200 on which it would pay tax of £100. X ought to pay Y £200 but as Y is not taxable on the receipt Y is better off to the tune of £100. Therefore it is necessary to exclude the gross up clause from such a covenant to pay.

Tax consequences of indemnity payments — consideration paid in cash

2.6 Before considering the tax implications of each type of indemnity it is useful to look at the development of tax law in this area. There are still a number of uncertainties especially where the consideration is given in shares or loan notes instead of cash, this is because for tax purposes there may not have been a disposal by the vendor and therefore no transaction with which to associate the indemnity payment (see 2.8 and 2.9).

History of the tax treatment of indemnity payments

2.6.1 The history of indemnity payments falls neatly into three parts:

(a) the period before the decision in *Zim Properties Ltd v Proctor*;

(b) the period after the *Zim* decision; and

(c) the period after extra-statutory concession D33.

Pre-Zim Properties Ltd v Proctor

2.6.1.1 In the period before the case of *Zim Properties Ltd v Proctor* [1985] STC 90 reliance was put upon *TCGA 1992 s 49(1)* which provides that:

> 'In the first instance no allowance shall be made in the computation under this chapter—
>
> (a) . . .
>
> (b) . . .
>
> (c) for any contingent liability in respect of a warranty or representation made on a disposal by way of sale or lease for any property other than land.'

TCGA 1992 s 49(2) provides that:

> 'If it is subsequently shown to the satisfaction of the inspector that any such contingent liability has become enforceable, and is being or has been enforced, such adjustment, whether by way of discharge or repayment of tax or otherwise, shall be made as is required in consequence.'

The effect of *TCGA 1992 s 49* is that if a warranty is given, the potential liability under it is ignored for calculating the capital gains tax on the transaction in which it was given. However, where a payment is actually made under such a warranty, the capital gains tax position is recalculated to take account of it. The payment is not taxed as a taxable receipt. Although practitioners were concerned that a payment made under a deed of indemnity might not receive this treatment (it should be noted that *TCGA 1992 s 49* does not expressly extend to indemnity payments), in practice it was not a major point when considering a deed of indemnity.

Zim Properties Ltd v Proctor [1985] STC 90

2.6.1.2 The case of *Zim Properties Ltd v Proctor* resulted in practitioners having to reconsider their approach to indemnity payments. The facts of the *Zim* case are fairly straightforward. A property company contracted to sell three properties; completion was to take place twelve months later and the contract provided that time was of the essence. However, the company was unable to show good title, so the purchaser repudiated the contract as it was entitled to do. The property company then sued its solicitors for negligence. By the time the company was able to market the property with good title property prices had fallen. The action was settled by the solicitors making a payment to the property company of £69,000 payable in two instalments, one of £60,000 and one of £9,000. The Inland Revenue assessed the company to corporation tax on chargeable gains on the first instalment. It was held by Warner J in the High Court that the compensation payment was taxable. It was a capital sum 'derived' from an asset, the asset being not the property but the right to sue. He said (at p 106e):

> 'Either way it would in my view be inconsistent with the decision in *O'Brien (Inspector of Taxes) v Benson's Hosiery (Holdings) Limited* to hold that the right to bring any action to seek to enforce a claim that was not frivolous or vexatious, which right could be turned to account by negotiating a compromise yielding a substantial capital sum, could not be an asset within the meaning of that term in the capital gains tax legislation.'

The claim, or in the event of dispute the right of action, which arises under a deed of indemnity given in favour of the target company is therefore an asset for capital gains tax purposes (for an alternative analysis, see *Damages and Capital Gains Tax* by David Wilde [1991] BTR 5). This asset, having been acquired by the target company for nothing (the target company itself does not give any consideration for the indemnity), is disposed of for the amount of the damages or settlement and the whole of such amount is therefore taxable. There is no indexation allowance to reduce the taxable amount, the company has no base cost to which indexation can be applied. The *Zim* case is authority for the proposition that all rights of action are chargeable assets within the capital gains tax net. The decision that the compensation payment in the *Zim* case was taxable follows the general proposition that the tax treatment of damages should mirror the tax treatment of the underlying transaction. However, had the property company disposed of the property in the original sale for the full value it would have been the profit (the excess of sale proceeds over indexed acquisition cost) which would have been chargeable to corporation tax. Once it was decided that the right to sue was a separate asset, the acquisition cost of the building could not be brought into account. (The result of the *Zim* case was probably not unfair. The damages represented an amount of lost profit on the sale. Had the profit been realised at the time it would have been fully taxable.)

Post-Extra Statutory Concession D33

2.6.1.3 The ramifications of the judgment in the *Zim* case were thought to be horrendous. Let us suppose, for example, that the property in the *Zim* case had benefited from the exemption from capital gains tax for private residences in *TCGA 1992 s 222.* If the company had good title and the property was sold at the market price the sale proceeds would not have been subject to capital gains tax. If, on the other hand, the circumstances in the *Zim* case were repeated, the payment of compensation which would otherwise have been non-taxable consideration would be taxable.

The Law Society, *inter alios*, lobbied the Inland Revenue for something to be done about this worrying anomaly and on 19 December 1988 the Inland Revenue issued a press release clarifying the manner, in which it would interpret the *Zim* decision. The extra statutory concession set out in the press release is now published as ESC D33. The effect of the concession is to remove the notion in *Zim* that a right of action is a separate chargeable asset and instead states that one should treat damages or compensation received in respect of an underlying asset (ie the property in the *Zim* case) as though the damages or compensation related specifically to that underlying asset. The payment will generally therefore be exempt from tax if the proceeds of the sale of the asset would be exempt and taxable if the proceeds would be taxable. Where there is no asset underlying the right of action, the right of action will not be treated as a separate chargeable asset and any damages or compensation will fall outside the capital gains tax net.

The *Zim* concession is wide-ranging and specifically addresses the issue of indemnities customarily given on share acquisitions. Paragraph 13 of ESC D33 which is headed 'indemnity payments' reads as follows:

> 'The principle in *Zim Properties Ltd* is not regarded as applicable to payments made under a warranty or indemnity included as one of the terms of a contract of purchase and sale. If after the completion of the sale a payment is made under a warranty or indemnity by the vendor to the purchaser, the purchaser's cost of acquisition in the event of a further disposal is reduced by the sum received, and the sale proceeds of the vendor are adjusted under *TCGA 1992 s 49.* Where such a payment is not made in accordance with the terms of the contract, the principle in *Zim Properties* may apply and the sums received by the vendor or purchaser as appropriate may be identified

> as capital sums derived from the asset, or from the right of action, depending upon the facts of the case.'

No mention is made in ESC D33 where payment is made to the target company; however, the Inland Revenue has indicated in correspondence with the Law Society that a payment due to the purchaser, which is directed elsewhere, will be treated as constructively received by the purchaser. Furthermore, payments to a target are not regarded by the Inland Revenue as falling within the *Zim* doctrine and hence target companies are not referred to in the concession. The Inland Revenue stated:

> 'We do not consider that the treatment of payments to a target company is strictly a *Zim* matter, and so we have not expanded the concession to embrace this. If the payment to the target company arose as a term of the contract *Zim* would not apply and if the payment should properly have gone to the purchaser but is directed by the purchaser to the target company, we would regard the purchaser as having constructively received the payment.'

It must be remembered that this indication by the Inland Revenue does not form part of the concession and it is understood that the Inland Revenue has sought to charge a target company to tax on an indemnity payment. Each case will turn on its own individual facts. The extra statutory concession only operates in relation to seller and purchaser.

Inland Revenue's view

2.6.1.4 The Inland Revenue's view of the tax treatment of payments under tax warranties and indemnities is set out in paras 13040 to 13048 and paras 14800 to 14853 of the Capital Gains Tax Manual. The relevant parts are discussed at the appropriate place in the paragraphs that follow.

Tax treatment of payments under a target indemnity

2.7.2 Under a target indemnity the seller makes a payment direct to the target company.

The taxation of target

2.7.2.1 The target company is not a party to the sale and purchase agreement. The target company will have acquired a right of action under the indemnity. This right of action will be an asset for capital gains tax purposes and when a sum is received from the seller there will be a receipt of a capital sum derived from that asset (*TCGA 1992 s 22(1)*). Where the claim is settled there will be a disposal of the right of action (*Zim Properties Ltd v Proctor*). The right will have been acquired for no consideration by way of bargain not at arm's length. *Section 17(2),*

TCGA 1992 will apply and the right will therefore have no base cost. Consequently, the target company will be taxable on the receipt.

In order to fully recompense the purchase it is necessary to gross up the payment to be made by the seller. Gross up clauses are more fully dealt with in para 3.8.

The Inland Revenue set out in para 13046 of the Capital Gains Tax Manual their attitude towards payments which are made direct to the target company. The tax treatment will depend upon the character of the payment.

In the Inland Revenue's view:

(a) if the payment is a reimbursement of allowable expenditure incurred by a target trading company it will be treated as a trading receipt of the company;

(b) if the payment is a reimbursement of allowable expenditure of a target non-trading company, it will be offset against the company's management expenses; and

(c) if the payment is not a reimbursement of allowable expenditure, it will be treated as a capital sum derived from an asset, ie the indemnity acquired for nil cost, under *TCGA 1992 s 22(1)*.

In each case the payment will be taxable in the hands of the target company. The rationale behind this view is clearly right. In the first two examples, where a company has received a deduction in respect of a payment and subsequently receives reimbursement of that sum, it is clearly right that the target ought to be taxable on the receipt. In the third example the tax consequences follow from the *Zim* case.

The taxation of the seller

2.7.2.2 The position of the seller under a target indemnity is not clear: Paragraph 13048 of the Capital Gains Tax Manual states that where a payment is made by the seller, the seller's disposal consideration is adjusted under *TCGA 1992 s 49(1)(c)* irrespective of the treatment of the payment in the hands of the recipient. However, it is considered that a payment from the seller to the target should not give rise to a reduction in the consideration received by seller and consequently there should be no reduction in the original capital gains computation and no repayment. This is because *TCGA 1992 s 49* provides that '. . . no allowance shall be made in the computation of the gain for any contingent liability in respect of any warranty or representation made on a disposal by way of sale . . . of any property other than land' and it is considered that the section envisages a warranty or representation given to the purchaser under the contract of sale not to the object of the sale. Neither the concession not the subsequent Inland Revenue letter to the

Law Society deal with the issue. It is considered that it would be anomalous to adjust the purchase price by reference to a payment made by the seller to a third party ie the target.

The taxation of the purchaser

2.7.2.3 The purchaser will have an unadjusted acquisition cost. This is compatible with the fact that the target has been placed in the position that it would have been absent the tax liability. The purchaser therefore does not require an adjustment to its base cost.

Example B

Assume that the purchaser buys target for £100 and that subsequently a tax liability of £10 arises in target and that the seller has indemnified the target.

The target receives £10 on which it is taxable.

The seller pays £10 for which it does not receive a deduction (subject to the Inland Revenue's view).

If the indemnity includes a gross up clause then the seller will have to cover the further tax payments for which the target becomes liable and will not get a deduction.

The purchaser has a base cost of £100.

Tax treatment of payments under a purchaser indemnity, covenant to pay and hybrid indemnity

2.7.3 Under a purchaser indemnity, covenant to pay and hybrid indemnity the seller makes payments to the purchaser or at the purchaser's direction to the target. The measure of payment will vary depending upon the type of tax deed. The tax treatment of payments under each is the same and are therefore dealt with together.

The taxation of target

2.7.3.1 If the payment is made direct from seller to purchaser, there will be no consequence for the target.

If the payment is made to the target at the purchaser's direction, the Inland Revenue has expressed the view that a payment due to the purchaser which is directed elsewhere is constructively received by the purchaser. If the Inland Revenue's analysis is correct, there should be no capital gains tax liability on the target when it receives an indemnity payment provided that the original liability was a liability to pay the purchaser. However, unless an indemnity which has been drafted with the target as a party expressly states that the seller is to make payment to the target company *as directed by the purchaser*, it is considered that the payments are unlikely to be treated as constructively received by the purchaser and a tax liability is likely to result. If payment is made to the target at the purchaser's direction, an inter-company loan should be created between the purchaser and the target.

Whilst ESC D33 has gone a considerable way towards allaying fears that indemnity payments are taxable, the purchaser will quite reasonably take the view that any residual risk of a tax charge should be borne by the seller, and so require a gross up clause to be included (for a detailed discussion of gross up clauses see para 3.8 below). A seller facing this argument would be justified in adopting the pre concession position and insist upon payment being made to the purchaser rather than the target. The seller can defend this position on the basis that the concession itself requires payment to be made exclusively by the seller to the purchaser and the correspondence between the Inland Revenue and the Law Society may be difficult to rely on in the event of a dispute.

The taxation of the seller

2.7.3.2 For the seller 'the sale proceeds . . . are adjusted under *s 49, TCGA 1992*' and, in effect, the statutory rules on warranty payments are extended by ESC D33 to indemnity payments. *TCGA 1992 s 49(1)(c)* provides that '. . . no allowance shall be made [in the seller's capital gains tax computation] . . . for any contingent liability in respect of a warranty . . . made on a disposal by way of sale'. Hence, there is no immediate reduction in the proceeds of sale allowed in the seller's capital gains tax computation.

Example C

The seller sells the target company to the purchaser for £100 and a year later a tax liability of £10 arises in respect of which the purchaser is entitled to recompense under the tax deed. Under *TCGA 1992 s 49(1)(c)*, the seller would initially be treated as making the sale for £100 (even if the seller knew the liability of £10 was going to arise). *TCGA 1992 s 49(2)* goes on to provide that if the seller subsequently makes a payment to satisfy the contingent liability, the original assessment may be revised. Therefore, at the time that the seller makes the payment of £10 to the purchaser the seller may retrospectively adjust its capital gains tax computation to treat the proceeds as £90. This may result in a repayment of tax, the conversion of a tax liability into a loss, or the increase of a loss.

The tax treatment of the purchaser

2.7.3.3 Extra Statutory Concession D33 states that 'the purchaser's cost of acquisition in the event of a further disposal is reduced by the sum received'. In the example given in B above, the purchaser will be treated as having acquired the target for £90 for capital gains tax purposes. The tax position of the purchaser therefore mirrors that of the seller. It should be noted that *TCGA 1992 s 49* only applies to the seller; the reduction in base cost for the purchaser is effected under *TCGA 1992 s 38*, as the amount of consideration given by the purchaser for the acquisition of the asset has been reduced.

Consideration in cash — indexation

2.7.4 *TCGA 1992 s 49* does not address the question of indexation; however, as it imposes a retrospective adjustment to the sale and purchase proceeds it would be logical to assume that the purchaser's base cost is reduced from the date of the acquisition and indexation applies to the reduced base cost. The seller pays back part of the purchase consideration. The rebate of tax received by the seller or loss created by the sale should be unaffected by indexation.

Tax consequences of indemnity payments — consideration in shares

2.8 Where the target is sold in exchange for shares, it is likely that *TCGA 1992 s 135* would apply to the seller and consequently *TCGA 1992 s 127* would apply to treat the target shares and the consideration shares as the same asset. *TCGA 1992 s 135* creates the fiction that there is no disposal for capital gains tax purposes by treating the share for share/debenture exchange as a reorganisation. If there is no disposal, *TCGA 1992 s 49(1)* cannot apply. A payment under an indemnity cannot therefore, under ESC D33 go to reduce the disposal proceeds of the target company shares. This problem is addressed by ESC D52.

Extra Statutory Concession D52

2.8.1 Extra Statutory Concession D52 provides that where shares are disposed of under *TCGA 1992 s 135* '[a]ny [payments in respect of contingent liabilities as defined in *TCGA 1992 s 49(1)(c)* incurred as a result of a share exchange . . . within *s 135*] attributable to the new holding of the shares and/or debentures may be treated as consideration given for the shares or debentures'. The effect of this is to increase the base cost of the holding.

Example D

If the disposal is for cash:

A acquired target T for £10. A sells T to B for £100. Following the sale B claims under the indemnity for £10. A's gain of £90 is reduced to £80 under *TCGA 1992 s 49(2)* and A is refunded the tax on £10.

If the disposal is for shares:

A acquired target T for £10. A sells T to B for £100 satisfied by the issue to A of £100 of shares in B. *TCGA 1992 s 135* applies so as to treat the consideration shares and the target shares as the same asset. The consideration shares are therefore treated as having a base cost of £10. Following the sale B claims under the indemnity for £10. The £10 A pays to B is added to A's base cost in the shares in B ie the base cost becomes £20. On a subsequent disposal of the consideration shares, assuming no increase in their value, A would be taxable on £80 which is the same as if cash had been received.

Consideration in shares — indexation

2.8.2 One question which is not addressed under ESC D52 is when indexation is to apply from. Paragraph 14819 of the Capital Gains Tax Manual states that indexation will apply from the date that the warranty payment is made. As the purchaser will still have its base cost reduced from the date of acquisition, reciprocity demands that indexation should apply to the seller from the date of sale, rather than the date of payment.

Tax consequences of indemnity payments — consideration in loan notes

2.9 The tax consequences of an indemnity payment made by a seller who has received loan notes will depend upon three factors: first, whether the seller in question is an individual or a company; second, whether the loan notes are qualifying corporate bonds or not; and third, the mechanics of paying the warranty claim.

Individuals

2.9.1 Before *FA 1998*, where the seller was an individual, it was common practice to structure the terms of the loan notes received in exchange for the consideration shares so that they were not qualifying corporate bonds ('QCBs'). This was usually achieved by giving the holder of the note the right to subscribe for additional securities or by including in the redemption terms a foreign currency conversion clause. There were three reasons why this is done: first, the exchange of shares for QCBs results in any gain on the shares being held over until a subsequent disposal of the QCBs, if the purchaser were to default on the loan notes, the held over gain would still be chargeable notwithstanding that the seller received no cash for the original shares and the loan notes were now worthless. A second reason used to be that indexation would continue to accrue if the shares were exchanged for non-QCBs; whereas the tax charge would crystallise if the shares were exchanged for QCBs at the time of the exchange but would not be chargeable until the disposal of the QCBs. Any indexation in the meantime would not apply to the crystallised tax charge. Thirdly, in the case of an amount which fell to be dealt with under *Marren v Ingles* it ensured that any capital loss would not fall in a later period than the original capital gain. Following *FA 1998* and the replacement for individuals of indexation by tapering relief the benefits of having a QCB are marginal and each case will depend upon the individual circumstances of the taxpayer.

Non-QCBs

2.9.1.1 Where the seller sells shares in exchange for non-QCBs the loan notes will probably be debentures and the exchange will be a reorganisation by virtue of *TCGA 1992 s 135.* If the indemnity payment is paid in cash, ESC D52 would apply and the base cost of the new securities would be increased (para 2.8.1 above and Example D). If, instead of the indemnity payment being paid in cash, the purchaser has the right under the loan notes to set the amount of the indemnity claim against the redemption proceeds, this will be equivalent to a payment of cash (*Spargo's Case* (1873) LR 8 Ch 407). The date of payment will be the date on which set-off occurs and ESC D33 will apply *TCGA 1992 s 49(1)(c)*. Alternatively, the loan notes may be of small denominations and an amount of the loan notes equalling the indemnity payment may be cancelled; this is equivalent to early redemption and set-off and the same consequences should follow. Where the redemption price is adjustable under the terms of the note so that the notes are redeemed at a discount to their issue price, the sale proceeds will be reduced by this mechanism, the amount the seller receives will be reduced and relief for the indemnity payment given accordingly. The purchaser's base cost will similarly be reduced.

QCBs

2.9.1.2 Where an individual receives a QCB in exchange for the target company's shares, *TCGA 1992 s 116* will apply to disapply *TCGA 1992 s 135* and instead any gain on the disposal of the target company's shares will be held over until the QCB is disposed of. Unfortunately, it is not clear how relief is to be given for any indemnity payment. *TCGA 1992 s 116(10)* provides that '. . . the relevant transaction shall not be treated for the purposes of this Act as involving any disposal of the [target company's shares]. . .'. If there is no disposal, *TCGA 1992 s 49(1)(c)* cannot apply as this requires '. . . a warranty or representation made on a disposal by way of sale . . .'; neither can a ESC D52 apply because this requires a share exchange within *TCGA 1992 s 135* and *TCGA 1992 s 116* disapplies, *TCGA 1992 ss 127* to *130* as applied by *TCGA 1992 s 135*. Even if ESC D52 did apply, it would be of no use because the effect of ESC D52 is to add the indemnity payment to the base cost of the QCB; this would reduce the amount of gain chargeable on the disposal of the QCB but this is not a chargeable gain by virtue of *TCGA 1992 s 116(10)(c)*. The crystallised gain ie the one arising on the target company's shares, remains unaffected.

The Inland Revenue's Capital Gains Tax Manual states (at para 14821) that on a disposal of the QCB, the '. . . computation [of the gain crystallised on the disposal of the target company's shares] should take account of any warranty allowable under *TCGA 1992 s 49(1)(c)*. It may be necessary to use *s 49(2)* to give relief if some or all of the debentures have been disposed of before the warranty is paid'. Although this is helpful to the taxpayer, it is difficult to see what is the statutory basis for the statement. A clue to the Inland Revenue's thinking is to be found in para 14822 of the Capital Gains Tax Manual in which it is stated that '. . . the receipt of cash and/or QCBs represents a disposal or an event which under *TCGA 1992 s 116(10)(a)* is treated as though it were a disposal'. However, the gain is calculated as if the target shares had been disposed of for a consideration equal to their market value immediately before the disposal. The conflict lies in the fact that the gain is calculated as if there had been a disposal whilst at the same time *TCGA 1992 s 116* provides that for all the purposes of the Act the exchange of shares for QCBs shall not involve a disposal. A further problem is that *TCGA 1992 s 49(2)* applies to alter retrospectively the proceeds whereas the calculation of the gain is performed at the date of exchange under *TCGA 1992 s 116(1)*. Until the matter is clarified taxpayers will have to rely on the practice as set out in the Inland Revenue Manuals.

Companies

2.9.2 Where the seller is a company, all loan notes received by the seller will be QCBs (*TCGA 1992 s 117(A1)*) and the loan relationship legislation in *FA 1996* will apply.

QCBs

2.9.2.1 As a consequence of loan notes being QCBs payments made under an indemnity will be taxable as described in para 2.9.1.2 above.

Treatment under corporate debt legislation

2.9.2.2 Where the loan note provides for the indemnity claim to be settled out of the proceeds of a loan note, the question arises as to how that ought to be accounted for; this in turn will depend upon the terms of the loan note. If the loan note provides for the indemnity payment to be set off against the payment of the redemption proceeds, this is mutual payment of two separate debts and the loan note will be paid in full and no problem should arise. If, however, the terms of the loan note provides for it to be redeemed at less than face value does a taxable gain arise in respect of the difference under loan relationship legislation? It is though that the answer is no. The reduction in proceeds effectively represents a loss on an investment rather than a profit of a capital nature arising from a loan relationship (see *FA 1996 s 84*). In other areas, this has been confirmed by the Inland Revenue.

Tax consequences — mixed consideration

2.10 Where the consideration is mixed ie cash and/or share and/or loan notes, the question arises as to how the indemnity payments should be allocated. As the payment is likely to be in cash, it is advantageous to the seller for payment to be set against the cash element first. This will result in a repayment under *TCGA 1992 s 49(2)*. Because of the uncertainties surrounding QCBs it might be thought that it would be advantageous to apply ESC D52 to any share consideration next. However, as stated in para 2.9.1.2 above, the Inland Revenue's view expressed in para 14822 of the Capital Gains Tax Manual is that the calculation of the gain under *TCGA 1992 s 116(10)(a)* is upon the premise that there is a disposal and consequently *TCGA 1992 s 49(1)(c)* can apply. They therefore state that '[a]ny warranty payments allowable under *TCGA 1992 s 49(1)(c)* should be allocated to the cash and QCB element before relief is given under ESC D52 . . . *Section 49* relief must be given against these disposal before it can be extended by concession.

Payments under parent company guarantee

2.11 It is not unusual where the target is sold by a member of a group of companies for the purchaser to seek a guarantee from the parent company of the group. Where a payment is made under such a guarantee, no relief will be available under *TCGA 1992 s 49(2)* to the guarantor. Consideration should therefore be given to the parent lending the sum to the seller to on pay to the purchaser in which case the seller should get relief.

Indemnity as a contractual term

2.12 A further point arising from the application of extra statutory concession D33 is that to fall within it any indemnity must be a term of the contract. This has led some practitioners to argue that the indemnity must be an integral part of the sale and tax deed agreement rather than a separate document. In practice, the indemnity is generally scheduled to the sale and purchase agreement at the time that contracts are exchanged (the date of disposal for capital gains tax purposes under *TCGA 1992 s 28*) and is only separated at completion when it is put into a separate document and executed as a deed. Caution dictates that this is the best course or at least that the sale and purchase agreement should contain some wording to indicate that the execution of a tax indemnity is a contractual term. It is, however, considered that even if these steps are omitted, the correct analysis is that the contract for the sale of shares is comprised of the main agreement, together with all the ancillary documents including the tax deed of indemnity.

The above view, expressed in the first edition, is accepted by the Inland Revenue. In para 13042 of the Capital Gains Tax Manual they state:

> 'For Capital Gains Tax purposes we do not distinguish between payments made under a warranty or indemnity contained in the terms of a contract for sale as opposed to such a warranty or indemnity contained in a separate document as part of the overall terms of an agreement for sale.'

The real question, notwithstanding the number of documents, is: was the warranty or indemnity given as consideration for the purchaser buying the target company shares? If it was, the warranty or indemnity is a term of the contract.

Taxation of indemnities given by the purchaser to the seller

2.13 It is increasingly common for the purchaser to give indemnities to the seller. The type of indemnity is discussed in para 4.6 et seq. However, the taxation of payments under an indemnity from the purchaser to the seller is obscure.

An example of a situation where an indemnity might be given is under *s 767A*, or *ICTA 1988 s 767AA*. *ICTA 1988 s 767 B(2)* provides that where a seller makes a payment to the Inland Revenue, that payment will not be deductible for tax purposes. The Inland Revenue have stated in their Tax Bulletin No 16 dated 21/4/95, that the recipient of a payment under an indemnity would not be charged; this is so regardless of whether the payment is to the seller or a member of the seller's group. Notwithstanding this statement, given ESC D33 it is difficult to see what underlying asset would have been disposed of in order for a tax charge to arise. Similarly, the purchaser should not get an adjustment to the base cost of the shares.

There is a trend towards inserting a clause in the indemnity given by the purchaser to the seller to the effect that any payment made by the purchaser to the seller shall be treated as an adjustment to the price. This is an attempt to gain relief by increasing the base cost of the acquired shares. Although the indemnity is connected with the purchase of the shares, it is difficult to see how it can affect the purchase consideration. It is thought that such a clause would not be effective.

Should the target company be made a party to the indemnity for any other purpose?

2.14 It is only necessary to exclude the target company from the indemnity for the purpose of any payments being made, it is not necessary to exclude the target from being a party to the indemnity for any other purpose. Where the indemnity provides for the target company to undertake certain obligations eg the provision of information to the seller in the event of a tax claim arising, the obligations will be directly enforceable against the target company which is a party to the indemnity; where the target is not a party, the obligations can only be enforced *via* a provision that provides for the purchaser to procure the target company fulfil its obligations.

Another reason why the target company should not be made party to an indemnity for the purpose of making payments is that in doing so the indemnity is made freely assignable, the purchaser being able to sue under the indemnity in its own right regardless of the identity of the shareholders who sold the company. The assignment of rights under a tax indemnity is discussed in para 5.5.

Why a deed?

2.15 Traditionally tax indemnities were contained in a deed. This was because the target company was party to the indemnity but not to the share sale agreement and gave no consideration for the indemnity to the seller. In the absence of consideration the indemnity was contained in a deed so that the target company could enforce it. In most cases the target company is no longer a party to the tax indemnity for the purposes of enforcement and hence there is no longer any reason why the indemnity should be contained in a deed. As discussed earlier, the tax indemnity is usually a term of the share sale agreement and consequently the purchaser gives consideration for the sellers' promise to indemnify. There is no reason why the indemnity should not begin 'in consideration for the purchaser agreeing to purchase the sale shares the seller hereby covenants/agrees to pay to the purchaser etc. . .'.

Although the need for a deed has disappeared, market practice tends to dictate that the indemnity continues to be given in that form.

Enforceability — purchaser's concerns

2.16 Where there is more than one seller there are a number of issues which need to be addressed. Who should the purchasers pursue? And for how much? Should the liability of the sellers be joint and several or only several among all the sellers? Or joint and several in the case of some sellers and several in the case of others?

Whom to sue?

2.16.1 The purchaser's primary concern will be to be reimbursed quickly in the event that a claim arises. The purchaser will not be concerned as to how the liability is to be split between the various sellers and will want the liability of the sellers to be 'joint and several', ie for each seller to be liable for the entire amount leaving the seller whom the purchaser chooses to sue to pursue the other sellers for their share. Further, it means that, although each seller is liable for the whole amount of the liability, the fact that the purchaser chooses to go against X, a seller with 50% of the shares, and that X was only good for 75% of the liability, does not preclude the purchaser from going against the other sellers in order to recover the remaining 25% of the liability. The purchaser would normally expect the seller to concede this point unless there are special circumstances (see 3.3.2 below).

It is always worth remembering that an indemnity does not have any magical qualities, no matter how well-drafted it is, if the purchaser cannot find the seller when a claim arises or if when the purchaser finds the seller, the seller has disposed of the sale proceeds or are living in a remote corner of the world, the indemnity itself is worthless. If need be, a purchaser should not be afraid to back up the indemnity with a retention made from the purchase price (see 3.3.2 below).

Are the purchase monies paid in proportion to the shareholdings?

2.16.2 The purchaser will also be concerned that the full amount of the acquisition cost is recoverable as this may include loans repaid at completion. The existence of such loans often means that the amount of consideration received by each shareholder is disproportionate to the proportion of shares held.

Example E

X Limited has two shareholders, A and B, who are both directors. A owns 95% of the shares and B owns 5%. However, there is a debt owing to B of £100,000 on which the company pays interest at 12% p.a. The company is very profitable but apart from the directors' remuneration, all surplus cash is reinvested and hence it does not have £100,000 to repay the loan at completion. The purchaser agrees to purchase the company for £500,000 payable in proportion to the shareholdings and to procure repayment of the loan immediately after completion. This is achieved by the purchaser either loaning the cash to the company and thereby replacing one debt with another or by subscribing for shares.

A argues that as he was the primary shareholder having held 95% of the shares and was also responsible for the day-to-day running of the company, he should be the sole indemnor of the purchaser. However, from the purchaser's point of view the purchase price for the company is £600,000 of which 79.17% (£475,000) has gone to A.

If it is agreed that the upper limit on liability is £600,000, the purchaser will be concerned that A is good for the full £600,000. Unless A has other assets it is unlikely that he will be able to find the full £600,000 in the event of a claim.

Seller's concerns

2.17 Where there is more than one seller, each seller will want to ensure that the agreement does not make them liable for more than their share of the consideration monies and, in the event that they are liable for more than this proportion, they are able to recover from their co-sellers.

In some circumstances it may be unfair to ask minority shareholders to be exposed to the entire risk.

Example F

A number of members of a family own 90% of the target company and two unconnected 'outsiders' own 5% each. It may be considered appropriate for each outsider to have his liability limited to 5% of the amount payable under the indemnity and for each member of the family to have a joint and several liability for up to 90% of the total limit on claims.

Arranging the liability in this way will, of course, necessitate the purchaser suing three parties in the event of a claim for the maximum permitted amount under the deed. In practice, however, the claim will be far less than 100% of the purchase price and the purchaser would only need to pursue one family member for the full amount. Unless the two minority holders are jointly and severally liable, the family member will be unable to recover anything from them. To further facilitate claiming against only one party to the indemnity not only must the covenants be expressed to be joint and several but it is also prudent to include a clause which states:

> 'The purchaser may release or compromise in whole or in part the liability of any of the sellers under this deed or grant any time or other indulgence, but any such release, compromise or grant shall not affect the liability of any other of the sellers.'

This does not mean that the two 5% shareholders will not be pursued unless there is a very large claim but it will prevent the other sellers arguing that the purchaser ought to be pursuing them for a proportionate part of the liability.

A point that is often overlooked is that where there is more than one seller the indemnity will regulate the relationship between the sellers. In the absence of a separate agreement, the common law rules will prevail. Where liability is joint and several the right to recover from co-sellers arises from the rights and obligations arising under the agreement. Where the facts are as in example E above, A may find that he is liable for 95% of any claim although he has only received 79.17% of the consideration. In that example the minority shareholder gains. However, if the split was 51%/49% and the consideration was paid in proportion to the value that each of the shareholdings would fetch if placed on the open market and not in proportion to their relative sizes then the 51% shareholder would almost certainly receive more than 51% of the consideration. Consequently, the minority shareholders would wish to ensure that the liability between them and their co-sellers were limited to the amount of cash received and not to the proportion of the consideration represented by the size of the shareholding.

Trustees

2.18 Where the sellers include one or more trustees it may be inequitable for them to be made liable for the full amount in the same way as the two 'outsiders' in example F above. Indeed they may be in breach of trust if they expose the trust to a potential liability for the whole of the consideration. The purchaser may therefore agree to make the trustees severally liable ie liable only for that proportion of the consideration which they receive. Again, the disadvantage of this route to the purchaser is that the purchaser will have to go against two parties to make full recovery in the event of a large claim. A way around this, although one which might not necessarily be acceptable to the sellers, is to make one seller liable for the full amount of the claim and for the other sellers to indemnify that seller. This obviously causes problems for that one seller who will then need to take action against all the other sellers. This method may also be used where only one seller is UK-resident as this will obviate the need for the purchaser to bring proceedings outside the jurisdiction or as far as the purchaser is concerned for the other sellers to submit to the jurisdiction of the UK courts. Another alternative is for one seller to guarantee the liabilities of the others.

Sale of less than 100% of the shares

2.19 Occasionally the purchaser may not acquire all the shares of the target company. This type of sale frequently happens where shareholders of an ailing company seek outside investment. In order to facilitate this, the sellers sell a proportion of their shares to outside investors in return for an agreement to inject new capital into the company either by way of loan or by subscription for further shares. Such a sale is often coupled with either an option for the outside investors to take control of the target company at some future date by the purchase of the remaining shares, or alternatively, any preference shares issued when the new investment was made may be convertible at some future date. The outside investors will usually seek an indemnity from the sellers to further protect their position especially if the company is in a precarious financial position itself.

The problem in these circumstances is to quantify the loss in value of the purchaser's shareholding in the target company in the event that the target company incurs a tax liability. Assuming the purchaser has purchased 50% of the target company's shares and a tax liability arises in the target company, there are two ways in which the purchaser can be reimbursed: first, an amount equal to 50% of the tax liability can be paid to the purchaser; or second, an amount equal to the tax liability can be paid to the target company. The former method assumes that the loss in value of a 50% shareholding is equivalent to half the tax liability incurred. The latter method seeks to put the target company into the same position as it was prior to the tax claim. It is necessary to pay the target company 100% of the liability for which the seller will get 50% of the benefit as its shares were also devalued by the tax claim. It is, of course, not appropriate for the seller to pay 50% to the target company. However, if a large tax liability arises it may be necessary to put the target company back in funds in order for the company to continue in business. It will be necessary therefore, if a payment of 50% of the liability is paid to the purchaser, for the purchaser to undertake to put the 50% received back into the company. The seller must also undertake to put in 50% to make good the loss.

Where the seller retains control of the target company the purchaser may be reluctant to allow the seller to make good a tax liability by putting 100% of the amount of the liability into the company. The purchaser may be concerned that unless there is a contractual obligation for the money to be applied to discharge the liability the seller may exercise control to use the money for other purposes. What should not happen is for the indemnity to say that the seller will pay the purchasers 50% of the tax liability or if directed by the purchaser, the seller will pay the target company 100% of the tax liability. The danger here is that the Inland Revenue may treat the purchaser as having constructively received 100% of the tax liability. It is obviously dangerous to provide for the seller to pay 100% to the purchaser or at the purchaser's direction to the company because there is a risk that the purchaser will not direct the money to be paid to the company and as a result to have gained a windfall profit equal to 50% of the tax liability.

The acquisition of minority holdings

2.20 Where the purchaser acquires a minority holding in the target company the problem is one of quantification of the amount to be paid. A purchaser buying a 5% stake in the company will have the holding valued at less than 5% of the value of a 100% stake in the target company. It is possible that a tax claim against the target company may not affect the value of a 5% holding at all. If this is so, any indemnity drafted so as to provide recompense on the basis of the loss incurred by the purchaser would result in nothing being payable to the purchaser. However, if the indemnity is drafted as a covenant to pay a proportionate amount of the liability, it is arguable that the purchaser will receive more than it ought to. In general, where the purchaser own less than 50% of the target company, a covenant to pay a proportion of the tax liability equal to the proportionate shareholding will result in the purchaser receiving too much. Where the purchaser owns more than 50% it will result in it receiving too little unless it owns 100%.

The problem, where less than 100% of the shares are acquired — be it a controlling interest or a minority interest — is again the *Zim* case. The logical solution would be to put the company back into funds so as to put the company back into the same position as it was prior to the tax claim. However, this will probably render the payment taxable in the target company's hands. This could be avoided by the seller paying the purchaser. However, the seller is unlikely to want to covenant to pay the amount of the tax claim to the purchaser or to have it directed by the purchaser to the company as the purchaser may not direct the payment to go to the target company at all. Furthermore, in the event of the two parties agreeing to this route, the purchaser may be deemed to have constructively received the entire amount, which in the case of a minority holding may be far more than the amount paid for the holding in the first place.

Chapter 3

Tax Deeds: Introduction and Operative Part

Introduction

3.1 This chapter and the next two chapters consider some of the most common clauses found in tax deeds and examine the arguments advanced by both the purchaser and the seller during the course of negotiating such clauses. It is impossible to deal with all the possible variations of any particular clause as they tend to evolve over time as ideas are being borrowed and improved upon with each new transaction.

As a last resort (or even a first) the best way forward when faced with an unfamiliar clause, or an unfamiliar variation of a standard clause, is to ask the person who drafted it: 'what does it mean?' or 'what is its purpose?' or even 'what is the risk that the clause is meant to cover?' It is surprising how frequently an unsatisfactory answer is given to such questions as in many cases the clause in question has been copied from another tax deed on the basis that it must serve some purpose. The object is to have a workable document. In the event that the parties litigate, the court will need to understand and apply it.

Principal clauses

3.2 A comparison of two deeds may lead one to the conclusion that they are totally different documents. However, there are a number of clauses common to most deeds and which make up their basic structure. It is the form rather than the substance of these clauses which vary and evolve over time. A deed will usually have the following main clauses:

(a) *Parties* — These usually comprise the Purchaser and Seller. It may include the target Company (usually inserted by the purchaser and deleted by the seller) and may also include a Guarantor or where shares have been settled, the settlor.

(b) *Recitals* — These give a brief description of the circumstances by reason of which the purchaser and the seller have agreed to enter into the deed. These are often omitted in modern deeds or confined to a few lines and consequently are only dealt with briefly in the text that follows.

(c) *Definitions* — There is a tendency to define most terms at the outset. This leads to a long definition clause. Many definitions themselves contain defined terms eg Taxation, Relief, Subsidiary etc. There is an increasing tendency for definitions to be very detailed and contain real substance, enabling the operative provisions to be kept short. For this reason the adviser must give careful attention to the definition of key terms in the modern tax deed.

(d) *The operative clause* — This may be a covenant to pay or an old style indemnity. A third alternative sometimes adopted is a hybrid of the two ie a covenant to pay an amount equal to that which would have been paid had the company been indemnified.

(e) *Exclusions* — Sometimes known as vendor protection clauses. These clauses are intended to ensure that the seller does not suffer the consequences of the purchaser's actions rather than the seller's. In addition, the clauses should ensure that the deed merely restores the purchaser to the position it would have been in had no relevant tax liability arisen and prevents the purchaser using the tax deed to secure a windfall benefit.

(f) *Limits* — These clauses prevent the liability of the seller from being open ended and comprise time limits for making claims and financial limits and restrictions applicable to such claims.

(g) *Time of payment* — This clause provides for the date upon which the seller is obliged to pay the purchaser. It is particularly important for fixing a date where there is a deemed liability and for providing a date from which interest is payable.

(h) *Over-provisions* — As its name implies, the over-provisions clause provides that if the accounts of the target company have over-provided for tax then the over-provision can be set against tax liabilities of the target company thereby reducing the liability of the seller under the deed.

(i) *Third party claims* — The third party claims clause provides for the target company to take action against third parties in the event that the seller is liable under the deed because of a tax liability resulting from the negligence of a third party (eg the target company's tax advisers where they have given negligent tax advice).

(j) *Purchaser's Covenants* — Increasingly legislation such as *s 767A* and *ICTA 1988 s 767AA* can impose a post completion tax charge on the seller or a member of the seller's group as a result of default by the purchaser/target company. The seller will want to ensure that it is protected against such risks.

(k) *Mitigation* — This clause allows the seller to reduce or eliminate a liability, for example, by the surrender of group relief to the target company as an alternative to settling a claim in cash.

(l) *Conduct of tax claims* — This clause sets out the procedure for dealing with pre-sale tax liabilities: how they should be contested, which party should conduct the appeal etc.

(m) *General* — These clauses comprise a collection of miscellaneous 'boilerplate' provisions and usually provide for the procedure for the notification of claims, which country's courts are to have jurisdiction over any dispute etc.

The above provisions are discussed in detail in this chapter as well as in the following two chapters. This chapter deals with clauses mainly affecting the purchaser. Chapter 4 deals with the clauses in which the seller will have a greater interest and chapter 5 deals with the general clauses affecting both parties.

Parties to the deed

3.3 The question of whom should be a party to the deed has already been addressed in Chapter 2, 2.6 above dealing with the *Zim Properties* case and ESC D33. There, the question was whether a tax deed should be given by the seller to the purchaser alone, or whether it should also be given in favour of the target company, which would necessitate the target company being joined as a party to the deed. As was explained, in most circumstances the target company will be excluded. However, once the question of who should be a party to the deed has been resolved, the fact remains that the seller may be any one of a number of different legal entities. The seller may be an incorporated entity (termed 'corporates'), a trustee, an overseas individual and perhaps a personal representative. The legal personality of the seller may affect the ability of the purchaser to make a claim. The identity of the purchaser is less important although the purchaser's identity is becoming increasingly important as the list of liabilities for which a seller may be secondarily liable and, in respect of which it looks for a cross-covenant from the purchaser, continues to grow.

Corporate bodies

3.3.1 A corporate seller is perhaps the most frequently encountered type of seller and, unless otherwise stated, is assumed to be the seller throughout this book. A common concern is that the corporate seller of the target company's shares is often merely a holding company in a large group with little economic substance. In such circumstances, the proceeds of sale are likely to be passed to the ultimate parent, leaving the purchaser with a real credit risk in respect of the covenants given by the holding company/seller. The fact that large reputable groups mindful of their reputation will be concerned to honour their subsidiaries' contractual obligations, including those under any tax deeds, gives some comfort but it is not enough. In such circumstances the seller should be asked for a parent company guarantee of its obligations. The seller will not usually object to such a request and for the purchaser it may be the only means of protection (any objection by the seller may put the purchaser on enquiry as to why the request was refused). Where a seller is the parent company it would depend upon how widely held the shares of the parent are as to whether its shareholders should be sought to be made liable under a guarantee.

Another alternative is to obtain a retention of part of the purchase price as security for any tax claim that may arise. This will meet with firm resistance from the seller. With good reason, it will regard a retention from cash received as security against the remote contingent risk that the seller might not fulfil its obligations under the tax deed as excessive weighting of risk in the purchaser's favour. However, in the case of specifically identified risks which, for example, may be identified in the course of due diligence, the seller has fewer grounds for resistance. In such cases, the balance of risk may justify the purchaser's approach: there is a real prospect of an identified (and probably roughly quantified) tax charge arising which was not taken into account when agreeing the price.

Apart from the debate over whether or not a retention should be made, a retention will also give rise to a host of other issues: how large should the retention be? How long should it be held for? Who should hold it? What criteria must be met before it can be released to meet a liability?

For the above reasons a strong guarantee is to be preferred whenever it is commercially feasible.

Individuals

3.3.2 Another common type of seller is the individual who is selling the family company. For the purchaser the problem will be preventing the seller dissipating the purchase monies prior to any claim, or, alternatively, putting the assets out of the jurisdiction or emigrating. Once the seller has the purchase monies such action is easy and there is little the purchaser can do. Where there is an actual liability the purchaser may apply for a *Mareva* injunction. Where there is no actual liability there is nothing to prevent the seller dissipating the sale proceeds. In most cases the only practical solution for the purchaser is to obtain a retention from the purchase proceeds for as long as possible.

One way of achieving an effective retention is to pay part of the purchase monies in the form of interest bearing loan notes, the principal of which can be applied to discharge tax liabilities that arise prior to the redemption date. The redemption date can coincide with the normal time limit for tax claims. Although this still leaves an exposure, for example, for claims based on neglect made outside the normal time limits, in practice such claims are rare and their existence will often become apparent to the purchaser in the six years following completion. In some cases partial redemptions can be made prior to the final redemption date as the risk of liabilities crystallising recedes as the years pass. The receipt of such loan notes may allow a seller to hold over any capital gain realised on the disposal of shares to the extent that loan notes are issued as consideration rather than cash paid. The gain will only crystallise when the loan notes are redeemed or otherwise disposed of. A deferral of tax in this way may actually have some attractions to the seller. However, where, prior to the phasing out of retirement relief, the seller would be entitled to such relief he or she may need to consider electing under *TCGA 1992 Sch 6 para 2* that the provisions of *TCGA 1992 s 127* do not apply in order to preserve retirement relief in respect of the consideration replaced by the debentures. One also needs to consider the ramifications that receiving loan notes may have on taper relief. If the purchase has a large capital asset such as property it may also be possible to create a charge over such asset to secure liabilities under the tax deed.

In many cases the risk of a seller disappearing may not be as acute as it first appears. Often a seller continues to be employed by the target company. In such a case the purchaser will have a good idea (or should do) of the seller's whereabouts. However, what may at first sight appear to be an advantage may subsequently turn out to be a disadvantage. The purchaser may feel that it is unwise to enforce any indemnity. The seller is generally retained after the sale because the purchaser feels that the seller is important to the continued success of the target company's business. The seller's goodwill will evaporate if the seller is sued by his employer and taking action against the seller may only be worthwhile in the event of substantial claims.

The usual method of giving greater protection to the purchaser when there is more than one seller is to make the sellers jointly and severally liable. In this case the purchaser can pursue its remedy against the most substantial seller leaving it to claim from the others. This causes few difficulties when the sellers are connected but it may be unfair when some of the sellers are 'minority outsiders'. In such cases the minority outsiders will usually argue for several liability as between themselves and the other principal shareholders and joint and several liability as between the principal sellers. If there are a few controlling shareholders and a small group of minority shareholders who control a small percentage of the target company, it is often agreed that the major shareholders will give a 100% indemnity and the minority are ignored. This is an ideal practical solution and one that is not without some technical justification. The minority can often argue that they had no control or knowledge of the management of the target company or its tax affairs and that they should not be responsible if the management of its pre-completion tax affairs causes problems. Conversely, to the extent that the tax has been understated in the audited accounts the target company's perceived net asset value is artificially increased with the result that all shareholders, including the minority shareholders, receive more than they might otherwise have done for their shares.

Using guarantees as an alternative means of protecting the purchaser where the sellers are individuals is difficult as one seller is unlikely to be prepared to guarantee the liability of another seller, unless they are connected.

Trustees

3.3.3 Trustees may be a seller in one of two ways. First, when they have invested trust monies in the company as part of the ongoing investment of the trust fund and secondly, which is more common, when the shares have been settled upon the trustees before the sale as part of a tax planning exercise. In the latter case the trustees are usually overseas trustees. Although many such schemes were rendered ineffective by the enactment of the relevant sections of the *Finance Act 1991* they still exist.

In either case, the purchaser's concern will be that the proceeds of sale will be advanced to beneficiaries prior to any indemnity claim and the trustees may therefore have insufficient funds to meet the indemnity claim. From the trustees' point of view they will not wish to expose themselves to a personal liability because of a deficiency in the trust assets and will therefore more usually insist on limiting their liability to the assets in their hands. Also they will usually seek to make themselves severally liable, thus excluding the possibility of the trust fund being called upon to satisfy claims against other sellers.

Where the trustees have invested trust monies the purchaser will usually have to accept the situation and seek a retention for as long a period as possible. Where, however, the shares were settled prior to the sale as part of a tax planning exercise it is usual to make each settlor party to the deed and liable for the amount of any claim as if they themselves had been the seller. This has the added advantage of making someone within the jurisdiction liable instead of, as is usually the case where such tax planning is involved, an overseas trustee. (Although having settled their shares, they may have insufficient assets to satisfy subsequent claims in any event.)

A number of particular problems arise when trustees give tax warranties. These are discussed in para 6.7.1 below.

Overseas sellers

3.3.4 Where the sellers are resident overseas there are a number of special considerations quite apart from that of enforcing the deed against them. However, on the question of enforceability: the chose in action created by the deed will usually be enforceable in the country where the seller is resident and therefore it is necessary, if the purchaser is to be able to enforce the indemnity, for the seller to submit to the jurisdiction of the English courts. To strengthen further the position of the purchaser, it is usual for an overseas shareholder irrevocably to appoint a UK agent for service of process. However, even these measures may be of no use for any judgment debt will still need to enforced, usually in the country of residence of the seller.

Personal representatives/executors

3.3.5 It is rare to find personal representatives or executors as parties to a tax deed. Where they are, their position is similar to that of trustees in that they will not wish to expose the estate, or indeed themselves, to large claims in respect of other sellers' liabilities by accepting joint liability. Usually where the shares have been devised to a specific legatee the shares will be transferred, if at all possible, to the legatee who will make the sale. The purchaser will usually require the seller to give a warranty (see 7.14.5 below) that the shares are not subject to an Inland Revenue charge for unpaid inheritance tax or indeed give a specific covenant against such tax in the tax deed. The purchaser would be wise to seek such a warranty (or covenant) in any event where the target company is a private company and the shares may at some time in the last seven years have been the subject matter of a gift.

Guarantors

3.3.6 An indemnity is only worthwhile if it is enforceable against a person who has the means to satisfy the claim. The purchaser may take a number of measures to ensure that there is someone of substance who can be made accountable or, alternatively, the purchaser can take security, for example, by means of retention from the purchase price.

If the purchaser has reservations about the seller's ability to satisfy potential claims, the purchaser will try to identify a person of substance to guarantee the covenantor's obligations. Such person will be made party to the agreement and indemnity as guarantor to perform the obligations of the contracting party in the event of default. Where the seller is a company, for example, the purchaser may look to the ultimate quoted parent company or where the sellers are trustees, the wealthy settlor of the trust may be asked to guarantee the trustees' obligations. A typical guarantee can be worded as follows:

'X.1

(a) The Guarantor hereby unconditionally and irrevocably agrees that if for any reason the Seller does not perform or comply with any obligation on its part to be performed or complied with under this Deed by the time such obligation is due to be performed or complied with the Guarantor will procure the performance or compliance with that obligation forthwith upon demand by the Purchaser.

(b) Without in any way affecting the Seller's obligation, the Guarantor shall be liable under this Clause X.1 as if it were the sole principal obligor and not merely a surety.

(c) The Guarantor shall not be discharged, nor shall the liability under this Clause X.1 be affected, by anything which would not discharge it or affect its liability if it were the sole principal obligor, including (without limitation):

  (i) any time, indulgence, waiver or consent at any time given to the Seller; or

  (ii) any amendment to this Deed (other than this Clause X.1) save that the Guarantor's obligations shall be construed subject to the terms of that amendment; or

  (iii) the making or absence of any demand on the Seller; or

  (iv) the enforcement or absence of enforcement of this Deed or of any security or other guarantee or indemnity; or

  (v) the dissolution, amalgamation or reconstruction of the Seller or any other person.

(d) The Guarantor's obligations under this Clause X.1 are and will remain in full force and effect by way of continuing security until no sum remains payable and no obligation or covenant remains to be performed or complied with by the Seller or the Guarantor under this Deed. Furthermore, those obligations of the Guarantor are additional to, and not instead of, any security or other guarantee or indemnity at any time existing in favour of any person, whether from the Guarantor or otherwise.

(e) As a separate and alternative stipulation the Guarantor unconditionally and irrevocably agrees that any sum expressed to be payable by the Seller under this Deed but which is for any reason (whether or not now existing and whether or not now known or becoming known to any party to this Deed) not recoverable from the Guarantor on the basis of a guarantee shall nevertheless be recoverable from the Guarantor as the Guarantor is the sole principal obligor and shall be paid by the Guarantor on demand.'

Recitals

3.4 Recitals briefly set out the circumstances that have led to the various parties entering into the deed. Compared with deeds of 10 or 15 years ago the number and length of recitals is now greatly reduced and the trend is towards omitting them altogether. The fact that they can be omitted leads to the conclusion that they are of little significance. Their only function was to put the deed in context and to identify the transaction pursuant to which the deed was entered into.

A typical recital to be found in a deed can be worded as follows.

> 'Whereas by an agreement dated [ ] and made between the Seller [and] the Purchaser [and target company/guarantor] (the "Agreement") the Purchaser has agreed inter alia to complete today the purchase from the Covenantor of the Shares (as defined in the Agreement) in reliance inter alia upon the covenants contained in this deed.'

If there is any value in this, it is to tie the tax deed in with the purchase contract (being part of the contractual arrangements it is important to ensure problems are not encountered with the *Zim* doctrine and that ESC D33 can be relied upon) and that there is consideration (ie agreeing to enter into the share sale agreement). However, as the share sale agreement generally specifically refers to entering into the tax deed as a condition of the sale and as it is a deed (which does not need consideration to be binding in any event) the recital is not really material. There is a tendency to include the tax deed as a schedule to the Agreement which serves to strengthen the link but again this is probably not necessary.

Definitions

3.5 In recent years there has been a trend towards shorter operative clauses and longer definitions. The first few pages of the tax deed are usually filled with definitions and it is important to understand the extent of the particular definition in question. The danger is that hard fought concessions won on the operative part of the deed are thrown away by insufficient attention to the four or five pages of definitions that typically are found in a deed. It is increasingly common to negotiate heavily to agree the definitions following which the main operative clauses become relatively uncontentious.

Definition of taxation or tax

3.5.1 A typical definition of taxation can be worded as set out below:

> '"**Taxation or Tax**" means:

(i) within the United Kingdom all taxes, levies, imposts duties and charges (including, but not limited to) income tax (including income tax required to be deducted or withheld or accounted for in respect of any payment) corporation tax, advance corporation tax, capital gains tax, inheritance tax, value added tax, customs and other import and export duties, excise duties, stamp duty, stamp duty reserve tax, landfill tax, insurance premium tax, any liability arising under *ICTA 1988 s 601*, national insurance contributions and any other taxes, levies, imports, duties and charges corresponding to, similar to, replacing or replaced by any such taxes;

(ii) outside the United Kingdom, all taxes, levies, imposts, duties and charges of any nature (including but not limited to) taxes on gross or net Income, Profits or Gains and taxes on receipts, sales, use, occupation value added, franchise, net or gross value or worth, personal property; and

(iii) all penalties, interest, fines and charges in connection with such Taxes regardless (in both cases) whether such Tax is chargeable directly or primarily to the company or any other person and of whether any amount is recoverable from any other person.'

Arguably the words from 'including' to 'similar contribution' add nothing. From the opening words all taxes are covered and so if a tax is excluded from the list its omission is irrelevant. Sometimes the words 'but without limitation' are inserted after the word 'including' which merely emphasises this point. However, such long definitions are commonplace and it is market practice to include them although the current trend is towards a shorter definition such as:

> '"**Taxation or Tax**" means any form of taxation, levy, duty charge, contribution or impost of whatever nature (including any penalty, fine, surcharge or interest relating thereto imposed by any Taxation Authority).'

If it is intended that a particular tax is to be excluded, it is this clause which ought to be amended. Taxes may be excluded for a number of reasons, eg where the target is the subject of a management buy-out and the managers have been responsible for the day to day compliance with PAYE, VAT and NIC legislation and regulations, these may be excluded, especially where the purchasing managers are the only people who know whether such liabilities may arise.

Sometimes a seller will argue that advance corporation tax should be excluded on the basis that as it can be credited against mainstream corporation tax, (for example, by carrying it back or forward against future mainstream corporation tax liabilities) it is not a real absolute cost to the purchaser. This argument ignores the carrying cost, ie until the mainstream corporation tax becomes payable, the purchaser is out of the money. This is especially so where there has been a large pre-sale dividend of distributable reserves, or where the company has foreign tax credits which will be set against mainstream tax in priority to credits in respect of advance corporation tax. In such circumstances the offset of advance corporation tax may be deferred for so long that the purchaser can legitimately regard the payment of ACT as commercially tantamount to an absolute cost. Furthermore, many auditors will not be prepared to recognise the value of the carried ACT credits in the accounts unless there is a reasonable prospect of their use within a reasonable period (whilst there are no hard and fast rules most auditors will regard the treatment of carried ACT as an issue if the likelihood is that the ACT credits will not be used within two years). The effect of this is to add to the adverse effect of carrying ACT: not only will the unindemnified purchaser have paid tax (ACT) with no immediate prospect of recovery but it will not be able to reflect the resulting credit in the accounts.

For companies with an ACT surplus this will remain a consideration notwithstanding the abolition of ACT on distributions paid after 6 April 1999 as the Shadow ACT regime may prevent the rapid utilisation of any carried forward ACT surplus.

Following the introduction of FA 1997 Sch 7 and prior to 6 April 1999 one must also bear in mind that ACT paid on a pre-sale dividend may be treated as paid on a deemed foreign income dividend which can restrict its usefulness still further.

It is considered that with few exceptions advance corporation tax should be included together with a clause providing for repayment as and when the credit against mainstream corporation tax is obtained. Further, where there has been a large pre-sale dividend prior to 6 April 1999, it may be prudent to retain out of the purchase monies an amount equal to the advance corporation tax on the dividend. This may be expressed as an interest-free loan from the seller to the purchaser or more usually to the target company repayable as and when the advance corporation tax is used. The use of the interest-free loan allows for flexibility of repayment and, in the event that the advance corporation tax becomes irrecoverable, it obviates the need for the purchaser to make a claim. This is to be compared with retentions from the purchase price which are usually repayable after a fixed period of time regardless of whether there is any doubt as to the recoverability of the advance corporation tax.

Where a pre-sale dividend is paid after 6th April 1999 the purchaser will have to assess the consequential effect that the resulting Shadow ACT will have on its ability to utilise surplus ACT within the target company.

The end of the 'Taxation' definition usually includes words to the effect that reference shall include any interest which results from late payment. This should be looked at very carefully. The seller should seek to exclude interest where that interest accrues as a result of the failure by the purchaser to pay money which has been received from the seller, to the relevant revenue authority. The exclusion can be worded as follows:

> 'Except to the extent that the same [ie the interest] arises by reason of any failure or delay on the part of the Purchaser or any of the Companies [this assumes the target company has at least one subsidiary] in paying over to the relevant body or authority any payment made hereunder by the Seller.'

The exclusions clause may include an exclusion to the effect that no liability shall arise to the extent that the liability for which the seller is sought to be made liable arose because of a voluntary act or omission of the purchaser following completion. The increase in the liability of the seller because of the non-payment by the purchaser would be caused by the voluntary act of the purchaser ie the non-payment. However, exclusions for voluntary acts occasionally become obscure because of amendments and the insertion of the above saves arguments later. No reasonable purchaser would resist such wording. Where the purchaser objects on the grounds that such liability is already excluded, the seller should seek to insert words, 'And for the avoidance of doubt no liability shall arise,' in the above clause in place of the word 'Except' which occurs at the beginning of the clause.

Reliefs

3.5.2 The current trend is to define 'Relief' simply as follows:

> '"**Relief**" means any loss, allowance, credit, deduction or set off'.

One then deals with the distinction between Reliefs which arise before and after completion in the definition of tax liability.

Business days

3.5.3 Generally time limits and other financial periods are set by reference to 'Business days' rather than just days. This avoids situations such as, for example, where there is a requirement to provide a cheque to meet a liability three days before the due date to pay tax and the cheque arrives after banking hours on the Friday before a Bank Holiday weekend. In such a case, the payment meets the contractual requirement but deprives the recipient of the opportunity to pay from cleared funds. Hence, the tendency to stipulate periods in business days. Business days are generally defined as:

> '"**Business days**" means a day which is not a Saturday or Sunday or a bank or other public holiday in England.'

This may have to be modified to include public holidays in other jurisdictions where target companies are resident outside the UK.

Accounts

3.5.4 The function of the indemnity is to allocate risks between the seller and the purchaser and is therefore drafted by reference to one specific set of accounts upon which the purchaser has based its offer price for the target company. This set of accounts effectively gives a 'snapshot' of the target company at a point in time and the risks can then be allocated either side of this line. However, 'Accounts' is often defined in the main agreement and may refer to the accounts of a number of years. Therefore one sometimes finds that the set of accounts which are to be used for the purpose of the deed are defined as either 'relevant accounts' or 'indemnity accounts'. A typical definition can be worded as set out below.

> '"**Accounts**" means the audited balance sheet and profit and loss account of the company for the [year] [period of [ ] months] ended [ ].'

The seller will often try and extend such definition, either in the definitions or in the accounts exclusion to catch the notes to the accounts. This is, inter alia, to try to include provisions for deferred tax (see Chapter 10).

Where the company being sold has a number of subsidiaries it is necessary to consider whether it is the consolidated accounts of the group or the individual accounts of each of the constituent members that are to be used. The decision to use consolidated accounts will have far wider implications than just the definition of accounts.

The following issues will need to be addressed:

(a) Should the availability of a relief in one company (that is a pre-completion relief) be available to set against the liability which arises in another subsidiary? If consolidated accounts are used this may already have occurred in the consolidation.

(b) Should the limits and *de minimis* limits apply to each company separately? It may be that the consideration has been apportioned between the various companies and that each has a separate *de minimis* limit. If this is the case it would be expected that each limit would be lower than one global limit (which would be the sum of the individual limits) and a claim would arise much earlier than would be the case if consolidated accounts were used.

(c) To the extent that a tax liability has been provided for in the accounts, it is usually excluded from any potential claim under the tax deed. This is because the tax deed is intended only to catch unexpected tax liabilities not taken into account by the purchaser when setting the price for the shares in the target company. Depending upon the level of profitability of the various companies, a target company in which a liability arises may have no provision for tax whereas another company in the group may. If the consolidated accounts are used there will be only one global provision for taxation which may be quite high and the company in which no provision is made in its own accounts will benefit from the provision for tax exclusion by virtue of the accounts used for the purpose of the tax deed being the consolidated accounts.

(d) The converse of the *de minimis* argument applies to the 'cap' on liabilities. When each individual company has its own 'cap' on liability it is possible for a liability of one company to exceed the limit thus reducing the recovery. It is very rare for the 'cap' to be apportioned in this way and should usually be resisted by the purchaser. This is especially so where the price has been apportioned by the seller to suit its own tax requirements.

A possible definition having considered these issues and consulted with the parties to determine which accounts were used as the basis of the offer is as follows:

> '"**Accounts**" means the audited [consolidated] balance sheet of the Company [and the Subsidiaries] as at the Accounts Date and the audited [consolidated] profit and loss account of the Company [and the Subsidiaries] for the financial year of the Company ended on the Accounts Date and the directors' report and other documents annexed thereto [and the [separate] audited balance sheet[s] as at the Accounts Date and profit and loss account[s] of the company and each of the Subsidiaries for their financial years ended on the Accounts Date and the directors' report and other documents annexed thereto.'

Completion accounts

3.5.5 The use of '**completion accounts**' is becoming more popular. Usually the method of producing the completion accounts is provided for in the main agreement (see paras 9.17 and 9.18 below). They are normally compiled on the same basis as the statutory accounts and also provide for tax in the same way as it would be provided for in the statutory accounts. Because they cannot be compiled until after the transaction, the agreement will usually provide for some compensating payment to the purchaser if the net assets as shown in the completion accounts do not reach a certain level. This may be done by the seller warranting the net assets. To the extent that the net assets fall below the warranted amount, the purchaser has suffered damage, ie the shortfall, and the consideration is reduced accordingly. To the extent that the net assets exceed the warranted amount, the purchaser has made a good bargain. Sometimes, there is no provision in such warranty clauses for the purchaser to pay the seller in the event of such a windfall. In such cases no additional consideration will be paid in the event that net assets exceed the contracted sum and the seller will therefore aim to either hit the warranted amount exactly or to fall below it. To do otherwise will be to give assets to the purchaser without a corresponding payment.

In other cases the agreement provides for additional consideration to be paid if the net assets are in excess of the predetermined level.

A transaction where the price varies on the basis of completion accounts is usually referred to as a 'net assets deal' and often some element of the consideration is left outstanding until the completion accounts have been compiled and the amount payable is then adjusted by reference to the completion balance sheet. The amount left outstanding is usually more than the anticipated compensating payment. Thus, if the seller has warranted net assets of £1 million, the purchaser may pay £800,000 initially. The final aggregate payment, depending upon the level of net assets may, say, be £750,000, £900,000 or £1.2 million. Leaving an element of the consideration outstanding in this way acts as an incentive to the seller to procure the early completion of the accounts. The effect of completion accounts on the provisions of a tax deed are discussed later in the context of limiting the provision of the tax deed in respect of tax arising on liabilities provided for in 'accounts' and in respect of tax arising on ordinary trading profits since the last audited accounts of the target company. The definition of '**completion accounts**' is usually given by cross-reference to the clause in the Sale and Purchase Agreement which deals with preparation of these accounts. For example, a typical clause might be worded as follows:

> '"**Completion accounts**" means the [audited balance sheet] [and profit and loss account of the Company] prepared as at Completion in accordance with clause [ ] of the Agreement.'

Events

3.5.6 The definition of an **'Event'** (or sometimes dealt with under the definition of a '**Transaction**') needs to be looked at very carefully. A liability under the deed usually arises by reference to Event occurring on or before completion.

It is common for the definition of 'Event' to include 'Completion'. The effect of this is that if the very act of selling the shares gives rise to a liability to tax this will be an '**Event**' under the terms of the deed and the seller will be immediately liable. This wording is specifically aimed at liabilities arising under *TCGA 1992 s 179*. If the purchase price for the shares is set by reference to a previous set of accounts it is doubtful whether any provision for this liability will have been made. If the purchase price is to be calculated by reference to a completion balance sheet any increase in the provision for tax that is made as a result of s 179 will result in a reduction of the purchase price and the purchasers will obtain immediate recompense. Liabilities under *TCGA 1992 s 179*, are dealt with more fully in 3.6.6 below.

An 'Event' is often defined to include 'the result of a series or combined result of two or more events, the first of which was an event occurring on or before Completion or the commencement of which shall have occurred on or before Completion'. The use of this type of wording is on the increase. Given that most deeds now include specific provisions dealing with secondary liabilities arising as a result of a combination of pre and post completion events (eg under *TCGA 1992 s 190*), it is difficult to identify which legitimate concerns for the purchaser are necessary if not covered by such specific clauses and why the 'combined events' wording is necessary. Secondary liabilities linked with pre-completion acts tend to be specifically identified and addressed in the modern tax deed, in a manner which leaves each party clear as to the extent of the indemnity being given. The definition above is very wide and its scope unclear which leads to uncertainty as to the precise scope of the tax deed.

For example, if chargeable gains are rolled over by the target in the pre-completion period under *TCGA 1992 s 152* and then realised as a result of a post completion disposal, does the combined events clause give rise to a claim? The exclusion for voluntary acts may not help as it may not apply to voluntary acts in the ordinary course of business. Further, if the roll-over was actually a hold-over into a depreciating asset under *TCGA 1992 s 154*, the liability may arise not due to the actions of the purchaser or target but as a result merely of the effluxion of time (ie the ten year anniversary of its acquisition). If the purchaser intended the deed to catch such items its intention should be clear and it should be discussed.

When acting for the seller, wide combined events clauses should be resisted. Apart from the uncertainty, the usual arguments for restricting its scope are: first, why, if the seller did something in the ordinary course of business prior to completion, should it have to pay if this leads to a liability because of something the purchaser does after completion? Secondly, why, if the purchaser does something outside the ordinary course of business, should the seller have to pay when the company is now outside the seller's control? The posing of these questions can lead to the offer of compromise by amendment of the clause by the insertion of the words 'but only to the extent that the first mentioned transaction is outside the ordinary course of business of the company and the second or successive transactions are effected after completion and are inside the ordinary course of the business of the company'. A further refinement is to make the second or successive transactions effected after completion, 'in the ordinary course of the company's ordinary course of business as carried out at completion'. This is to prevent, for example, the purchaser altering the nature of the company's trade from, say, a trading company, to an investment company and then arguing that the transaction is in the ordinary course of an investment company's business.

One way of combatting such clauses is to ask for specific examples. It is very hard to think of any (apart from secondary liabilities dealt with separately) and any request for examples is usually met by the comment that the deed is to counter unexpected tax liabilities and the fact that no examples can be thought of does not mean that there won't be any. The seller should seek to exclude the combined events clause and at the very least limit the scope of such clauses in the manner described above.

A typical example of a definition of an 'Event' is set out below.

> '"**Event**" includes (without limitation) the death of any person, any transaction (including the execution and completion of all provisions of the Agreement), event, act or omission (including omitting to comply with its obligations under the Pay and File regime) and includes further any change of residence of any person for the purposes of any Tax and becoming, being or ceasing to be a member of a group of companies (howsoever defined) for the purposes of any Tax and references to an Event occurring on or before Completion shall include the result of a series of Events, the first of which was an Event occurring on or before Completion.'

Tax liability

3.5.7 The modern trend of short operative provisions and detailed substantive clauses contained in the definitions is particularly clearly illustrated in the definition of 'Tax liability'.

The modern tendency is to define a tax liability as not only catching actual payments of tax but also deemed payments, which will be treated as though they were tax liabilities. The best way of considering what is permissible and what is not is to give an example of the type of clause commonly used and then analyse its contents.

The type of clause commonly used may be as follows:

> 'references to any "**Tax liability**" of the Company shall include not only liabilities of the Company to make payments of or in respect of Tax but also:

(i) the loss, for whatsoever reason, whether by set off against Income, Profits or Gains (whether present, past or future) or by set off against Tax Liabilities or otherwise of any Relief, which would (were it not for the loss or set off) have been available to the Company [and has been taken into account in computing (and so reducing) any provision for deferred taxation which appears (or which but for such Relief would have appeared) in the Accounts or has been treated as an asset therein];

(ii) the loss of a right to repayment of Tax [which has been treated as an asset in the Accounts] or the setting off of any right to repayment of Tax against any actual liability in respect of which the Purchaser would, but for that setting off, have been able to make a claim against the Seller under this Deed; and

(iii) the setting off against Tax Liabilities, Income, Profits or Gains earned, accrued, incurred or received before Completion of any Relief, which was not available before Completion but arose in respect of any event occurring after Completion in circumstances where, but for such setting off, the Company would have had an actual Tax Liability in respect of which it or the Purchaser would have been able to make a claim against the Seller under this Deed.

in the cases described in this Clause [x] the amount of the Tax Liability shall be:

(i) in any case falling within Clause X(i) the amount of Tax which could thereby have been saved (on the assumption (whether or not it is the case) that there are sufficient Income, Profits or Gains against which to set off the Reliefs lost) on the basis of the tax rates current at the Accounting Date;

(ii) in any case falling within Clause x(ii) the amount of the repayment which would otherwise have been obtained; and

(iii) in any case falling within Clause x(iii) the amount of Tax which has been saved in consequence of such set off.'

Clause X(i) is designed to indemnify the purchaser against the loss of a relief in the target company resulting from setting it against tax liability which would otherwise have given rise to a straightforward claim under the tax deed. The purchaser's argument is that if there would have been a claim under the tax deed in respect of a tax liability had that tax liability crystallised and been settled in cash, a claim should not be excluded simply on the basis that rather than allowing a tax assessment to arise the purchaser has utilised its valuable reliefs to extinguish it. In principle the seller should have no great objection to this concept provided that the reliefs are clearly defined in the accounts and the purchaser paid for them. If, for example, the target company had surplus ACT carry forward which the auditors had taken the view would not be used for three or four years such ACT would not be shown as an asset in the audited accounts. It may have been that during the course of negotiations the seller suggested to the purchaser that notwithstanding the fact that the ACT was not shown as an asset the purchaser should add to the purchase offer an additional sum to pay for the ACT credits. If one assumes, for the sake of illustration, that this was rejected by the purchaser, the seller would have strong grounds for arguing that in the event that the purchaser subsequently used such ACT credits to discharge a pre-completion tax liability it should have no redress for those lost credits against the seller. The seller's argument would be that in the example given the advance corporation tax clearly did not add to the assets of the company, nor could the purchaser claim to have paid for the ACT credits and the purchaser suffers no economic loss when the target company uses them. The seller will argue, with some justification, that the purchaser has received something for nothing and if it loses that item it should have no financial redress. The words in brackets in the specimen clause X(i) make it clear that where the relief in question has been reflected in the accounts and the purchaser has a legitimate argument that it paid for those reliefs, there should be financial redress.

Clause x(ii) deals with the loss of a right to repayment of tax. Again the wording in parenthesis is important, if it is clear that the right of repayment has been shown as an asset of the company (it is likely that it would have done), the purchaser paid for that asset and should it be lost the purchaser has suffered real economic loss and should be entitled to be reimbursed by the seller.

Clause x(iii) deals with deemed tax liabilities which frequently cause most difficulty.

The clause is aimed at situations where, for example, the purchaser makes losses in the target company after completion and carries back those losses against a pre-completion liability that, had it crystallised, would have given rise to a claim under the tax deed. The purchaser's argument in such circumstances is that it should make little difference to the seller whether it pays under the covenant in respect of a cash sum paid to the Inland Revenue to discharge the liability or, alternatively, whether it pays the purchaser for reliefs that it made available to extinguish the liability that would otherwise have arisen.

It is difficult for the seller to resist this reasonably, although some sellers take the view that the tax deed should be to reimburse or protect against loss not to enable the purchaser to make a profit by turning what might otherwise be a valueless relief (because a purchaser could not utilise such relief) into cash. Frequently, this argument is supported by a suggestion from the seller that in some way the purchaser should share the benefit with the seller in return for the seller agreeing to the inclusion of the clause. Where this is the case the purchaser may feel that in the circumstances of the transaction that it is not realistic to expect to persuade the seller otherwise. The compromise is often to incentivise the seller by agreeing that the seller need only pay the purchaser for the losses on the later of the date when the tax liability that would otherwise have arisen under the deed would have crystallised, or the date upon which the purchaser would otherwise have used the reliefs. In this way the use by the purchaser of its relief offers the seller the prospect of deferring payment beyond the date which it would otherwise have had to settle a tax claim under the indemnity had no utilisation of relief taken place.

Apart from objecting to this compromise in principle, the purchaser may be concerned that if it used the relief sufficiently far into the future, the terms of the tax deed may have expired and with it the purchaser's contractual rights to claim payment. There is also a credit issue to consider: whilst the seller may be in a position to pay a tax claim under the indemnity or for reliefs used today, will it be in a position to make a payment for relief at some stage in the future?

Income profits and gains

3.5.8 The trend to shorten the operative clauses has also led to a move to define the income, profits, gains, distributions etc in respect of which a tax liability arises and which fall within the ambit of the deed. In this way it is possible to restrict the operative provisions to a simple statement that the covenant is in respect of Tax Liabilities arising from **Events or Income, Profits or Gains** occurring on or before Completion. A typical definition is set out below:

> 'reference to:
>
> (i) "**Income, Profits or Gains**" include (without limitation) revenue profits, chargeable gains, and any other similar measure by reference to which Tax is chargeable or assessed;
>
> (ii) Income, Profits or Gains earned, accrued or received on or before a particular date or in respect of a particular period shall include Income, Profits or Gains which have been deemed to have been earned, accrued or received at or before the date or in respect of that period for the purposes of any Tax assessment;
>
> (iii) any payment or distribution made on or before a particular date shall include:
>
> (a) any payment or distribution which on or before that date has fallen due to be made; and

(b) any act or transaction which has occurred on or before that date and is or has been deemed to be a payment or distribution for the purposes of any Tax assessment; and

(iv) any "**Dividend**" shall include anything which has been deemed to be a dividend or distribution to shareholders or others for the purposes of any Claim to Taxation and shall also include any other event which gives rise to an obligation to account for advance corporation tax or amounts corresponding to or similar to advance corporation tax'.

Tax claim

3.5.9 The mechanism by which the seller is made liable under a deed is usually triggered by the target company receiving a 'tax claim' or 'claim for taxation'. What is meant by a 'tax claim' or 'claim for taxation' should be carefully defined for the rights and obligations of the various parties depend upon this trigger mechanism. Some deeds seek indemnification against tax claims ie assessments. This seems to be incorrect as an indemnity should be given against an actual or deemed tax liability arising as a consequence of an assessment being raised and not against the assessments themselves. Further, following the introduction of the self-assessment system and for larger companies, quarterly accounting for tax, this seems even more inappropriate. The need for a definition of a tax claim however, continues as a company will still receive notification if the Inland Revenue or other tax authority feels that it has not properly accounted for tax.

A definition of a tax claim may be worded as set out below.

'"**Claim**' means:

(i) any assessment, notice, letter, determination or other document issued or action taken by or on behalf of any taxing for other competent authority (whether within or outside the United Kingdom and whether issued or taken before or after the date hereof and whether satisfied or not at the date hereof); and

(ii) any return, amended return, computation, accounts or any other documents required for the purposes of Taxation (whether within or outside the United Kingdom)

from which (in any case) it appears that a Tax Liability has been or may be imposed on the Company or increased or further payment to such authority or body required to be made.'

Remaining group

3.5.10 Sometimes it is necessary to refer to the seller's group which is not being sold, for example, if the purchaser gives cross covenants. A simple definition would be:

> '"**Remaining group**" means the Seller and all companies (other than the Company) which at or within [four] years of completion were 51% subsidiaries (as defined in *s 838 of the Taxes Act 1988*) of the Seller'.

The operative clause

3.6 The operative clause is probably the most important in the entire tax deed. In the event of this clause being defective nothing can be recovered by the purchaser. There has been a recent tendency to move towards shorter operative clauses by using a greater number of defined terms.

The first point to consider is whether the operative clause is to be an '**indemnity**' or a '**covenant to pay**'. If it is an indemnity, what does it indemnify? It may be an indemnity against any '*loss occasioned as a result of a Tax Claim arising out of any transaction prior to completion*'. As mentioned earlier, it is arguable whether any such loss has actually been occasioned or whether the purchaser just entered into a bad bargain. This is even more arguable where the indemnity is expressed to be against any other 'reduction in the value of the shares' as arguably there has been none. On the other hand, if such an indemnity is effective and the target receives adverse publicity as the result of a tax claim and in consequence the value of the whole group is reduced, is this a 'loss' resulting from a tax claim? Should the purchaser be put in the position it would have been in had the tax claim not arisen or should it be the target company that is compensated?

The whole purpose of a tax deed is to provide a quick and efficient method of collecting a quantified sum. It is arguable that this purpose is undermined by the use of a wide indemnity to compensate for a reduction in the value of shares as it raises many of the uncertainties mentioned above, not the least of which is the difficulty in establishing the diminution in the value of the shares. Just as in the case of a warranty claim, the claimant will have to establish the level of its loss and that the loss stemmed from the claim for taxation.

Notwithstanding the practical difficulties of an indemnity against loss, there is also the more theoretical point. Is an indemnity from A to B really apt to cover a liability of a third party, possibly the target company not party to the sale of shares in the context of which the tax indemnity was given? Sometimes one encounters clauses whereby the seller covenants to pay the purchaser such sums as would, if paid to the target company, indemnify the target against loss arising from tax claims. The arguments about establishing the quantum of loss if anything would seem to be intensified by such a clause.

To avoid uncertainty the alternative to an indemnity is to draft the tax deed as a 'covenant to pay'. It is now rare to encounter a tax deed drafted as an indemnity rather than as a covenant to pay. A covenant to pay makes the seller liable to pay an amount equal to the tax charge levied on the company (or which would be levied but for some relief) in the event of certain occurrences. The amount is limited to the amount of the tax liability, the idea being that if the company is put back into the position it was prior to the claim, there is no loss. This can be achieved by a payment to the purchaser which can pass funds onto the target company to enable it to pay its tax bill either by loan, subscription for new shares or otherwise. By using a covenant to pay the amount of the liability is quantified (ie the amount of the assessment) and there is no need to value the target company, or argue about the value by which the target company's shares have been diminished. In other words, the covenant ensures that the tax deed provides a quick easy means of recovery as it is intended to do.

A typical 'covenant to pay' could be worded as set out below.

> 'The Seller covenants with the Purchaser and (as separate covenants) with each Company that subject to the following provisions of this deed the Seller will, as directed by the Purchaser, pay to the Purchaser or a Company, an amount equal to [ ].'

There then follows a list of the liabilities which are to be covered. This covenant assumes that the target company has a number of subsidiaries; hence the reference to 'each Company'.

There are two points to note.

(a) First, the 'covenant to pay' is entered into with the purchaser and the target company or companies (if the target company has subsidiaries). When acting for the seller it is strongly advisable to remove the covenant to the target company and, if relevant, its subsidiaries in view of the *Zim* decision. However, it is thought that the risk of the *Zim* decision applying is reduced, by making the payment to the company at the direction of the purchaser, which as a matter of law should amount to constructive receipt by the purchaser. Although the *Zim* risk is reduced most sellers will still insist on a simple covenant in favour of the purchaser only, to minimise the risk as far as possible. If a payment is made to the purchaser it is easy for the purchaser to fund its subsidiaries tax bill. The seller does not care what the purchaser does with the money provided that this does not entail the seller making a bigger payment (ie under the gross-up clause).

(b) Secondly, the tax liability is payable under the tax deed whether or not the target company can claim reimbursement from a third party (see the definition of Taxation). This ties in with the third party claims clause and the corresponding benefits clause (see paras 4.4.2 and 4.4.3 below). The idea is that the purchaser should be able to seek immediate recompense from the seller regardless of whether the claim arises from the fault of another person. An example would be where the target company has received negligent tax advice on a transaction from which an unexpected tax liability arises. The target company is able to claim for its loss from the negligent tax adviser but would prefer the seller to refund the loss immediately. As a claim for negligence may take years to settle, the target company will need to pay the tax liability promptly in order to avoid interest and penalties. If there is a suitable provision in the deed, the target company will take action against the third party at the expense of the seller, which will be reimbursed to the extent that recovery is made from the third party. The effect of this is that the purchaser is not forced to pursue potentially long drawn out arguments with the third party before it can recover the liability under the tax deed. In any event, the purchaser may be unaware of what has happened in the past and may be unable to mount the claim against the third party as effectively as the seller. Furthermore, the purchaser should not be concerned with the problem of pursuing people in respect of events that took place prior to its ownership. The seller should be prepared to accept a clause giving the purchaser an immediate right of recovery provided the seller is given a fair chance, through the third party claims clause, to recover the money paid to the purchaser.

General indemnity clauses

3.6.1 The operative clause can be divided into two parts: covenants which deal with general concerns, albeit arising under specific provisions of the Taxes Acts; and secondly specific covenants which are tailored to meet specific issues of the transaction or which arise from particular circumstances or from particular incidents in the target company's past, (for example, a specific covenant to cover the tax consequences of a pre-sale reorganisation).

There are broadly two approaches to a general covenant which, for convenience, are described for the purposes of this chapter as the standard approach and the varied approach.

The standard approach to a general covenant

3.6.2 In recent years the operative clause covering general tax liabilities has been in the form of a promise to pay an amount equal to tax arising from actual or deemed profits, income or gains arising on or before completion or otherwise resulting from pre-completion events. This covenant is subject to the exclusions and limitations contained in the rest of the deed, for example, in respect of tax provided in the last audited accounts. A typical example of this clause would be to covenant to pay an amount equal to:

> 'any Tax Liability of the Company arising as a consequence of any Event which occurred or was deemed to occur on or before Completion or arising in respect of or with reference to any Income, Profits or Gains which were earned, accrued or received on or before Completion or arising as a consequence of a Dividend declared on or before Completion.'

This clause illustrates the trend of keeping the operative provision short by using defined terms. Whether or not any reasonable seller should object to this clause depends not on the drafting of the operative provision itself but upon what is included in the defined terms 'Tax Liability', 'Event', 'Income, Profits or Gains' and 'Dividend'. The negotiation will centre around what is included in those terms (see the earlier discussion of the definitions in a tax deed). Provided that these terms are construed sufficiently narrowly, the seller should have little objection.

The varied approach to the general covenant

3.6.3 As set out above the standard approach comprises a general blanket covenant up to completion (subject to the normal limitations and exclusions).

The difference between this approach and the varied approach (which is increasingly common) is the manner in which the period between the last accounts date and completion is dealt with. It should therefore be noted that the varied approach can only apply where there are no Completion Accounts. Increasingly the trend is to break up the pre-completion period into two periods: the period up to and including the date of the last audited accounts and the period between the date of the last audited accounts and completion. An example of such a clause is to covenant to pay an amount of tax equal to:

> 'any tax liability of the Company arising:
>
> (1) as a consequence of any Event which occurred or was deemed to occur on or before the Accounts Date or arising in respect of or with reference to any Income, Profits or Gains which were earned, accrued or received on or before the Accounts Date;
>
> (2) as a consequence of any of the following occurring or being deemed to occur after the Accounts Date but on or before Completion:

(i) any Event which results in a Tax Liability arising in the Company where such liability is chargeable or attributable primarily to a person other than the Company (including any liability under *Pt VII* of the *Taxes Management Act 1970* (charges on non-residents));

(ii) any Event which gives rise to a Tax Liability or deemed Tax Liability (as opposed to actual liability) on Income, Profits and Gains;

(iii) any distribution (as defined in *s 209,* of the *Taxes Act 1988*) or deemed distribution for tax purposes;

(iv) the disposal acquisition or deemed disposal or acquisition of any asset other than trading stock; and

(v) the Company ceasing for tax purposes to be a member of any group or associated with any other company.'

The blanket coverage in Clause 1 above covering the period up to the Accounts Date is satisfactory as far as it goes. What is unsatisfactory, when acting for the seller, is accepting an indemnity only against specified events between the Accounts Date and Completion.

Traditionally, the period between the last Accounts Date and Completion is covered by a blanket covenant subject to an exclusion for transactions outside the ordinary course of business (see the discussion in para 4.3.7). The logic of this approach is that as a general rule if the company is being purchased on the basis of the last audited accounts, any further profits that accrue are an unexpected, unpaid for windfall for the purchaser and it is not reasonable to expect the purchaser to pay the tax on such profit, except where the tax bill was in respect of something out the ordinary. For example, if an asset was sold at an undervalue to a connected party the Inland Revenue may substitute open market value with the result that a tax liability arises in excess of the cash actually received. In such circumstances the purchaser would expect the seller to be liable for the tax.

Superficially the varied approach covers the same ground in as much as, prima facie, in the period between the Accounts Date and Completion only tax arising from 'unusual' events or activities is covered. However, what the varied approach does is put the emphasis on the purchaser to specifically identify and list all of those activities of the seller between the Accounts Date and Completion which are to be covered by the indemnity. The purchaser should object to this on the basis that the seller has run the company in the relevant period and has full knowledge of precisely what happened in that period and will know whether or not the list of specific events is comprehensive.

The purchaser will acknowledge that the list included in the above clause will cover most foreseeable events but there is always the danger that something unforeseen and unusual has happened which would not be covered by the listed categories. In circumstances where such an unusual, unforeseen event has occurred, the purchaser's attitude will be that the seller should meet any consequential liabilities and such event would certainly have been included in the list of seller's liabilities had the purchaser known. It would seem out of keeping with the spirit of a tax deed to place the onus on the purchaser to ensure that it has covered everything, which it can never be certain of, where the basic premise upon which the tax deed is drafted is that, save as provided for in the Accounts, all pre-completion tax has been paid.

Specific covenants

3.6.4 Although the deed is usually drafted in general terms, it is common practice to include clauses tailored to the specific circumstances of the target company. A common example is where there is a known or expected liability under *TCGA 1992 s 179*, or, alternatively, where there has been a group reorganisation or some other tax planning by the seller prior to the sale. Other less commonly found examples are transfer pricing under *ICTA 1988 s 770* (or *s 770A*), and, prior to 6 April 1999, advance corporation tax arising on pre-sale dividends.

Before considering particular examples, it is first worth considering the advantages and disadvantages of identifying specifically risks. In favour of covering specific liabilities is the argument that identification of those risks when negotiating the terms of the deed forces the parties to focus upon the potential liability and deal in detail with the respective rights and obligations in the event of the liability arising. Furthermore, the purchaser will often want to exclude specific identified risks from the *de minimis* limits and exclusions. The rationale for this is that the *de minimis* limits are only intended to exclude nuisance claims in respect of unexpected liabilities and generally the exclusions should not extend to an identified problem which, if it crystallises, is a type of liability which the purchaser should reasonably expect to be covered by the tax provision in the accounts. To include identified liabilities in the *de minimis* limit or make them subject to exclusions may involve the purchaser paying the target company's expected tax liabilities.

An argument often levelled against identifying specific potential liabilities is that this may alert the Inland Revenue to the potential liability and thus make the liability more likely to crystallise. An example of this is where the target group has been engaging in intra-group transactions which may be subject to attack under *ICTA 1988 s 770*. The seller may believe that it has very good arguments against the application of the transfer pricing provisions (and after the introduction of self-assessment will have had to have been confident enough of its position to make a nil return). However, if the purchaser insists upon identifying the liability in a specific covenant, this may alert the various authorities to the existence of a potential problem. This is a difficult issue to resolve. On the one hand, specifically identifying the liability may alert the authorities to the problem, the purchaser wants to be absolutely certain that the risk is covered. Further, how can the *de minimis* financial limit and exclusions be disapplied if the risk in question cannot be specifically identified? The purchaser may have some sympathy for the seller's predicament but its priority is to ensure that it is fully and unambiguously indemnified. The purchaser would be ill advised to accept the seller's argument if in doing so it faced the possibility of the seller pleading at a later time that the liability is not covered by the general covenant. In any event, the argument that identification of such specific liabilities in the tax deed may alert the authorities may turn out to be spurious if the seller has to disclose the liability in the disclosure letter for the purpose of the warranties.

One method of addressing this problem, often suggested in the UK, is the use of a side letter. It is difficult to see how this helps. To ensure that it is protected, the purchaser will want the side letter to be contractually binding (see *Kleinwort Benson v Malaysia Mining Corporation* [1988] 1 All ER 714) and to form part of the transaction documentation. On this basis, if the Inland Revenue wish to see the documents relating to the transaction, the side letter will need to be disclosed. The fact that the liability is separated out and dealt with in a side letter will only serve to draw attention to it. If the side letter is not one of the documents relating to the transaction and is not disclosed, it is difficult to see how either side could rely upon it or why they entered into it in the first place. Any other interpretation could be fraudulent.

It is often better to try and steer a middle course, ie to draft a clause which although alluding to the problem does not specifically identify it or mention any specific set of circumstances. In the context of *ICTA 1988 s 770*, such a liability might be covered by the sellers covenanting to pay:

> 'any liability arising from the application of ss 770–774, *Income and Corporation Taxes Act 1988* or any equivalent provisions applicable in a foreign jurisdiction.'

Such a wording may be sufficient to cope with the problem.

It should give the purchaser adequate protection and is not as obvious as saying that the purchasers are indemnified against the application of *ICTA 1988 s 770*, to a particular, described transaction undertaken prior to completion. It could be said that the mention of *s 770* may be sufficient to alert the Inland Revenue that there is a problem. However, it is difficult to see how the conflicting requirements of the parties: the purchaser's desire to clearly identify a given risk and the seller's desire to be as vague as possible, to avoid alerting the Inland Revenue, can be reconciled. The compromise is not perfect but is as far as the purchaser can reasonably be expected to go. If it is necessary to remove any liability under this contract from the *de minimis* provisions, it is then merely a matter of stating that the *de minimis* limits do not apply to any liability indicated in identified clauses.

Specific covenants in respect of pre-completion surrenders of group relief and surrenders of ACT

3.6.4.1 It is not unknown for indemnities to extend to cover circumstances where, for example, the target company has paid for group relief where it proves that the losses concerned are unavailable. The seller will often make the comment in this context that there is no need for such an indemnity; to the extent that losses purported to be surrendered are unavailable the result will be a liability which is not provided for in the accounts. Thus, the seller will argue a tax liability will arise which will be covered by the general covenants. This is correct but overlooks the fact that it is possible that more than the tax value of those losses would have been paid. For example, suppose that before completion the seller surrendered £1m of tax losses to the target company for which it was paid £1m (notwithstanding the fact that the actual tax saved as a result of the group relief claim was only £310,000 at current corporation tax rates). Thus, in the event that the losses proved to be unavailable the target company would receive a tax assessment for £310,000 on profits which were assumed to have been sheltered by the losses and the purchaser would have a claim for that amount under the tax deed. However, even if this claim were satisfied it would still leave the target's net asset value depressed by £690,000. Consequently, the purchaser will be keen to ensure that in such circumstances the difference between what it loses commercially and what it can recoup under the general tax liability provisions can be claimed.

A common clause to catch this might be as follows:

> 'Any amount paid (or payable to the extent that it is actually paid) by the Company for a surrender to it of group relief or advance corporation tax in respect of any periods or accounting periods ended on or prior to Completion to the extent that such group relief or advance corporation tax is lost, cancelled or disallowed or otherwise proves to be unavailable to set off against Income, Profits or Gains or Tax for the period in respect of which the surrender is made together with interest calculated in accordance with clause [number of interest clause] from the date of payment for such surrenders by the company until a claim under this clause is satisfied PROVIDED THAT any claim under this clause shall arise only to the extent that the amount paid for group relief or advance corporation tax exceeds any satisfied claim made under clause [main operative

clause in respect of pre-completion tax liabilities] in respect of taxation assumed to have been discharged by the group relief or surrendered advance corporation tax which is lost, cancelled, disallowed or otherwise unavailable.'

Although people may dispute the precise wording of the provision the principle would seem to be fundamentally fair as one is only reinstating the target company to the position it would have been in had the group relief claim not been made. However, more problematic is the covenant that one sometimes sees where the purchaser tries to claim amounts equal to,

> 'any liability of the Company arising from an obligation to repay the whole or any part of any payment received for group relief pursuant to an arrangement entered into by the Company on or before completion.'

The purchaser will argue that it expected to have a sum of cash in the target attributable to payments received for surrendering losses and if this proves not to be there, (because upon failure of the group relief claim it is obliged to repay money it received for its losses under the group relief agreement) it should be reimbursed under the tax deed. The seller will argue that if this clause is included in the tax deed it will effectively pay for losses it does not receive and the purchaser will not have been restored to parity but will actually show a profit. The seller's argument must be right. If the claim were allowed in the form set out above then the target company would potentially end up with all the losses that it purported to surrender. Arguably this restores parity although the purchaser anticipated having cash not losses the value of which may be discounted because they cannot be used immediately elsewhere. If the purchaser does receive a sum of cash then whatever the discount factor applied the purchaser must end up in profit.

A compromise that is sometimes reached is to exclude this risk from the covenants and instead give a warranty in respect of group relief. This warranty enables the purchaser to argue that it has suffered loss as a result of the target having to repay money it received for group relief which proved to be unavailable, and to rely upon the general doctrine of having to establish the quantum of damage to ensure that it is adequately compensated.

Covenants based on specific sections of the Taxes Acts

3.6.4.2 Traditionally, it was generally regarded as unacceptable to extend the covenant to cover events occurring beyond completion because of uncertainty as to what may be caught. However, as a result of changes in law there are increasing numbers of sections in the *Taxes Act* where a liability attributable to the seller's actions or omissions could arise and devolve upon the target company after completion. Such liabilities the purchaser would rightly expect the seller to meet. The purchaser should be able to clearly identify specific concerns that it has and ensure that the drafting of the covenants covering the concerns are sufficiently specific to ensure that the seller is reasonably comfortable about giving the covenants required. However, the purchaser will be tempted to adopt a more global approach to ensure that it catches any post-completion events which could rebound upon the target and which it cannot specifically identify. The seller will generally resist such an approach on the basis that covering post-completion Events should be very much a rare exception and will only be agreed where the case is clear and justified.

A typical covenant would be an agreement to pay tax liabilities arising or deemed to arise at any time after completion:

'(a) Under *s 132 of the Finance Act 1988* by virtue of the relationship on or at any time before completion of the company with the migrating company (referred to in that section) where such migrating company is not the company [or any of the subsidiaries]; or

(b) as a result of the making by the seller or a member of the seller's group of any such payment or deemed payment as constituted as a chargeable payment for the purposes of *s 214, ICTA 1988;*

(c) as a result of the disposal by the seller or any member of the seller's group of any asset or of any interest or right over any asset.'

This latter provision is designed to catch the sort of situation envisaged by *TCGA 1992 s 190.* If corporation tax on a chargeable gain of a group member is not paid within six months of the time when it becomes payable, then, within two years the tax may be assessed on (a) the principal company of the group when the gain accrued or (b) any other company which at any time in the two years preceding the time the gain accrued was a group member and owned the asset disposed of (or the right, interest etc therein). Thus, if prior to the sale the target transferred an asset to the Seller who disposed of it after completion but failed to pay the resulting tax, the liability could devolve upon the target. Although the target then has a statutory right of recovery from the seller (to which the gain accrued) or from the principal company of the group at the time the gain accrued, it is thought to be much easier to enforce a contractual obligation.

Identifying specific liabilities where there are completion accounts

3.6.4.3 Where the price is to be determined by reference to a completion balance sheet, the existence of specific liabilities or potential liabilities may cause problems. Where the specific liability is sufficiently certain then arguably it should be taken into account in the completion balance sheet. The effect of providing for such liabilities in this way means that, as the price is being determined by the net assets shown by the completion balance sheet, the purchase price will be reduced by an amount equal to the liability. Therefore, if the liability materialises the purchaser will suffer no economic loss. Where such a liability is taken into account by specifically indemnifying against it, the amount of any payment to be made by the seller in the event of a claim under the deed should be restricted to the excess of the tax liability arising from the specified risk over the amount of the provision made in the completion balance sheet. One should also ensure that this amount is not subject to the general limitations and exclusions. Occasionally, it has been argued that such a liability should not be included in the completion balance sheet on the basis that to the extent that there is a potential liability to tax there is a corresponding asset, namely the deed. Even if this were true, the tax deed would not be an asset of the target company's (on the assumption that the target is not party to the deed) but an asset of the purchaser's. It should not, therefore, impact upon the target's balance sheet. Any such argument merits little consideration.

Specific covenants — pre-sale dividends

3.6.5 Prior to disposal of a target company it is common for the seller to declare a dividend to eliminate undistributed profits. In this way, monies that would otherwise increase net assets (and hence the price and capital gain for the seller) can be received as franked investment income. However, such pre-sale dividends give rise to a number of issues which the purchaser will need to ensure are covered by the tax deed. If, prior to 6 April 1999, the dividend purports to be paid under a group income election, the purchaser will want to be satisfied that the election is effective. If the election fails, or if no group income election is in place the purchaser will want to ensure that the economic carrying cost of the resulting advance corporation tax is borne by the seller.

Pre-sale dividends: the position where the target company is not a member of a group or ICTA 1988 s 247 does not apply

3.6.5.1 Provided that *ICTA 1988 s 245* does not apply, any advance corporation tax payable by the target company as a result of a pre-sale dividend will not be an absolute cost to the target company because it can be set against mainstream corporation tax of future accounting periods (or carried back to accounting periods commencing in the previous six years by virtue of *ICTA 1988 s 239(3)*). However, it is the seller which benefits from such a dividend by a reduction in income tax liabilities because of the tax credit, or if the seller is a company, by the receipt of franked investment income.

If the target company cannot utilise the advance corporation tax immediately (eg by carrying it back to previous accounting periods and reclaiming mainstream corporation tax already paid) it will need to be financed (eg by borrowing) or the target company will lose the opportunity of using the funds, used to pay the tax, elsewhere in its business. In effect the target company will be financing the seller's reduced income tax liability or, if the seller is a company, the advance corporation tax paid by the target will frank the seller's advance corporation tax on its own dividends and therefore allow the seller to pay dividends without the disadvantage of paying advance corporation tax.

If the target company's profits decline, the carrying cost of this may be considerable. The introduction of the Shadow ACT regime will ensure that the allocation of ACT will not enable the use of such carry forward ACT to be accelerated.

It is also worth noting that if the target company's auditors take the view that the advance corporation tax paid by the target will not be recovered in the foreseeable future, they may not allow the target to reflect the value of the tax credit in its accounts. Thus, the target suffers a double disadvantage: the cost of the funds tied up in paying the advance corporation tax and the adverse impact on its balance sheet. As a result the payment of advance corporation tax on a pre-sale dividend is sometimes one of the liabilities specifically indemnified. The specific covenant dealing with the liability will provide that the seller will incur an immediate obligation to pay an amount equal to the advance corporation tax, which is then reimbursed under the corresponding benefits clause as and when it is credited against mainstream corporation tax. An example of a clause where the seller agrees to pay the purchaser an amount equal to the advance corporation tax arising out of a pre-sale dividend can be worded as set out below.

> 'The Seller agrees to pay the Purchaser an amount equal to the Advance Corporation Tax [arising in respect of the dividend of [£1,000,000] declared on [30 January 1998] and paid on [3 February 1998] or [arising in respect of any qualifying distribution as defined in *ICTA 1988 s 209* on or before Completion] (subject always to the provisions of [corresponding benefits clause]).'

If such a clause is inserted the seller will want to ensure that the corresponding benefits clause is particularly strong and imposes clear obligations upon the purchaser to procure that the target company utilises the advance corporation tax credits and makes reimbursement as soon as reasonably practical. Conversely, the purchaser will want to ensure that payments made under the specific covenant do not count towards the financial cap under the deed as the net overall effect once the credits are used and the seller repaid should be neutral. The purchaser would not want to find that in receiving then repaying a sum in respect of advance corporation tax it has exhausted all or any part of the cap which could prevent future claims. The purchaser will also want to ensure that the exclusions are disapplied.

An alternative to giving a specific covenant is for the seller to provide the purchaser with an interest-free loan to fund the tax payment such loan to be repaid when the purchaser or target company receives the benefit of the resulting tax credits see para 3.6.5.2 below.

Following the abolition of ACT and the introduction of the Shadow ACT regime by the Corporation Tax (Treatment of Unrelieved Surplus Advance Corporation Tax) Regulations 1998 the position will generally be easier when a pre-sale dividend is paid as the cash cost of funding the ACT charge is eliminated. However, the seller will have to consider its view on any carry forward ACT surplus. If the target company has such a surplus, the payment of the pre-sale dividend may inhibit its ability to utilise such surplus. How the purchaser reacts will depend upon the extent to which such surplus was recognised when setting the purchase price. If the surplus had no (or very little effect) on the price then the purchaser has few grounds for complaint as the payment of a pre-sale dividend and the consequential generation of Shadow ACT has not affected the bargain struck with the seller. However, if assumptions were made about the utilisation of the surplus ACT when setting the price and such assumptions are upset by an unexpected pre-sale dividend the position is more difficult. It is hard to see how this can be dealt with through the tax deed as a pound for pound adjustment is inappropriate (the purchaser would not have paid any more than a discounted present value for the ACT surplus based on when the purchaser anticipated it would be used). Further, if the 'loss' to the purchaser caused by the creation of Shadow ACT has to be agreed and quantified it would seem more appropriate to deal with this during the negotiation by way of an adjustment of the purchase price.

An ACT loan

3.6.5.2 Where the target company pays a pre-sale dividend to its parent shortly prior to completion (upon which advance corporation tax is payable), the purchaser has two choices: it could seek a specific indemnity of the type described above or it could try to retain an amount out of the sale proceeds equal to any advance corporation tax liability of the target company as an interest-free loan (the 'ACT loan'). The seller should not object to this as the advance corporation tax charge is a direct result of its action in reducing the size of its tax bill. The loan will be repaid by the purchaser as and when the target company receives credit for the advance corporation tax. Although this protection may be included within the tax deed, such a clause is sometimes included in the main agreement as it requires a loan from the seller to the purchaser (instead of to the target company which has the advance corporation tax liability). Care should be taken to tie this clause in with a corresponding benefits clause otherwise there may be room for the seller, at least on the wording of the deed, to recover the amount twice: once as a repayment of the loan and again as a credit against the mainstream corporation tax liability under any corresponding benefits clause.

It is also necessary to check the exclusions clauses. Where the deed is drafted by reference to the last audited accounts there is usually a clause which excludes any liability of the seller in respect of any tax paid in the ordinary course of business between the accounts date and completion. Without suitable changes in the drafting of the tax deed it could be argued that although the liability for advance corporation tax on the pre-sale dividend is specifically identified in the operative clause, any liability of the sellers to pay is excluded because the advance corporation tax is a tax payable in the ordinary course of business. It is arguable that dividends are not payable in the ordinary course of the target company's business and therefore tax referable to dividends is also outside the ordinary course of business. It is better to avoid such controversies by excluding dividends from any definition of 'actions in ordinary course of business'.

The advantage of an ACT loan is that by taking it outside the ambit of the indemnity the problems of adjustment to the purchase price under *TCGA 1992 s 49* (upon payment of the claim and upon subsequent readjustment when the advance corporation tax credit is used and the seller repaid) are avoided. In addition the financial limits can be left untouched. This mechanism will not be used once ACT is abolished.

Pre-sale dividends: the position where the target company is a member of a group

3.6.5.3 When a pre-sale dividend subject to advance corporation tax is paid the purchaser's options are relatively clear. However, the position is more difficult when the seller purports to pay the pre-sale dividend under a group income election, prior to the introduction of the Shadow ACT regime, thus eliminating the target company's obligation to pay advance corporation tax. The purchaser must decide whether there is a material risk of the group income election failing and in the light of that evaluation decide whether or not the risk is sufficiently grave that it must be dealt with specifically under the tax deed.

Apart from ensuring that the group income election is in place, the purchaser will be concerned to ensure that *ICTA 1988 s 247* is not disapplied because the dividend is paid so soon before completion that the seller no longer beneficially owns the shareholding in the target company. The risk of this has been increased following the introduction of *Sch 7* of the *Finance Act 1997* which excludes only those pre-sale dividends made within 14 days of the actual sale thus, forcing the seller to leave making pre-sale dividends to the last possible moment so increasing the risk of beneficial ownership having already passed.

Under *Finance Act 1997 Sch 7 para 1(3)*, a pre-sale dividend may be treated as if it were a foreign income dividend ('FID'). For the seller, this would have the consequences of a 'real' FID: namely, a non-taxpayer would not be able to reclaim the tax credit and non-residents would not be able to claim the tax credit back under a double tax treaty. For the purchaser, however, the only concern would be to ensure that a valid group income election is in place. This is because, under Sch 7, a pre-sale dividend can be treated in one of two ways: it can either be excluded from the ambit of Sch 7 by virtue of para 6 (pre-sale distributions) or it can be treated as a deemed FID paid under the group income election (by virtue of *ICTA 1988 s 247(5A)* to *(5D)*).

If the seller wishes to ensure that the pre-sale dividend is not treated as a deemed FID, the key issue is timing. Under para 6 of Sch 7, a pre-sale distribution does not fall within the ambit of para 1(3) of Sch 7 if the distribution is made within a 14 day period prior to the date of the change in ownership of the company. The concern for the seller is that unless the distribution is left until the last possible moment a problem in the final negotiations may lead to the date of exchange being pushed beyond 14 days of the dividend.

Thus, the seller is likely to leave it to the last possible moment before making the pre-sale dividend, say, for example, the very day of the exchange and simultaneous completion of the sale. The purchaser will need to think carefully about whether or not the beneficial ownership still exists with sufficient certainty to ensure that the normal provisions of s 247 can apply. Conversely, if the seller is happy for the pre-sale dividend to be treated as a deemed FID, it can still be paid under a group income election long before the sale election provided that the seller is resident in the United Kingdom and holds *all* of the ordinary share capital of the target company. The purchaser will therefore have to be satisfied that there is no small minority holding which could prejudice this position.

Provided that the purchaser can be satisfied that the group income election is valid and in place, it should generally be possible to meet any concerns regarding ACT payable in respect of pre-sale distributions by including a specific indemnity rather than pursuing a loan and retention route.

Once the Shadow ACT regime is introduced this area will be simplified. Intra group dividends will not attract ACT and will de facto be paid under a group income election unless such dividends are paid from franked investment income and an appropriate election is made.

Specific covenants — TCGA 1992 s 179

3.6.6 A liability under *TCGA 1992 s 179* triggered by the sale will usually be covered by the general covenant as the tax liability will arise as a consequence of an 'Event occurring on or before Completion'. It is worth noting that unless there is a simultaneous exchange and completion, it is execution of an unconditional contract which causes the target to leave the group and triggers the s 179 charge. Where the purchaser has a particular concern in this respect, it can be dealt with by way of a specific indemnity in respect of s 179 liabilities. This will also facilitate the exclusion of any charge under s 179 from the exclusions or any *de minimis* limit.

A clause to cover a liability under *TCGA 1992 s 179* can be worded in one of the following ways.

> 'The Seller covenants to pay the Purchaser an amount equal to any tax arising under *TCGA 1992 s 179* as a result of entering into or performing this Agreement.'

or

> 'The Seller covenants to pay the purchaser an amount equal to any liability arising under *TCGA 1992 s 179* in respect of the property owned by the Company as a result of entering into or performing this Agreement.'

It is often the case that where the seller anticipates that there may be a liability under s 179 it will enter into a pre-sale reorganisation in order to reduce or eliminate the charge. In such circumstances it is right for the purchaser to identify the reorganisation as a specific risk and seek protection from any tax liability which may arise as a result of that reorganisation as well as any liability arising under s 179.

Specific covenants — pre-sale reorganisations

3.6.7 Occasionally there may have been a reorganisation prior to the sale. This may either be a commercially driven reorganisation, for example, to extract companies and assets to be retained by the seller from the target group, or, the result of some tax planning exercise by the seller. There is usually a specific clause put into the deed to indemnify the purchaser from any liability arising out of such a reorganisation. The purchaser will want to ensure that there is no risk that a claim could be denied because, for example, it is arguable that the liability arises from something that the purchaser does after completion. The purchaser may also want to specifically identify the tax risks of the reorganisation so that they can be carved out from the exclusions and limits. The seller may wish to seek an indemnity from the purchaser to ensure that the purchaser does not do anything to undo what the seller has done.

The answer to these issues lies in the general approach to the deed. The purchaser is buying an asset which it hopes to use to generate profits. Should it be fettered in its use of the asset by what the previous owner has done? Should it have to consider whether what it does will have an adverse effect on the seller? Conversely, should it be able to do something which it knows will adversely affect the seller and which is not done for any good commercial reason. Outside the context of the pre-sale reorganisation these questions can be dealt with by the following type of exclusion clause:

> '[Exclusion for any taxation] "which would not have arisen but for a voluntary act carried out by the Purchaser or the Company after the date of this deed being an act which:
>
> (i) is not in the ordinary course of the normal business of the Company [as carried on at the date of this deed];
>
> (ii) could reasonably have been avoided; and
>
> (iii) the Purchaser was aware would give rise to the Taxation in question."'

However, where there has been a pre-sale reorganisation different considerations come into play. The seller wants both the cash from the sale and for it to be taxed at the lowest rate. Although this is a common aim on the part of seller, should the purchaser have to co-operate in the seller's tax planning? Further, should the purchaser bear the cost if a liability which arises after completion is a result of the reorganisation? Should the purchaser indemnify the seller if it goes wrong? There is no reason in principle why the seller should not indemnify the purchaser for tax liabilities arising after completion in respect of a reorganisation prior to completion. The way this can be done is by defining the reorganisation, by setting out the various steps and then by putting in a clause which specifically identifies as a risk 'tax arising out of the Reorganisation whenever arising'. Again the identification of this specific risk means that it can easily be excluded from the *de minimis* limits and certain exclusions can be disapplied.

The seller may object to setting out the steps of the reorganisation on the basis that it invites attack from Inland Revenue. However, should the purchaser's protection be limited in order to help the seller's tax planning?

The fact that the purchaser may not have a full picture of the pre-sale reorganisation and the question of whether an indemnity should be given to the seller are issues which must be considered together. It is one thing to say the seller will not be liable if the purchaser's acts give rise to a liability, it is a totally different matter to go on to say that the purchaser will pay the seller if subsequent acts by the purchaser damage the seller. The seller is in a far better position to know what future acts are likely to cause problems. Such acts can be divided into two classes.

Those acts which give rise to a liability in the target company and those acts which give rise to a liability on the seller, (in respect of which the seller is seeking an indemnity). The first category can be dealt with by the seller stating which acts are likely to cause problems and requiring the purchaser not to do them. The purchaser will then need to decide how likely it is that it will need to do the various acts and assess the risk. Assuming that the seller and purchaser can agree, liability can be excluded by specific exclusions for those acts. If the seller and purchaser cannot agree, the purchaser has to decide whether it wants the target company with those particular fetters, whether the price needs to be renegotiated, or indeed whether it wants the target company at all. It is not unknown for the seller's tax planning to cause unnecessary problems for the purchaser and thus reduce the value to the purchaser of the target company.

As far as the purchaser indemnifying the seller is concerned this is not a course which would usually be recommended. If one act of the purchasers were to give rise to a liability for both the seller and the purchaser it would be unfortunate for the purchaser to have to pay the seller and yet to have no claim against the seller because of an exclusion.

As far as the seller is concerned the views expressed above would imply that there is no sympathy for the seller in such cases. Certainly, faced with arguments such as those expressed above it is difficult to justify a case for the seller. However, at the end of the day it is all down to bargaining and what the seller can get away with. This depends on the need of the purchaser to buy the company.

Suggested approach to reorganisations

3.6.7.1 A suggested approach to dealing with a pre-sale reorganisation is summarised as stated below.

(a) Define 'Reorganisation' by describing the various steps in the definitions clause.

(b) Indemnify against any tax arising out of the reorganisation.

(c) Decide whether the clause should include any tax liability arising after completion.

(d) Decide whether the clause should describe acts which the purchaser should not do and exclude any liability resulting from such acts.

(e) Decide whether the reorganisation indemnity should be excluded from the financial limits or time limits.

(f) Decide whether there should be a contest clause establishing which party has the right to conduct any disputes with a taxing authority. Such a clause usually imposes limitations on the party conducting the dispute and it is usual for 'contest clauses' to give the seller the right to conduct the dispute in respect of pre-completion liabilities. However, if the seller wishes to have the conduct for the reorganisation the clause may have to be modified as the tax liability may arise post-completion. It is hard for the purchaser to resist this where the seller will ultimately have to pay the tax cost of the reorganisation, under the provisions of the tax deed.

Cost clause

3.7 Whichever approach is adopted on the general and specific covenants, most deeds will contain a cost clause and a gross up clause.

On the basis that the tax deed should fully protect a purchaser against the adverse effect of pre-completion tax liabilities, it is difficult for the seller to resist the argument that this protection should extend to associated costs. However, the precise extent of any indemnity against costs will be the subject of negotiation.

The seller will want to ensure that the purchaser's costs are reasonable in quantum and justifiably incurred. For example, if an inconsequential claim, for say £5,000, is made as a result of a straightforward adjustment (which does not have wider ramifications and which the taxpayer clearly has little grounds to contest), the seller would not want to find itself having to pay an amount in respect of the tax and also, say, the substantial fees of a leading tax QC needlessly instructed by the purchaser. To protect against situations such as this: where costs are out of proportion to the size and importance of the issue, the seller will generally expect to limit the purchaser's indemnity to 'reasonable costs properly incurred'. A purchaser will sometimes argue that it does not want to debate the quantum of costs as the issue should be simply whether it was reasonable and proper for it to incur them. If the answer to this question is that the purchaser was acting reasonably when it decided to incur them, arguably the quantum is irrelevant. On this basis the purchaser will change the limitation to 'costs reasonably and properly incurred'. The seller will argue that if the purchaser is not paying the bills it may not pay proper attention to ensuring that costs are at an appropriate level which the former wording protects against.

The seller will also need to ensure that the provision dealing with costs only requires it to pay the purchaser, where there is a bona fide claim under the tax deed, or there would have been one had the purchaser not successfully contested an assessment from a tax authority. If the purchaser takes advice in connection with a potential claim which proves to be outside the tax deed (eg because it is covered by an exclusion), the seller will not expect to have to meet the purchaser's costs.

One issue which can cause difficulty is whether or not the indemnity against costs should cover just external costs or should extend to the target company's and purchaser's internal costs: the cost of management time etc. The seller sometimes takes the view that dealing with past issues is part and parcel of the routine management involved in running a company and therefore the purchaser should accept that it is liable to meet such cost. This argument is sometimes motivated by the concern that an unscrupulous purchaser may seek to pass on general management costs unassociated with any claim to the seller.

The purchaser may take the view that if it has to tie up valuable resources, for example, the time of its Finance Director, dealing with a claim and possibly helping the seller to put together a case to contest an assessment then that should be for the account of the seller. If, for example, the seller contests an assessment before the Courts, the purchaser will need to make the target's financial records available and those personnel involved at the relevant time may be required to give evidence etc. This commitment coupled with the time spent by the purchaser monitoring the claim will represent a costly exercise for the purchaser's group. As a practical matter the purchaser is unlikely to co-operate to the extent required by the seller if it is meeting the cost. As a matter of principle, assuming that the claim under the deed is justified, the purchaser's view will be that associated costs whether external or internal stem from the unprovided for pre-sale tax liability, which the seller had promised would not arise. Therefore, the seller should meet such costs. A compromise may be for the seller to agree to meet such costs only when they are incurred in connection with a hearing before a Tribunal, the Commissioners or the Courts, on the basis that in such circumstances the co-operation and internal management costs go beyond normal tax compliance.

Another issue to be considered is whether the seller should provide security for costs? Prior to the seller undertaking the conduct of the tax claim it is usual to secure the purchaser against any costs that may be incurred. Such clauses are usually qualified by securing the purchaser to its 'reasonable satisfaction', thus preventing the purchaser from claiming extortionate amounts from the seller.

A typical cost clause involves the seller covenanting to pay the purchaser an amount equal to:

> 'any [[reasonable] costs or expenses [properly] incurred] [costs and expenses reasonably and properly incurred] by the Purchaser or the Company in connection with any Tax Liability the subject of a valid claim under this deed or in connection with any action taken in avoiding, resisting or settling any action under this deed.'

Gross-up clauses

3.8 The modern tax deed generally contains a group of clauses protecting the seller from the risk that payments under the deed will be devalued because of their tax treatment leaving the purchaser with an insufficient sum to meet the liability giving rise to the claim.

Example

A Ltd buys B Ltd from C Ltd and obtains a full tax indemnity in favour of itself and B Ltd but without a gross-up clause. B Ltd makes a claim for £100,000 which C Ltd settles. The payment from C Ltd is taxed in B Ltd. Consequently, the net of tax payment from C Ltd that B Ltd is left with is £69,000 (assuming a corporation tax rate of 31%) to discharge a pre-completion tax liability of £100,000. The net effect is that B Ltd is only partially indemnified.

The provisions deal with two situations: first, a deduction or withholding from a payment under the deed and, second the situation where a gross payment is taxable in the hands of the recipient. Under current UK law it is difficult to see how a deduction of tax could be required to be made from a payment (unless and to the extent that the payment contains a sum of contractual (annual) interest because it is paid late). The position could change if there is a change in law. The second risk that the payment may be taxed in the hands of the recipient is more serious (see below).

These risks are dealt with by:

(i) requiring the seller to make all payments gross unless a deduction or withholding is required by law;

(ii) stating that if a deduction or withholding is required by law, or if a payment is subject to tax upon receipt, the seller will gross up to ensure that sufficient additional sums are paid to ensure that the amount received by the purchaser net of all taxes is equal to the liability in respect of which the claim is made.

Prior to the *Zim* case concession (ESC D33) the gross-up was often a contentious area. Currently, where there is a seller/purchaser only deed (ie the target company is not party to the deed) then the problem should not arise. However, where the purchaser insists upon an indemnity in favour of the target company then it is perfectly proper for the seller to refuse to give a gross-up. It is unreasonable for the purchaser to expose the seller to the easily avoided risk of having the payment taxed and then insist that the seller bears the cost.

Even where the deed would appear to fall within the concession to the *Zim* case, most purchasers will insist on still including a gross-up clause. Their argument is that if the seller accepts that it indemnifies on a full indemnity basis, then however remote the risk of a payment under the tax deed being taxed in the purchaser's hands, it should be covered. If it is not, the purchaser risks being only partially indemnified.

There are two types of gross-up clause in common usage. The first type states that the seller will pay such amount as after deduction of tax will leave the purchaser with an amount equal to the tax liability. The problem with this type of clause is that it will not be known at the time of the claim whether an assessment will be made upon the recipient and, if so, at what rate. If no assessment is made the seller will need to be reimbursed if it was assumed a gross-up would apply when a payment was made. An example of this sort of clause can be worded as set out below:

> 'If any sum payable by the Seller under this Deed shall be subject to tax in the hands of the recipient, the Seller shall be obliged to pay such sum as will after such Tax be the same amount as the recipient would have been entitled to receive in the absence of the tax charge.'

Another type merely provides that the sellers will pay an amount equal to:

> 'any liability to tax resulting from the receipt by the purchaser of any payment under this deed.'

It should be noted that this will include a payment under this particular clause itself. Thus, where a payment is made under the tax deed which is taxed in the purchaser's hands, the clause above operates and a further payment is made equal to the tax on the original payment which additional payment is itself taxed, the clause operates again and the gross-up payment is taxed and so on. The obvious problem with this type of clause is that it needs a number of payments.

In fact the ultimate amounts payable under each type of clause are the same; for proof of this see appendix 4.

A variant of the second type of clause is merely to undertake that the seller will pay tax on any of the other claims other than on the gross-up. This will mean that only one payment need be made. Although the purchaser is not fully recompensed for tax on the payment under the gross-up clause, it is simpler and, provided the magnitude of the claims is not too great, the tax on the second and subsequent amounts and thus the costs to the purchaser should not be too large.

A typical deduction/withholding/gross-up clause is as follows:

> 'A. Deduction from Payments and Gross-up.

A.1 All sums payable by the Seller to the Purchaser (or vice versa) under this Deed shall be paid free and clear of all deductions or withholdings whatsoever save only as may be required by law.

A.2 If any such deductions or withholdings as are referred to in sub-clause A.1 are required by law the Seller or the Purchaser (as the case may be) (the 'Paying Party') shall be obliged to pay to the other party (the 'Receiving Party') such sum as will after such deduction or withholding has been made leave the Receiving Party with the same amount as it would have been entitled to receive in the absence of any such requirement to make a deduction or withholding.

A.3 If any amount payable under this Deed shall be subject to Taxation in the hands of the Receiving Party, the amount payable shall be increased so as to ensure that the net amount retained by the Receiving Party after taking such Taxation into account is equal to the full amount which would have been retained but for such Taxation.'

Sometimes the seller will also wish to ensure that if it is forced to deduct tax and gross up it is reimbursed if the purchaser receives the benefit of any tax credit in respect of the sums deducted. It is hard for the purchaser to resists this. In the absence of such a provision the purchaser could end up with an overall benefit as a result of the tax claim. The gross up would ensure that cash received equalled the tax liability yet in addition the purchaser will have a tax credit. A typical clause dealing with this may be as follows:

> 'If the Paying Party makes an increased payment pursuant to Clauses [ ] in respect of which the Receiving Party obtains a tax credit the Receiving Party shall reimburse the Paying Party such amount as the Receiving Party shall (acting in good faith) determine so as to leave the Receiving Party in the same position it would have been in had no such deduction or withholding been made but only to the extent that the Receiving Party can do so without prejudicing the retention of any credit or relief obtained as a result of the deduction or withholding.'

When presented with such a clause the purchaser may wish to add wording to make it clear that reimbursement will be given only once a tax credit is actually utilised, not simply when it becomes available.

Time for payment

3.9 Once a liability under the deed has arisen the question arises as to when payment should be made. The purchaser will normally require the cash to be made available in time to pay the tax liability. The seller will normally wish to leave payment as late as possible. It is relatively easy to specify a date when payments should be made if there is an actual liability for tax for which the company must account. However, the deed must also cater for the possibility that a liability has been eliminated by the use of some relief, or alternatively, the liability arises because of a loss of a repayment or credit. Deeds tend to vary on the dates for payment. However, some frequently encountered clauses are set out in the following paragraphs.

Where there is an actual payment of tax due it is usual to provide that the seller will pay the purchaser 'X days before the day on which a payment of tax becomes due'; X is a variable figure open to negotiation. Obviously the seller will err towards a smaller number of days; the purchaser towards a larger number of days. Sometimes it is the practice to define 'days' as 'Business Days'. The seller will also want to ensure that it is not prejudiced by any delay of the purchaser in notifying it of the potential claim. A Seller will usually want to specify that its obligation to pay is the later of [X] days before the tax becomes due and [X] days of being notified.

Another variant is to state that 'the seller shall make payment in respect of the claim on the date on which that taxation becomes due'. At first sight this may look unduly beneficial to the seller. However, it is usually qualified by some wording which states 'no payment shall be treated as being made until cleared funds in respect thereof are available to the purchasers'. In effect this recognises that the purchaser should not really care upon which date the money is paid provided that on the date that the payment becomes due they have cleared funds to pay the bill. It is up to the seller to put the purchaser in funds. The usual reason for providing a number of days prior to the date of payment is in order to allow a cheque to clear. Where no payment is made until cleared funds are available the number of days prior to payment becomes irrelevant. The 'cleared funds' wording can be further refined by stating that any payment which becomes due from the seller on a day which is not a business day shall be treated as paid on the next following business day, and any payment which is made after 3 pm on any day shall, for the purposes of calculating interest, be deemed to have been paid on the next following day.

Where there would have been an actual payment of taxation but that payment has been eliminated by the use of a relief there are two alternative dates for payment. The first is usually expressed as set out below:

> '[X] days before the day on which the payment would have been due had the claim been satisfied by the company by payment rather than by utilisation of a relief and for these purposes it is assumed that the claim would have been made and tax would become due at the earliest possible date (assuming no application for postponement).'

The alternative is to state that the tax shall be 'deemed to be due on the date on which the tax which would otherwise have been relieved but for the utilisation of the relief concerned is itself due'.

The philosophy behind these two clauses can be most readily seen by taking an example. Assuming that a target company makes losses following completion and the tax liability arises pre-completion the target company would have the option of either paying the liability or carrying the loss back under *ICTA 1988 s 393A* . Usually the deed will provide that where the company elects to carry the loss back then there will be a deemed liability for taxation for which the sellers are liable. Under the first type of clause the seller must pay the tax as if no losses had been carried back and utilised. The purchaser therefore receives the money immediately upon the date when tax would otherwise be payable even though the losses which have otherwise been utilised could not have otherwise been used. In effect the purchaser is receiving an accelerated receipt for the use of those losses.

The second type of payment clause states that, even though losses have been carried back and the taxation has been eliminated, the seller is not liable to pay anything until such time as the losses which were carried back would have been used by the purchaser to reduce an actual liability for taxation in the target company (or in a member of any group of which the target company is a member). In the example given, if the target company continued to make losses for a number of years then, until such time as it makes profits and the carried forward losses could have been utilised, there is no obligation on the seller to make a payment under the deed. There would appear to be no middle ground between the two clauses. However, if the second type of clause is adopted there is no incentive on the purchaser to carry back the losses. As the purchaser must elect to carry back the losses, a failure to do so will expose the seller to an immediate liability. Unless a clause in the deed obliges the purchaser so to do, the seller is helpless in this matter. In any event, it can be argued that there is no reason for the seller to be given the benefit of the purchaser's losses. Where the target company is a member of a group, the second type of clause may not be as detrimental to the purchaser as first may appear because the losses may otherwise have been utilised by way of group relief by surrender to another group company, in which case the purchaser should then be able to claim from the seller. All that happens in this case is that a tax liability of the target company is eliminated at the expense of creating a liability in another group company.

A further point to note is that utilisation of the relief should only affect the date for payment and not the actual timing of the liability. The reason for this is that if the deed is limited by time then a liability must arise within the time limit. The fact that a date for payment does not arise within the time limit does not absolve the seller from a liability to pay; whereas, if the liability is actually put off until such time as the relief is utilised, that liability could conceivably fall outside the time limits.

Where there is no actual payment of tax to be made because the potential liability which would have given rise to a payment under the tax deed is prevented from crystallising by utilisation of a pre-completion relief, which has been paid for by the purchaser or because the claim is for the loss of a repayment of tax, there needs to be a deemed date for payment. Where there is a loss of repayment it is usual to deem the date to be the date upon which the repayment would have been made though this may be difficult to determine as there is no due date for a repayment of tax. Where there is a loss of a pre-completion relief then payment should be made by the seller upon it becoming clear that the relief has been lost. The reason for this is that the purchaser, having paid for the relief, requires its money back.

Default interest

3.10 In the event that payment is made late then it is usual to provide for a rate of default interest. This is interest over and above any interest that is payable to the appropriate revenue authority for late payment of tax.

In the definition of Taxation (see para 3.5.1 above) it will be remembered that the seller would like to protect itself from a situation where having paid an amount to the purchaser, the purchaser has not paid the Inland Revenue and so incurs interest for late payment. In such circumstances the seller should not be liable for any interest becoming payable to the Inland Revenue after they have put the purchaser in funds.

An example of a typical clause dealing with default interest in the event of late payment of claims under the tax deed is set out below.

> 'If the Seller fails to pay any sum due under this Deed on the due date of payment, the Seller shall pay interest on that amount from the due date until actual payment at the rate of [X] per cent per annum above the Base Rate for the time being of [ABC] Bank PLC compounded monthly.'

Default interest is intended to make the seller pay sooner rather than later. Without default interest it could be beneficial for the seller to invest an amount which is due to the purchaser rather than to pay the purchaser. If, for example, the official Inland Revenue rate of interest for late payments for a tax liability is (say) 10% pa and the seller can invest the amount needed to satisfy the claim of, say, £1 million at 12%

pa then no matter how late it pays the claim it will still make a profit. However, the seller will have to pay tax on any interest earned. It will only be beneficial where the seller has losses with which to shelter any tax liability. Assuming this to be the case, then if the seller paid promptly it would cost the seller £1 million. If the seller satisfied the claim two years later it will cost the seller £1 million plus interest on overdue tax of £200,000, less the interest on money invested of £240,000. Thus, by delaying the seller, saves £40,000.

It is occasionally argued that there is no need for a default rate of interest. The reason being that the deed is drafted so as to cover the purchaser for interest on late payment of the tax. As a result, the purchaser need not pay the relevant revenue authority until any dispute regarding the liability is resolved, whereupon the purchaser pays the relevant revenue authority the tax (if any) plus interest and penalties and the seller merely reimburses the purchaser. In effect the seller dictates when the purchaser pays the relevant revenue authority. The problem with this is that the purchaser may have other claims against the Inland Revenue and failing to pay this liability may create ill-feeling. Further, the purchaser may be entitled to repayments from the Inland Revenue in respect of another company or other companies in the purchaser's group and a failure to pay may prejudice these repayments. Arguments against any default rate should be rejected by the purchaser. The purchaser requires the cash and a default rate encourages the seller to pay.

A further reason why the argument should be rejected and a default rate included is that it does not cater for the position where there is no actual liability of tax to be paid and a liability under the deed only arises because of the loss of a relief or the loss of the repayment. In these cases there is no incentive at all for the seller to pay the purchaser.

Rate of interest

3.10.1 The rate of interest to be used is a matter of negotiation. The debtor should wish to pay rather than invest elsewhere. However, the rate should not be so penal that a court would not enforce it. Usually 2% or 3% over base rate is the norm. However, if the seller is a bank a higher rate should be considered. Further, where the seller is a foreign company, consideration should be given to the comparative rates of interest depending upon in which currency it is payable.

Chapter 4

Tax Deeds: Protecting the Seller

Introduction

4.1 The sale and purchase agreement is based on the broad premise that, apart from tax which has been provided in the accounts or which arises in the ordinary course of the target's business since the date of those accounts, the company should suffer no tax liability. The seller accepts that the tax deed puts this principle into effect. However, the seller must ensure that the tax deed contains limitations and exclusions which prevent the purchaser exploiting the terms of the tax deed to secure an advantage which was not intended and to which the purchaser is not entitled. For example, the seller would not expect the purchaser to be able to claim for a readily avoidable tax liability triggered by the purchaser's deliberate post-completion actions outside the ordinary course of business. The seller would also want to ensure that to the extent a claim could be made under either the warranties or the tax deed, there is an exclusion which prevents a claim in respect of the same liability being made under both. The clauses containing limitations and exclusions preventing the tax deed extending beyond what is intended are commonly referred to as 'vendor protection clauses'. This chapter examines some of the general and specific issues arising from the drafting of vendor protection clauses.

General consideration — the interaction of vendor protection clauses with the sale and purchase agreement

4.2 A practical difficulty that frequently arises when negotiating vendor protection clauses in the tax deed is the vexed question of how they interact with the exclusions and limitations contained in the sale and purchase agreement and what drafting is required to ensure that the two sets of provisions are complimentary.

The sale and purchase agreement will contain many of the vendor protection clauses one would expect to find in the tax deed. These limitations and exclusions generally purport to cover the warranties and sometimes even purport to extend to the tax deed. If this point is not carefully addressed it can lead to the unfortunate position where advisers specialising in company law negotiating the sale and purchase agreement, agree the form of limitations and exclusions which apply to the tax warranties and possibly to the tax deed. As non-tax experts they will make such agreements without fully appreciating the ramifications of what is agreed. Apart from the risk that what is negotiated will be unsuitable, this can give rise to a number of other issues.

One likely difficulty is that having concluded considered negotiation and drafting of vendor protection clauses in the tax deed, the tax advisers are informed that these agreements must be scrapped as the position has already been agreed 'commercially' in the context of the sale and purchase agreement. Invariably what is agreed in the main agreement is not specifically geared towards tax as the limitations and exclusions apply to a host of other warranties and consequently they are not particularly well drafted in the tax context. An alternative problem arises if the clauses are not conformed and the exclusions and limitations in the agreement and the tax deed both purport to apply to tax warranties and the tax deed but are not identical, leading to possible conflicts.

To avoid these potential difficulties it is important that the corporate advisers and tax advisers agree at the outset that the tax advisers will be responsible for negotiating exclusions and limitations applicable to tax. One possible exception are the financial (and time) limits, which are essentially a straightforward commercial point where the tax adviser should agree to follow what is agreed in the context of the sale and purchase agreement. However, the tax adviser should ensure that the client knows the statutory time limitations for making tax claims and advises the purchaser to agree longer time limitations for tax matters. Having agreed the areas of responsibility it is advisable to insert a clause in the tax deed stating:

> 'The exclusions and limitations in clauses [ ]–[ ] of this Deed shall apply to the Tax Warranties in the Agreement *mutatis mutandis*'.

The agreement should make it clear that its limitations and exclusions do not apply to the tax warranties which are governed by the limitations and exclusions in the tax deed. Another alternative is to put in wording to the effect that if there is a conflict between the provisions of the tax deed and agreement, the provisions of the deed will take priority as regards tax and the tax warranties.

General consideration — general drafting

4.2.1 It is quite common for the purchaser's advisers to include some vendor protection clauses in their preliminary draft of the tax deed. The seller should consider the wording of these clauses carefully to ensure that they are not unduly restrictive and should consider what further provisions may be necessary. When inserting new provisions, the seller's advisers must ensure that their standard precedent wording conforms with the terminology used in the purchaser's deed.

Specific exclusions and limitations

4.3 Broadly the tax deed draws a line in time and allocates risks either side of that line. Without more, the seller would be liable for an unlimited time and for an unlimited amount. Further, there are certain liabilities which, if not excluded, would expose the seller to risks which were not intended. Therefore, there are a number of exclusions which are usually included in the tax deed.

Financial limits

4.3.1 Most tax deeds include financial limits for claims. Commonly clauses setting out such limits are divided into three parts:

(a) a minimum limit below which individual claims cannot be made (sometimes referred to as the '*de minimis* limit');

(b) a minimum limit for the aggregate of all claims below which claims cannot be made (sometimes also called the '*de minimis* limit' and sometimes referred to as a 'cushion' or 'threshold'); and

(c) a maximum or cap for the aggregate of all claims, above which claims are excluded.

Sometimes there is a fourth part which excludes specific identified risks from any of the limits.

A typical financial limits clause is set out below:

> '(a) [Subject to Clauses (b) and (c) the liability of the Seller[s] under this Deed shall not (when aggregated with any liability under the Warranties) exceed £[consideration];
>
> (b) The Seller[s] shall [only be liable under this Deed to the extent that] [or] [not be liable under this Deed unless] the amount of any Tax Liability subject to the covenants contained in this Deed (when aggregated with any liability under the Warranties) exceeds in aggregate [£500,000];
>
> (c) The Purchaser shall not be entitled to recover any sums whatsoever in respect of any particular Claim under this Deed in respect of which the amount claimed does not exceed [£5,000] and such Claims shall be disregarded for the purposes of sub-Clauses (a) and (b).'

Where there is an exclusion for specific risks a clause worded as set out below can be added:

> 'To the extent that a claim arises under clause [ ] of this deed, the limits in this clause [ ] shall not apply and such a claim shall be disregarded when aggregating claims for the purposes of the sub-clauses.'

Small claims

4.3.1.1 Broadly, the seller can argue in favour of (c) above on the basis that it is unreasonable for the purchaser to have the ability to make a 'nuisance' claim knowing that they will be fully indemnified against tax and the costs of the claim, when the value of the claim is such that it is of no real significance in the context of the transaction, but the claim would nevertheless put the seller to great administrative inconvenience and expense. Below a certain level it is more inconvenient for the seller to deal with and settle a claim than it is for the purchaser to bear the cost of it. The purchaser's argument to counter the above reasoning is that as it is the purchaser who will suffer the economic loss through the target company, it is for the purchaser to decide whether such a loss is material. Furthermore, whereas a small claim under the warranties may involve establishing a breach and loss stemming from such breach, which then has to be quantified, the administrative burden imposed by a tax deed, which provides a quite easy means of recovery of a liquidated sum, is considerably reduced.

If the purchaser decides to accept the inclusion of (c), it must consider the risk of multiple small claims being made. For example, if, in the preceding years, the target had made a large number of annual payments to different parties and failed in each case to deduct an amount in respect of basic rate income tax under *ICTA 1988 s 349*, the aggregate of the individual claims may amount to a substantial sum, although each is under the £5,000 floor set by the above clause. The purchaser may insist on wording being inserted to catch this eventuality, or alternatively, insist that the document makes it clear that, whilst small individual claims cannot be recovered, they count towards the *de minimis* limit in (b) (although they would then also count towards the maximum limit in (a)).

Cushion or threshold

4.3.1.2 The arguments used by the seller and the purchaser for and against the inclusion of (b) are largely the same as those discussed in relation to (c). Again the purchaser may argue that if it suffers economic loss by virtue of the target company incurring an unprovided for tax liability, it should be able to recover its loss pound for pound. The seller can use the arguments discussed above and in addition will be able to point to the fact that it is market practice to include such a *de minimis* limit.

One point to be noted in the context of (b) is that the limitation can take the form of a 'cushion' or a 'threshold' (sometimes also referred to as a 'buffer' or in the USA as a 'basket'). In the example above the second alternative, which does not allow claims 'unless' a given sum is exceeded, is a 'threshold' and the clause operates so that once the tax liabilities exceed a certain sum the whole amount becomes payable. When the provision is drafted as a 'cushion' the words, 'only be liable under this deed to the extent that' are included and the words 'not be liable under this deed unless' are deleted. Where there is a cushion the liability of the seller only arises if, and to the extent that, tax payable exceeds a certain sum. For example, if the *de minimis* limit was a 'cushion' and was set at £100,000, then a successful tax claim for £120,000 would make the sellers liable for only £20,000. In general, the purchaser should insist upon, and a reasonable seller should agree to, a threshold rather than a cushion.

The 'cap'

4.3.1.3 The figure inserted as the maximum limit for claims (in (a) above) is a matter of negotiation but generally it is accepted that the absolute maximum for claims should be the amount of consideration paid by the purchaser. There may be exceptions to this rule; where for example, the target company has had a large business hived-out of it so that its past tax liabilities are potentially much larger than the target company's current net asset value and profits would indicate. Such cases are the exception. One of the more common exceptions is the case where the purchaser expects the value of debts assigned with the target company to form part of the maximum limit or where the purchaser repays inter-company indebtedness pursuant to a term in the sale and purchase agreement.

Example

Company 'A' agrees to buy the target company for £3m on the basis that the target company is free of debt. In fact, however, the target company owes a member of the seller's group £1m. In these circumstances, Company 'A' may agree to pay £2m for the target company's shares and to procure the repayment by the target company of the £1m debt to the former group member. The purchaser may well select this route because the consideration for stamp duty purposes will be taken at £2m (provided the agreements are properly structured and drafted following the case of *Spectros International plc (in voluntary liquidation) v Madden (Inspector of Taxes)* [1997] STC 114). The advantage to the seller is that it lowers any capital gain on the disposal of the shares. In such a case Company 'A' would expect the cap on liability to be £3m and not to be restricted to the £2m which was the sum paid for the shares.

The link between financial limits and corresponding benefits and savings

4.3.1.4 The tax deed often contains clauses which provide that if the purchaser or target company receives a repayment or benefit in respect of a claim made and settled under the tax deed, the amount of such repayment or benefit should flow through to the seller (see 4.4.1 and 4.4.2 below). In such circumstances it is reasonable for the purchaser to require that this is reflected in the limits. For example, a seller pays a purchaser £1m in respect of a tax claim made under the tax deed where the maximum limit is also £1m. Subsequently, the Inland Revenue agree that the tax was not properly due and refund the tax to the purchaser. The purchaser, pursuant to the provisions of the tax deed, refunds the money to the seller. One would expect that as parity has been restored the tax deed should operate as if no claim had ever been made. However, whilst this may be true in cash terms, when the purchaser comes to make another claim it may find (in the absence of an express provision to the contrary) that it cannot make such a claim, as it has already exhausted the maximum limit of £1m. The purchaser has the right to expect that the financial limits in the tax deed will operate in respect of the real net financial losses. The following clause could be added by the purchaser to the end of the financial limits clause in (a) (see 4.3.1 above) in order to give it this protection:

> 'The amount in this sub-clause [(a)] shall be increased by an amount received by the Seller by way of payment or set-off under clauses [x or y] of this deed.'

The references to clauses [x or y] are to the clauses dealing with corresponding benefits, savings and refunds.

An alternative way of dealing with this problem is to disregard any amounts which are paid and subsequently refunded under the corresponding benefits, savings and refunds clauses. Such a clause would be worded as set out below:

> 'Any amounts paid pursuant to clause [operative provision] and subsequently refunded and/or set-off under either clause [ ], [ ] or [ ] [the corresponding benefits, savings and refund clauses] shall be disregarded to the extent of the refund and/or set-off for the purpose of clause [a] in the event of any further claim under clause [operative provision].'

Although there is no difference in substance between this and increasing the amount of the financial limits, a seller may be prepared to accept the latter clause more readily because psychologically they do not feel they are exposing themselves to any greater liability. This is even more likely to be the case where the purchaser seeks to extend the limits where the tax claim is in respect of a secondary liability (see below).

The problem of the limits not reflecting real financial loss is not restricted to cases where there is a repayment or a corresponding benefit in respect of a claim, but also extends to situations where a claim is the primary liability of a party other than the target company, and the target's liability to tax results from a secondary claim. For example, in certain circumstances an unscrupulous seller could manipulate its own tax affairs or those of its group to ensure that a secondary liability devolves upon the target company and the resulting claim is satisfied under the tax deed. Unless specific provision is made, this has the effect of satisfying the liability at the same cost to the seller as if it had settled the primary liability but with the side effect of exhausting the limit for claims under the tax deed. This is best illustrated by example.

Example

X Ltd owns 3 subsidiaries; A, B and C Ltd. A Ltd owns Blackacre which in October 1998 it transfers to C Ltd under *TCGA 1992 s 171*. In January 1999 X Ltd sells A Ltd and B Ltd for £5m to Mr P. There is a cap on claims agreed at the purchase price of £5m. There is no *TCGA 1992 s 179* liability upon the sale as C Ltd does not leave the X Ltd Group. In February 1999, C Ltd sells Blackacre and is subsequently assessed for £5m for corporation tax on the capital gain. C Ltd at X Ltd's direction wilfully refuses to pay the tax. Under *TCGA 1992 s 190* the Inland Revenue seek to recover the tax from A Ltd as it both owned Blackacre and was a member of X Ltd's group within the two year period prior to the crystallisation of the gain. Mr P claims against X Ltd under the tax deed and the claim is satisfied. However, X Ltd points out that having settled the claim no further liability can arise under the tax deed or warranties as the cap on claims has been reached.

As the number of sections under which secondary liability can arise continues to increase it is important to cover the sort of risk highlighted in the example above. The following clause can be adopted:

> 'The amount in sub-clause [a] shall be increased by the amount of any liability of the Seller arising under this deed in respect of Taxation which is primarily the liability of or is attributable to a person other than the Company.'

The seller may also wish to add wording to ensure that the *de minimis* limits are similarly increased to prevent the purchasers exhausting the *de minimis* limits but leaving the maximum limit unaffected. As stated above, the seller may find it more acceptable if, instead of increasing the limits, any payments for secondary liabilities are disregarded. It is not unknown for the seller to argue that an extension of the 'cap' will result in the possibility of the seller paying back more than the consideration received. In reality any extension will only arise because the target company has discharged some other liability of the seller, a fact which the seller will often ignore!

Time limits

4.3.2 A tax deed is generally limited by time. The seller will want to be certain that at a given point in time it has no further liability for taxation in respect of the disposal of the target's shares. The period usually chosen for making claims (not determining their outcome) is six years which is intended to reflect the ordinary time limits for an assessment for corporation tax to be raised in the absence of fraud or neglect. In fact, *TMA 1970 s 34* states that in such cases the assessment to corporation tax can be raised, 'six years after the end of the accounting period to which it relates'. For this reason the purchaser will generally ask for seven years as this allows for the settling of six full accounting periods of the target company. If, for example, the target company has an accounting period corresponding to the calendar year and is sold on 30 March 1997 an assessment in respect of the pre-sale period from 1 January 1997 to 30 March 1997 can be raised at any time up to 1 January 2004 being six years following the end of the 1997 accounting period. If claims were limited to a six year cut off period then no claims could be made after 30 March 2003. This would leave the purchaser exposed to an assessment being raised in the ordinary course between 31 March 2003 and 1 January 2004 in respect of a pre-completion liability. It has been suggested that the case of *Glaxo Group Ltd and Others v Inland Revenue Commissioners* [1996] STC 191 (where in a transfer pricing dispute the Inland Revenue were allowed to amend an existing open assessment more than six years after the accounting period) is authority for the proposition that, de facto, there is no real time limit for making claims and that consequently there should be no limit in respect of a tax deed or a tax warranty. Whilst this argument has some merit, it is largely of academic interest as under current market practice and as a practical matter, a well-advised seller will not extend its exposure under the tax deed or the tax warranties indefinitely. Realistically, the most a purchaser can expect to achieve is extending the time limits to 22 years in the case of fraud or neglect by the target company. This is on the basis that *TMA 1970 s 36* allows assessments in respect of the loss of corporation tax attributable to fraud or neglect of the taxpayer or the taxpayer's agents to be made 'twenty-one years after the end of the accounting period to which it relates'.

Although it is difficult for the seller to object on technical grounds to extending time limits to cover assessments arising from misconduct during its period of ownership, in practice, many sellers object on practical commercial grounds. The seller will often argue that it is not feasible for it to have an exposure, albeit a highly contingent one, extending over such a period.

A seller may sometimes argue in favour of a three-year period on the basis that although technically, in the absence of fraud or neglect, claims can be made within six years of the end of an accounting period, in practice if the claim does not come to light within three years of completion (assuming that the target company's tax affairs were reasonably up to date at completion) it is unlikely to come to light at all. Clearly, the seller wants to limit the period of time during which a contingent liability may be outstanding. This may be particularly relevant if, for example, the seller anticipates that it may be listed on the stock exchange within a six-year period in which case it may wish to avoid mentioning contingent liabilities in its listing particulars. Whether such an approach would be accepted depends upon the history of the target company and the outcome of negotiations. A clause dealing with time limits including a provision dealing with fraud or neglect is set out below:

'The liability of the Seller[s] under this Deed shall terminate on:

(i) the twenty-second anniversary of Completion in any case attributable to fraud or negligent conduct of the Company or person acting on its behalf except in respect of any claim under this Deed of which notice in writing is given to the Seller[s] before that date containing to the extent reasonably practicable a description of the Claim and the estimated total amount of the Claim;

(ii) the tenth anniversary of Completion the case of consequential group relief adjustments mentioned in *Finance Act 1990 s 96*; and

(iii) the seventh anniversary of Completion in any other case'.

The seller may object to the exception in (i) on the basis that the purchaser needs only to give notice to extend the period. The seller will want to ensure that the restriction in (i) applies equally to (ii) and (iii) but may also wish to add a long-stop date so that notwithstanding that notice of a claim has been given within the period specified in the clause, its liability finally and absolutely determines within a year of such seventh (or later) anniversary unless the purchaser has commenced proceedings in respect of the tax claim. Suitable wording can be added to the end of the clause to ensure this as set out below:

'. . . and the liability of the Seller shall absolutely determine if proceedings in respect of such claim shall not have been commenced within twelve months of service of such notice.'

Limitation by reference to the accounts: the position where there are no completion accounts or completion balance sheet

4.3.3 Most purchasers will accept the principle that they cannot claim in respect of tax which has been provided for in the last set of audited accounts. Insofar as a tax liability has been recognised and provided for, the net asset value of the target is reduced and consequently such tax liability is taken into consideration when agreeing the purchase price. This assumes that the purchaser's offer is based on the last audited accounts of the target company and is linked to net asset value. Increasingly, a company's worth is based on turnover and profitability not the net assets, as was the case with the capital intensive manufacturing companies in the past, and in consequence this assumption looks increasingly ill founded. Take, for example, the case of a sale of a successful high technology company where the share value is based on a multiple of projected profitability and turnover rather than net asset value, which is comparatively low. In such a case one is led to question why, where there is no clear link between the purchase price and net assets, the tax provision in the accounts should limit exposure under the deed. The seller will claim that even in such a case, where price is principally determined by turnover/profitability, the accounts position is still a factor. The seller will argue that if, when looking at turnover, it recognised that an unprovided tax liability would arise, this would be factored in to its determination of the price. In practice, even in the clearest cases where it is apparent net asset value did not determine the price, a purchaser will find it extremely difficult, however technically strong its argument, to persuade a seller to abandon the exclusion. The market practice is overwhelmingly supportive of the seller.

If the price is determined by reference to net assets and the indemnity does not exclude liabilities provided for in the accounts, the seller would incur the economic costs of such liabilities twice: once in respect of the reduced purchase price and then again when the liability materialised, resulting in a claim under the tax deed. Whilst it is hard for a reasonable purchaser to resist this basic principle, there are still a number of difficult questions that should be addressed.

The basic limitation clause states that a claim cannot be made in respect of a tax liability of the target company 'to the extent that provision or reserve for payment is made in the Accounts'.

Often, however, the limitation is much wider and seeks to exclude matters contained in notes to the accounts or otherwise reflected in the accounts. For example, the limitation may exclude claims for tax:

> 'To the extent that provision or reserve for such Tax liability was made or reflected in the Accounts [(including any provision or reserve made in respect of deferred tax)] or referred to in the notes thereto or to the extent that payment or discharge of such Tax Liability has been taken into account in the Accounts.'

Before becoming too embroiled in theoretical discussions, the adviser should first attempt to secure a copy of the latest accounts if he or she has not already done so in order to see what is contained in the notes to the accounts and in the body of the accounts.

There is often debate between the seller and the purchaser about extending the accounts exclusion and in particular including matters 'reflected' in the accounts or otherwise 'taken into account'. Leaving aside the vexed question of deferred tax, much of such debate is often ill considered. The fact is that many tax liabilities may be fully provided for in the accounts and the impact of such provision is that the net asset value of the target company is depressed notwithstanding that there is not a specific tax provision or reserve against such liability. For example, PAYE and VAT liabilities do not appear in tax provisions but are shown in the accounts as liabilities. Further, if for example the target company has taxable trading profits of £2m and carry forward trading losses of £1m, the tax provision will be set at £300,000 (assuming a corporation tax rate of 30%). In this way although tax (of £600,000) on the full year's profit of £2m has not been provided for, the discharge of the tax has been taken into account and it would be incorrect to allow the purchaser to disregard the loss offset (subject to what the purchaser has been told and agreed about excess carry forward losses).

The question of whether a reference to the notes should be included is principally determined by the provisions for deferred tax (where the notes are particularly germane). The issue of deferred tax is considered in more detail in Chapter 10.

The problem of the global approach

4.3.4 In the second set of specimen wording given in 4.3.3 above, the clause provides that no claim arises in respect of 'such tax liability' ie tax liabilities specifically provided for. Sometimes a seller adopting a more general approach will seek to couch the limitation in terms that a claim cannot be made until it exceeds the aggregate of all provisions or reserves made for taxation in the accounts. In this way if the seller has, for example, over-provided £100,000 for corporation tax and under-provided £100,000 for income tax, the two figures are netted-off and there is no resulting claim under the tax deed. Under the more specific approach there is potentially a claim for an income tax liability of £100,000 coupled with a potential claim by the seller in accordance with the clause dealing with over-provisions.

The seller sometimes seeks to justify this global approach on the basis that as in the example given above, the purchaser has suffered no economic loss. The purchaser bought the target on the basis that there was no additional tax to pay beyond that provided for, which is the case in the example. In principle the seller has good reason to argue that the global approach should be adopted. However, the purchaser should normally resist such an approach and the seller may well be advised to reconsider in view of the potential practical difficulties that can arise from the 'global' approach.

Example

The target company's accounts provided for £1m for corporation tax on trading activities for the year ended 31 December 1998. The target is sold and the tax deed provides that a claim can only be made once the aggregate of all tax provisions or reserves are exceeded. The purchaser then receives unexpected demands for:

(a) VAT together with penalties and interest of £600,000;

(b) income tax of £350,000 not deducted from royalty payments to different parties under *ICTA 1988 s 349*, made up of a claim for £120,000, ten claims of £15,000 and another of £80,000;

(c) stamp duty of £10,000;

(d) stamp duty reserve tax of £10,000; and

(e) a demand for employer's National Insurance Contributions for 1996 of £30,000 including penalties and fines.

Since the global approach was adopted in the tax deed none of these liabilities can give rise to a claim as in aggregate they total £1m which is not more than the provision for tax. The purchaser pays the liabilities from its own resources and gives the seller no notice under the deed of a potential claim. In September 1999 the liability to corporation tax of £1m for which the provision in the accounts was made becomes due and the provision having already been used, the purchaser makes a claim under the tax deed.

In these circumstances the seller would immediately respond to the purchaser's claim by stating that the liability was provided for in the accounts. The purchaser would then have to establish that the provision is exhausted. The seller would want to have full details of the previous tax paid and could question whether the claims were justified and should have been settled. The seller is also deprived of the right to fight the claims which have already been settled and which resulted in a subsequent tax liability.

Another problem with the global approach is that the seller will also find it difficult to establish that an over-provision has arisen until all open years are finally settled. This is because there will always be the possibility of further claims arising which the purchaser can use to deny credit for such over-provision. Conversely, where the global approach is rejected and there is a specific provision for corporation tax in a particular year and that corporation tax is settled at a lesser figure, there will be an over-provision irrespective of undetermined liabilities for other taxes.

An alternative is to provide in the claims clause that the purchaser should notify the seller of any claim for taxation regardless of whether it is within the limit of the provision for tax in the accounts. This creates more administration for the purchaser but prevents the problems outlined above. Following the target's acquisition the purchaser may have copies of the working papers which indicate how the provision for taxation was calculated in which case unexpected or unprovided for claims may be easier to identify. It may be tempting in such circumstances for the purchaser to agree to notify the seller of a claim in the event that the working papers lead to the conclusion that a liability for taxation was not provided for. Such arguments should be resisted. In the event that the purchaser fails to identify such a liability then the seller may argue the purchaser is at fault. This will only lead to further arguments and create more uncertainties in a document which is intended to create certainty.

Where a global approach is taken, the purchaser will suffer a cashflow disadvantage. In the example given above, the purchaser would have to settle all liabilities (which it would otherwise expect the seller to pay under the tax deed, because it had not been provided for), from the purchaser's own resources. It would find that it could only recover these sums subsequently when the liabilities in respect of which the provision was made actually crystallise and a claim under the tax deed arises as the provision has already been used. The purchaser also has the practical difficulty of establishing that the provision has been exhausted. The seller may question whether or not the claims settled by the purchaser were justified and withhold payment until the purchaser can convince the seller that the claims should have been met. In the event that paying such claims was not justified, the purchaser could argue that all it was doing was paying tax in accordance with the terms of the deed which was freely negotiated between two parties and that if the seller wanted it to operate in a different way it should have identified the problem during the negotiations and dealt with it. To avoid these practical problems the purchaser may take a prudent view and notify the seller of all claims not provided for. This would give rise to the rather anomalous position that the conduct of the claims provisions would apply notwithstanding that there was no question of a claim being made in respect of the subject matter of the notification. For the reasons above most tax deeds do not adopt the global approach and look instead at specific provisions against particular types of liabilities.

Completion accounts

4.3.5 Increasingly, a feature of company acquisitions is the preparation of a completion balance sheet, whereby a non-statutory set of accounts is drawn up as at the date of completion using the same accounting principles generally adopted by the target company. The price to be paid is then adjusted up or down depending upon whether the completion balance sheet shows net assets to be greater or less than the price paid. In the context of the tax deed this has two important consequences:

(a) first, the rationale for giving a seller credit for the provision for taxation in the accounts by reference to which the consideration is determined (which is discussed above) dictates that it is the provision in the completion accounts which limits the liability and not the provision in the last audited accounts; and

(b) second, the purchaser must ensure that the normal limitation to exclude taxation arising in the ordinary course of business or trade since the last audited accounts date is removed. All such activities should be reflected in the completion accounts and a tax provision should be included in the completion accounts for the resulting tax liabilities. The purchaser would expect to be indemnified to the extent that these liabilities are not provided for.

It is sometimes argued by the seller that if the profits giving rise to an unprovided for tax liability are not reflected in the completion balance sheet there should be no liability under the tax deed. This argument should be resisted by the purchaser and it would normally be abandoned by the seller when it is pointed out that recipricosity involves a return of the purchase price if the profits are overstated or assets undervalued in the completion balance sheet. Completion balance sheets are usually prepared, in the first instance, by the seller's accountants. It is therefore arguable that it is for the seller to ensure that the figures are correct and that if the actual profits exceed those shown in the accounts it is the seller's fault. Where a completion balance sheet is prepared by the seller's advisers, it is usual to include provisions enabling the purchaser's accountants to question and discuss the figures prior to agreement of them.

Before accepting the determination of the purchase price and liabilities the parties will usually require the completion balance sheet to be prepared after a proper audit to ensure the accuracy of the figures in the completion accounts. Failing this, the sale and purchase agreement can specify that the completion balance sheet is to be prepared as if it is to be audited in accordance with accepted accounting practice and consistent with accounting procedures previously adopted by the target company. Preparation of the completion balance sheet is fertile ground for dispute because the way in which it is prepared can directly influence the price paid. Professional advisers of the highest integrity, complying with the requirements of the accounting standards, can still differ on how such procedure should be applied to a given set of figures. To narrow the ground for dispute, although much will still depend upon the good faith of the parties, it is sensible to insert a clause setting out in as much detail as possible the accounting practices to be adopted particularly in potentially contentious areas such as the valuation of stock in trade. Such a clause should also include a formal consultation procedure.

Management accounts

4.3.6 With increasing computerisation of accounting systems, many companies now produce regular management accounts. There is a trend towards the adjustment of the purchase price by reference to such accounts with a corresponding adjustment in the drafting of the tax deed. The use of management accounts to determine the purchase price or the provision for taxation for the purposes of the deed should be resisted by the purchaser. Management accounts are not audited: they are prepared internally and do not have the safeguard of an external independent check. The accuracy of the management accounts depends upon the accuracy and completeness of the information on which they are prepared, the competence of the staff preparing them and the adequacy of the computing system producing them. Generally, the purchaser has no way of evaluating any of these factors. It is not unknown for management accounts to be manipulated to give a less than accurate picture. In most circumstances a purchaser should be reluctant to accept any drafting adjustments to the tax deed and purchase price by reference to the management accounts. However, in some instances the management accounts can be used; the degree of such use depending on the confidence of the parties in their accuracy.

Transactions in the ordinary course of business since the last accounts date

4.3.7 Where the purchase price is determined by reference to a set of audited accounts, a reasonable purchaser will accept an exclusion clause that a liability will not arise in the following circumstances:

> 'The Seller will not be liable to the extent that the liability arises as the result of transactions in the ordinary course of normal business of the Company since the Accounts Date and which is not interest or a penalty, surcharge or fine in connection with Taxation.'

The reason why this is acceptable is that as a general principle a purchaser will base the purchase price for the target company on the last set of audited accounts, hence any profits made in the period between the date of those accounts and completion is an unexpected and welcome bonus for the purchaser. It would clearly be unfair if, as a result of ordinary trading activities, the company made £1m of profit prior to completion and the purchaser then claimed the corporation tax of £300,000 (based on a 30% rate) on such profits which it neither expected nor paid for. It would be more equitable if the purchaser paid the tax on its windfall still leaving it £700,000 better off than it expected.

Whilst this general principle should be readily accepted by the purchaser in respect of ordinary trading activities, the question becomes more difficult when extended to business activities generally. If, for example, the exclusion applied to all tax liabilities arising from 'business activities' there could be unfortunate consequences: the seller could agree to sell the target company which owns assets having a book value of £10m at a time when the open market value of such assets is £50m. In these circumstances the purchaser will expect to acquire such assets through the target company albeit with locked-in capital gains. However, if before completion the assets are sold, the purchaser will not acquire the target company with £50m worth of assets with a potential capital gain but will instead, in the absence of roll-over relief, find itself with cash of £50m plus an immediate tax charge. Conversely, if the clause is restricted to trading activities it may exclude profitable and beneficial matters which are arguably business but not trade and certain borderline activities. The clause given above is a reasonable compromise.

A clause of this type is often criticised on the basis that the concept of the 'ordinary course of normal business' is too vague. Whilst this criticism is justified, it is difficult to find a better solution. However, the more obvious areas which are not intended to be regarded as the ordinary 'course of normal business' can be expressly identified. Thus, the current market practice has developed of excluding tax arising from the 'ordinary course of business' then going on to specifically identify particular matters which fall outside this description. A typical clause is:

> 'To the extent that such Tax Liability arises as a result of transactions in the ordinary course of business the Company after the Accounting Date but on or before Completion PROVIDED THAT (without prejudice to the generality of the foregoing) any Claim for Taxation arising from any of the following shall not be regarded for the purposes of this clause [ ] as arising 'in the ordinary course of business of the Company':
>
> (a) any event which results in a Tax Liability arising in the Company where such liability is chargeable or attributable primarily to a person other than the Company (including any liability under Part VIII of the Taxes Management Act 1970 (charges on non-residents));
>
> (b) any liability under Part XVII of the Taxes Act 1988 (tax avoidance);
>
> (c) any liability in respect of any distribution (as defined in *s 209* of the *Taxes Act 1988*) or deemed distribution for tax purposes;
>
> (d) any liability arising as a result of the Company ceasing for tax purposes to be a member of any group or associated with any other company;

(e) the disposal of any asset (including trading stock) or the supply of any service or business facility of any kind in circumstances where the consideration actually received (if any) for such disposal or supply is less than a consideration deemed to have been received for the purpose of any tax but only to the extent the tax liability is attributable to the difference between the consideration actually received and the consideration deemed to have been received for the purpose of any tax.'

The above are only a few of the acts which might be considered to be outside the ordinary course of the normal business of the company. A purchaser may consider that by including a long list of excluded acts it is gaining extra protection. However, the danger, for the purchaser is that in the event of a dispute the list may be considered to be exhaustive and therefore anything which is not included is in the ordinary course of the normal business of the target company. To prevent such an interpretation the hallowed words 'without prejudice to the generality of the foregoing' can be inserted in the introduction to the specific acts.

The purchaser sometimes includes a provision that any disposal of a capital asset is outside the ordinary course of business. The seller may have difficulty accepting such a limitation as the target company is likely to dispose and acquire capital assets as part of its routine activities. Thus, the disposal of such assets could be in the ordinary course of the normal business of the company. Very often the seller will give a warranty that no assets have been disposed of since the Accounts Date and then disclose against it. The purchaser may be happy to accept this as an alternative to a blanket exclusion of capital assets as being in the ordinary course of trade.

In the past, the list of activities outside the ordinary course would include close company apportionments although as these were abolished for accounting periods ended after 1 April 1989, the purpose of including such a provision has effectively disappeared.

Retrospective changes in taxation

4.3.8 Retrospective changes in taxation can mean either a change in the substantive law or alternatively a change in the rates of taxation. Although retrospective changes in substantive tax law are still the exception, there is an increasing trend towards such changes. Fifteen or twenty years ago discussion on apportioning the risk of retrospective changes was largely hypothetical. Today it is a real practical consideration. For example, *Finance Act 1990 s 57* stated that changes introduced by that section to the deep gain legislation introduced in the *Finance Act 1989* 'shall be deemed always to have had effect'. By way of illustration the *Finance Act 1997* alone introduced at least five changes which were deemed always to have effect (in addition to numerous other provisions which to some extent had retrospective effect) namely: *FA 1997 s 71* which affected *ICTA 1988 s 242(6)*; *FA 1997 s 78* which affected *ICTA 1988 s 349(3)*; *FA 1997 s 79* which affected *ICTA 1988 s 541*; *FA 1997 s 75(1)* and *(2)* which affected *ICTA 1988 s 842AA(5A)*, *(5B)*, and *(6)* and *FA 1997 s 89* which introduced *ICTA 1988 s 138A*. As well as rules treated as always having effect, there are those which go back in time to a fixed date such as the rules on pre-entry losses introduced as *TCGA 1992 s 177A* and *Sch 7A* by *FA 1993 s 88(1)* and *Sch 8* which apply to losses of a company joining a group after 30 March 1987. Many other changes whilst purporting not to be retrospective have that effect. For example the rules on finance leases in *FA 1997 s 82* and *Sch 12* catch existing leases which may have run for many years before the legislation was introduced. The current trend is to announce changes in rates of tax in advance so reducing the risks posed by sudden unexpected changes. However, the danger for the purchaser is that as a result of a retrospective change in taxation, whether it is substantive or only a change in the rate, the provision for taxation in the relevant accounts, which when prepared covered all liabilities, may become inadequate following the sale. The question then arises as to whether it is the seller or the purchaser who should bear the risk of such changes.

The seller's argument is that, as at the date of completion of the accounts, provision was properly made to cover all taxes and it is the purchaser which must assume the risk of subsequent changes in tax legislation, just as it bears the economic risks taken over in respect of all business activities of the target company after completion. The purchaser's argument will simply be that as the company was bought on the basis that it would not have to pay any pre-completion tax and that as the seller enjoyed the profits (either by extraction or by virtue of the enhanced value of the target company's shares) upon which the retrospective tax is levied, it is the seller that should suffer any extra burdens in respect of them. Whilst this is not a point which can be regarded categorically as one upon which the seller's view should prevail, in general it is accepted that the seller's argument is slightly the stronger and it is rare to find a deed in which the seller bears the risk of extra taxes.

A basic clause states that a liability will not arise under the indemnity 'to the extent that it arises or is increased as a result only of a retrospective change in the law of taxation announced after the date of the deed'.

Sometimes, but rarely, the exclusion for tax provided for in the accounts and the exclusion for retrospective changes in taxation are included together. This type of exclusion can be worded as set out below:

'. . . to the extent that provision or reserve in respect thereof has been made in the [Relevant/Audited Accounts] which is insufficient only by reason of any increase in rates of Taxation or change in law [or practice] of any taxation authority after the date hereof having retrospective effect'.

This clause should be rejected by the seller as it requires that a provision has been made in respect of a liability which proves to be inadequate because of changes in law. Arguably this will not exclude a liability which is created in its entirety due to a change in law and in respect of which no provision was made at all, as it did not exist when the accounts were prepared.

Under current market practice, most clauses seek to extend the exclusion not only to retrospective changes in legislation but also to retrospective changes in published Inland Revenue, Customs & Excise or other taxing authority's practice, or even wider still to retrospective changes in treatment agreed specifically by a tax authority with the target company. In such cases the purchaser should consider resisting the extension of the clause even if they agree with the basic principle. Changes in Inland Revenue practice, are far more likely to occur than changes in legislation, and the risk of the clause applying is therefore increased. However, it is usual for Inland Revenue Statements of Practice to be effective from a certain date and it is unusual for the introduction of a Statement of Practice to impose a harsher regime in respect of periods prior to its introduction. Similarly, the withdrawal of an Extra Statutory Concession will be with effect from a stated date. Most purchasers will be prepared to accept the extension of the clause to published concessions and practices but will reject any references to informal unpublished concessions. This latter category is simply too vague and uncertain to rely upon.

An example of a more widely drafted clause is set out below:

'To the extent that such Tax Liability arises or is increased as a result of a change or changes in the tax rates or in legislation made after the date of this Deed (whether relating to Taxation or otherwise) or to the change or the withdrawal after the date of this Deed of any previously published practice or concession of any taxing authority with retrospective effect.'

One point that should be considered is the position when an indemnity is being negotiated in the period between the Budget and enactment of the resulting Finance Act (roughly March to July). One should consider whether any provision introduced in the Budget statement or Finance Bill would, if enacted, become effective from an earlier date, giving rise to specific problems. Where this is the case the negotiation surrounding the clause dealing with retrospective changes in taxation will be more difficult since the risk of being caught by the clause will be real and ascertainable rather than hypothetical. Alternatively, the fact that the risk is real and ascertainable may mean that one side or the other is more ready to take it on.

Limiting the tax deed by reference to disclosure

4.3.9 Frequently the seller will amend the tax deed so that it contains an exclusion which prevents a claim in respect of any matter stated in the disclosure letter. It is often suggested that such clauses are not considered the norm. An example of such a clause is to exclude all liabilities from a claim to the extent that the claim arises from any act, omission or event stated in the disclosure letter or such a liability is stated in the disclosure letter. The seller will argue that to the extent that the purchaser was made aware of the risk before it committed to the purchase of the target company, it should not have any cause for complaint, nor means of redress, should the risk disclosed materialise. From the purchaser's point of view there are compelling arguments against this and, as a general rule, a purchaser should firmly reject a tax deed limited by reference to disclosure.

The purchaser will argue that the purchase price was set on the basis that (save as provided in the accounts) there would not be any pre-completion tax liabilities. If such liabilities were known to exist at the time the purchase price was agreed, they would have been taken into consideration. Their existence would have reduced the net asset value of the target company and in consequence the purchaser would reduce the purchase price. If having set the price, the purchaser accepts that it is liable for disclosed liabilities, it goes against this fundamental agreement. In effect it allows the seller to reduce the value of the target company without suffering any consequential reduction in the price.

From the purchaser's point of view the fact that there may be liabilities which were not provided for in the accounts is the *raison d'etre* for the tax deed. The tax deed is intended to provide a means of making good a loss in value caused by unexpected tax liabilities that should have reduced the price at the outset had they been known about. The liabilities the seller is likely to disclose are the very liabilities the purchaser would expect to be indemnified against.

Often the inclusion of an exclusion clause which seeks to limit the deed by reference to disclosure is merely a negotiating position and the deletion of such an exclusion clause by the purchaser will be met with little or no opposition from the seller.

From a purely practical point of view there are a number of reasons why a purchaser should resist accepting a deed limited by disclosure.

(a) Once the seller knows that it is absolved from liability in respect of everything contained in the disclosure letter the temptation will be to include a reference to every transaction ever undertaken by the target company on the basis that such an approach would guarantee total immunity from any claims under the indemnity. Thus, instead of making a proper disclosure in reply to specific questions in the warranties the risk is that the purchaser will be given a mass of information much of which may prove to be irrelevant.

(b) Even assuming that a serious attempt is made at disclosure the onus on the purchaser will be considerable. Generally, a purchaser and its advisers will peruse a disclosure letter carefully and try and obtain clarification, where practicable, on areas of uncertainty. However, the purchaser will conduct such an exercise on the basis that having obtained a reasonable degree of clarity it can proceed as it has a safety net in the form of the tax deed. Without the benefit of an indemnity against matters disclosed, the purchaser will feel compelled to evaluate exhaustively every potential point raised in the disclosure letter, which will result in considerable additional delay and cost. As in practice the disclosure letter is usually produced at a fairly late stage of negotiations it is commercially undesirable for the transaction to be delayed at such a stage whilst further detailed information is requested and produced.

(c) Assuming that the purchaser is able to make a full analysis of the facts and information provided, the nature of taxation means that often the degree of risk of a tax liability arising and the likely *quantum* of the liability should it arise is impossible to predict with any confidence. The purchaser is likely to take a pessimistic view on the basis that it will have to suffer the economic loss of any liability and it will try and negotiate a reduction in the purchase price accordingly. Conversely, the seller is likely to take a more sanguine view as it is not at risk and it is likely to have decided that the tax risks are manageable when the transactions giving rise to the potential liability took place. The result can be that following the tax disclosure numerous points become subject to dispute.

(d) Even assuming that the purchaser and seller agree on the degree of risk, the likely *quantum* and then accept a variation of the purchase price, it is clearly undesirable for every potential tax liability stated in a disclosure letter to result in further adjustments of the purchase price.

The views set out above are, of course, based on a general position and there may be exceptions. In particular, although in practice it is rare, certain risks may be explained in detail to the purchaser early in negotiations and it is therefore understood from the outset that the seller is not prepared to accept any potential liability in the event that such risks crystallise. In such circumstances specific risks can be dealt with by specific exclusions from the tax deed, which would not require a comprehensive exclusion by reference to the disclosure letter.

In such cases the seller may argue that the best way of dealing with specific exclusions is simply to include a general statement in the tax deed that its scope is limited by disclosure and then only include those specific items in the tax section of the disclosure letter. If the purchaser accepts this approach it must ensure that the reference is to particular numbered paragraphs in the disclosure letter and that these paragraphs are studied carefully to ensure that only the subject matter, which it has been agreed should be excluded, is referred to in those paragraphs. It is not unknown for the seller to suggest that the indemnity is limited by reference to disclosure letter on the basis that only the risks known and discussed will be stated therein and then phrase the exclusion clause so that it extends to other tax risks in other parts of the disclosure letter.

Exclusion of warranty claims from claims under the tax deed

4.3.10 Most tax deeds contain a provision which prevents a claim being made and satisfied in respect of the same subject matter under both the tax warranties and the tax deed. Such a double claim is technically possible, particularly where the tax deed is expressed as a covenant to pay an amount equal to a tax liability in the target company. Under such a deed, there is no need for the purchaser to show loss and thus the fact that the loss has been recovered under the warranties does not appear to bar a claim under the tax deed. It is arguable that if such a claim were brought before the courts, the courts would have little sympathy for the purchaser but the risk exists that the court would feel compelled to adhere to the strict provisions of the tax deed, thereby allowing a double claim. To counter this possibility it is usual to find that the following clause is inserted:

> 'Where any facts or circumstances could give rise both to a claim under this deed and a claim under the Warranties, the Seller shall not be liable in respect of both claims.'

The purchaser should have no difficulty in accepting such a clause in principle. However, the scope of such clauses needs to be examined carefully, otherwise the purchaser may be left with a dilemma. This is because the measure of damage for a warranty claim is the loss flowing from the breach. It is therefore possible for the loss to be greater than the amount of the tax claim, eg where because of the publicity arising from an unusually large tax claim or one arising because of fraud, a large order is lost, whereas the amount payable under the tax deed is usually the amount of the tax liability suffered by the target company. A clause phrased like that above will present the purchaser with two options: first, to pursue a warranty claim with all its inherent difficulties for the whole of the damage suffered and second, to make a relatively simple indemnity claim for the amount of the tax liability.

To overcome the above concern an alternative method is to include one or other of the following type of exclusion:

> 'No claim shall arise under this deed to the extent that recovery is made under the warranties', or
>
> 'No claim shall arise under this deed to the extent that a claim arises under the warranties and such claim is satisfied.'

The insertion of such a clause will give the purchaser the opportunity of taking both a warranty and an indemnity claim in order to recover the full amount of the loss, but to the extent that recovery is made under one claim there will be a credit for any amounts paid or payable under the other. Usually the purchaser will choose to take the indemnity claim although, if it is considered that there is damage beyond the amount of the tax liability, a claim under the warranties may be preferred to an indemnity claim. The purchaser should be careful that the clause only prevents a double recovery in respect of any liability and does not also compel a claim to be first made under the warranties. These clauses have become unusual but are still encountered from time to time. They normally prevent a claim under the tax deed to the extent that the seller is liable to the purchaser under the warranties in respect of a liability to taxation. The purchaser should resist such a clause. Prior to the Inland Revenue concession (Concession D33 announced in the IR Press Release dated 19 December 1988) but post-*Zim Properties*, the seller would prefer a claim to be made under the warranties to avoid the risk of being forced to gross-up payments made to settle claims under the tax deed. However, following the concession the application of which is now tried and tested, this is no longer a concern where payments are made by the seller to the purchaser. This clause is still sometimes used because the seller recognises that by forcing a purchaser to claim under the warranties there are more obstacles in the way of a successful claim. The purchaser will have to show a breach of warranty and consequential loss rather than simply showing that a pre-completion tax liability not provided for in the accounts has arisen, as would be the case with a claim under the tax deed. If the purchaser accepts that it must claim under the warranties in priority to the tax deed, the value of the tax deed as a quick and efficient method of recovery is undermined.

Exclusions for tax arising as a result of post-completion changes in accounting policy and the accounting reference date for the target company

4.3.11 After completion many purchasers require the target company to bring its accounting policies and accounting reference date into line with the policies and accounting date used in the rest of the purchaser's group. Whilst this is a perfectly legitimate action for the purchaser to take, it may cause liabilities for tax in the pre-completion period which would not otherwise have arisen. The seller will be anxious to ensure that the post-completion business activities of the purchaser ie changing the accounting reference date and accounting policies, do not give rise to a claim for tax by the purchaser under the tax deed.

How a change of accounting date can give rise to such a liability is perhaps best illustrated by an example.

Example

A Ltd has an accounting reference date of 31 December. In the period from 1 January to 30 June, A Ltd does not make any profits on ordinary trading activities. However, between 1 April and 30 June A Ltd effects a series of transactions outside the ordinary course of its business from which it makes a capital loss of £1m. In the period from 1 January to 31 March A Ltd had disposed of a capital asset outside the ordinary course of business which gave rise to a capital gain of £1m.

A Ltd is sold on 1 July to B Ltd.

The seller took the view that in the period prior to completion there would be no taxable profits as the capital profits made on the extraordinary activities (£1m) would be offset by the capital losses made in the same accounting period of £1m. Because of this assumption, the seller was not concerned by the potential exposure on the £1m of capital profit which would not be caught by the usual exclusion for profits made since the date of the last accounts in the ordinary course of the target company's business. The seller was satisfied that the usual mitigation clauses would require the purchaser to set off losses in the pre-completion period against the profits made in the same period.

On 3 August, having purchased A Ltd, B Ltd changes (retrospectively) the accounting reference date of A Ltd to 31 March which can be done relatively easily in respect of any current accounting period. As a result, in A Ltd's accounting period to 31 March A Ltd made capital profits against which the capital loss of £1m made in the following period could not be set off by a carry-back. The effect of this is that the £1m profits made in the period from 1 January to completion would give rise to a tax liability. Due to the change in the accounting dates the capital losses are no longer made in the same accounting period as the pre-completion profits and they cannot be carried back to set against capital gains.

To avoid the risk of a change of accounting date giving rise to such liabilities an exclusion is often included to this effect to exclude a liability:

'to the extent that such Tax Liability results from or is increased or extended by the change of the accounting reference date of the Company on Completion or any subsequent change thereafter or by any change in the accounting policies of the Company after Completion'.

An alternative clause is:

'A claim cannot be made under the tax deed in respect of a liability to the extent that it arises or results from or as a consequence of a change in the date to which the company makes up its accounts.'

Sometimes the purchaser will argue that a liability arising from a post-completion change in accounting period does not need to be excluded by the type of clauses above as such liability will be excluded by the general exclusion for liabilities arising from post-completion voluntary acts. However, this is not clear as arguably the liability arises from the pre-completion disposal. To avoid such an issue the inclusion of a specific exclusion is to be preferred.

Changes in accounting policy can also cause potential tax charges. If, for example, the purchaser procures that the target company treats assets formerly treated as trading stock as part of fixed capital, expenditure formerly deducted may cease to be deductible, giving rise to tax liabilities in the pre-completion period. It is difficult to think of any examples of accounting policy causing retrospective changes in the tax treatment of the target company. Furthermore, it is often argued that any such changes will be covered by the exclusion for tax liabilities arising from voluntary acts of the purchaser after completion. However, the prudent view is that if there is a specifically identified risk it is better to deal with it specifically rather than rely upon a general clause.

To this end, a claim is often excluded to the extent it arises:

'as a result of any change in accounting policy or the basis upon which the company values its assets'

The purchaser will often add a proviso to make it clear that the exclusion will not apply if changes have to be made to correct deficiencies in the seller's accounting practice — such a proviso (to be added to the end of the clause) may read as follows:

'save where such change in accounting policy or basis of valuation is necessary to comply with generally accepted accounting standards and policies applicable to the relevant accounting periods'.

Post-completion voluntary acts

4.3.12 The seller will take the view that if the purchaser procures that the target company does something after completion which gives rise to a tax liability prior to completion, such tax liability is excluded from the tax deed. The purchaser will normally have no difficulty in accepting such exclusion.

A reasonable clause incorporating the conflicting requirements of the seller and purchaser might be to exclude a claim:

> 'to the extent that such Tax Liability would not have arisen but for a voluntary act [or omission] or transaction carried out [(other than in fulfilment of a legally binding commitment entered into by the Company on or before Completion)] by the Purchaser or the Company after Completion otherwise than in the ordinary course of business of such Company as such business is conducted at Completion and which the Company was aware [or ought reasonably to have been aware] would give rise to such a liability'.

A seller would normally reject a provision which stated that the purchaser had to be aware that its voluntary act would cause a tax liability before the purchaser is prevented from making a claim under the tax deed. Not unreasonably the seller would take the view that it will be extremely difficult to prove the purchaser's awareness, or lack of awareness, of the consequences of its acts and that including such a provision would dramatically undermine the value of the clause. However, the words 'was aware or ought reasonably to have been aware' are common and bring an element of objectivity to determining the seller's liability (if any) and therefore a clause which determines awareness on the basis of this test is more likely to be accepted by the seller.

Where the act is in the ordinary course of business, the purchaser would be aggrieved if the very carrying on of the business gave rise to a pre-completion tax liability for which no indemnity claim arose, hence the disapplication of the exclusion to events in the ordinary course of business. The inclusion of the words, 'as carried out at Completion' after the reference to the ordinary course of business, prevents the purchaser from changing the nature of the target company's business and the argument that the act, which would otherwise have been outside the ordinary course of business, was inside the ordinary course.

Disclaimer of capital allowances

4.3.13 Sometimes the seller will require any liability to be excluded to the extent that it arises from the disclaimer of capital allowances claimed prior to Completion or variation of a pre-completion claim. Arguably this is a voluntary act and may already be excluded but it is becoming increasingly common to identify the risk specifically. A typical clause might be to exclude Liability:

> 'to the extent that such Tax Liability arises by virtue of any voluntary disclaimer of or revision of a claim for industrial building or other

capital allowances after Completion which has the effect of increasing the Tax Liability of the Company in respect of any period ending on or before the Accounting Date'.

As capital allowances are claimed for accounting periods when the tax computations are submitted for such periods, it is inappropriate to cover the open period in which the sale takes place as no capital allowance claim will have been made.

Failure to make an election taken into account in the accounts

4.3.14 It is likely that the seller will require an exclusion from liability:

> 'to the extent that a Tax Liability would not have arisen or would have been reduced or eliminated but for a failure on the part of the Company to make any claim, election, surrender or disclaimer or give any notice or consent or do anything after Completion the making, giving or doing of which was taken into account in the [Completion/Audited] Accounts.'

The purchaser will usually accept this provided they know what claims, elections, surrenders etc need to be made and provided it and not the seller has control and conduct of pre-completion tax compliance. It is usual therefore for the seller to add the following words at the end of the Clause:

> '[. . . and full details of which are included in the Disclosure Letter]'.

Where the accounts are Completion Accounts the seller may argue that notification is impossible because the accounts will not be prepared until some time after Completion (the same may be true of Audited Accounts) and a compromise is therefore for the purchaser to add after the end of the clause the following words:

> '[. . . and full details of which are to be notified to the Purchaser in writing at least 30 [business days] prior to the last date upon which the claim, election, surrender or disclaimer may validly/legally be made, given or done]'.

Increase in assets

4.3.15 Occasionally the seller will ask for an exclusion clause worded in the following terms:

> 'No liability will arise if and to the extent that it corresponds to an increase in the value of the assets of the [Company] [Companies] resulting from a reduction in its liability to Taxation.'

At first sight this might seem reasonable. However, at the time the claim is made there may be no way of knowing whether a reduction will occur. For example, if the claim is for VAT where that payment of VAT is irrecoverable (therefore leading to a deduction in the corporation tax liability), at the time of that claim, the extent of the reduction in corporation tax arising as a result of the deduction may be unknown. Therefore, it is considered that such an exclusion is best dealt with by the corresponding benefits clause. When the deduction is given the purchaser repays an amount equal to the saving in corporation tax.

Another clause dealing with an increase in assets is one which excludes a liability:

> 'to the extent that the income, profits or gains in respect of which the Tax Liability arises were actually earned, accrued or received by the Company, but were not reflected in the Accounts'.

At first sight this would seem to be reasonable and follows the logic that excludes tax on profits since the accounts date. The seller will argue that if the purchaser receives an unexpected windfall it should not expect the seller to pay the tax. However, most purchasers would resist such a clause. If the profit arose prior to the Accounts Date it should have been included in the Accounts prepared by the seller. If the profit arose after the Accounts Date but prior to Completion then such profit should be caught by the exclusion of profits in the ordinary course of business and, if not, there should be an indemnity. Suppose the target company owns an item of plant, which is valued in the Accounts at £5m, has a chargeable gains tax base cost of £5m and has been fully depreciated for capital allowance purposes. The plant is disposed of prior to completion for £7m which, net of chargeable gains tax of £600,000 (at 30%) and a full balancing charge (ignoring indexation and other reliefs), leaves less than £5m. Does the clause mean that no claims can be made or only that no claim can be made for the tax on the £2m difference between the value of the asset in the Accounts (£5m) and the value actually realised?

A similar clause encountered periodically is a clause excluding tax liabilities covered by insurance. Again it is hard to see how this can apply and is probably just imported from the Agreement's warranty exclusions where it can be relevant to non-tax warranties. When acting for the purchaser one generally deletes such a clause as the seller can give no sound reasons for its inclusion.

Cessation of trade

4.3.16 If there are losses carried forward, the seller can reasonably expect these to be a buffer against claims unless they have been shown as assets in the accounts or otherwise paid for by the purchaser. The seller's concern is that following the sale and change in ownership the purchaser will allow the trade of the target company to cease or change such that losses cannot be carried forward from the last Accounts Date to cover the period from such date to completion (and to the extent the indemnity goes beyond completion, beyond such date). *ICTA 1988 s 768* states that if within a period of three years there is both a change in ownership or major change in the nature or conduct of the trade (or if the activities of the trade become small or negligible), *ICTA 1988 s 393* will be disapplied to the extent that it allows trading losses made in an accounting period beginning before completion to be set against profits of a period ending after completion. *Section 768(2)* and *(3)* state that losses shall be apportioned on a time basis for the period of completion, or, if this is unreasonable, on a just and reasonable basis. The usual expectation therefore would be (assuming no earlier change in ownership and no change in trade) that the apportionment would preserve the seller's losses. If the purchaser changes the trade the seller would not receive full benefit of the carried forward losses for the open accounting period (ie the period commencing prior to Completion), nor to the extent the seller is liable for post completion liabilities, would it be able to carry forward losses to post completion periods. *ICTA 1988 s 768A* also contains provisions which in the same circumstances prevents the carry back of losses from accounting periods ending after the change in ownership.

As with *s 768,* the seller's expectation would be that the losses arising between the last Accounts Date and completion would be fully apportioned to that period and available for carry back. The seller's fear is that the apportionment might be made on a basis which deprived it of such losses. To cover these risks it is quite usual to find an exclusion of liability:

'which would not have arisen but for a cessation of trade, or a change in the nature or conduct of trade by the company on or after the date hereof'.

Statutory rights of recovery: ICTA 1988 ss 767A, 767AA

4.3.17 A fuller discussion of *ss 767A* and *767AA* is set out below in paragraph 4.6.

Where a liability arises in the circumstances set out in *s 767A* or *s 767AA* and the target company is assessed as being secondarily liable, the purchaser will generally have a claim under the deed. However, if the Inland Revenue have in the meantime recovered the tax from the seller's group, the seller will want to avoid the possibility of still having to pay under the deed (which if in the form of a covenant to pay is still technically permissible as the purchaser does not have to establish loss). To cover this possibility it is becoming usual to include an exclusion of liability:

> 'to the extent that the seller or a member of the Remaining Group [ie the sellers post sale group] has satisfied such Tax Liability by

> reason of being liable for such Taxation under *ICTA 1988 s 767A* or *s 767AA*.'

Similar concerns arise whenever there is a statutory right of recovery and the seller may therefore consider extending the clause to catch any situation where the liability has already been satisfied under a statutory right of recovery. Thus, after the specific reference to *ss 767A* and *767AA* could be added 'or liable to the Purchaser under any statutory provision'.

Compensation at no expense to the purchaser or a company and insurance

4.3.18 A rather innocuous exclusion occasionally required by the seller can be worded as set out below:

> 'No liability will arise if and to the extent that the liability has been made good or otherwise compensated for at no expense to the Purchaser or a Company.'

It is difficult to imagine how this exclusion can apply save in respect of a statutory right of recovery. It could be that a former group member may cover the liability by the surrender of group relief for no payment, although such matters are normally dealt with separately under a mitigation clause.

Failure to act by the purchaser

4.3.19 The seller may be concerned that a failure by the purchaser to act in accordance with the conduct of tax affairs clause may prejudice it and increase its liability. To counter this problem the following exclusion clause may be included:

> 'No liability will arise where the Purchaser and/or the Company fail after due warning to act in accordance with the reasonable instructions of the Seller in conducting any dispute referred to in [Conduct of Tax Affairs Clause].'

A purchaser should resist such a clause. The clause has the effect that a simple failure by the purchaser, (for example, to submit a document to a revenue authority), for whatever reason, may result in the total exclusion from liability for the seller. In practice, such a failure may make no difference to the level of the claim and may not prejudice the seller. If the seller feels that it has been prejudiced by the purchaser's actions, it has perfectly adequate remedies at common law: the deed being a contract and any failure by the purchaser being a breach of contract. The seller can therefore refuse to pay over any increased liability arising out of the purchaser's failure to act and meet any claim by the purchaser with a counterclaim for damages for breach of contract. A claim for breach of contract will result in damages equal to the loss suffered by the seller, which is equitable and which should be contrasted with the position when a failure by the purchaser triggers the total exclusion of liability for the seller under the above exclusion. In such circumstances even though the purchaser's failure may, for example, only result in interest for the late payment of tax, the exclusion does not confine itself to excluding a claim for the actual loss (ie the interest on late tax). A more reasonable clause which should be acceptable to a purchaser is a clause which excludes liability:

> 'to the extent that such Tax Liability [is in respect of interest or penalties which] arise[s] or [is/are] increased in consequence of any failure by the Purchaser to comply with, or failure to procure the compliance of the company with, any of their respective obligations under the Deed'.

Third party exclusions

4.4 The seller will occasionally seek an exclusion which prevents the purchaser making a claim if the target company has a claim against a third party. Such an exclusion may directly contradict the words of the covenant, which will usually provide that the seller will pay irrespective of whether or not the target company has a right to reimbursement from any other person. The whole point of the indemnity is to provide the purchaser with the means to pay a tax liability in the target company. If a claim is excluded where the target company has a claim against a third party, or, more unusually, because of the existence of an insurance claim, then it has not achieved its aim. Such exclusions should be resisted by the purchaser. The ability to claim from third parties are usually covered by a specific third party claims clause (see para [4.4.1]).

The seller expects to indemnify the purchaser against unexpected tax liabilities. However, it will wish to ensure that purchaser does not simply recover under the deed because it is quick and easy to do so and ignores its rights against third parties which, if enforced, could relieve the seller from liability. Moreover, the seller will want to ensure that the purchaser does not recover the same loss twice: once under the deed and once against third parties thereby receiving a windfall as a result. An obvious example of this type of liability is where the pre-completion tax liability arises as the result of the negligence of the target company's tax advisers. Generally, the seller will be liable to pay immediately under the terms of the indemnity but the target company will also have a right of action against the tax advisers for negligence. The target company will be able to pursue the tax advisers and recover an amount in respect of the liability that the seller had previously paid to the purchaser thus recovering the amount twice.

A windfall for the purchaser could also result from the target company receiving a credit for a payment made by the seller (eg where the liability under the deed was for advance corporation tax which is later set off against a mainstream corporation tax liability) or, the seller may by having over-provided for taxation in the accounts of the target company received too little for the target company. The types of clauses which are usually included in the deed to protect the seller in such circumstances are dealt with in the paragraphs below.

Third party claims clauses

4.4.1 There are two types of third party claims clauses. The first, which is not very satisfactory for the seller, imposes a passive obligation: that in the event the target company receives an amount from a third party in respect of a liability that has been satisfied under the deed, the company shall reimburse the seller to the extent of the recovery, subject to a cap equal to the liability paid by the seller. The problem with such a clause is that there is no obligation upon the purchaser or company to take positive action against the third party. Unless the amount recoverable from the third party is far in excess of the amount already recovered from the seller, there is no incentive upon the purchaser to pursue the third party. The seller has no *locus standi* in the matter and therefore cannot sue the third party. The seller is therefore left with a theoretical possibility of recovering the amount paid to the purchaser under the deed but no practical way in which it can enforce recovery.

The second type of clause imposes upon the purchaser a positive duty to pursue the third party at the expense of the seller. This can be done either by the seller financing the action, or by the seller securing the purchaser against all costs and expenses it incurs. The purchaser may further protect itself by providing that it can recover any costs to the extent that they have not been recovered from the seller out of the proceeds of the action against the third party.

This latter type of clause can be worded as set out below:

> 'Without prejudice to the Seller's obligation to make any payment hereunder, where the Company is entitled to recover from some other person (other than the Purchaser but including any taxing or other competent authorities) any sum in respect of any such Tax Liability as is mentioned in Clause [reference to operative provision], the Purchaser shall procure that the Company shall as soon as reasonably practicable following it becoming aware of its entitlement notify the Seller and if so required by the Seller and at its expense, take all appropriate steps to enforce such recovery (keeping the Seller fully informed of the progress of any action taken) and shall account to the Seller for any amount so recovered together with any interest or repayment supplement received in respect of the sum so recovered forthwith [PROVIDED THAT the amount so repaid in respect of such Tax liability less any interest and repayment supple-

ment shall not exceed the amount paid by the Seller hereunder in respect of that Tax Liability and so far as not repaid or paid, the amount of the sum recovered (including any interest or repayment supplement) shall be set against the liability of the Seller in respect of any future claims under this Deed].'

The clause can be extended by the proviso in parenthesis which provides that to the extent that if there is any excess over and above the amount of the settled claim it shall be set against any future liability. Provided that the sum recovered is limited to the claims settled and the purchaser is secured to its reasonable satisfaction, or the seller is fully accountable for costs and expenses, the purchaser should have no reasonable objection to such a clause. Sometimes clauses provide that the whole amount of whatsoever nature recovered from third parties in respect of the subject matter of a tax claim satisfied under the deed (less expenses) should be paid to the seller, irrespective of the quantum of the claim under the deed satisfied by the seller. This should be rejected by the purchaser.

Example

Purchaser buys X Ltd from seller. As a result of pre-completion negligent tax advice given by Grabbitt & Scarper, X Ltd is assessed to tax of £1m. As a result of the assessment X Ltd is branded as a 'fraudulent, immoral company' in the local newspapers. As X Ltd's business is giving advice on investments in companies which do not pollute the environment or invest in countries where there are oppressive political regimes, its image is very important and is badly tarnished as a result of the handling of its tax affairs. In the six months following the newspaper articles its turnover drops by 50% even though the market is buoyant. The purchaser claims £1m under the tax deed and pays its tax. It then procures that X Ltd sues Grabbit & Scarper for the loss of tax (£1m) and damages for the loss of turnover attributable to the damage of its reputation.

The High Court awards X Ltd damages of £5m and costs. The purchaser offers to refund the seller the £1m it paid under the deed but the seller claims that the recovery stems from an action it requested in respect of a pre-completion tax liability and that it should therefore receive the whole £5m.

In the above example the excess is clearly to compensate the purchaser for its loss. Thus, any clause which requires the purchaser to account fully for all sums recovered from a third party should be rejected. Similarly, even if the clause restricts itself to requiring the payment of all sums recovered in respect of tax, the purchaser would usually take the view that such sums shall be for its account as owner of the asset not for the seller. The purpose of the deed is not to allow the seller to profit. The compromise generally arrived at is to give the seller credit for the sum recovered against potential future claims.

Corresponding benefits clauses and over-provisions

4.4.2 Some deeds do not include a corresponding benefits clause. This is usually justified on the basis that a corresponding benefit is too vague a concept and, to the extent it covers something more concrete, such matters are already covered by the third party claims clause. However, it is necessary to read the third party claims clause very carefully to make sure this is the case. A typical example of a liability covered by the corresponding benefits clause is where the liability under the deed is for advance corporation tax. This may arise where a dividend is paid after the latest accounts (by reference to which the deal was done) but prior to completion. The liability under the deed arises because the advance corporation tax on such a dividend would not be provided for in the accounts and the advance corporation tax payable on the dividend is arguably not tax in the ordinary course of business (usually the declaration and payment of dividends are specifically identified as being acts outside the ordinary course of business). When the advance corporation tax (in respect of which the seller has made payment under the indemnity) is offset against mainstream corporation tax, the corresponding benefits clause would operate to reimburse the seller the amount of the credit offset against mainstream corporation tax, thus ensuring that the purchaser does not receive a windfall. Another area where a corresponding benefit may arise is where the indemnity payment is in respect of VAT which turns out to be irrecoverable but which is consequently deductible for corporation tax purposes.

The third party claims clause outlined in para [4.4.1] above may be inadequate to deal with recovery of benefits or credits such as the offset of advance corporation tax against corporation tax liabilities. Although third party clauses make provision for payment to be made to the seller when 'the company is or becomes entitled to recover from a person (including the Inland Revenue or any other taxing authority, but excluding the seller) a sum in respect of any claim for taxation', it could be argued that a credit against a mainstream corporation tax liability is not an amount that the company can be said to 'recover' from the Inland Revenue and that it is merely set off against another liability.

The mechanics of establishing that there has been a corresponding saving and, if so, its quantum, generally requires the target company's auditors to provide confirmation. Rather than set out the mechanics for obtaining such confirmation in a corresponding benefits clause then duplicate the mechanics in the clause dealing with over-provisions, the modern trend is to deal with corresponding benefits and over-provisions in the same clause thus enabling the draftsman to use one set of procedural provisions to govern both.

Over-provisions

4.4.3 Over-provision clauses have become increasingly popular and are now usually included in the deed as a matter of course. However, as far as the purchaser is concerned it is arguable whether such a provision should be included at all. The question arises as to whether the seller should be protected against its own mistake of over-providing and hence selling the target company for less than it is actually worth. Furthermore, if the price is based on turnover or profits it is arguable that the over-provision did not effect the price. There are arguments both for and against such a clause. It can be said that prudence dictates that provisions are more likely to be over-provisions than under-provisions. On the other hand, where there is a completion balance sheet there would be a tendency for the seller to under provide for taxation, so as to obtain the greatest price possible for the company, which leaves the purchaser to make a claim to the extent that tax liabilities are not provided for in the completion balance sheet. It should be remembered that the existence of a *de minimis* limit may make this course of action preferable for the seller. In any event, the inclusion of the over-provision clause has become market practice and in most cases it will merely be a question of deciding how extensive the over-provision clause is to be.

Once it has been accepted that there is to be an over-provision clause, drafting it in relation to a single target company with no subsidiaries is quite straightforward. Where, however, the target company has one or more subsidiaries the matter is more complex.

The principal questions which arise are as follows:

(a) Should an over-provision in the accounts of one company be set against a liability in another company?

(b) Should the consolidated accounts of the group be used or the individual accounts of the various companies?

(c) Who is to decide whether in fact there has been an over-provision?

(d) Once there has been a decision that there has been an over-provision, can that decision be revisited subsequently?

(e) If the over-provision arises in the accounts of a company which has subsequently been sold, should the seller still obtain the credit?

A suggested clause for over-provisions and corresponding benefits is set out below:

'*Over-provision and Corresponding Benefits*

4.4.3 *Tax Deeds: Protecting the Seller*

1. If the Company's auditors for the time being shall (at the Seller's request and expense) certify at a time when the Company is a 75 per cent subsidiary of the Purchaser that:

1.1 any provision for Tax contained in the Accounts [(other than a provision for deferred Tax)] is an over-provision otherwise than by reason of:

1.1.1 a reduction in the rates of Tax or other change in legislation made after Completion with retrospective effect; or

1.1.2 any Relief arising after the Accounting Date; or

1.1.3 any act of the Purchaser or the Company carried out after the Accounting Date; or

1.2 any Tax Liability which has resulted in a payment being made by or becoming due from the Seller under this Deed has given rise to a corresponding saving for the Company;

then an amount equal to the value (as certified by the Company's auditors for the time being) of such over-provision or corresponding saving shall be set off first against any payment then due from the Seller under this Deed and secondly (to the extent there is any excess) against any payment(s) already made or subsequently due under this Deed in chronological order until exhausted PROVIDED THAT to the extent that such over-provision or corresponding saving is set off against any payment already made by the Seller that payment shall forthwith be repaid to the Seller.

2. Where the Company's auditors have certified as mentioned in Clause 1 the Seller or the Purchaser may on or before the [seventh] anniversary of Completion request the auditors for the time being of the Company to review (at the expense of the party requesting the review or where payment is required to be made pursuant to Clause 3, the party making such payment) the certification given pursuant to Clause 1 in the light of all relevant circumstances at the time of the review and certify whether in the light of such circumstances the original certificate should be amended.

3. If the certificate given following a review pursuant to Clause 2 certifies that the original certificate should be amended an adjusting payment equal to the difference between the sum in the original certificate and the sum in the amended certificate shall be made by the relevant one of the Seller or the Purchaser (as appropriate) as soon as reasonably practicable'.

The clause attempts to restrict its application only to over-provisions as the position stood at completion excluding post-completion reliefs and change of law etc is perfectly reasonable. There is no reason why the seller should benefit from matters outside its control after completion particularly as usually the seller will exclude its liability for post-completion events over which it has no control. For example, there will generally be a specific exclusion for tax caused by post-completion legislative changes. By the same token, just as the seller excluded itself from post-completion liability, it should also be excluded from post-completion benefits.

The disadvantage of the clause is that it puts the onus on the seller to enquire whether there is an over-provision and pay the expense of an auditors determination. Post-completion the seller will have little or no knowledge of the target company's tax affairs, short of periodic, speculative enquiries, there is no way to establish the position. Consequently, the seller will often bolster the opening of the clause by requiring the purchaser to notify it if it becomes aware of a potential over-provision or corresponding benefit as follows:

> '1. If the Purchaser of the Company become aware that any provision for Tax contained in the Accounts is likely to be an over-provision (the "**Over-provision**") or that any Tax Liability which has resulted in a payment being made by or becoming due from the Seller under this Deed has given rise to a corresponding saving for the Company, the Purchaser shall forthwith give details thereof to the Seller and the Seller may upon receiving such notice or in the absence of such notice at any time request that the Company's auditors for the time being certify the extent of such over-provision or corresponding saving in which event an amount equal to the value (as certified by the Company's auditors for the time being) of such Over-provision or corresponding saving shall be paid forthwith to the Seller to the extent that the Seller has already made any payment(s) under this Deed and to the extent that there is any excess such excess shall be carried forward and set against any future payment or payments which become due from the Seller under this Deed in chronological order until exhausted.
>
> 2. The amount of the Over-provision shall be calculated on the basis that no Over-provision will arise or be increased. [EXCLUSIONS AS PER ABOVE].'

The former over-provision clause provides for repayment only in the event that the target company in which the over-provision has arisen is still a subsidiary of the purchaser. The reason for this is that in the event that it is no longer a subsidiary it may be impossible for the purchaser to procure that the target company repay the amount of any over-provision.

The question of how over-provisions should be dealt with where one of the companies is a foreign subsidiary and the accounts of the foreign subsidiary are in a foreign currency are dealt with in Chapter 12.

Mitigation

4.5 The seller of a target company giving a tax deed will be concerned to ensure that where a tax charge can be avoided or partially mitigated, the purchaser should take such steps as are necessary to mitigate the liability before attempting to make a claim under the tax deed.

Example

In 1998 two companies, Company A and its 100% subsidiary Company B, with the same accounting periods, are sold to a purchaser in a single transaction. In the year ended 31 December 1997 Company A made taxable profits of £10m for which a provision for tax was made in the accounts on the basis of taxable profits of £9.9m. Company B made losses in the same period of £100,000. In the circumstances it is not unreasonable for the seller to expect the purchaser to procure that Company B surrenders losses to Company A to cancel the potential tax charge before making a claim under the tax deed. (This assumes, which is usually the case, that the purchaser does not purchase tax losses.)

In the situation described above, unless a suitable provision is made in the tax deed the purchaser may fail to procure that the target company makes the necessary claim for group relief, with the result that an extra tax liability of £31,000 (at 31%) arises in Company A. This liability could, subject to *de minimis* limits, be claimed under the tax deed while the tax loss is retained in Company B and is available for carry-forward relief.

Unless losses and other tax reliefs have been taken into account when setting the purchase price, a purchaser should generally accept that before they claim under the deed they must first utilise available reliefs and only if, and to the extent that, a liability to tax exceeds such reliefs, can it make a claim under the tax deed.

In addition to ensuring that the purchaser procures that the target group uses all losses and reliefs before making a claim under the tax deed, the seller may wish to go further. The seller may seek the purchaser's agreement that in the event that a tax liability arises in the target group, despite utilising all reliefs, any remaining tax liability may be satisfied by the seller by a surrender from the seller or by a member of the seller's group of losses or of advance corporation tax. Clearly most sellers would prefer to use losses or advance corporation tax to discharge a tax liability which would otherwise give rise to a claim under the tax deed, than let such liability arise and pay cash to settle the resulting claim.

The purchaser will find it hard to resist the seller's request for such provisions to be included in the tax deed. On the basis that the purpose of the indemnity is to ensure that the purchaser does not suffer any tax charge, it should not matter to the purchaser whether such liability is settled in cash or never arises in the first place as a result of the surrender of losses. A purchaser may wish to ensure that the surrender of losses or of advance corporation tax by the seller in such circumstances still constitutes a claim under the deed and counts towards satisfying the *de minimis* limit. If this is not the case, the purchaser may feel prejudiced by procuring that the companies accept a surrender of losses rather than receiving a cash payment in settlement of a claim under the tax deed. However, the purchaser must bear in mind that whilst claims settled by a surrender of losses or of ACT from the seller may count towards exhausting the *de minimis* limit and make future claims easier, at the same time the maximum financial limit is being exhausted. On balance most purchasers and sellers will accept that extinguishing potential tax liabilities using a seller's reliefs should constitute a claim under the deed. Logically, accepting a surrender to satisfy a liability should leave the parties in exactly the same position they would have been in had a tax liability arisen and a claim made and satisfied by a cash payment under the deed.

Sometimes a purchaser will try to resist the inclusion of a mitigation clause, on the basis that allowing the seller to surrender losses or ACT may prevent it from using post-completion reliefs and demanding payment under the tax deed for the reliefs used. The seller should resist such arguments as the purpose of the tax deed is to ensure that the purchaser does not suffer any fiscal disadvantage as a result of unforeseen tax liabilities arising in respect of events prior to completion. It is not the purpose of the tax deed to provide a mechanism for converting the purchaser's reliefs into cash.

A typical example of a mitigation clause is set out below:

'1. The Purchaser shall at the Seller's request procure that the Company:

1.1 uses such Reliefs (other than Reliefs arising in the Company by reference to an accounting period commencing or expenditure incurred after Completion) available to them (including by way of surrender from one Subsidiary to another or between [the name of the Company] and any Subsidiary and vice versa) such Reliefs to be used in priority to Reliefs arising after Completion.

1.2 make all elections, save in respect of matters after the date of this Deed, so as to reduce or eliminate the liability under this Deed.

1.3 at the Seller's request and expense deliver to the Seller a certificate from the Company's auditors for the time being confirming that all such Reliefs have been so used and elections made.

2. The Seller may by notice in writing to the Purchaser elect to mitigate or eliminate any liability under this Deed by surrendering or procuring the surrender to the Company of group relief (as defined in *s 402* of the *Taxes Act 1988*) or ACT to the extent permitted by law but without any payment being made in consideration of the surrender and the Seller shall be absolved from liability under this Deed to the extent of the amount of Taxation relieved by such surrender. The Purchaser shall procure that the Company takes all such steps as the Seller may reasonably require to permit and effect any surrender and claim of such Relief including (but not limited to) making a claim in a corporation tax return.'

Indemnities given to the seller by the purchaser

4.6 The modern tax deed will generally contain indemnities from the purchaser in favour of the seller. Whilst such indemnities may be relevant only in the context of a given transaction, there are some indemnities which are found more generally.

Cancellation of tax advantages

4.6.1 The first type of indemnity protects the seller against the adverse effects of *ICTA 1988 s 703* when such adverse effects are caused by post-completion acts of the target company. A detailed examination of *s 703* is beyond the scope of this book. However, put simply, a seller receiving a capital sum for shares may be concerned to ensure that part of the sum is not re-categorised as income. At the time when the rate of tax on capital gains was considerably lower than the rate of tax on income there was obviously an advantage in categorising a payment as capital rather than income. As the rates of tax for income and capital gains is now the same for individuals and for companies, this advantage has been largely eroded and much of the debate concerning *s 703* has disappeared. However, notwithstanding the fact that the same tax rate applies, there may still be advantages in obtaining capital treatment for a payment where indexation and the annual exemption etc may be available or where the seller has carry forward capital losses. A particular difficulty arises where the target company pays the purchaser an 'abnormal dividend' after completion. This means broadly that the purchaser receives more by way of dividend than could be reasonably expected given the period of the purchaser's ownership of the target and the normal profit levels of the target. If such an abnormal dividend is declared and paid, the Inland Revenue may decide that the seller has inflated the capital sum paid for its shares in the target by failing to distribute profits in the pre-completion period. The Inland Revenue may then seek to re-categorise part of the sum received for the shares as capital to be payment of income.

To protect against the risk discussed above the seller may seek a covenant worded as set out below.

> 'The Purchaser covenants with the Seller to pay a sum equal to any payment of Taxation made pursuant to *ss 703–709, Income and Corporation Taxes Act 1988* arising in respect of the consideration received under the Agreement to the extent that such taxation would not have arisen but for the payment of an abnormal amount by way of dividend by the Company after Completion.'

The purchaser may resist giving this covenant on the basis that if the seller had a concern under *s 703* then an application for clearance should have been made under *ICTA 1988 s 707*. Should it fail to do this, then, rather than expect the purchaser to restrict its future actions, the purchaser may take the view that the seller must accept the consequences of its failure to make distributions and its failure to make an application for a clearance under *s 707*. The purchaser can argue with some justification that it should not restrict its future actions to accommodate the seller's pre-completion tax avoidance. It would seem hard for the seller to resist such arguments. If a covenant is given in respect of *s 703*, the seller will wish to ensure that the provisions on gross-up, costs and conduct apply *mutatis mutandis*.

An alternative approach is for the purchaser to ask what acts the seller is worried about and then give a warranty that it will not do them. From the purchaser's point of view this is more acceptable because it puts the onus upon the seller, who is in the better position to know, to list those acts it considers dangerous. It also means that the purchaser can look at the list and weigh up the risks and decide whether it wants the target company subject to those restrictions, and provides the purchaser with a defined set of parameters within which it may act. Any warranty should therefore be in narrow terms and not merely state that the purchaser will not do anything which may give rise to a liability under *s 703*.

Value Added Tax

4.6.2 The second common type of covenant sought by a seller from a purchaser is in respect of value added tax. This is sought where the seller and the target company are members of a value added tax group of which the seller is a representative member. As all value added tax on supplies made by the target company is payable by the seller in such circumstances, the seller will want to ensure that it does not bear the cost of paying value added tax that should properly be borne by the target. Such a situation could arise where in the pre-completion period value added tax is due in respect of supplies by the target company in its ordinary course of business but not accounted for to Customs & Excise prior to completion. The seller's view should be that the target has had the benefit of the profits and inputs generated by such activities and therefore the value added tax should be for its account.

Where, as in the case of the example quoted above, taxable supplies have been made by the target company prior to completion but value added tax does not have to be paid to Customs & Excise until after completion, the seller will, in the absence of an indemnity, have no means of recovering the value added tax liability which it has to pay to Customs & Excise as a representative member of the group. At the time the payment of tax is made by the seller, the seller cannot control the target company and procure that it repays the value added tax paid on its behalf as it did for value added tax periods prior to completion. Reasonable purchasers should not have any objection to this in principle and a clause to cover this point could be worded as set out below:

> 'The Purchaser hereby covenants with the Seller to hold the Seller and each company in the Seller's group (other than the Companies) fully indemnified against any value added tax recoverable from the Seller or any other group companies under *Value Added Tax Act 1994 s 43* attributable to imports or supplies actually made by any of the Companies during the VAT return period of the VAT group in which completion falls (whether or not such imports or supplies are treated as made by the Seller or any other group companies under that section).'

ICTA 1988 ss 767A and ss 767AA

4.6.3 It has become market practice for the purchaser to indemnify the seller against a potential tax charge under *ICTA 1988 s 767A*, which was introduced by the *Finance Act 1994*. Following the introduction of *s 767AA* by the *Finance Act 1998* one can reasonably assume that it will become equally common to see an indemnity in favour of the seller in respect of *s 767AA*.

ICTA 1988 s 767A

4.6.3.1 *Section 767A* applies if a seller sells a target to a purchaser, bringing about a change in ownership, and a tax liability arises in certain prescribed circumstances, which remains unpaid after six months of the due date for payment. In such circumstances, the Inland Revenue may assess the seller for such tax on the basis that the seller is a person who had control of the target in the three years prior to the change in ownership.

The tax charge can arise where:

(a) at any time during the period three years before the change in ownership the target company's activities cease or become small or negligible and no significant revival of those activities occurs during that period and a tax liability arises and is not paid. Thus, suppose for example, part of the target group comprises a company which became dormant a year before the sale. Two years before that when the company was still trading tax liabilities arose but these were fully provided for in the accounts but remain unpaid pending resolution of a few outstanding issues with the Inland Revenue. Following completion the tax position is agreed at the sum provided in the accounts and an assessment is raised. The purchaser then fails to discharge the tax bill to the Inland Revenue. Notwithstanding that there could be no possible claim by the purchaser on the seller (as the tax was provided for in the accounts), the Inland Revenue would be able to look to the seller to discharge the tax, even though it no longer owned the target company at the relevant date. Of all the specified circumstances in *s 767A* this is the most likely to apply;

(b) at a time after the change in ownership of the target company but under arrangements made before the change, the activities of the trade or business for the target cease or became small or negligible and the purchaser fails to procure that the target pays a tax liability. The Inland Revenue ask the seller to discharge such liability. In practice, it is difficult to see how 'arrangements' could exist where there is a normal open market sale; and

(c) during the period beginning three years before any change in ownership and ending three years afterwards (ie a six-year period) there is a major change in the nature or conduct of the trade or business. This change is coupled with a transfer of the target's assets to the person controlling the target, or someone connected with that person, and such transfer occurs during the three years before the change in ownership or after the change but under arrangements made before the change. The major change must be attributable to the transfer of assets. Again, the possibility of such arrangements existing between two parties dealing in the 'arm's length' seems small.

It would seem that realistically the only time a liability is likely to arise under *s 767A* is when dormant subsidiaries are sold as part of the target group. However, notwithstanding this, it has become accepted market practice for the purchaser to indemnify the seller against these risks and it is hard for the purchaser to resist as a liability can only arise in the event that the purchaser procures that the target company defaults in its obligation to pay tax.

ICTA 1998 s 767AA

4.6.3.2 The risks posed to the seller by *ICTA 1988 s 767AA* introduced by *Finance Act 1998* are far more acute than those posed under *s 767A.* As with *s 767A, s 767AA* applies where there is a change in the ownership of the company and tax remains unpaid more than six months after it was assessed. It applies where it is reasonable to infer that, given terms of the sale which gave rise to the change in ownership and given any other circumstances, the transaction was entered into by one or more of the seller and purchaser on the assumption that a tax liability would be unlikely to be met or met in full were it to arise. *Section 767AA(3)* makes it clear that the tax liability must be reasonably foreseeable at the time of the change in ownership or that there was a reasonable foreseeable risk.

Although the Inland Revenue have made encouraging noises about the section being unlikely to be applied when the transaction is at 'arm's length' (see IR Press Release of 19 August 1998), the actual wording of the section means that potentially it could apply in a wide range of circumstances. What is reasonably foreseeable at the time of the change in ownership is a wide and uncertain test, particularly as one party may be held responsible for what is deemed to be the reasonably foreseeable acts of another party. Because the ambit of the section is so wide, all well-advised sellers should seek an indemnity against a charge under *s 767AA.*

The sort of clause that may be appropriate may be something along the lines of a covenant to pay:

> 'any Tax assessed on the Seller or a member of the Seller's Group under *ss 767A, 767AA (or 767B)* of the *Taxes Act 1988* to the extent that such Tax is not of a type which would allow it to be claimed by the Purchaser from the Seller under Clause [ ] of this deed'.

Other indemnities

4.6.3.3 Other areas where the seller may seek an indemnity from the purchaser depending upon the specific circumstances of the target company are:

(a) *ICTA 1988 s 776*: a disposal of land otherwise than in the ordinary course of business by the purchaser may give rise to a liability on the seller;

(b) disclaimer of capital allowances: the seller may have an increased liability to corporation tax as a result of a reduction in group relief in consequence of the target disclaiming capital allowances following completion;

(c) pay and file returns: where the seller is responsible for submitting returns for pre-completion periods there should be a provision in the sale contract binding the purchaser to sign them; and

(d) *ICTA 1988 s 751*: where the target group includes CFCs, the seller should ensure that the purchaser procures that any CFC persues an acceptable distribution policy for pre-completion periods.

Taxation of the seller

4.6.3.4 Payments made to the seller are not specifically dealt with under ESC D33 although the Inland Revenue have stated how they will deal with payments under *ICTA 1988 s 767B(2)* in their Tax Bulletin No 16 dated 21 4 95; however, it would be wise for the seller to seek a gross up clause.

Chapter 5

Tax Deeds: Mechanics, Notice Provisions etc

Introduction

5.1 The two previous chapters discuss the clauses which provide the purchaser with a claim and protect the seller from paying the purchaser any more than the purchaser's real economic loss. Having established the circumstances in which a liability will arise, the tax deed must also provide the mechanics for making a claim. These clauses are very important and in practice difficult to negotiate. Their importance is that to provide effective protection for the purchaser, it is not enough for the tax deed to give the purchaser the means of recovering economic loss, it must also provide a practical, quick and effective way of enforcing such claims. From the seller's perspective, protection against unjustified claims is worthless if the deed fails to provide it with the means contesting liability. The difficulty of agreeing clauses dealing with conduct of disputes stems from the fact that the purchaser's position and the seller's can be diametrically opposed. The purchaser may take the view that having bought the target company it should exercise full control and discretion over its affairs including its tax affairs. The purchaser may regard the prospect of handing over full control of the target's tax affairs, when there is a contested claim, to the former owner as unacceptable and undermining its ownership rights. Conversely, the seller will often take the view that having agreed with the purchaser that it will meet the full costs of any claim it should have the right to ensure that those costs are minimal. The seller may take the view that the purchaser has no vested interest in reducing the target company's contested tax claims. A contested tax claim represents only a commitment of management time and effort for the purchaser with no benefit for the purchaser as the seller meets the final cost whatever the level of such cost.

This chapter examines the mechanics of how a claim is to be made and some other relevant clauses which are usually included in order to make the deed a stand alone document.

Conduct of tax affairs

5.2 As stated above, a result of the importance of having conduct of the target's tax affairs and the difference in approach between the parties is that the conduct of tax affairs clause is often one of the most contentious and difficult areas to negotiate. In drafting the clause the following questions, *inter alia*, need to be considered:

(a) Should the purchaser notify the seller whenever an assessment relating to a pre-completion period arrives or only when the purchaser believes that there is a genuine claim ie it is not covered by one of the exclusions?

(b) How much notice of claims should the purchaser give the seller in view of the time limit for appeals?

(c) If the seller disagrees with the assessment should it have control of the dispute?

(d) If either the seller or the purchaser fails to follow the correct procedure under the conduct clause, what happens?

(e) Should the seller be able to control the dispute without taking professional advice on the validity of the dispute and the possible chances of success?

(f) Should the purchaser have the power of veto if the seller's actions prejudice the target company?

(g) If the purchaser has control of the dispute should the seller have a power of veto to prevent the purchaser settling a claim so as to prejudice the interests of the seller?

(h) Who should bear the cost?

(i) How far should the appeal process go? The Commissioners, the High Court or the House of Lords?

Control over disputes

5.3 The purchaser will be reluctant to relinquish one of the privileges of ownership of the newly acquired target company by allowing the seller the ability to interfere in the target company's tax affairs. The purchaser's concern may be that the seller's objective will be simply to reduce its exposure under the tax deed to a minimum, irrespective of the damage that may be caused to the target company's future relationship with the Inland Revenue or other revenue authority. The purchaser may be concerned that the seller will concede points to reduce an immediate tax liability at the expense of the creation of future problems. If, for example, the seller agrees a particular tax treatment for a given type of expenditure, such treatment may be applied to the target company in future accounting periods resulting in additional tax liabilities. Conversely, the seller is generally reluctant to allow the purchaser to have control of the tax dispute as the purchaser has nothing to gain by disputing the revenue authority's claim, assuming that when the dispute is finally determined the seller bears the cost. The seller will be concerned that if it bears the cost of any tax liability, the purchaser will want to settle the claim without the bother of disputing it. It is because the purchaser has no vested interest in pursuing a defence against a claim from the revenue authorities that the seller will wish to ensure it controls the running of the dispute. It is considered that since, ultimately, the seller will pay all the costs and any tax liability borne by the target company (subject to limitations and exclusions in the tax deed) it should decide whether it wishes to dispute the assessment from the revenue authority and, if so, to what extent and how it will contest the claim.

Given the complexity and the numerous permutations which can arise, it is impossible to go into great detail on clauses other than the more common types of conduct of claims clauses which may be inserted in the tax deed. The best way to examine the problem is chronologically and to start from the time that the purchaser first becomes aware that a potential problem has arisen which could give rise to a claim under the tax deed.

Notification

5.3.1 The conduct of a claims clause generally begins with a statement relating to notification of liabilities. A typical clause can be worded as set out below:

> 'If the Company or the Purchaser (as the case may be) shall become aware of a Claim in respect of a Tax Liability relevant for the purposes of this Deed (including any determination or direction in respect of losses which could increase such tax liability) of which the Seller is not then aware it shall as soon as reasonably practicable give written notice thereof to the Seller and in any event within [14] days of receipt.'

It should be noted that such a clause gives a degree of discretion to the purchaser. The purchaser must decide that the claim is in respect of a Tax Liability which is 'relevant for the purposes of this Deed'. If the purchaser believes that an exclusion applies or that the liability is covered by the provision for tax, there would be no need to notify as it would not result in a claim. In practice, unless it is absolutely clear that no claim can be made, the purchaser should inform the seller.

In practice the purchaser will often inform the seller when any assessment whatsoever in respect of a pre-completion period is raised in the hope that a claim can be made and the burden of settling the liability passed on to the seller. It should be noted that, although the amount of the claim falls within the *de minimis* limit, the seller may still wish to dispute it. If the assessment is potentially erroneous then a successful appeal will leave the *de minimis* limits intact in the event of a further claim arising. Further, it is necessary to consider the time limit 'as soon as reasonably practicable'.

The seller may feel that the purchaser should be obliged to notify the seller of a potential issue within a definite period. The words most commonly used to achieve this are 'and in any event within [14] days of receipt' added to the end of the clause above. The object of this amendment is to protect the seller against delay caused by the purchaser which could result in a loss of the right to appeal against an assessment. When these words are added, the purchaser often argues that 14 days is not a sufficient period to establish what action it must take. It may argue, for example, that if an assessment arrives at its accounts office at the time when staff are on holiday, 14 days would not be enough time for the purchaser to comply with its obligations to notify the seller. Whilst one can sympathise with such an argument, the seller's likely response is that given that there are only 30 days to appeal against an Inland Revenue assessment and it has only half the permitted time to consider, draft and lodge an appeal, it is more than equitable to expect the purchaser to forward the assessment with a covering letter in the first half of the permitted time. The compromise might be to add a proviso worded as set out below:

> 'Provided that in a case involving an assessment with a time limit for an appeal notification is made within [14] days of receipt and in any other case within [30] days of the receipt of the [notice, demand, letter, assessment or other document from which it appears that the company may become, subject to a liability for taxation] [Claim].'

Alternatively, it may be agreed that a clause which provides for the making of a protective appeal and application for postponement of taxes in an assessment in respect of pre-completion matters is inserted and the time limits are therefore extended. Most companies would make such a protective appeal on the basis that the assessment was, taking all the circumstances into account, excessive.

The response: where the revenue authority's claim is not contested

5.3.2 If the seller receives a notice from the purchaser and decides to accept the validity of the tax authority's claim, the question is simply one of establishing whether or not such an admission gives rise to a claim under the indemnity given the *de minimis* limits etc. If the seller fails to respond within a specified time, the purchaser will expect to be free to settle the claim, as the purchaser will not wish the tax affairs of the target to remain outstanding indefinitely pending a reply from the seller. It is hard for the seller to resist such a request. One question to be determined is: what time span should be regarded as a reasonable opportunity for the seller to respond? Another question is whether, if the seller fails to respond, should the purchaser have an unfettered discretion to settle the claim? To settle these questions the purchaser will seek to introduce a clause as set out below:

> 'The Purchaser and the Company shall be free to pay or settle any tax claim on such terms as they may in their absolute discretion think fit and without prejudice to their rights and remedies under the deed if:
>
> (a) within [14] days of service of the notice under sub-clause [reference to the sub-clause containing the obligation to notify] the Seller fails to notify the Purchaser of its intention to dispute the tax claim; or
>
> (b) the Seller fails to comply with the provisions of sub-clause [reference to any sub-clause which requires the seller to provide security for costs, take professional advice etc before the purchaser and the target company co-operate with the Seller.]'

The seller may argue that, whilst appreciating that at some stage the purchaser has to be able to settle the target company's tax affairs in the event of a failure to respond, 14 days is too short a period. It is hard to see how the purchaser will be unduly prejudiced if the period is extended to, say, 30 days. The seller may also try to impose a requirement that the purchaser must exercise reasonable discretion rather than absolute discretion when settling the tax claim. For example, if the purchaser receives an estimated assessment for a figure which is patently absurd (it is not unknown for the Inland Revenue to raise high estimated assessments to provoke a response from the taxpayer) it should not accept the figure without questioning the *quantum*, notwithstanding the fact that the seller has failed to respond. The problem for the seller is that such an issue will arise from its own failure to respond within a reasonable time to a notice from the purchaser. It is therefore difficult for the seller to insist that the onus is on the purchaser to show that it has reasonably exercised its discretion to settle a claim.

Where the revenue authority's claim is contested

5.3.3 If the purchaser accepts the basic principle that the seller should be able to contest the claim from a revenue authority, the problem then arises in deciding the extent to which the seller should be able to exercise that right and, in particular, to what extent the seller's discretion should be fettered. The clause is usually divided into two parts. The first part is a general statement of the seller's right to contest the claim while the second part imposes a number of restrictions and limitations on the general right to contest.

The general right to contest can be contained in a clause which can be worded as set out below.

> 'Subject to [the sub-clauses containing limitations or conduct] on the giving of the notice specified in sub-clause [reference to the sub-clause containing the obligation to notify] the Seller shall be entitled to resist the Tax Claim in the name of the Company at its own expense and can conduct any appeal, dispute, compromise or defence of the Tax Claim and of any incidental negotiations and the Purchaser will give and procure that the Company gives the Seller all reasonable co-operation, access and assistance as may be requested by the Seller for the purpose of considering and resisting the Tax Claim.'

Sometimes the purchaser will try to amend the clause to ensure that the seller is responsible for both the purchaser's and the target company's internal costs for providing the assistance referred to in the clause. The seller is often reluctant to agree to this on the basis that the purchaser may exploit the seller's need for assistance and charge large fees. Sometimes a compromise is reached where the seller agrees to pay all the external costs reasonably incurred by the purchaser together with any reasonable internal costs. Often the seller will offer this compromise only where the claim involves an appeal before a tribunal, the Commissioners or the courts on the basis that anything short of this is routine administration. The seller may refuse to meet the purchaser's internal costs in general on the basis that the cost of dealing with tax affairs of the target company is part of the routine administrative overheads associated with company ownership which should be borne by the purchaser. The problem in sustaining such an argument is that the seller is unlikely to secure the desired degree of co-operation if it involves the purchaser and the target company incurring major expenses which cannot be recouped by them. This is particularly so where the seller expects to take a tax claim before the courts.

Restrictions on the seller's right to conduct a claim

5.3.4 There are numerous possible restrictions which can be imposed upon the seller by the purchaser and most of them are the subject of keen negotiation. Some of the more common types of restriction are set out below.

It is quite common for the purchaser to insert a clause which can be worded as set out below. The more usual form of this clause uses the words 'Tax Counsel' with the prefix 'Leading' or the addition of the words 'of at least ten years standing':

> 'Sub-clause [the clause which gives the seller the general right to have conduct] shall not apply unless the Seller has been advised by [Leading] [Tax Counsel] [of at least ten years' standing] [Independent Tax Advisers (which shall include the Seller's solicitors and accountants)], after disclosure of all relevant information and docu-

> ments, that any appeal against the Tax Claim will, on the balance of probabilities succeed.'

The seller may have strong objections to such a clause for a number of reasons. First, the seller will regard it as unreasonable that a relatively small assessment for, say, £10,000 has to be submitted to a Tax Counsel for his opinion. Secondly, the seller could argue that given the time limits for lodging an appeal it is totally impractical to obtain the advice of a Tax Counsel before at least lodging notice of appeal and making an application for postponement of tax. Thirdly, the seller may argue, with some justification, that many Tax Counsel will be extremely reluctant to give an opinion that an appeal is likely to succeed in all but the most obvious cases (in which case there would be no need for his opinion). Even if a Tax Counsel is prepared to opine on the possibility of success, he is likely to restrict his comments merely to saying that there is a reasonable chance of success or that the appeal is worth contesting, rather than to say that it is likely that the appeal will succeed. More fundamentally, the seller's attitude will be, assuming that the purchaser is fully indemnified against costs and against any tax liability ultimately borne by the target company, that it is for the seller to decide whether it feels it is reasonable to resist a tax claim. If, for example, a target company is assessed for tax of £25 million and a Tax Counsel opined that there was only a 30% chance of success, the seller may quite reasonably regard an appeal as fully justified taking into account the *quantum* of the claim.

Whilst the seller may recognise that the purchaser does not want to be involved in needless expense and time in pursuing a claim which, on any reasonable basis, is not worth pursuing, the seller can argue with some justification that given the cost of making an appeal (even before the Commissioners of Inland Revenue), it is extremely unlikely that the seller will embark upon such a course without careful consideration of the merits of making an appeal. Furthermore, in any dispute before the Courts consulting Tax Counsel (or a qualified advocate with rights of audience) is mandatory in any event. In the light of the above comments, the seller can argue that a clause requiring it to take Tax Counsel's advice should be deleted. However, where for example, the purchaser cannot be persuaded that the seller will act properly, a more limited clause might be substituted which states that the seller should not be allowed to contest the claim except in the circumstances stated below:

> 'The Seller cannot contest the claim unless they have been advised by independent tax advisers reasonably acceptable to the Purchaser, after disclosure of all relevant information and documents, that it is reasonable to resist the Tax Claim in the manner proposed by the Seller.'

Occasionally the seller will enquire as to what is meant by 'independent'. Are the solicitors/accountants who advised on the transaction independent? The answer to this question is normally in the affirmative. The word 'independent' is used to prevent the seller consulting its own in-house tax advisers whose interests are identical to those of the seller.

Obviously, if the seller is a large, reputable PLC, the purchaser may take the view that it is unlikely that the seller will not obtain good advice and it will not be too concerned whether a restriction clause is included. Conversely, if the seller is an individual who is selling his interests in a relatively small company, the purchaser may feel that there is a risk that the seller may take action without seeking professional advice and that this could waste the purchaser's time and money and the restriction clause should therefore be included.

If the clause is inserted, the seller may be concerned to ensure that there is some mechanism which enables a holding appeal to be made prior to obtaining an opinion. This will prevent the risk of missing a time limit for an appeal due to the need in the first instance to obtain professional advice.

Notwithstanding any indemnity for costs the purchaser may have under the general indemnity clauses, the purchaser may require the seller to provide security against the costs and potential tax charges that could result from the claim before embarking upon any defence. This will be particularly important if, for example, the seller is non-resident. To ensure adequate protection, the purchaser may require the insertion of a clause which provides that the purchaser shall not be required to procure that the target company takes any action unless security is given. Such a clause is set out below:

> 'The Purchaser [and the Company] must be secured to their satisfaction by the Seller against any liability in respect of the Taxation the subject of the Tax Claim and against all losses (including additional liability to taxation), costs, damages and expenses which may be incurred in resisting the Tax Claim.'

It is hard for a seller who is an individual or a small company reasonably to resist this request although some sellers, particularly if they are large, reputable companies, take exception as it implies that in some way such seller might not honour its obligations. Large companies will often refuse to give security. Often a less substantial seller will agree to such a clause provided that it is limited by stating that the purchaser must be secured only to 'their reasonable satisfaction'. This prevents the purchaser from rejecting an appeal through the back door by demanding such a high level of security that the seller cannot provide it.

Of all the limitations, by far the most difficult area to negotiate is that dealing with the extent to which the purchaser is able to influence the seller's conduct of the dispute. As a minimum the purchaser will try to ensure that the seller keeps it informed but the purchaser may also try to require the seller to seek its views on how the claim should be handled. A fairly typical clause is that the seller shall not be entitled to resist the tax claim unless there is consultation. A qualification of this type can be worded as set out below:

> 'The Seller shall keep the Purchaser and the Company fully informed and shall consult with the Seller about the conduct of the Tax Claim.'

It is considered that the right to be informed and consulted is pointless if the seller can then ignore the purchaser's views. Thus, frequently the purchaser should not only request that it is consulted before action is taken but should also seek to give itself the right to veto the seller's actions. For example, the purchaser may insert a clause as set out below:

> 'No material communication, written or otherwise pertaining to the dispute shall be sent to the Inland Revenue or other Revenue Authority without having first been submitted to and approved by the Purchaser such approval not to be unreasonably withheld or delayed.'

The purchaser will want this right of veto to ensure that the seller does not agree anything which may be used as the basis for an unfavourable assessment on the target company in future. The seller's view will be that as it will pay the costs of any dispute and all tax liabilities, it should be free to settle the claim as it thinks fit. The seller will not want to have the evidential burden of proving that the purchaser withheld consent unreasonably. The purchaser may, for example, object to a proposed basis of settlement of a claim as it may cost the target company (say) £10,000 in future if the treatment of an item of expenditure is applied to such items in future accounting periods. However, a failure to settle on the basis of such treatment could give rise to an immediate cost to the seller of, say, £500,000. It would be difficult to say in such circumstances that the purchaser was being unreasonable. The position could be improved for the seller by making it clear that equal regard should be paid to the position of the seller and purchaser and a balance of convenience test applied to determine whether consent has been withheld unreasonably.

Often clauses are inserted by a purchaser to the effect that the seller can have conduct provided such conduct does not 'prejudice the company or create any future Tax Liabilities'. The seller should treat any such wording with caution. Often it is phrased widely enough to allow the purchaser a right of veto. The purchaser has only to claim that the dispute may prejudice the target company's good standing and relationship with the Inland Revenue to deny conduct. Alternatively, even something such as agreeing a liability and using pre-sale losses (which the purchaser did not pay for) to shelter it can create future liabilities for the target company and potentially deny the seller conduct. At the very least the seller should insist that the 'prejudice' or 'Tax Liability' resulting from its conduct must be material. The next step would be to introduce a balance of convenience test ie if the seller's proposed course of conduct saves it, say £1m, at a cost to the target of upsetting its Inspector of Taxes, it should be allowed to proceed.

Another possible compromise could be for the seller to pay the purchaser an amount equal to the sum for which the claim could have been compromised by agreement with the Inland Revenue, whereupon the seller's liability is discharged but the purchaser can continue to pursue the claim. An example of such a clause is set out below:

> 'The Purchaser shall not be obliged to procure that the Company compromises any claim if the Purchaser takes the view that such compromise could have adverse effects for the company in which event the Seller shall if it desires be discharged from all liability under this deed in respect of such claim upon paying to the Purchaser the amount which the relevant Revenue Authority has indicated it is prepared to accept in settlement or compromise thereof.'

Failure to comply with conduct clause

5.3.5 A point which is sometimes not considered is what is to happen if either party fails to perform their part of the bargain. What happens if notice is given in 15 instead of 14 days, or it transpires that the Tax Counsel used was only of nine years call instead of ten? More fundamentally what if a failure on the part of the purchaser increased the amount payable by the seller?

Seller's failure

5.3.6 Sometimes the matter is taken care of by stating that if the seller fails to do something it forfeits its right to conduct the dispute. In para [5.3.2] above, the inclusion of a clause was suggested that allowed the purchaser to settle in the event that the seller failed to comply with certain provisions. A seller should normally resist such a clause as it is extremely harsh: a failure on the part of the seller may not prejudice the purchaser in any way. If a failure by the seller cannot cause any damage to the purchaser then arguably all the clause does is to present an obstacle to the seller. It does not provide the purchaser with any protection. The answer probably lies in the fact that the tax deed is a contract between the purchaser and the seller. If the seller breaches the contract does that breach cause damage to the purchaser? If it does the purchaser has a remedy at common law for the damage suffered. In general, therefore, a breach by the seller should not excuse the purchaser from performance, or prevent the seller from continuing with the conduct of the dispute unless the breach is so fundamental that it prevents the purchaser from performing. A purchaser may therefore ask: why have obligations imposed on the seller if a failure to fulfil those obligations does not give the purchaser the right to settle? The answer to that question is that if a failure by the seller to perform its obligations causes the purchaser or the target company no loss, there is no need for such a clause and if it does the damage can be repaired through a claim for contractual damages.

The position of the target company in the deed

5.3.7 Where the deed is drafted as a covenant to pay, the only parties will be the purchaser and the seller. The damage caused to the purchaser will therefore be a diminution in the value of the target company's shares. An argument for including the target company as a party to the deed is that it could sue the seller directly in the event that a breach by the seller causes it damage. The fact that the target company has given no consideration for the right will not matter because there is no legal requirement for consideration when a contract is executed as a deed.

Purchaser's failure

5.3.8 A failure by the purchaser to do some act or other will, like a break by the seller, be a breach of contract. If that breach results in an increased liability for the seller then that increase can be claimed from the purchaser. Where the increased liability arises in the target company the seller simply has to refuse to pay for the liability. The seller can meet any attempt by the purchaser to recover the amount through the courts with a counter-claim for breach of contract. Often failure by the purchaser will simply result in interest on overdue tax or other increases in the liability such as a penalty. This can be covered by an exclusion from the main operative clause of the deed for tax arising from the defaults of the purchaser.

Best approach

5.3.9 As it is impossible to provide for all the different permutations and combinations of action that may be taken by the seller or the purchaser, the best approach is to draw up a list of issues to be addressed on a 'what if ?' and 'who is ?' basis (ie what if the purchaser wished to settle and the seller does not? Who is to bear the cost? Who is to conduct the dispute?) If such questions are addressed when the deed is drafted, no matter how vigorous the negotiations, in the event of a claim arising, each party will know their rights and obligations and the conduct of any dispute will be smoother. The last thing that either party wants is to have a dispute over how the dispute should be conducted.

Notice provisions

5.4 To avoid doubt the deed should provide for the manner in which the notices required under the deed should be served and the time when a notice served in a particular way is deemed to have been received. Establishing exactly when a notice shall be taken to have been served is particularly important in the context of the conduct of the tax claims clause, which generally lays down strict time limits for parties to comply with their obligations.

When drafting a notice clause it is important to ensure that, not only does it correspond with the notice provisions in the Sale and Purchase Agreement, but also that it provides adequately for all the modern methods in which notice may be served, notably, facsimile etc. A standard form of notice clause can be worded as set out below:

'(i) Any notice or other document to be served under this deed may be delivered personally or sent by pre-paid first class recorded delivery post or facsimile process to the party to be served at his address appearing in this deed or at such other address as he may have notified to the other parties in accordance with this clause.

(ii) Any notice or document shall be deemed to have been served:

- (a) if delivered personally, at the time of delivery; or
- (b) if posted, at 10 am on the second Business Day after it was put in the post; or
- (c) if sent by facsimile process at the expiration of two hours after the time of despatch if despatched.

(iii) In proving service of a notice or document it shall be sufficient to prove that delivery was made or that the envelope containing the notice or document was properly addressed and posted as a pre-paid first class recorded delivery letter or that the facsimile message was properly addressed and despatched as the case may be.

(iv) If a notice which is delivered personally or by fax is given:

- (a) on a day that is not a Business Day the relevant notice still be deemed to be given by the Business Day next following that day;
- (b) after 5.30 pm on a Business Day the relevant notice shall be deemed to be given at 9.30 am on the Business Day next following such Business Day.'

The notice provisions rarely cause any difficulty although the clause set out above may have to be modified to take into account special circumstances. For example, if a purchaser was a foreign corporate body, the deemed service of notice by posting will be inappropriate as the seller will be deemed to have received notice before it can possibly have done so or *vice versa.*

Assignment of a tax deed

5.5 The purchaser (Purchaser A) will wish to ensure that in the event it sells the target company's shares during the currency of the tax indemnity given by the seller, it can pass on the benefit of such indemnity to its own purchaser (Purchaser B). In this way Purchaser A can avoid any involvement in tax disputes arising from the period before its ownership. This will not only remove Purchaser A from the administrative burden of the claim but will ensure that on the subsequent sale to Purchaser B (provided Purchaser B accepts Purchaser A assigning the benefit of the tax deed from the seller and does not seek further indemnification), Purchaser A's exposure will be limited to tax indemnification only for the period of its ownership of the target.

It is possible, although the cocktail of statute law, common law and equitable principles leaves the position far from clear, that in the absence of an express prohibition on assignment in the tax deed, the deed is anyway capable of assignment under the general principles of law. However, the purchaser may be reluctant to rely on such unclear principles of law and will seek to reduce the uncertainty by inserting a specific provision in the tax deed under which the contracting parties agree to the deed being assigned. Such a clause could be worded as set out below:

> 'The benefit of this Deed may be assigned in whole or in part without any restriction by the person for the time being entitled thereto.'

The seller will generally expect to resist successfully the insertion of such a clause. The seller's view will be that it agreed a level of protection in the context of the circumstances of a particular transaction with a particular purchaser and that an indemnity so tailored should not be used as a precedent for a separate transaction with different facts. For example, the seller may sell a target company to a purchaser with whom it has had a great number of dealings over several years and which it knows to be a reputable and well-established quoted company, which is likely to use the tax deed responsibly. It may be that the seller would not have been prepared to give the same tax deed to a purchaser with a lesser reputation who was unknown to it.

The seller may also argue that a tax deed is designed to compensate the purchaser to the extent that the price it paid for the shares was excessive by reason of an unforeseen tax liability, which reduces the value of the shares of the target company. The reason for the indemnity is reduced once the purchaser has sold on the shares, possibly at a considerable profit. Furthermore, the seller will argue that the indemnity was never intended to be a transferable asset acquired with the shares.

Against the seller's argument, the purchaser will argue that the net economic effect on the seller will be the same whether or not the deed is assigned, but that where it is not assigned Purchaser A will simply be involved in a much greater degree of administration. In the absence of assignability, Purchaser A is likely to give Purchaser B a tax deed in the same or comparable terms as the tax deed it received from the seller. Hence, in the event of a claim resulting from an event during the seller's period of ownership, Purchaser B will claim against Purchaser A, who in turn will claim against the seller. The seller will argue that the administrative burden is simply a consequence of Purchaser A's decision to sell the target company's shares. The seller's view is that it is only prepared to deal with the party with which it negotiated the tax deed.

An absolute prohibition on assignment could be worded as set out below:

> 'None of the rights or obligations hereunder may be assigned or transferred to any person without the written consent of the other party hereto.'

The seller should check that there is no provision in the main agreement which governs the deed which provides that where consent is to be given, such consent is not to be unreasonably withheld.

Sometimes a compromise is reached which enables a purchaser to assign the indemnity within its group of companies but only for so long as the assignee remains a member of the group. A suitable clause could be worded as set out below:

> 'The benefit of this deed may be assigned to any member of the Purchaser's group at the date of this deed (a group being the Purchaser and its effective 51 per cent subsidiaries for the purposes of *s 170(7)* of the *Taxation of Chargeable Gains Act 1992*) in whole or in part and without restriction by the person for the time being entitled thereto provided that should the assignee cease to be a member of the Purchaser's group the company shall reassign such part of the benefit of the deed assigned to it to the Purchaser.'

It is important that reassignment be included or that the deed is expressed to terminate if the assignee leaves the group. It is surprising how many clauses are defective in this way. A clause which allow a purchaser to assign within the group without any restriction is open to abuse in the following way. A purchaser acquires a new shelf-subsidiary which then buys the target company and takes the benefit of the deed (assignment within the group). Such a purchaser then sells the new shelf-subsidiary out of the group with the target company as subsidiary and the deed is thereby effectively assigned.

Payment free of deduction

5.6 Under current UK law there is no duty to deduct income tax from indemnity payments. Although in the event of late payment and the imposition of default interest, *ICTA 1988 s 349* will require the seller to deduct income tax at the basic rate from interest payments. To ensure that indemnity payments are not subjected to any deduction of income tax or withholding tax, the following clause is sometimes inserted:

> 'All sums payable by the Seller to the Purchaser [or the Company] under this deed shall be paid free and clear of all deductions or withholdings whatsoever save as may be required by law.'

Attestation

5.7 As discussed earlier it is often no longer necessary for tax indemnities to be in the form of a deed. However, until this becomes accepted in the market, tax indemnities will continue to be drafted in deed form. Furthermore, there will still be cases where the target company will be party to the document and because there is no consideration to support the promises made to the target company, such a document needs to be in the form of a deed if the promises are to be binding.

The *Law of Property (Miscellaneous Provisions) Act 1989* (*LP(MP)A 1989*) *s 1*, the *Foreign Companies (Execution of Documents) Regulations 1994 (SI 1994/1995)* (the 'Regulations') and *Companies Act 1989 s 130*, introduced changes in the way in which individuals and companies may execute deeds and required certain drafting changes to be made to documents purporting to be deeds. The changes introduced by these Acts need to be considered in particular when determining how a tax deed should be executed.

LP(MP)A 1989 s 1(2) states that to ensure a document purporting to be a deed is not void it must be 'clear on its face that it is intended to be a deed' by the persons making it and must be validly executed as a deed. What is meant by 'clear on its face' is not set out in the Act, so to avoid any doubt the wording must make it unambiguous that all the parties intend the document to be a deed. Thus, it is strongly inadvisable for some parties to execute the tax deed as a deed and others to execute it under hand.

Execution by individuals

5.7.1 Prior to the changes in the law, an individual had to execute a deed under seal (which in modern times meant affixing a small waifer seal opposite the signature). This requirement was abolished by *LP(MP)A 1989 s 1(1)(b)*. Under *s 1* an individual may validly execute a deed:

(a) by signing in the presence of a witness who attests this signature; and

(b) in certain cases (eg blind or illiterate signatories) if it is signed at his direction and in the presence of two attesting witnesses.

Changes also meant that a deed does not have to be 'delivered' as in the past but this is of little practical significance. The only point to note is that when execution is on a different date from completion one must ensure that the operative date is the date of the completion meeting.

The point to note under *LP(MP)A 1989 s 1,* is that the witness to any particular signature must attest and must be present when the signature is executed, which whilst customary in the past was not mandatory. Unlike the formalities for the execution of wills, there is no prohibition on who may sign as a witness although common sense dictates that whenever possible an independent third party should be used. In the event of any dispute regarding the execution, the evidence of an independent witness would carry far more weight than someone connected to one of the signatories who may have a vested interest in the outcome of any such dispute.

The following are some examples of the type of clauses that can be used by signatories.

Where an individual signs on his own behalf:

SIGNED as a deed by IVOR HEADAKE in the presence of: } ....

....

Witness's Signature: ....

Name: ....

Address: ....

Where an individual signs on behalf of someone else:

SIGNED as a deed by IVOR HEADAKE at the direction of HENRY DOOLITTLE and in his presence and in the presence of: } [Henry Doolittle by Ivor Headake]

Witness's Signature:	Witness's Signature: ....
Name:	Name: ....
Address:	Address: ....

It has become customary to omit the occupation of witnesses although the considered view is that this is worth including as it can help trace a witness should the need arise. If, for example, the witness is a solicitor, he may be traced through the Law Society notwithstanding the fact that he may have changed firm or address since witnessing a deed.

Execution by companies

5.7.2 The *Companies Act 1989 s 130,* came into force on 31 July 1990 and abolished the requirement for companies to have a common seal. In practice, many companies retain a seal because their articles require it or simply because it gives the company greater flexibility as to who can execute documents on its behalf.

Often a company's articles permit non-directors/company secretaries to execute documents on behalf of the company as authorised signatories. However, *CA 1985 s 36A(4),* requires either a director and a company secretary or two directors to execute a document and express it to be executed by the company where no seal is affixed and the articles cannot override that provision. Hence, if a company wants to use authorised signatories other than the directors and the company secretary, it must use a common seal. It is also worth noting that often a UK company operating in a foreign jurisdiction is only empowered to appoint a person to act as its attorney to execute deeds in that foreign jurisdiction by writing under its common seal or it may find that it is obliged under the laws in a foreign jurisdiction to affix a seal to documents executed there.

For a company to validly execute a deed since the introduction of *LP(MP)A 1989 s 1(2)(a),* and *CA 1989 s 130,* the following conditions must exist:

(i) it must be clear on the face of the document that it is intended to be a deed by the person making it; and

(ii) it must be executed under seal as in the past or it must be signed by two directors or a director and a company secretary and must be expressed to be executed by the company.

Suitable attestation clauses for use by the company are set out below:

Not using a seal

EXECUTED as a deed
by A COMPANY LTD
acting by IVOR HEADAKE
and HENRY DOOLITTLE }

Director....................................... Director/Secretary......................

Using a seal (subject to provision in the articles of association)

The Common Seal of
A COMPANY LTD was affixed
to this deed in the presence of: } [COMMON SEAL]

Director....................................... Director/Secretary......................

Foreign corporations

5.7.3 It will often be the case that one or both parties to a UK tax deed will be companies incorporated outside the United Kingdom ('foreign corporations'). The adviser then has to consider how such corporations must execute the deed.

The Regulations came into effect on 16 May 1994. The Regulations were made under *Companies Act 1989 s 130(6),* and apply *Companies Act 1985 ss 36–36C,* to foreign corporations. The Regulations provide that a document may be validly executed:

(a) by the company fixing its common seal (if it has one); or

(b) in any manner permitted by the laws of the territory in which the company was incorporated for the execution of documents by such a company; or

(c) if it is executed and expressed (in whatever form of words) to be executed by the company and, if signed, is signed by person(s) who (in accordance with the laws of the territory in which the company is incorporated) is or are acting under the authority (express or implied) of that company.

As with documents executed in the United Kingdom, the document must make it clear on its face that it is to take effect as a deed. However, there is no requirement for a witness although as a practical requirement, rather than strict technical matter, it may be better to have one in case there is a dispute over whether the deed was validly executed.

Tax deed made by foreign corporations

SIGNED as a deed under seal by A GERMAN GmbH and signed and delivered as a deed on its behalf of AN AGENT in the presence of:	}	Signature of an Agent WAFER SEAL

Witness's Signature:..

Name:..

Address: ....

When using the attestation clause suggested for foreign corporations the UK tax adviser must always ensure that he has taken foreign legal advice to ensure that such a form of attestation is permitted under the company's constitution and its domestic law and that no additional formalities are required for valid execution under the laws of such jurisdiction. Further, such legal advice should confirm that any person executing is acting with due authority under the laws in question. The UK tax adviser wishes to ensure that the deed is validly executed under both UK law and the laws of the foreign jurisdiction to ensure no potential conflict of law issues arise.

Chapter 6

Warranties given on the Sale of Shares in a Private Company

Introduction

6.1 This chapter and the next, chapter 7, examine the tax warranties given in a typical share sale and purchase agreement. The negotiation of the tax warranties can be a time-consuming exercise. In the past there has been a tendency to have a large number of warranties many of which were irrelevant but were included either because the purchaser's advisers were adopting the 'catch all' approach or because the purchaser's advisers were not confident when advising on tax matters and therefore did not have the confidence to allow warranties to be deleted. More recently, there has been a tendency to focus upon the purchaser's concerns and to target the warranties at these. This has cut down the time taken to negotiate the warranties and produces a sale and purchase agreement which is more relevant to the actual transaction.

What is a warranty?

6.2 Although warranty is a legal term, clients often want legal jargon put into a commercial common sense language.

Tax warranties — commercial rationale

6.2.1 Stripped of all the legal jargon, a tax warranty is no more than a statement of fact made about the tax affairs of the company. It can be either positive or negative. Thus:

> 'the target company's tax affairs are up to date';
>
> and
>
> 'the target company is not a close company',

are both capable of being given as tax warranties. The factor that elevates them above a mere statement of fact is that they are made to the purchaser and the purchaser relies upon them when entering into the contract. If they are untrue, the purchaser can sue the seller for any resulting loss.

Tax warranties — legal rationale

6.2.2 Traditionally, the terms of a contract have been categorised as either 'warranties' or 'conditions'. This distinction seeks to recognise that the clauses in a contract are not all of equal importance. Terms which represent the substance of a contract and go to its foundation are classified as conditions. A breach of a condition undermines the very purpose of the contract and permits the innocent party to repudiate the contract as well as to claim damages. A warranty is a lesser term which is often said to be collateral to the main purpose of the agreement and a breach of which is not as serious for the injured party as a breach of a condition. The remedy for a breach of warranty recognises the lesser importance of a warranty and the innocent party can claim damages but cannot treat the contract as repudiated. Repudiation excuses the innocent party from further performance of the contract; whereas, if there has been a breach of warranty, the innocent party is still obliged to perform any outstanding obligations and the innocent party's only remedy is to sue for damages.

Warranty

6.2.2.1 A warranty is a contractual term which the other party relies on when entering into a contract but is not sufficiently significant to allow the other party to treat the contract as repudiated. Lord Denning MR in *Dick Bentley Productions Ltd v Harold Smith (Motors) Ltd* [1965] 2 All ER 65 at 67 put it thus: '. . . it seems to me that if a representation is made in the course of dealings for a contract for the very purpose of inducing the other party to act on it, and actually induces him to act on it by entering into the contract, that is prima facie ground for inferring that the representation was a warranty. It is not necessary to speak of it being collateral. Suffice it that the representation was intended to be acted upon and was in fact acted on.' To put the question of reliance beyond doubt, the sale and purchase agreement will usually have a clause in the following terms:

> 'The seller acknowledges that the Purchaser has entered into this Agreement in reliance upon the Warranties set out in Schedule [ ].'

Condition

6.2.2.2 A condition is a contractual term which goes '. . . so directly to the substance of the contract or, in other words, [is] so essential to its very nature that [its] non-performance may fairly be considered by the other party as a substantial failure to perform the contract at all.' (*Wallis, Son & Wells v Pratt & Haynes* [1910] 2 KB 1003 at 1012 per Fletcher Moulton LJ). It is very rare for there to be a contractual condition relating to tax.

Innominate term

6.2.2.3 This simple and practical doctrine which enables a distinction to be drawn between conditions and warranties is still of considerable importance. However, it has proved to be too simplistic to be capable of universal application in the modern commercial world, where commercial arrangements are increasingly sophisticated. Consequently, the common law has given birth to a hybrid term known as an 'innominate term'.

The concept of the 'innominate term' was formulated in the case of *Hong Kong Fir Shipping Co Ltd v Kawasaki Kisen Kaisha Ltd* [1962] 1 All ER 474 which concerned a two-year charter contract for a ship. For the first six months of the charter the ship spent most of the time undergoing repairs with the result that the charterers repudiated the charter. The plaintiffs, whilst admitting that they had breached a term which stated that the ship was suitable 'for ordinary cargo service', sued for breach of contract and claimed for wrongful repudiation. The court upheld the plaintiff's claim and accepted that the breach allowed a claim for damages but not repudiation by the defendants.

Under the traditional approach to the law of contract the breach of contract in the *Hong Kong Fir Shipping* case would have been characterised as a breach of warranty. However, the Court of Appeal showed itself reluctant to make such a categorisation. Diplock LJ's judgment made it clear that the court felt that such a distinction was inappropriate when dealing with complicated clauses in a contract. At p 487 he said:

> 'There are, however, many contractual undertakings of a more complex character which cannot be categorised as being 'conditions' or 'warranties' if the late nineteenth century meaning adopted in the *Sale of Goods Act 1893* be given to those terms.'

Identifying warranties through drafting

6.2.2.4 Despite the muddying of the waters, most contracts still lend themselves to the traditional classification and in practice it is rarely difficult to distinguish between a warranty, a condition and an innominate term. The reason for this is primarily that most well-drafted contracts expressly identify warranties as such. It is therefore implicit that the parties recognise them as such and accept that the remedy for the breach of such a term is damages. Most contracts go as far as stating that a breach of warranty as stated therein will only give the innocent party a right to sue for damages.

Authority for the proposition that identifying a term expressly as a warranty ensures that it will be categorised as such by the court is generally thought to be found in the case of *Heilbut, Symons & Co v*

Buckleton [1913] AC 30. In the case Lord Moulton (at p 49) referred to the judgment of Lord Holt in earlier cases (*Cross v Gardner* (1689) Holt KB 5 and *Medina v Stoughton* (1700) Holt KB 208) and stated that the court accepted that an affirmation at the time of sale is a warranty, provided that it appears on evidence that it was intended to be a warranty. However, Lord Holt does not appear to have said any such thing. In fact it appears that Lord Moulton, like most lawyers, attributed words to Lord Holt which are perhaps more correctly attributed to Buller J's judicial gloss on Holt's words in the case of *Pasley v Freeman* (1789) 3 Term Rep 51.

Identification of the intention of the parties aside, there must in any event be comparatively few instances where the aggrieved party will not receive adequate redress for a breach of a tax term by a payment of damages. Even if the claim is very large, the damage ultimately sustained by the aggrieved party is a requirement to pay an amount to a taxing authority, which can fully be made good by payment of an equal amount plus any incidental costs by the party in breach.

Taxation of warranty payments

6.3 Unlike payments under an indemnity, under a warranty payment there should be no question of the seller paying an amount to the target company. Consequently, the tax treatment of payments made by a seller to a purchaser under a warranty is governed by *TCGA 1992, ss 49, 116* and ESC D52. These are dealt with in [2.8], [2.6.1.1] and [2.9.1.2] respectively.

Function of tax warranties and their interaction with the deed of indemnity

6.4 Notwithstanding the right to sue for damages, the primary function of tax warranties is to elicit information. The use of warranties to make a claim for breach of contract in respect of pre-completion tax liabilities from the seller is only a secondary function. There are a number of reasons why the information gathering function of warranties takes precedence over the damages function.

The tax deed is a quick and efficient way for the purchaser to obtain redress from the seller when contrasted with the cumbersome procedure for making a claim under the tax warranties. To make a claim under the tax warranties, the purchaser must establish that a particular warranty has been breached, that a loss has been suffered as a result of the breach, the extent of that loss and that the purchaser's duty to mitigate that loss has been discharged. As potential claims can often be pursued either under the tax warranties or the tax deed, the purchaser will generally prefer to seek financial redress under the tax deed, where it is often sufficient to show that a valid assessment for tax has been made for a pre-completion tax liability which was not provided for in the accounts.

Another reason why undue emphasis cannot be put on a warranty as a means of obtaining financial redress is that a warranty's usefulness in gathering information can be undermined. Unlike the tax deed, tax warranties are invariably expressed to be subject to disclosure. Consequently, the seller is encouraged to co-operate and provide a wealth of valuable information safe in the knowledge that the provision of information limits any potential exposure under the warranties, although it should be noted that specific indemnities are sometimes included in the tax indemnity as the result of disclosure made against the warranties.

If the warranties are drafted and negotiated on the basis that they are there primarily to pursue potential claims against the seller, the seller may resist inclusion of warranties and make limited disclosure against them. This would undermine the purchaser's objective of obtaining a detailed financial picture of the target company via the warranties and the disclosure letter so as to facilitate the running of the target company's tax affairs by the purchaser following purchase of the company. This is particularly important in the period following completion when the purchaser's financial advisers will not have had the opportunity of familiarising themselves with the target company.

Having said that the primary function of the warranties is to elicit information, the purchaser's advisers should always be aware of the fact that certain matters may be subject to a claim under the tax warranties which cannot be the subject of claim under the tax deed. Generally, a claim can only be made under the tax deed if it arises as a result of pre-completion events. However, it is possible for a liability to taxation to arise after completion as a result of something done before completion.

Example

The target group comprises the target company X and its subsidiary company Y. On the sale of company X the seller warrants that there have been no transfers, to which *TCGA 1992 s 171* would apply, between company X and its subsidiary company Y. The seller gives the standard form of indemnity which contains an exclusion for tax liabilities arising from voluntary post-completion events outside the ordinary course of the target company's business. In fact, despite the seller's warranty, most of the assets owned by Y were acquired from X in the six years before completion and *TCGA 1992 s 171* applied. On the purchase of X and its subsidiary company Y, no charge under *TCGA 1992 s 179* will arise by virtue of the exclusion in *TCGA 1992 s 178(2)*. If the purchaser subsequently procures that X disposes of Y so triggering a *TCGA 1992 s 179* charge, the purchaser will be precluded from making a claim under the deed of indemnity by virtue of the fact that the sale is a transaction occurring after completion. However, the purchaser may be able to claim for breach of warranty, although it would have to persuade the court that its loss ie the *TCGA 1992 s 179* liability stems from the breach of warranty.

Another example where a warranty is more likely to provide financial redress than the tax deed is where the seller warrants that the target company has made no claims or elections to roll-over capital gains under *TCGA 1992 ss 247, 248, 152–158, 161* and *162* prior to completion. Another way of doing this is to warrant the base cost of the target company's capital assets for the purposes of corporation tax on chargeable gains. Following the sale of the target, the purchaser may have the choice of procuring that the target dispose of any one of a number of identical assets, although, due to roll-overs, capital gains realised on the disposal of one such asset would be larger than the capital gain realised on the disposal of an otherwise identical asset. If the purchaser opted to dispose of an asset which triggered a larger tax charge having relied on the warranty from the seller that no roll-over claims have been made in respect of that asset, there is a potential claim under the warranty. Again this is a post completion event.

As well as eliciting new information the warranties give the purchaser an opportunity to obtain further details of known problem areas. The accountants' due diligence exercise may have provided some detail of potential problems upon which more information is required. In such circumstances warranties can be tailored to extract the desired information.

Apart from obtaining information that would be useful to the purchaser in running the company, the information can also be used to draft specific indemnities against problems identified in the disclosure exercise, possibly putting such specific indemnities outside the usual *de minimis* financial limits. If a risk revealed by the warranties is thought to be serious enough, the purchaser may require a retention from the purchase price or reduce the purchase price or ultimately even withdraw from the transaction.

The measure of damages

6.5 Having established that a particular contractual term is a warranty, and that its breach will result in a claim for damages, it is then necessary to consider what the aggrieved party has to do in order to claim damages. To obtain damages for a breach of warranty the aggrieved party must establish:

(a) that a warranty has been breached ie that it is untrue;

(b) that damage has been suffered;

(c) that the damage stems from such breach; and

(d) the *quantum* of damage.

Whether there has been a breach of a tax warranty is a question which must be decided on the facts of any particular case and it is incapable of further constructive analysis. The question of whether damage has resulted from the breach, whilst again relying heavily on the facts, is also dependent upon the application of established principles of law.

Remoteness of damage

6.5.1 A layman may think that the unforeseeable and bizarre consequences of a breach of warranty are matters of pure fact and result, albeit indirectly, from a particular breach of a warranty. However, the law requires that a line is drawn at a particular point with the result that certain types of loss, whilst undeniably resulting from a breach, do not qualify for compensation. Practicality demands that such a line is drawn as otherwise the judicial process would be trapped in the complex web of examining consequences of consequences.

The common law has drawn the line, beyond which damages cannot be claimed, at the point where the damage becomes sufficiently remote to be disregarded. The case of *Hadley v Baxendale* (1854) 9 Exch 341 is the recognised authority on the question of remoteness of damage. The case laid down two rules: first, that damages are recoverable only when they may 'fairly and reasonably be considered arising naturally, ie according to the usual course of things' from the breach; and second, as an alternative to the first rule, damages may be recoverable when they may 'reasonably be supposed to have been in the contemplation of both parties at the time they made the contract'. An attempt to explain the inter-relation of these two rules was made in the case of *Victoria Laundry (Windsor) Ltd v Newman Industries Limited* [1949] 2 KB 528; [1949] 1 All ER 997 where Asquith LJ stated the following classic test:

> 'In cases of breach of contract, the aggrieved party is only entitled to recover such part of the loss actually resulting as was at the time of the contract reasonably foreseeable as liable to result from the breach.
>
> What was at that time reasonably so foreseeable depends on the

> knowledge then possessed by the parties or, at all events, by the party who later commits the breach.
>
> For this purpose, knowledge "possessed" is of two kinds; one imputed, the other actual. Everyone, as a reasonable person, is taken to know the "ordinary course of things" and consequently what loss is liable to result from a breach of contract in that ordinary course. This is the subject matter of the "first rule" in *Hadley v Baxendale.* But to this knowledge, which a contract-breaker is assumed to possess whether he actually possesses it or not, there may have to be added in a particular case knowledge which he actually possesses of special circumstances outside the "ordinary course of things", of such a kind that a breach in those special circumstances would be liable to cause more loss. Such a case attracts the operation of the "second rule" so as to make the additional loss also recoverable.'

The House of Lords in *Kovfos v C Czarnikov Ltd* [1967] 3 All ER 686 (the *Heron II* case) criticised Asquith LJ (possibly a little unfairly given his comments reported at p 540 in the *Hadley v Baxendale* case) as confusing a breach of contract with the commission of a tort. The House of Lords said in effect that the rules in *Hadley v Baxendale* only apply, whether in respect of damage arising naturally or within the contemplation of the parties at the time of the contract if, in either case, the damage was a serious possibility as a result of the breach. Under the law of tort, if the damage is foreseeable, it can be claimed no matter how unlikely. Despite such criticism the basic rule remains as stated by Asquith LJ ie that the reasonable horizon of contemplation, which allows damage to be claimed as not too remote, starts at damage that can easily be expected to arise from a breach in the ordinary course of things and such horizon is then extended by any special knowledge possessed by the defendant. If as a result of such knowledge, whether usual or special, the damage from the breach could be said to have been 'on the cards' to quote from Asquith LJ, a colloquialism criticised by the House of Lords in the *Heron II* case but not substituted by anything better, then it is not too remote and can be the subject of a claim.

Quantum of damages

6.6 Having established that a warranty has been breached and that damage stems from the breach and is not excluded as being too remote, the successful plaintiff must then quantify the damage in cash terms. The question of the measure of damages is decided on the basis that the injured party must be put into the position he would have been in had the contract been performed in accordance with its terms.

Damages for a breach of contract are compensatory, ie for the loss suffered, and there is no concept of punishment by awarding exemplary damages as there is in the law of tort. However, this does not mean that damages should only compensate for financial loss stemming from the breach. For example, the judgment in the case of *Jarvis v Swan Tours Ltd* [1973] QB 233, where a holiday which fell short of the type of holiday described in the firm's holiday brochure, resulted in the holidaymaker recovering not only the cost of his holiday but also an additional sum to compensate for the disappointment he suffered.

When considering the *quantum* of damages two factors are taken into consideration by the courts: first, the duty on the injured party to mitigate the loss; and, secondly, the impact of taxation on the damages awarded.

There is a common law duty on the party suffering damage resulting from a breach of warranty to mitigate the loss. (There is no such common law duty under the tax deed see *White & Carter (Councils) Ltd v McGregor* [1962] AC 413). For example, assume a tax liability of £100,000 arises in a company recently acquired by the purchaser in respect of which the seller gave a warranty that no such liability would arise and the purchaser ignores the assessment in respect of the liability for a year before notifying the seller. The seller could reasonably claim that whilst accepting payment of damages of £100,000, the liability for any interest and penalties levied by the relevant tax authority is incurred solely as a result of non-payment due to the purchaser's delay in settling the liability itself or notifying the seller. The seller's view would be that the purchaser cannot expect compensation for a loss which stems from the purchaser's default in not acting reasonably by informing the seller of the liability in time.

Although there is an obligation on innocent parties to mitigate their loss, this does not mean that they must go to extreme lengths to do so. The party breaching the warranty must accept the pecuniary state of the innocent party. If, therefore, the innocent party has no cash to pay the tax bill and is unable to raise the necessary funds, interest and penalties suffered by the innocent party would be recoverable. Likewise, if the innocent party borrows the money any interest incurred would also be recoverable provided the rate was reasonable compared with rates prevailing at that time for that sort of borrower.

In making awards of damages the court will also consider the impact of tax on the award. The leading authority in this area is the case of *British Transport Commission v Gourley* [1956] AC 105. In awarding damages for loss of earnings the court looked at the plaintiff's net loss ie gross earnings less income tax and national insurance contributions. In the context of damages for breach of a tax warranty the doctrine is, however, largely otiose. An examination contrasting the taxation of damages in respect of a warranty claim with the taxation of the proceeds of a claim made under the tax deed can be found in Chapter 2 above.

Position of the warrantors

6.7 Warranties are devalued if the status of the warrantors means that there is little prospect of recovering damages from them. However, particular considerations arise in respect of trustees who give warranties.

Trustees as warrantors

6.7.1 Where shares are purchased from trustees, it is likely that those shares were gifted into the settlement. If the settlor subsequently becomes insolvent *Insolvency Act 1986 ss 342* and *425* give a court extremely wide powers to set aside transactions at an undervalue which have prejudiced the creditors of a person making the undervalue transfer. The court's task is to restore the position to what it would have been had the transaction at an undervalue not taken place. In doing so, the court may exercise its powers against a third party such as a person who has purchased shares from trustees, possibly even if that third party has subsequently sold the relevant shares. The court can exercise these powers:

(a) at any time, if the donor becomes bankrupt as a result of a crime, ie the bankruptcy test (*IA 1986 s 341(4)* although this is to be repealed by the *Criminal Justice Act 1988* from a day to be appointed);

(b) at any time, if there has been a transaction at an undervalue and the court is satisfied that it was entered into by the donor for the purposes of denying present or future creditors of the assets or it has otherwise prejudiced their interests. This is sometimes called the motive test (*IA 1986 s 423*);

(c) at any time within two years of the transaction at an undervalue. It can be set aside once a bankruptcy petition is presented in relation to the donor. In this period of two years there is no requirement that the donor must have had any intention of prejudicing the interests of creditors or was insolvent at the time of the transaction at an undervalue;

(d) in the period from two to five years from the transaction at an undervalue the court can set aside the transaction where a bankruptcy petition is presented in relation to a donor and the petition proceeds to actual adjudication of bankruptcy. However, in this two-to-five year period, the donor must have been insolvent at the time of the transaction at an undervalue or become insolvent as a consequence of it.

The purchaser can be protected if it can be shown that the purchaser acquired the property from the donee, ie the trustees, in good faith, for value and without notice of the 'relevant circumstances' ie broadly, those circumstances enabling the courts to exercise its powers. *Section 342(2A)* inserted by the *Insolvency (No 2) Act 1994* creates a presumption of bad faith only where there was both knowledge of the relevant surrounding circumstances and relevant proceedings.

The problem for the purchaser is that the purchaser may be imputed to have constructive knowledge and this makes it easier for the purchaser to decide that it must ask the relevant questions in warranties in order to find out whether there is likely to be a problem under the *Insolvency Act 1986.*

To protect itself a purchaser should ensure that a warranty is obtained that none of the target company shares have ever been subject to a transaction at an undervalue (nor do they represent assets which have been the subject of such a transaction). To the extent that there have been transactions that are at an undervalue, the purchaser should be satisfied that the donor has never been insolvent nor that it was the purpose of the transaction to put the assets beyond the reach of creditors as envisaged by *Insolvency Act 1986 s 423.*

The other potential problem for a purchaser of shares from a trust is the possibility that there is a charge over the shares under the *Inheritance Tax Act 1984* (*IHTA 1984*). Under *IHTA 1984 s 237* where shares have been subject to a chargeable transfer and any inheritance tax remains unpaid, the unpaid tax is secured by an Inland Revenue charge over the shares which were the subject of the transfer. The charge will follow the property unless the purchaser of the shares does not have any knowledge of the facts giving rise to the charge. Alternatively, the purchaser is protected where a certificate of discharge has been given by the Inland Revenue under *IHTA 1984 s 239* and the purchaser has no notice of any facts which may render the certificate invalid. Tax advisers should be particularly careful when asking for a warranty on this topic that the trust documents disclosed do not constitute a deemed disclosure of a transfer of the shares into the trust which could constitute a valid disclosure against the warranty and may easily be overlooked.

Limitations on warranties

6.8 The tax adviser should ensure that time limits, financial limits and the exclusions dealt with when discussing the tax deed are applied to the tax warranties. These exclusions are included in the main body of the agreement and should duplicate those in the tax deed *mutatis mutandis.*

Chapter 7

Specific Tax Warranties

Introduction

7.1 This chapter we look at the typical warranties given on a share sale and examine them in order to ascertain what they are intended to achieve, how they do it and, on the basis that they are usually drafted by the purchaser, the ways in which a seller may wish to amend them.

Disclosure against tax warranties

7.2 Traditionally the purchaser provides a set of warranties to the seller and the seller makes disclosures against them. The purchaser seeks information from the seller by providing a number of factual statements, ie the warranties, which the purchaser believes to be true. The onus is thereby transferred to the seller to state if the warranties are not true. If the seller is to avoid a liability for a breach of the warranties, disclosure must be made against them. This can be done in one of two ways. The warranty can be amended or, as is more usual, disclosure is made in a separate document. The issues arising from disclosure are dealt with in the next chapter. If the seller can temper the severity of the warranties by making disclosures, why should the seller object to giving warranties? There are two main objections. First, to the extent that disclosure is not made and a warranty proves untrue a legal liability does arise. However, against this, it can be said that the seller, having been given ample opportunity to disclose against the warranties, should not then complain if the liability arises following a failure on the part of the seller to make disclosure. Secondly, the breadth and scope of the warranties makes the investigative work which the seller has to undertake extremely onerous, for example, a warranty may state that a certain fact is true and has been true for the previous twelve years. Proper disclosure against this warranty will require scrutiny of all the relevant files which may be contained in archives, misplaced or even lost. A further argument, which may be advanced against the inclusion of a warranty, is that it is not relevant, although until the purchaser has asked the question and received a disclosure (or not as the case may be) this may not be apparent. To delete a warranty exposes the purchaser to a potential liability if it was in fact germane. Against this it can be argued that where a matter is covered by a warranty it is also, usually, covered by the tax deed and that the purchaser has no increased exposure as the *de minimis* limits under both are usually the same.

Standard forms of warranties

7.3 With the increased use of word processors and photocopiers there is a tendency for advisers to send out a large number of standard form warranties which at the outset are identical for every transaction. However, there is an increasing trend away from acquiring information for information's sake and towards pinpointing exactly what the purchaser requires to know and then amending the warranties, if necessary, in the light of the disclosures made.

Production by sellers of contract containing warranties

7.4 Normally the contract, which will include the tax warranties, is produced by the purchaser's solicitors. Occasionally, where for example, a company is sold by tender, the seller's solicitors will produce a standard contract to be sent to all prospective purchasers. The seller may take one of two different views on producing the warranties. The first is to give the absolute minimum. Although at first sight this may appear attractive, in practice all bidders will usually purport to accept the warranties offered and when a preferred bidder has emerged and 'knocked the others out of the ring' an attempt will then be made to expand on the warranties. Often this will involve deleting those that have been provided by the seller and producing the purchaser's set of standard warranties. The second route, which is preferred but which involves more work at the outset, is for the seller to examine the usual purchaser's standard set of warranties and amend them so as to tailor them to the conditions applicable to the company being sold. The seller should give the widest warranties possible and present them to the purchaser on a 'take it or leave it' basis. It is surprising how many sellers prefer to take the first route believing it to involve less work, only to find that they have to perform the exercise of going through a standard set of purchaser's warranties anyway as and when they are produced by the preferred purchaser.

Usual types of warranties

7.5 This chapter contains some of the more usual warranties found in a typical share sale and purchase agreement together, where relevant, with comments. It is not intended to be an exhaustive list; however, it highlights some of the contentious areas and explains some of the more common arguments advanced for making amendments to certain warranties. It is usual to include a provision in the sale and purchase agreement which makes it clear that the headings used in the warranties section are for the sake of convenience only and are not to be regarded as part of the warranties nor should they be regarded as an aid to their interpretation.

Residence

7.6 Often it is obvious where a company is resident; however, it is desirable for the seller to warrant the company's residence status.

UK residence

7.6.1 'The Company has never been resident for tax purposes in any jurisdiction other than the United Kingdom.'

Where the purchaser is acquiring a group of companies, it is necessary to ascertain the residence status of each of them. Instead of giving warranties in respect of each company in the group, it is usual to give a global warranty and for the seller to disclose in respect of each group company for which the warranty is inapplicable. Such a warranty applying to residence might be as follows:

> 'Each Company is and has throughout the past six years been resident in the United Kingdom for corporation tax purposes and if any of the Companies is not so resident it is not a company incorporated in the United Kingdom.'

The purchaser will wish to ensure that the target company is not, nor has been, resident outside the UK which could render it liable to tax in the jurisdiction in which it is or was resident. More important perhaps, the purchaser will wish to ensure that the target company is not exposed to a potential charge to UK tax for a period when it purported to be, but was not, non-UK resident.

Companies are normally taxed in the country in which they are resident. A company is resident in the UK if it is incorporated in the UK or if it is managed and controlled in the UK. Where a company is resident in more than one jurisdiction because, for example, it is incorporated in the UK but managed and controlled in another jurisdiction. *FA 1994 s 249* provides that where a double tax treaty treats a company as resident outside the UK and not resident in the UK, for all UK tax purposes the company is to be treated as resident in the jurisdiction in which it is resident for the purpose of the treaty. A company may also be taxed if it carries on business through a branch or agency or has a place of business or permanent establishment another territory.

Where the company has been acquired by the seller, the seller may only be prepared to give a warranty for the period of ownership.

Branch or agency

7.6.2 'The Company has no branch, agency, place of business or permanent establishment outside the UK.'

The fact that the company is resident in the UK does not preclude it from being taxed on branch profits outside the UK. This warranty seeks to establish if there are any other jurisdictions in which the activities of the company may be taxed notwithstanding its UK residence status.

Dual residence

7.6.3 'The Company is not nor has it within the past six years been a dual resident company within the meaning of *ICTA 1988 s 404(4)* and the Company has not been involved in a transaction to which *ICTA 1988 s 404* or any other provision (including any exclusion from a provision) relating to dual resident investment companies as defined in *ICTA 1988 s 404(4)* could apply.'

Where a dual resident investment company makes a loss, that loss is unavailable for surrender to other members of a UK group. The seller may object to giving such a warranty where it is not warranting losses.

Following a change in the UK company residence rules in 1988, it became possible for a company to be a member of an UK group and yet be non-resident for the purposes of any applicable double taxation treaty. This enabled an asset to be transferred intra-group to that company without incurring a charge to capital gains tax and for the asset to be transferred abroad free of tax under the applicable double tax treaty. In order to prevent this avoidance technique, provisions were included in the *Finance Act 1990* which make the disposal to the dual resident company a chargeable disposal at full market value. The purchaser will therefore require to know whether any such transfers have been made. A typical warranty can be worded as set out below:

> 'The Company has not since the Accounts Date disposed of an asset or acquired an asset in circumstances such that the reliefs contained in *TCGA 1992 ss 139, 171* or *175* are not available as a result of the acquiring company being regarded for the purpose of any double taxation arrangements having effect by virtue of *ICTA 1988 s 788* as resident in a territory outside the United Kingdom and as not liable in the United Kingdom to tax on a gain arising on a disposal of the relevant asset occurring immediately after its acquisition.'

Tax administration, returns, payments and appeals

7.7 Having established the liability to UK tax, the starting point for most sets of tax warranties is to ensure that the day to day tax housekeeping has been correctly carried out.

Returns

7.7.1 'All necessary information, notices, accounts, statements, reports, computations and returns which ought to have been made have been properly and duly submitted by the Company to the Inland Revenue, HM Customs & Excise and any other relevant taxation or excise authorities whether of the United Kingdom or elsewhere and all information, notices, computations and returns submitted to the Inland Revenue, HM Customs & Excise and such other authorities are true and accurate and are not the subject of any material dispute nor [so far as the seller is aware] are likely to become the subject of any material dispute with such authority.'

This warranty is intended to ensure that the target company has dealt properly with all administrative matters. Disclosure against such a warranty could impose a considerable administrative burden on the seller and consequently it is usual for the seller to qualify the first part of the warranty by stating that all information, notices, computations and returns are 'true and accurate in all material respects'. The insertion of such a qualification obviously leads to the question what is 'material'. One answer may be that a matter is 'immaterial' if the seller felt that it did not need to disclose it, although taking this to its logical conclusion would mean that the seller would never disclose anything and would thus avoid any liability. One possible solution is to agree a level of materiality between the parties. It should also be noted that as far as VAT is concerned a number of immaterial errors may lead to a material penalty. It is for this reason that the seller is usually asked to give warranties with regard to VAT returns separately (see para [7.18.4] below).

The last part of the warranty, although appearing slightly innocuous, is asking the seller to warrant something which is outside the seller's knowledge. It is therefore usual for the seller to insert the words 'so far as the seller is aware' wherever a warranty refers to something that might happen in the future. In the above example the last two lines would read 'nor so far as the seller is aware are the information, notices, computations and returns likely to become the subject of any material dispute with such authority'. The term 'so far as the seller is aware' often appears in a number of warranties and should be a defined term. Whilst the exact meaning is a matter for negotiation, in general it imposes an obligation on the seller to make some enquiry.

A typical clause found in the main body of the sale and purchase agreement would be:

> 'where any statement is qualified by the expression "so far as the [seller[s]/warrantor[s]] [is/are] aware" or any similar expression that statement shall be deemed to include an additional statement

that it has been made after reasonable enquiry of the matters in question.'

It should be noted that such a clause may put an obligation on the seller to make enquiries of the Inland Revenue whether there is a potential dispute. This may itself be detrimental and an obligation to make enquiry of the tax authorities should be excluded in the case of tax warranties.

Outstanding claims and elections

7.7.2 'The Disclosure Letter gives full details of all matters relating to taxation in respect of which the Company (either alone or jointly with any other person) has or on the basis of law and practice operative at Completion has an outstanding entitlement:

(a) to make any claim (including a supplementary claim) for relief under any taxation statute;

(b) to make any election for one type of relief, or one basis, system or method of taxation as opposed to another;

(c) to make any appeal (including a further appeal) against any assessment to taxation; or

(d) to make any application for the postponement of taxation.'

When the purchaser acquires the target company, it will be necessary to ascertain the precise position of the target company's tax affairs. During this transitional period when the purchaser is becoming familiar with the target company's tax affairs, the concern is that an important time limit for making a claim or election or appealing against an assessment may be missed. Consequently, the purchaser will seek a warranty which in effect requests the seller to put the purchaser on notice of procedural matters which must be undertaken in the period immediately following completion.

Whilst the seller will not normally have any objection to providing information requested in (c) and (d) they may take the view that (a) and (b) are too vague and the purchaser should specify those elections and claims they have in mind.

Disclosure of notices and elections

7.7.3 'The Disclosure Letter gives full details of every notice, clearance application or election made by the Seller in respect of the sale.'

Although the purchaser could claim to be entitled to see notices, clearance applications and elections which directly affect the target company, it is doubtful whether the seller would want to divulge all the details of the sale or even whether it is necessary for them to do so. The seller's own tax planning may involve clearance applications which have no bearing on the target company. There is no reason why the purchaser should see these.

Claims and election

7.7.4 'All claims and elections which have been made by the Company are valid and have been made within the statutory time limits, all consents to the surrender of losses given by the Company or for the benefit of the Company have been made within the statutory time limits; none of the claims, elections or surrenders are in dispute and none of the claims, elections or surrenders will be withdrawn.'

This warranty provides comfort to the purchaser that the tax affairs of the Company are not going to be altered due to a missed time limit. Often the issue of withdrawal of tax surrenders is dealt with as a specific term of the contract; although, any such withdrawal by a member of the seller's group would probably give rise to a tax liability in the target company with a resultant claim under the tax deed.

Payment of tax liabilities

7.7.5 'All Taxation of any nature whatsoever whether of the United Kingdom or elsewhere for which the Company is liable including amounts becoming due since the Last Balance Sheet Date or for which any Company is liable to account has been duly paid and the Company has not incurred any liabilities to interest or penalties in respect of them (insofar as such taxation ought to have been paid) and without prejudice to the generality of the foregoing the Company has made all such deductions and retentions as it was obliged or entitled to make and all such payments as should have been made including those pursuant to the provisions of *ICTA 1988 ss 42A, 43, 118A–118K, 119, 129, 123, 348, 349, 350, 524, 555–558, 582, 733* and *737.'*

This warranty gives the purchaser comfort that tax payments are up to date. Again, if this warranty was breached, it is likely that there would be a claim under the tax deed. Interest and penalties would not normally be considered as tax liabilities arising in the ordinary course of business since the accounts date, if the tax deed is drafted by reference to the last set of accounts. Alternatively, if a completion balance sheet is used, provision should be made and the price adjusted accordingly.

The purchaser should not allow any qualification to this warranty as the seller should know whether or not the tax has been paid.

The part of the warranty starting 'and without prejudice to the generality of the foregoing . . .' can be deleted without affecting the sense of the warranty. Lists of section numbers are usually included only to provide a check list for the seller.

Liabilities not understated

7.7.6 'The Company has not received from any tax authority any payment to which it was not entitled nor has the Company received any tax assessment in which its tax liability was understated.'

This is a catagoric statement and it would be prudent for the seller to qualify this warranty with the words 'so far as the seller is aware'.

Secondary tax liabilities

7.7.7 'The Company is not, nor will it become, liable to pay, to reimburse or to indemnify any person (including a Tax authority) in respect of the taxation liability of any other person as a consequence of that other person failing to discharge the liability where that other person is or may become primarily liable for the taxation in question including without prejudice to the generality of the foregoing any liability under *ICTA 1988 ss 767A, 767AA* and *777(8), TCGA 1992 ss 189, 190* and *191* and *FA 1990 s 96*.'

Increasingly, tax legislation provides for the Inland Revenue to assess another member of a group of companies where one member of the group defaults; this is so regardless of whether that other company is still a member of the group. To the extent that the remaining group remains under the control of the seller, the seller should have no objection to such a warranty. However, it is possible for the seller to become liable under this warranty as a consequence of a default by a company sold to a third party. The seller should ensure that in such circumstances recovery can be made against the third party.

Penalties and interest

7.7.8 'The Company has not within the past six years paid or become liable to pay, nor are there any circumstances by reason of which the Company is likely to become liable to pay, any penalty, fine, surcharge or interest whether charged by virtue of the provisions of the *TMA 1970* or the *VATA 1994* or otherwise.'

This warranty serves not only to indicate how the tax affairs of the company have been run but also the likely relationship of the target company with its inspector of taxes. To the extent that disclosure is made against this warranty, any liabilities should have been provided for in the Accounts. Penalties due since the Accounts Date will have to be dealt with separately and may need to be excluded from any *de minimis* limits.

Investigations including back duty investigations

7.7.9 'The Company has not within the last twelve months suffered any investigation audit or visit by the Inland Revenue, HM Customs & Excise, Department of Social Security or other taxation or excise authority and neither the Seller nor the Company is aware of any such investigation audit or visit planned in the next twelve months and without prejudice to the generality of the foregoing the Company has never been the subject of an investigation by or involving any of the Special Investigations sections of the Inland Revenue or Customs and Excise and no circumstances exist which make such an investigation likely.'

This warranty does nothing other than seek information, it is difficult to see what damage would be suffered by a purchaser if it was untrue. However, by means of such a warranty, the purchaser will be able to ascertain the dates and frequency of pay-as-you-earn audits and VAT control visits. Such information will be useful to the purchaser and will prevent the purchaser being surprised by a routine visit from the Revenue Authorities in the period immediately following the purchase at a time when the purchaser may be trying to integrate the target company into the acquiring group. Furthermore, a recent visit on, say, PAYE matters which results in no or only minor points being raised gives the seller some degree of confidence that such matters have been properly dealt with and that there are no undetected liabilities. If disclosure is made against the latter part of the warranty, thorough investigation of the facts and circumstances should be made.

Corporation tax on income

7.8 The purpose of the next set of warranties is to ensure that tax has been accounted for properly on the transactions that have been entered into. The relevance of any particular warranty will obviously depend upon the activities of the company in question.

Sale and lease-back of land

7.8.1 'The Company has not entered into any sale and leaseback arrangements to which *ICTA 1988 ss 779* and *780* have been or could be applied.'

ICTA 1988 ss 779, 780 apply to sale and lease back transactions in land. *ICTA 1988 s 779* restricts the amount of rental paid which will qualify as a tax deduction. *ICTA 1988 s 780* deals with leases that have not more than 50 years to run which are surrendered or assigned for a capital sum and following the surrender or assignment a new lease not exceeding 15 years is granted. The section taxes as income part of the consideration received on such a transaction.

Taxpayer required to account as agent or lessee

7.8.2 'The Company is not liable as lessee or agent for any Sch A tax under *ICTA 1988 ss 23* or *42A*.'

ICTA 1988 s 23 (now repealed) and *s 42A* provide a mechanism for collecting unpaid tax from people other than the landlord where the landlord has defaulted on payment of Schedule A tax.

If the company does not occupy premises as lessee, the warranty is unlikely to apply and the seller should delete it. If the warranty is given and a payment has to be made, there should be a mechanism for the purchaser to reimburse the seller out of subsequent payments to the landlord. *ICTA 1988 s 42A(3)* would give the seller a right of indemnity against a non-resident landlord. However, this indemnity is only effective if there are continuing payments being made to the landlord; hence, the need to put an obligation on the purchaser provided, of course, that the purchaser remained in occupation as lessee continuing to pay rent.

Grant of lease at a premium

7.8.3 'The Company has not been and will not be charged to tax by reason only of any transaction which has taken place and which falls within *ICTA 1988 ss 34–36*.'

Under these provisions, certain land transactions are treated a being effected on revenue account instead of on capital account.

ICTA 1988 s 34 applies to the receipt of a premium on the creation of a lease for a period not exceeding 50 years and taxes as income 2% of the premium for each full year, except for the first, for which the period of the lease is less than 50 years.

ICTA 1988 s 35 applies where a lease not exceeding 50 years' duration is granted at an under-value and is then assigned at a premium. In such a case the assignee can be charged to tax under Sch D Case VI on a proportion of the difference between the open market value of the lease granted and the premium actually charged on the grant.

7.8.3 *Specific Tax Warranties*

ICTA 1988 s 36 provides that where land is sold subject to a right of reconveyance at some future date either back to the seller, or to a person connected with the seller, the seller is chargeable to tax on income under Sch D Case VI on a proportion of the premium.

The seller may regard this warranty as unnecessary as it duplicates the warranty which is usually given to the effect that either all tax due has been paid (see para [7.7.5] or provision or reserve has been made for all tax due (which is usually the subject of an accounts warranty).

The purchaser may require this warranty purely for information purposes. Any information disclosed will enable the purchaser to complete any pre-completion tax returns. It should also enable the purchaser to check whether the tax has been computed correctly. Any tax liability arising from breach of this warranty should be covered, in any event, by the tax deed.

Disallowance of Revenue items

7.8.4 'No rents, interest (including any amounts treated as interest under *ICTA 1988 s 730A*), annual payments or other sums of an income nature which have been paid or are payable by the Company or which the Company is under an obligation to pay in the future are wholly or partially disallowable as deductions or charges in computing profits for the purposes of corporation tax by reason of the provisions of *ICTA 1988 ss 74, 79, 125, 338, 577A, 770, 770A, 779, 781–784* or *787, Sch 28AA, FA 1996 Sch 9 para 13*.'

This warranty aims to establish that there are no payments which the target is obliged to make which will not be allowable as either a deduction from trading profits or as a charge on income. The seller can make disclosure of those payments which are not deductable.

ICTA 1988 s 74 describes the payments which are not deductible in computing Sch D1 profits.

ICTA 1988 s 79 denies a deduction for contributions to a local enterprise agency unless the agency is approved and certain conditions are fulfilled. The seller should not accept liability under this part of the warranty if the agency's approval is withdrawn after the sale. The seller would have no control over this and the risk should pass to the purchaser when the target is acquired.

ICTA 1988 s 125 denies a deduction as a charge on income where an annuity or other annual payment (except interest) is paid to a person who is not required to bring the payment into charge to income or corporation tax.

ICTA 1988 s 338 determines whether a charge on income is tax deductible for UK resident companies. *Section 338* is not as important as it was following the introduction of the loan relationship provisions in *FA 1996.*

ICTA 1988 s 577A denies a deduction for any payment the making of which constitutes the commission of a criminal offence; an example might be a payment to a terrorist group which had threatened to damage business premises unless the payment was made.

ICTA 1988 s 770 allows the Board of the Inland Revenue to make a direction where the company is involved in transfer pricing. Excessive payments to a connected company can be disallowed. *ICTA 1988 ss 770–773* were replaced by a new *s 770A* and *Sch 28AA* was introduced by *FA 1998 s 108* which provides for an adjustment to the profits of a company where a potential advantage in relation to UK taxation is conferred.

ICTA 1988 ss 779–784 restrict the amount of rental paid which is deductible where the transaction involves the sale and leaseback of real property and other assets.

ICTA 1988 s 787 denies relief where arrangements have been made solely or mainly to obtain relief from the payment of interest. Since the introduction of *FA 1996* most companies well get relief on an accruals basis; consequently, *ICTA 1988 s 787* is no longer as relevant as it once was.

FA 1996 Sch 9 para 13 disallows a deduction for interest where the interest either accrues or is payable on a loan which was taken out for an unallowable purpose. This is an anti-avoidance provision and its exact scope is still far from clear. The legislation states that an unallowable purpose is one which 'is not amongst the business or other commercial purposes of the company'.

Generally, the seller will have no objection to giving the purchaser information regarding disallowable items. However, it is not necessary to give the warranty in respect of past disallowable items as these will be covered by the other warranties. The warranty really seeks to gather information. The purchaser might argue that past information allows the purchaser to analyse the potential impact in the future.

No compensation for loss of office

7.8.5 'The Company has not made any payment to, or provided any benefits for, any officer or employee or any former officer or employee, of the Company which would be disallowable for corporation tax purposes nor has the Company agreed to make a payment of an income nature in excess of [ ] except in the ordinary course of the Company's business which would not be allowable as a deduction in computing corporation tax.'

This is quite a wide warranty. It covers compensation for loss of office and ex gratia payments to former employees. It could also extend, in the case of family businesses to excessive remuneration, and the provision of benefits to directors. Payments of an income nature could even extend to entertainment costs, and gifts.

The seller will no doubt seek to disclose against this warranty. The words '. . . nor has the Company except in the ordinary course of business', are very wide and may include redundancy payments.

Again, any reference to disallowable items in the past should already be covered by the warranty which provides that full provision for tax has been made.

Pension contributions

7.8.6 '*FA 1993 s 112* does not and will not apply so as to restrict any deduction in respect of employers' contributions to an exempt approved pension scheme.'

FA 1993 s 112 provides that for periods of account ending after 5 April 1993, tax relief for employers' contributions to an approved exempt scheme is only to be given for sums actually paid into the scheme and not for any provisions for payments to the scheme.

The seller should look at the wording of this warranty carefully. As worded, the seller could be warranting that a deduction will be obtained for payments made whilst in the purchaser's ownership. The seller should restrict it to payments made before completion.

Liability for released debts

7.8.7 'The Company has not been released from any debt either in whole or in part to which *ICTA 1988 s 94* could apply nor has the Company been released from a debt either in whole or in part which is a loan relationship for purposes of the *Finance Act 1996*.'

ICTA 1988 s 94 applies where a deduction has been allowed for a debt which has been incurred for the purposes of a trade, profession or vocation and which is then released. The amount which has been released is treated as a receipt of the trade, profession or vocation arising in the period in which the debt is released.

When a loan relationship under *Finance Act 1996* is released, in certain circumstances the credit arising on the release can give rise to a tax charge. Usually, this will be where the parties to the loan relationships are not connected under *FA 1996 s 87(3)*.

Trading losses

7.8.8 'The amount of trading losses available to the Company for carry forward has been and will not be less than £[ ] and nothing has been done which might cause the disallowance of the carry forward of such losses under the provisions of *ICTA 1988 s 768* and there are no grounds for believing that the Inspector of Taxes may discover that the amount is, or may become, excessive.'

It is very rare for a seller to warrant the amount of trading losses to be carried forward unless the purchaser is paying for them. Occasionally, the purchaser will provide a standard set of warranties which include a warranty for trading losses with the amounts left blank. Under no circumstances should the seller insert what they feel to be the correct amount because to do so would be to effectively guarantee that amount of loss. Unless the seller is prepared to warrant the losses, any such warranty on those terms should immediately be deleted.

However, for the sake of completeness, in the event that the purchaser has agreed to pay for losses, such a warranty could be worded as set out above.

Disallowance of trading losses

7.8.9 'There are no circumstances which might cause a disallowance of the carry forward of losses, expenses of management, debits in respect of loan relationships or excess charges under *ICTA 1988 ss 393, 768, 768B* or *768C* or the carry back of losses under *s 768A*.'

ICTA 1988 s 393 allows losses to be carried forward against profits of the same trade. Where the trade has changed, such carry forward would be disallowed.

ICTA 1988 ss 768, 768B and *768C* restrict the carry forward of losses to a future accounting period where within a period of three years both before and after a change of ownership there has been a major change in the nature or conduct of the trade. Whether there has been a change in ownership is determined by *ICTA 1988 s 769* and this essentially requires the acquisition of more than 50% of the ordinary shares of the company. Whether there has been a major change in the nature or conduct of a trade is a question of fact and was discussed in the cases of *Purchase v Tesco Stores Limited* [1984] STC 304 and *Willis v Peeters Picture*

Frames Limited [1983] STC 453. The Inland Revenue have issued a statement of practice SP 10/91 setting out their interpretation of the term 'a major change in the nature or conduct of a trade or business'.

ICTA 1988 s 768 disallows the carry back of losses where there has been a change in ownership and in the three years before or after the change of ownership where there has been a major change in the nature or conduct of the trade or business.

As stated above in para [7.8.8] it is very unusual for the seller to warrant the amount of losses carried forward unless they are being paid for. Consequently, the seller should not accept this warranty or any associated indemnity. Neither should the purchaser insist on this warranty if the losses are not being paid for.

No application of ICTA 1988 s 343(4)

7.8.10 'There are no circumstances in which any losses carried forward will be restricted or disallowed under the provisions of *ICTA 1988 s 343(4)*.'

Section 343(4) restricts the losses which are available to carry forward on a reconstruction where the transferee does not take over the whole of the liabilities of the transferor which are attributable to the trade.

If the seller is being paid for the losses, there is no reason why this warranty should not be given. If the loss is not being paid for, the warranty should be deleted. The purchaser would probably have a similar attitude.

Valuation of trading stock on a cessation of trade

7.8.11 '[The Company has not within the last six years discontinued any trade.] or [The Disclosure Letter contains details of any trade that has been discontinued: no adjustment in the value of trading stock from the discontinuance of that trade is or has been required to be made under *ICTA 1988 s 100*].'

ICTA 1988 s 100 provides how, when a trade has been discontinued, any trading stock belonging to the trade at the discontinuance is to be valued. The stock is deemed to have been realised at market value unless the stock is transferred to a person carrying on a trade in the U.K. If this happens, the actual value of the consideration is taken. Where the parties to the transaction are connected, the stock is treated as having been realised at an arm's length price; however, the parties may elect to substitute the higher of the sale price or book value. The election is joint and must be made within two years of the transfer. The same value is used in both the seller's and the purchaser's computations.

Deductibility of investment company outgoings

7.8.12 'The company is not an investment company as defined by *ICTA 1988 s 130*.'

or

'The company is an investment company as defined by *ICTA 1988 s 130* and all outgoings of a revenue nature are deductible in computing its profits.'

This warranty merely seeks confirmation that any management expenses or charges on income incurred by an investment company are deductible. The provisions applicable are *ICTA 1988 s 75* (deductibility of investment company management expenses) *ICTA 1988 ss 338* and *339* (charges on income) and *FA 1996 Pt IV Chapter II* (loan relationships).

Deep gains and deep discounts

7.8.13 'The company did not, before April 1 1996 issue or own any:

(a) deep discount securities (*ICTA 1988 s 57* and *Sch 4*);

(b) deep gain securities (*FA 1989 Sch 11*); or

(c) convertible securities (*FA 1990 s 56* and *Sch 10*).'

Special regimes applied to the above securities. Under *FA 1996* these regimes ceased to apply from 1 April 1996; however, accrued discounts up to that date were frozen and became chargeable on some future event eg the sale of the security or its redemption.

Futures and options

7.8.14 'The Company has not entered into any transaction to which *ICTA 1988 Sch 5AA* applies.'

Schedule 5AA was introduced to attack schemes where the disposal of futures or options comprise part of a transaction designed to produce a guaranteed return. The Schedule charges profits or gains of a capital nature to tax under Sch D Case VI if not taxed under Sch D Case I or Case V.

Life policies

7.8.15 'The Company is not liable nor will it become liable to taxation in respect of any policy of insurance including life insurance policies, contracts of life annuities and capital redemption policies whether or not acquired as original beneficial owner.'

ICTA 1988 ss 539–554 tax profits arising from life assurance policies, contracts for life annuities and capital redemption policies in certain circumstances.

To the extent that the company is liable, provision or reserve should be made in the Accounts. To the extent that a liability might arise between Accounts and Completion, consideration should be given to excluding the liability from the *de minimis* limits.

Foreign exchange gains on losses

7.8.16 'The Company is not nor has it been since the Accounts Date:

(a) the holder of a qualifying asset;

(b) subject to a qualifying liability; or

(c) a party to a currency contract;

for the purposes of *FA 1993 Pt II Chapter II.*'

This warranty seeks to discover whether the foreign exchange gains and losses legislation in *FA 1993* will apply to the company. If the seller makes no disclosure against this warranty, it will be sufficient protection because any foreign exchange gains or losses arising will result from a breach of the warranty. However, if the seller makes disclosure against this warranty, the purchaser will need to seek further information and perhaps seek further warranties.

The purchaser will need to know whether:

(a) the transitional rules in *SI 1994/3226* as amended by *SI 1996/1349* apply;

(b) in respect of eligible assets as defined in *SI 1994/3227*, if the company has made a matching election;

(c) the company has made any claims to defer unrealised exchange gains within *FA 1993 s 139*;

(d) the Company has made a local currency election under *SI 1994/3230*; and

(e) the anti-avoidance provisions in *FA 1993 ss 135–18* apply.

Interest rate and currency contracts and options

7.8.17 'Since the Accounts Date the Company has not been a party to a contract which is a qualifying contract for the purposes of *FA 1994 s 147*.'

This warranty seeks to discover whether the financial instruments legislation in *FA 1995* will apply to the company. If the seller makes no disclosure against this warranty, it will be sufficient protection because any liabilities which arise from the application of the legislation will result in a breach of the warranty. However, if the seller makes disclosure against this warranty, the purchaser will need to seek further information and perhaps seek further warranties.

The purchaser will need to know whether:

(a) the transitional rules in *ICTA 1988 s 158* apply;

(b) the company has any quasi-qualifying contracts within *FA 1994 s 148(3)* in respect of which no election has been made; and

(c) the anti-avoidance provisions in *FA 1994 ss 165–168* apply.

Loan relationships — creditor relationships

7.8.18 'Since the Accounts Date the Company has been taxed on an authorised accruals basis in respect of all loan relationships which are creditor relationships as defined in *FA 1996 s 103* and in respect of each such relationship the accruals are computed only by reference to interest, no tax (other than tax on interest) would be payable if the debt was repaid at face value, and the Company is not connected with the debtor within *FA 1996 s 87*.'

This warranty seeks information regarding the company's loan relationships. Unlike the foreign exchange gains and losses and the financial instruments legislation, it is highly unlikely that the target company will not be a party to a loan relationship even where the company has only traded in the UK.

This warranty looks at those loan relationships which are creditor relationships, ie those under which the company is owed money and receives interest. It seeks to ascertain that there will be no gain on the disposal of the debt, other than interest and that the company is not connected with the debtor.

The purchaser may seek further warranties in respect of creditor loan relationships, for example:

> 'The authorised accounting method used for the purposes of *FA 1996 s 86* is the accounting method used in the Company's statutory accounts.'

This merely seeks to ascertain that there is no discrepancy between the accruals made for tax purposes and those made in the company's accounts. The reason for this is that *FA 1996 s 86* permits different methods to be used for different loan relationships.

Convertible securities

7.8.19 Either:

'The Company does not own any convertible securities';

Or

'*FA 1996 s 92* applies to all convertible securities owned by the Company.'

FA 1996 s 92 defines convertible security for the purposes of the loan relationship legislation. A security falls within *FA 1996 s 92*, if amongst other things, there is more than a negligible likelihood that the conversion right will be exercised to a significant extent and the asset is not one the disposal of which would be treated as a disposal in the course of activities which form an integral part of a trade carried on by the company. If a security falls within *FA 1996 s 92* the company will only be taxed on the interest on the security. Any gains or losses are dealt with under the capital gains tax regime, for which purposes, the securities are not treated as qualifying corporate bonds.

Loan relationships — debtor relationships

7.8.20 'Since the Accounts Date the Company has obtained relief on an authorised accruals basis in respect of all loan relationships which are debtor relationships as defined by *FA 1996 s 103* and in relation to each such relationship, the deduction for which the Company obtains relief is not less than the interest accruing for the period. There would be no adverse tax consequences if such debts were to be repaid at face value other than that the interest accrued would cease, and there is no connection between the Company and the creditor as mentioned in *FA 1996 s 87*.'

This warranty seeks information about the company's debtor loan relationships, ie those under which it owes money and pays interest. It seeks to identify the amount of relief which the company is receiving and that this is consistent with the deduction taken in the company's accounts. It also seeks to ascertain that the company is not connected with the creditor.

The purchaser may seek further warranties in respect of debtor loan relationships, for example:

> 'The Company has not accrued a debit for interest which is unpaid or likely to remain unpaid for a period of 12 months after the end of the accounting period in which it was accrued.'

This seeks to ascertain that there are no debits which are likely to be cancelled and which would lead to a tax charge under *FA 1996 Sch 9 para 2.*

> 'The Company has not been and is not a party to any loan relationship which was for an unallowable purpose (as defined in *FA 1996 Sch 9 para 13*).'

Finance Act 1996 Sch 9 para 13 is a wide-ranging anti-avoidance provision. To the extent that a loan relationship is for an unallowable purpose, the deductions to which a company is entitled are reduced on a just and reasonable basis. To a certain extent the matters covered in this warranty are covered in 7.8.4 above.

Capital gains

7.9 The capital gains tax warranties generally seek to ascertain whether there are any latent tax charges which would arise on the disposal of capital assets. Whether a provision has been made for these tax charges will depend upon whether the target was intending to dispose of any capital assets in the short term. The capital gains tax warranties are important because to the extent that a liability arises, it is likely to arise as a result of an act of the purchaser after completion and consequently will not be covered by the tax deed.

Book values

7.9.1 'The book value shown in or adopted for the purpose of the Accounts as the value of each of the assets of the Company on the disposal of which a chargeable gain or allowable loss could arise does not exceed the amount which on a disposal of such asset at the date of this agreement would be deductible under *TCGA 1992 s 38.*'

It is highly unlikely that the book value of each asset in the accounts will correspond with its cost for capital gains tax purposes, either because of roll-over relief, hold-over relief, the application of the indexation allowance, or because the assets have been transferred intra-group under *TCGA 1992 s 171.* The purchaser may not be concerned to know the capital gains base cost of all the assets of the target company. However, there will be numerous occasions when this information is vital, either generally or because there are specific assets which the purchaser intends to sell after completion.

This warranty requires the seller to disclose any assets where the book value is in excess of the base cost for capital gains tax purposes.

Roll-over and hold-over claims

7.9.2 'The Disclosure Letter sets out full particulars of all claims and elections made (or assumed in the Accounts to be made) under *TCGA 1992 ss 23, 152–162, 165, 247, 247A* or *248* insofar as they could affect the chargeable gain or allowable loss which would arise in the event of a disposal after the Accounts Date by the Company of any of its assets, and indicates which assets (if any) so affected would not, on a disposal, give rise to relief under *TCGA 1992 Sch 4*.'

TCGA 1992 s 23 allows a company to claim roll-over relief where the proceeds of an insurance claim are used either to restore an asset or replace an asset which was lost or destroyed.

Where there has been a deferral of a liability to capital gains tax under *TCGA 1992 ss 152, 153* the base cost for CGT purposes will be lower than the acquisition cost shown in the accounts. If an asset is disposed of and the base cost of that asset has been reduced as a result of a hold-over from a previous gain, and the asset is then disposed of following completion, the capital gain arising would be larger than would otherwise be anticipated. Such a liability would not be caught under the tax deed as it is a tax liability arising as a result of an event occurring after completion.

It is very likely that disclosures will be made under this warranty and as a result it should be possible for the purchaser to calculate the inherent tax liability and to determine whether there is a need to seek a reduction in the purchase price as a result. Where there are large held over gains there may be tax liabilities, not taken into account in the accounts, which materially reduce the realisable value of the company's assets. Particular attention should be given to any claim under *TCGA 1992 s 152* or *s 153* where the gain has been rolled over into the purchase of plant or machinery, or any other asset which is or will within ten years become a wasting asset ie an asset with a predictable life not exceeding 50 years. This will include short leases or leases which will become short within ten years. Under *TCGA 1992 s 154* liability to tax on such assets is only deferred and, unless the gain is subsequently rolled into another asset, the capital gains tax charge will automatically arise on the expiry of ten years.

TCGA 1992 ss 247, 247A and *248* apply roll-over relief where land is compulsorily purchased by an authority having or exercising compulsory purchase powers and the proceeds are reinvested by the seller.

TCGA 1992 Sch 4 provides relief where the company holding an asset acquired it on or after 31 March 1982 and that acquisition was either treated as being for such consideration that no gain or loss accrued or a claim was made to hold over a gain made on the disposal of another chargeable business asset. The rebasing legislation applies if the person disposing of an asset held it on 31 March 1982 and assumes that where this is not the case, the acquisition cost after 1982 would be fully indexed. Where the acquisition cost is reduced by reason of a deemed no gain/no loss disposal or a hold-over claim, the indexation relief is reduced accordingly. *Schedule 4* deems no gain/no loss acquisitions to have taken place at the time of the original acquisition and allows an increase of half the difference between the reduced acquisition cost and the disposal proceeds where a hold-over claim has been made.

Rebasing

7.9.3 'No election under *TCGA 1992 s 35* has been made in relation to any company, and the Accounts are prepared on the basis that no such election will be made.'

TCGA 1992 s 35 permits a company (or the parent company of a group) to make an election to the effect that all assets owned by the company (or the group) were disposed of and reacquired for market value on 31 March 1982. It will be important for the purchaser to find out whether such an election has been made for the purposes of future disposals.

Of course, if such an election has been made, it will be for the seller to either disclose the fact in the disclosure letter or to delete the warranty and to give the following warranty:

> 'An election under *TCGA 1992 s 35* has been made and the Company owns no asset which is not subject to the election.'

In the event that no election has been made, it will be necessary for the purchaser to determine the date upon which the first disposal under the rebasing regime was made so that the expiry date of the two-year period mentioned in *TCGA 1992 s 35* can be calculated. Accordingly, where no election has been made it is usual to seek a warranty worded as set out below:

> 'The Disclosure Letter gives the date of the first disposal (if any) made by the Company to which *TCGA 1992 s 35* applies, and the period during which an election under *s 35* could be made in relation to the Company has not [and will not at completion have] expired.'

Transactions not at arm's length

7.9.4 'The Company has not disposed of or acquired any asset in circumstances such that the provisions of *TCGA 1992 s 17* could apply to such disposal or acquisition nor given or agreed to give any consideration to which the provisions of *TCGA 1992 s 128(1)(2)* could apply.'

Where a person acquires or disposes of an asset by way of a non-arm's length transaction, for example as a gift, or by way of distribution from a company in respect of shares in a company, or where the consideration cannot be valued, or where the transaction is in connection with a person's loss of office or services rendered, *TCGA 1992 s 17* operates to substitute the market value for the consideration actually given or received.

TCGA 1992 s 128(2) limits the consideration which may be added to the base cost following a reorganisation of share capital to the increase in value of the holding. A typical example would be where a worthless debt owed by a subsidiary is capitalised and the shares in the subsidiary subsequently disposed of. The base cost for the purposes of the disposal will be restricted to the acquisition cost of the original holding plus any increase in that cost as a result of capitalising the debt. If the debt was in fact worthless, there will be no increase. To a certain extent, where the seller has warranted the base cost of the assets, there is no need for a warranty of this type. However, such a warranty is useful for the purposes of gathering information.

Transactions between connected parties

7.9.5 'The Company is not entitled to any capital loss to which the provisions of *TCGA 1992 s 18(3)* are applicable.'

Where a capital loss arises to a person as a result of a transaction with a connected person, that loss may only be set against a gain made on a transaction between the same persons at a time when they are still connected.

The seller may object to such a warranty if it is not warranting capital losses. Alternatively, the warranty is not necessary where the company is neither carrying forward any capital losses nor has made any capital losses since the accounts date.

Gifts involving companies

7.9.6 'The Company does not own nor has it owned any shares on the disposal of which *TCGA 1992 s 125* could apply nor has the Company received any assets by way of gift as mentioned in *TCGA 1992 s 282*.'

Where a close company transfers an asset at an undervalue, *TCGA 1992 s 125* provides that a proportion of the gain accruing to a company will be treated as reducing the base cost of the shares in the company to the shareholder. As a result of *TCGA 1992 s 282*, where a donor of a gift has failed to pay the tax on chargeable gains arising as a result of the gift, the Inland Revenue is able to recover the amount due from the donee. Where, therefore, the company has been the recipient of a gift, a tax liability could arise on that company in the event of the donor of the gift not paying any tax due.

Disposal of debts

7.9.7 'No chargeable gain will accrue to the Company on the disposal of any debt owed to it.'

In general, the repayment of a debt to the original creditor (or other disposal by him) will not give rise to a chargeable gain or allowable loss except in the case of a debt on a security. A chargeable gain on repayment may arise in particular where the creditor has taken an assignment of the debt at a consideration which is, or is deemed to be, less than the amount expected to be received on its eventual repayment. The purchaser will therefore usually seek disclosure of any debt where the disposal of the debt and, in particular, where repayment of the debt to one of the companies, may result in a chargeable gain. Following the introduction of the loan relationship legislation in *FA 1996*, many debts will be taken out of the CGT regime.

Part disposals under TCGA 1992 s 42

7.9.8 'The Company has not made a part disposal of any asset which required or will require the gain to be computed under *TCGA 1992 s 42*.'

This warranty is an information gathering warranty. The seller would probably delete it on the grounds that to the extent that any such disposal has been made, the tax will have been provided for and will be covered by other warranties or the tax deed.

The purchaser may require the warranty in order to check that the calculations are correct for any disposals disclosed against it.

Negligible value claims under TCGA 1992 s 24(2)

7.9.9 'The Company has made no negligible value claims under *TCGA 1992 s 24(2)*.'

This warranty seeks information. However, if the company has made a negligible value claim and the asset in question subsequently increases in value, the whole of the increase will be chargeable to tax in the event that the asset is disposed of. Such a disposal will take place after completion and the liability will not be caught by the tax deed. Whether the claims are valid or not is therefore irrelevant.

The seller may object to this warranty on the grounds that the purchaser is not paying for capital losses.

Wasting assets

7.9.10 'The Company does not own any asset which is a wasting asset (other than plant and machinery eligible for capital allowances) within *TCGA 1992 s 44* or a lease to which *TCGA 1992 Sch 8* applies.'

This is an information seeking warranty. It is also important if gains on the disposal of other assets have been rolled into wasting assets. If they have, the gain will become chargeable if the wasting asset is disposed of or on the expiration of a period of ten years.

Debts from connected persons

7.9.11 'The Company has not acquired any debt from a connected party such that a loss on the disposal of the debt will not be an allowable loss by virtue of *TCGA 1992 s 251*.'

Normally, a debt is a chargeable asset if acquired for value; however, where the debt is acquired from a connected party within *TCGA 1992 ss 18* and *286* any loss on a subsequent disposal will be disallowed. Following the introduction of the loan relationship legislation in *FA 1996*, nearly all such debts will be taken out of the CGT regime.

Debts

7.9.12 'No chargeable gain will arise on the disposal of any debt by the Company.'

This is an information seeking warranty. However, to the extent that a gain arises on a disposal of a debt after the completion, any gain would not be covered by the tax deed. Again, many such debts will no longer be in the CGT regime.

Loans to traders

7.9.13 'The Company has not claimed any relief under *TCGA 1992 s 253*.'

Where money is lent to a UK resident for the purposes of that person's trade or the trade of other companies in the same group, *TCGA 1992 s 253* gives relief where the loan becomes irrecoverable. This warranty seeks information. It is difficult to see what damage would arise if the loan had become irrecoverable unless the relief, for some reason, was not due.

Payment by instalments

7.9.14 'The Company has made no election or arrangement for the payment of taxation by instalments under *TCGA 1992 ss 280* and *281*.'

TCGA 1992 s 280 allows corporation tax on chargeable gains to be paid by instalments over a period not exceeding eight years if the consider ation payable on the disposal of an asset is payable over a period exceeding twelve months. It is no longer necessary to show hardship in order to make the election.

TCGA 1992 s 281 allows tax to be paid by ten equal interest bearing instalments where capital gains tax is payable on a gift, on a deemed disposal on the termination of a life interest under a settlement and when a person becomes absolutely entitled to settled property provided, in each case, hold-over relief cannot be claimed.

The seller may seek to delete this warranty. Provision should have been made for the tax notwithstanding that it is payable by instalments. To the extent that tax is underprovided, it will be covered by other warranties and by the tax deed.

Pooling

7.9.15 'The Company has made no election under *FA 1983 s 34* and *Sch 6* or under *TCGA 1992 Sch 2*.'

The election under *FA 1983 s 34* has effect with respect to all disposals of qualifying securities made after 31 March 1982. An election under *TCGA 1992 Sch 2* can be made in respect of the first relevant disposal of quoted securities after 19 March 1968 to substitute the market value as at 6 April 1965 for the securities' cost. For most companies it is no longer possible to make the election.

The seller ought to know whether such an election has been made and will make disclosure of that fact.

The purchaser is unlikely to recover a substantial amount under this warranty. The base cost of the assets will normally have been warranted elsewhere.

Corporate bonds

7.9.16 '*TCGA 1992 s 116* could not apply to any corporate bond owned or loan relationship of the Company by reason of any reorganisation, reconstruction or conversion of securities.'

TCGA 1992 s 116 caters for reorganisations, reconstructions and conversions of securities which involve qualifying corporate bonds. Where QCBs are converted into shares, this is treated as a disposal of the QCB and any gain is exempt. Where shares are converted into QCBs, any gain or loss is calculated and is charged on a subsequent disposal of the QCB. This warranty seeks information as to past events which might mean there is a charge to tax. Such a charge should have been provided for, and is likely to be caught under other warranties and the tax deed.

Appropriation to trading stock

7.9.17 'Since the Accounts Date the Company has not appropriated any of its assets to or from trading stock.'

Under *TCGA 1992 s 161*, where an asset is appropriated to trading stock there is a deemed disposal and reacquisition at market value. However, the company can elect to bring an asset which has been appropriated to trading stock into the accounts at market value less any capital gains or plus any allowable loss for Sch D Case 1 purposes; thus, converting the capital gain or loss into a revenue gain or loss. This warranty seeks to ascertain the values of stock and assets and whether the election needs to be made.

Pre-entry losses

7.9.18 'As at completion the Company will have no unrelieved capital losses nor will it own any assets which if disposed of at completion would give rise to a capital loss.'

Where a company has unrelieved capital losses, those losses are not available to use against gains otherwise than those made in the group with the losses. *TCGA 1992 Sch 7A* is an anti-avoidance provision which prevents companies being acquired for their capital losses.

The seller might take the view that as the losses cannot be transferred otherwise than for use in the groups in which they arise, this warranty is irrelevant. The purchaser is not paying for the losses.

Attribution of gains of non-residents

7.9.19 'The Company does not own any shares in a non-resident company which if resident in the UK would be a close company and in respect of any such shares as are disclosed, no gain has accrued to the non-resident company on which the Company may be liable to corporation tax on chargeable gains by virtue of *TCGA 1992 s 13*.'

TCGA 1992 s 13 applies where chargeable gains accrue to a non-resident company where that company would be a close company if resident in the UK. Subject to certain conditions, participators in such a company can be assessed as if part of the gain had accrued to them.

Where an amount in respect of the chargeable gain is distributed by the non-resident company, either by way of dividend or distribution of capital, or on the dissolution of the company, the tax paid is applied to reduce any tax liability arising by reason of the distribution.

To the extent that gains have been attributed, any tax should have been provided for and the seller may resist this warranty. To the extent that tax has not been provided for, it might be because the seller is expecting a distribution before the tax is due; in which case, the seller should ensure that if the target company controls the non-resident, the purchaser causes the non-resident to make the distribution or the seller is absolved from responsibility if it does not.

Companies ceasing to be resident in the UK

7.9.20 'The Company has not made any deemed disposal of assets either by the Company ceasing to be resident in the UK or by the Company ceasing to be liable to UK tax.'

It is unlikely that this warranty will apply if the seller has warranted that the company is UK resident. However, where a group is being purchased it is possible that one of the subsidiary companies may have ceased to be UK resident. Where a group is being purchased, the word 'Company' usually refers to each company in the group, hence the seller would need to disclose if it applied to any company in the group.

Capital allowances

7.10 Capital allowances warranties are usually concerned with the discrepancy between the book value and tax written down value of assets qualifying for allowances. Whether or not this discrepancy will give rise to a tax liability will depend upon a number of factors. Normally, accelerated capital allowances will be dealt with in the deferred tax charge; this means that the company will have provided for balancing charges which are likely to arise in the foreseeable future, which is usually two to three years. However, many companies will anticipate that the capital spend in those two or three years will be such that the new allowances given will more than cover the anticipated tax charge and therefore no provision need be made.

Other warranties seek to ascertain whether the necessary claims and elections have been made.

Tax written down values

7.10.1 'No balancing charge under *Capital Allowances Act 1990* (or other legislation relating to any capital allowances) would be made on the Company on the disposal of any pool of assets [save that no warranty is given in respect of assets whose value is below £[ ] (that is to say all those assets expenditure relating to which would be taken into account in computing whether a balancing charge would arise on a disposal of any of those assets) or of any asset not in such a pool, on the assumption that a disposal made for a consideration equal to the book value shown in or adopted for the purpose of the Accounts for the assets in the pool [or as the case may be for the assets [whose value exceeds £[ ]].'

It is usual for the purchaser to require details of all capital allowances claims. The purchaser will want to know when any capital allowances have been claimed, particularly where the book value of assets exceeds the tax written down value (and therefore where a balancing charge may arise on a disposal). Depending upon the type of company and the assets that it holds the purchaser may not require detailed disclosure. Where, however, the purchaser expects to make a disposal of the target company's assets after completion, they will wish to know the potential recovery of capital allowances which will take place as a result. Conversely, the seller may not be willing to go through the exercise of preparing detailed calculations for capital allowances on minor assets. For example, where the company being purchased is a rail freight company with a large number of wagons each of which is a capital asset upon which capital allowances have been claimed. Although a total disposal of all the assets at the same time from the capital allowances pool may give rise to a large balancing charge, the normal turnover of wagons in the ordinary course of business of the company may not give rise to a substantial charge at any one particular time. In a situation such as this, the warranty will need to be modified to exclude assets below a certain value or a statement will need to be included to the effect that disclosure will only be made in respect of specified material assets. The seller may also argue that it is selling the shares in the company with an underlying business sold as a going concern. On this basis, if the purchaser intends to sell the underlying assets, it is for the purchaser to undertake the task of ascertaining the capital allowance analysis of its intended post completion voluntary acts.

Claw-back of capital allowances

7.10.2 'No event has occurred since the Accounts Date otherwise than in the ordinary course of business by reason of which any balancing charge may fall to be made against or any disposal value may fall to be brought into account by any Company under *CAA 1990* (or other legislation relating to any capital allowances).'

The purchaser will be concerned to know whether any event has happened between the accounts date and completion which may give rise to a claw-back of capital allowances.

Capital allowances on leased assets

7.10.3 'The Company has not made any claim for capital allowances in respect of any asset which is leased to or from or hired to or from the Company and no election affecting the Company has been made or agreed to be made under *CAA 1990 ss 53* or *55* in respect of any such assets.'

There are numerous anti-avoidance provisions in relation to capital allowances on leased assets. It is necessary to ascertain the position of all leased assets of the company being purchased.

Notification of plant and machinery allowances

7.10.4 'The Company has notified its Inspector of Taxes of all expenditure incurred which qualifies for plant and machinery allowances pursuant to *FA 1994 s 118*.'

FA 1994 s 118 provides that expenditure on plant and machinery can only qualify for first year allowances or writing down allowances if notification is given to the company's Inspector of Taxes.

The seller should know whether these notifications have been made. If they haven't, any allowance claims might be invalid (the notification must be made within three years of the end of the chargeable period) with the consequence that the tax charge in the accounts is under provided.

Short life assets

7.10.5 'The Company has not made any election under *Capital Allowances Act 1990 s 37* nor is it taken to have made such an election under *s 37(8)(c)*.'

It is possible to elect for short life assets, eg desk-top computer hardware, to be dealt with outside the normal capital allowances pool if the capital expenditure is incurred on or after 1 April 1986. If the asset is disposed of within four years after the end of the tax year of the acquisition at less than the written down value for tax purposes, the balancing allowance (not normally available for pooled assets) can be claimed. However, it should be noted that if the disposal is at more than the written down value, a balancing charge will be made (such a disposal would otherwise only decrease the value of the pool).

Long life assets

7.10.6 'The Company does not own any long life assets as defined by *CAA 1990 s 38A(2)*.'

CAA 1990 Part 1 Chapter IVA, inserted by *FA 1997 Sch 14* with effect in relation to chargeable periods ending on or after 25 November 1996, introduced the concept of long life assets. A long life asset is plant and machinery having an expected useful economic life when new of at least 25 years. In general, long life assets go into a separate pool and qualify for a reduced rate of allowance of 6% instead of 25%.

The seller should know which assets are long life assets and make disclosure accordingly.

Disclaimer of allowances

7.10.7 'The Disclosure Letter gives full details of all disclaimers of capital allowances and writing down allowances on plant and machinery and of any reduction in initial allowances on industrial holdings and agricultural buildings.'

A taxpayer is not obliged to take the full amount of an allowance and can disclaim allowances if this is more advantageous. This warranty seeks information regarding disclosures that have been made so that the purchaser can ascertain the allowances still available to be claimed.

Fixtures

7.10.8 'The Company is not in dispute, nor could it be in dispute with any person as to the availability of allowances under *CAA 1990 s 51*.'

CAA 1990 s 51 provides detailed rules as to the availability of allowances on fixtures in buildings. Following the case of *Stokes v Costain Property Investment Co Ltd* [1984] STC 204 there was doubt over who was entitled to allowances when plant and machinery became a fixture in a building. *CAA 1990 s 51* seeks to overcome this. However, where there is a dispute, *CAA 1990 s 51* provides a mechanism for resolution (*CAA 1990 s 51(7)*). This warranty merely seeks to confirm that there is no dispute so that allowances being claimed are not likely to be withdrawn.

Disposal value of fixtures

7.10.9 '*CAA 1990 ss 59–59B* do not apply to any fixtures acquired by the Company for a capital sum so as to determine the disposal value of the seller of the fixture.'

CAA 1990 ss 59–59B apply where one person succeeds to another's qualifying interest so as to determine the amount of consideration to be apportioned to fixtures comprising part of that interest. Under *CAA 1990 s 59B*, where a fixture is sold with land, the seller and the purchaser can elect how much of the purchase price is to be apportioned to the fixture provided the amount so apportioned does not exceed the cost to the seller of the fixture or the amount to be apportioned.

The seller will know whether *CAA 1990 s 59B* has applied to a fixture and whether an election has been made.

Industrial buildings

7.10.10 'None of the Company's assets, expenditure on which has qualified for a capital allowance under *Pt I* of the *Capital Allowances Act 1990*, has at any time since that expenditure was incurred been used otherwise than as an industrial building or structure.'

Where an industrial building is temporarily not used for industrial purposes it is possible to continue to claim writing down allowances except where the building is for the time being used for some other purpose. The purchaser will usually need to know the status of the various buildings owned by the seller.

Connected persons

7.10.11 'The Company has not been party to a transfer of asset to or from a connected person with *CAA 1990 ss 157* or *158*.'

CAA 1990 s 157 applies to substitute market value for the actual consideration where a sale is between connected persons.

CAA 1990 s 158 provides for a different value to be substituted where the parties elect. In general, it substitutes the lower of the price actually paid and the tax written down value.

Again, this is an information seeking-warranty.

Distributions

7.11 The tax deed will only catch pre-completion transactions or, if the word 'transaction' is defined to include a number of events some of which occurred pre-completion and some of which occurred post-completion, it will catch post-completion events only to the extent that those events can be said to be connected. It is possible therefore that the target company may have done something in the past which may cause a future tax liability which is not caught by the tax deed. In the event of the seller warranting a state of affairs which has an impact upon a post-completion act, it may be difficult for the purchaser to prove damage, especially if it can be shown that the act would have been carried out in any event. However, it is advantageous for the purchaser to have the information to make an informed decision as to whether to act in a certain way and to form a view as to how much it will cost.

Repayments of share capital

7.11.1 'No company has at any time after 6 April, 1965 repaid, redeemed or purchased or agreed to repay, redeem or purchase, or granted an option under which it may become liable to purchase, any shares of any class of its issued share capital nor has any company after that date capitalised or agreed to capitalise in the form of shares or debentures any profits or reserves of any class or description or otherwise issued or agreed to issue any share capital other than for the receipt of a new consideration (within the meaning of *Pt VI* of the *Income and Corporation Taxes Act 1988*) or passed or agreed to pass any resolution to do so.'

Sections 210 and *211* treat a bonus issue which occurs after a repayment of share capital or a repayment of share capital following a bonus issue as a distribution. Whether or not the purchaser is contemplating a bonus issue by the target company at the time of the transaction, it will be important for the purchaser to find out by means of a warranty whether there has been a previous repayment of share capital both to ascertain the amount, if any, of any advance corporation tax which would be payable and also to ensure that it is paid in order to prevent any penalties for late payment (this will not be relevant after 6 April 1999). It is important to note that those receiving the bonus issue do not need to be the same people to whom the repayment of share capital was made. The target company will also need to inform any shareholders where the purchaser is acquiring less than 100% of the target company's shares that they may have a liability to tax on receipt of any subsequent bonus issue. This may be the case where the other shareholders are higher rate taxpayers and their liability is not covered by a tax credit provided by the advance corporation tax. *Finance Act 1997 Sch 7* prevents a person who sells shares to the company from reclaiming the tax credit.

Interest treated as a distribution

7.11.2 'No securities (within the meaning of *Pt VI* of the *Income and Corporation Taxes Act 1988*) issued by any company and remaining in issue at the date of this agreement were issued in such circumstances that any interest or other distribution out of assets in respect thereof falls to be treated as a distribution under *ICTA 1988 s 209*.'

It will also be necessary to ascertain whether the interest which is either paid or payable by the company is to be treated as a distribution and therefore not allowable as a charge on the company's profits.

Distributions referable to a transaction in securities

7.11.3 'The Company has not paid, nor will it pay before completion, any dividend or other qualifying distribution which is, or will be, deemed to be a Foreign Income Dividend under *FA 1997 Sch 7*.'

FA 1997 Sch 7 provides that where a distribution is made by a company and the distribution is referable by way of whether the distribution is made, the time when it is made, its form or its amount, to a transaction in securities, the distribution is treated as a foreign income dividend. Again this warranty is for information purposes. The foreign income dividend provisions will be repealed from 6 April 1999 after which the need for this warranty will diminish.

Capital distributions

7.11.4 'The Company has not received any capital distribution to which the provisions of *TCGA 1992 s 189* could apply.'

TCGA 1992 s 189 allows the Inland Revenue to recover from the target company any tax on chargeable gains due from a company in which it has an interest. Such recovery is possible where the target company receives or has become entitled to receive in respect of shares a capital distribution (other than one representing a reduction of capital) and the capital so distributed constitutes a disposal of assets or derives from the disposal of assets in respect of which a chargeable gain accrued to the other company. It is therefore necessary to ascertain the circumstances in which a charge could arise.

Groups of companies

7.12 It is possible that the target company is a stand alone company and has therefore never been a member of a group. There are different types of group depending upon the shareholding relationships and the rights attaching to the shares.

Where the company is a stand alone company it is sufficient to warrant:

> 'The Company is not, nor has it ever been, a member of a group of companies however defined.'

If the company has ever been a member, the warranty will be breached and any damage flowing will be recoverable.

Where the company has been a member of a group it will be necessary to determine what types of group they were and the likely consequences.

Capital gains tax group

7.12.1 'The Company is not and has not [since its incorporation] [within the last [twelve] years] been a member of a group of companies as defined in *s 170* of the *Taxation of Chargeable Gains Act 1992*.'

If a company is not and has not been a member of a capital gains tax group it is sufficient for the seller to warrant the fact.

If this is false, any tax charge which arises from the company having been a member of a capital gains tax group would arise from a breach of this warranty.

Where a company has been a member of a capital gains tax group it is usual for the purchaser to seek warranties in order to obtain information.

No TCGA 1992 s 179 charge

7.12.2 'No asset of any company shall be deemed under *TCGA 1992 s 179* to have been disposed of and reacquired by virtue of or in consequence of the entering into or performance of this agreement or any other event since the Accounts Date.'

Where assets are moved around a capital gains tax group they are deemed to be disposed of and acquired at such value that neither a gain nor a loss will accrue to the company making the disposal; in effect, the transferee acquires at the transferor's indexed base cost (*TCGA 1992 s 171*). Where a company leaves a capital gains tax group with an asset which it acquired from another member of the group within the previous six years, it is treated as disposing and immediately reacquiring the asset at market value at the time of the original intra-group transfer. However, the capital gain or loss which arises on the deemed disposal or acquisition is deemed to arise on the later of the beginning of the accounting period in which the company left the group and the date of the intra-group transfer.

The date of disposal for capital gains tax purposes is the date when the contract is made not the date of completion. Therefore, in the majority of cases the *s 179* charge will arise pre-completion and any liability to tax will be covered by the tax deed. It is increasingly common to have simultaneous exchange of contracts and completion, and in such cases it is therefore important to ensure that the tax deed covers completion itself and not just events prior to completion.

However, it is important for the purchaser to check any disclosures against this warranty. The purchaser may wish to include a specific clause in the tax deed to cover any tax liability which may arise as the result of a company leaving a group and perhaps to exclude the liability from the financial limits. Otherwise, a known *s 179* liability will become a cost to the purchaser.

Group income elections

7.12.3 'The Disclosure Letter contains full particulars of all elections made by the Company under *s 247* of the *Income and Corporation Taxes Act 1988* (Dividends etc paid by one member of a group to another) and all such elections are now in force but no assessment has been or may be made on the Company in respect of Advance Corporation Tax which ought to have been paid or Income Tax which ought to have been deducted.'

Where the target company is a subsidiary of another company, the purchaser will wish to ascertain whether or not any dividends or any interest payments have been paid by the target company under a group income election. The purchaser's concern will be to ensure that where such a payment has been made, the group income election was valid and applicable to the payment in question. If a dividend or interest was paid and which was purported to be paid under a valid group income election which, for whatever reason, was not applicable to the payment, the target company would be liable for advance corporation tax or income tax (currently at 20%) which should have been, but was not, remitted or deducted together with any resulting interest and penalties for late payment of taxation.

If the target company is long-established and has been a member of a group of companies for a long period, the seller may try to restrict the application of the warranty to, say, the last six accounting periods. In the absence of such a restriction, the seller may feel that undue onus is placed on it to find out what group elections were made in respect of distant accounting periods which are unlikely to be of any real practical significance, given the length of time which has elapsed since they were made. In general, the purchaser would agree to such a restriction provided that it is not for too short a period.

On or after 6 April 1999 the group income elections shall cease to apply to dividends following the abolition of ACT.

Effective 51% subsidiary test

7.12.4 '*ICTA 1988 s 247(8A)* does not apply to prevent any Company from being a 51% subsidiary of another company in the group.'

This warranty should be included where a group is being bought. *ICTA 1988 s 247(8A)* prevents a company from being a 51% subsidiary of another company unless that other company not only owns 51% of the ordinary share capital but also is entitled both to more than 50% of profits available for distribution and to more than 50% of the assets available to members in a winding up.

It seeks to confirm that dividends paid throughout the acquired group were properly paid without advance corporation tax.

Group relief and surrenders of advance corporation tax

7.12.5 Group relief warranties are primarily concerned with obtaining information, particularly in relation to post accounts date periods.

There are three reasons why a purchaser would be interested in finding out what group relief claims and surrenders of advance corporation tax have been made.

First, to the extent that losses or advance corporation tax have already been paid for, the purchaser will wish to ensure that they are available. The purchaser will wish to avoid a situation where the target company has paid for losses or for the surrender of advance corporation tax prior to completion and, for whatever reason, the surrender is ineffective and the target company has also to pay the tax that such surrender was supposed to discharge. This situation would reduce the net asset value of the target company.

Second, the purchaser will want to ensure that to the extent that the target company has surrendered or agreed to surrender losses or advance corporation tax itself, where the company accepting the surrender is not to be part of the group being sold, it will receive payment from the company to which it makes its surrender. The purchaser will not wish to find itself in a position of having assumed a given surplus of advance corporation tax or losses that such advance corporation tax or losses are diminished or are unavailable due to contractually binding agreements to surrender to members of the seller's group, where such surrender is not for the market value of the losses or advance corporation tax being surrendered.

Third, the extent that losses have been surrendered for value the purchaser will wish to ensure that such value is received by the target company.

Notwithstanding these reasons for a warranty in respect of group relief or the surrenders of advance corporation tax, there may be other reasons why a warranty is required. For example, where the target company has profits which may be relieved by claiming group relief, the decision by the seller to relieve these profits may have important consequences if the purchaser is a foreign company. If the target company has distributable reserves which have not been taken out by way of a dividend strip prior to the sale, a dividend declared post-completion to a foreign company would have the effect not only of allowing any advance corporation tax on the distribution to be carried back to previous accounting periods and so enable a repayment of mainstream corporation tax but may also have the advantage of allowing a part of the advance corporation tax credit to be repaid under any applicable double taxation treaty. The amount of this credit will be restricted from April 1999. It is not unknown for companies to have large distributable reserves of this type. The surrender of group relief immediately prior to completion in respect of the two years immediately prior to completion will reduce the taxable profits and thus reduce the ability of the target company to carry back advance corporation tax. The potential for a dividend strip post-completion would thus be severely reduced. However, because the dividend would be out of pre-acquisition profits there is a danger that it would be abnormal for the purposes of *ICTA 1988 ss 703–709*.

A typical warranty on group relief would be worded as set out below:

> 'No Company has within the last six years surrendered or claimed or agreed to surrender or claim any amount by way of group relief under the provisions of *s 402* to *s 413* (inclusive) of the *Income and Corporation Taxes Act 1988* or any amount of advance corporation tax under the provisions of *s 240* of the *Income and Corporation Taxes Act 1988* nor made or received or agreed to make or receive any payment in respect of any such surrender.'

An alternate warranty could be worded as set out below:

'The Disclosure Letter contains full and complete particulars of all arrangements and agreements relating to group relief (as defined in *s 402* of the *Income and Corporation Taxes Act 1988*) to which the Company is or has been a party and:

(a) all claims made by the Company for group relief were, when made, valid and have been or will be allowed by way of relief from Corporation Tax;

(b) the Company has not made nor is liable to make any payment under such arrangement or agreement; and

(c) the Company has received all payments due to it under any such arrangement or agreement for surrender of group relief made by it.'

This warranty can be repeated, *mutatis mutandis,* for surrenders of advance corporation tax.

Special arrangements for groups under pay and file

7.12.6 'The Company is not a party to any arrangement under SP10/93.'

Statement of Practice 10 of 1993 provides a simplified procedure for making and revising claims to group relief and for the giving and revising notices of consent to surrender relief under pay and file where the companies in the group are dealt with mainly in one tax district. This warranty is for obtaining information.

Surrender of tax refund

7.12.7 'The Company has not surrendered, agreed to surrender, claimed or agreed to claim any tax refund.'

FA 1989 s 102(3) allows companies within a group to jointly elect for a repayment which is due to one company to be surrendered to another company provided it is within the group relief group. This is to deal with the differential rates of interest paid and receivable or under and over payments of tax under pay and file.

Where disclosure against this warranty is made and the target company is claiming a refund, the purchase of the target may amount to arrangements. It is therefore necessary to ascertain whether the surrender was made before arrangements came into force. It is also necessary for the purchaser to consider whether the refund of tax will be available. If the surrendering company goes into receivership or liquidation, the refund may never be paid. Consideration should be given to whether provision for the tax payable should be made in the accounts or whether there should be a retention from the purchase price until the surrender is actually made.

Liability for capital gains tax for other group members

7.12.8 'No tax has been or may be assessed on the Company pursuant to *TCGA 1992 s 190* in respect of any chargeable gain accrued prior to the date of this agreement and the Company has not at any time within the period of six years ending with the date of this agreement transferred any asset other than trading stock, including without limitation any transfer by way of share exchange within *TCGA 1992 s 135*, to any company which at the time of disposal was a member of the same group as defined in *s 170, TCGA 1992*.'

In certain circumstances, one member of a group of companies may be held liable for corporation tax on chargeable gains payable by another group member even though, at the time the gain arises, the company is no longer a member of the same group.

Such a warranty would force disclosure of any circumstances in which a charge as described above could apply. It also provides information to enable the purchaser of a group of companies to ascertain whether a charge under *TCGA 1992 s 179* would arise on the subsequent sale by the purchaser of one of the companies being purchased.

To a certain extent this warranty duplicates that given in 7.7.7 and the seller may seek to delete it.

Employees

7.13 Warranties relating to employees usually seek to ensure that the administrative processes have been complied with. Although this may appear to be a matter of detail and involve small amounts, often substantial liabilities can arise, for example where employees have been treated as self-employed. There are also substantial penalties in this area.

Compensation for loss of office

7.13.1 'The Company is not under an obligation to pay nor has it since the Accounts Date paid or agreed to pay any compensation for loss of office or any gratuitous payment not deductible in computing its income for the purpose of corporation tax.'

In the case of *Snook v Blasdale* (1952) 33 TC 244 it was held that the compensation paid to retiring directors on a change of control was allowable only if the company could prove first, that the question of payment had not been affected in any way by the terms of the sale of shares; and second, that the decision to pay the compensation had been made solely in the interests of the company's trade. It is quite common for a seller who is a director of the company to receive a termination payment for loss of office. The purchaser will therefore be concerned that any such termination payments are deductible.

On a non-tax note it will be necessary to check that the provisions of *CA 1985 s 151* (financial assistance generally prohibited), have not been breached.

Give As You Earn

7.13.2 'The Company does not participate in a scheme under *ICTA 1988 s 202,* and in relation to any such scheme disclosed the company has given effect to the scheme in accordance with the contract and has complied with that section and all regulations made under it.'

It is usual for the purchaser to require a warranty to the effect that any give-as-you-earn scheme has been properly operated. Obviously if there is no such scheme the words after '1988' can be deleted.

Profit related pay

7.13.3 'No scheme registered under *Chapter 3 of Pt V* of *ICTA 1988* applies to the Company or any of its employees and no application for registration of a scheme so applying has been made.'

If the target company operates a registered scheme for profit related pay the purchaser will be concerned to ensure that it has been properly operated and that the terms of the scheme and statutory requirements have been complied with.

PAYE and National Insurance

7.13.4 'The Company has properly operated the Pay As You Earn and National Insurance systems deducting and accounting for tax and maintaining records as required by law.'

Proper operation of the PAYE system and accounting for tax under that system is probably already covered under the general warranties which seek confirmation that tax returns have been submitted and are accurate and that all tax that should have been paid has been paid. However, it is becoming increasingly common to have a specific warranty on the operation of the PAYE system.

Expense payments and benefits in kind

7.13.5 'The Disclosure Letter sets out full details of all current dispensations and notices granted by the Inland Revenue relating to the target company under *ICTA 1988 ss 144* and *166* and full details of any annual settlement arrangements.'

The purchaser may also be concerned to ascertain whether any special basis has been agreed between the target company and the Inland Revenue in respect of the expenses or provision of benefits to employees. In particular, *ICTA 1988 s 166* enables inspectors of taxes to agree that there is no liability to Sch E taxation or on the employer to include such payments in P11D Forms in respect of particular payments or benefits provided to employees in respect of expenses wholly, exclusively and necessarily incurred in relation to that employment.

The wording of an alternate warranty is set out below:

> 'There are no current dispensations or notices granted by the Inland Revenue relating to the Company under *ICTA 1988 ss 144* and *166*.'

Liability insurance

7.13.6 'The Company paid no premiums in respect of directors' or officers' liability insurance before 6 April 1995 and any premiums paid since that date fall within *ICTA 1988 s 201AA*.'

ICTA 1988 s 201AA allows a deduction from emoluments for policies of insurance which cover the holder of an office of employment against liabilities incurred when acting as an officer or employee.

Share option schemes

7.13.7 The purchaser will want to know whether there were any share option schemes or profit sharing schemes. Warranties tend to ask for disclosure of any such schemes and a statement that the rules and legislation have been properly applied. A typical warranty would be:

> 'The Disclosure Letter contains full details of any approved share option scheme and the Company has complied with all statutory requirements in respect of any such scheme disclosed.'

An identical form of wording can be used for unapproved share schemes, profit sharing schemes, ESOTs, save-as-you-earn share option schemes and approved or unapproved retirement benefit schemes. In relation to retirement benefits schemes, the purchaser should also seek confirmation that the company is not liable for any tax in relation to payments into or out of such schemes.

Close companies

7.14 When there was a big discrepancy between the rates of income tax and corporation tax, it would have been possible, without the close company provisions for the owners of companies to reduce their income tax bills by incorporating their business and for that company not to pay dividends. The capital value of the company would increase and could be realised later at the lower rate of capital gains tax. The close company provisions provided a mechanism whereby the Inland Revenue could apportion the undistributed income to the shareholders in the close company and tax them as if they had received the income. With the reduction in the rates of income tax and the assimilation of the rates of income tax with those of capital gains these provisions became less important; consequently, the apportionment rules were repealed with effect from 31 March 1989 and it is now no longer necessary to seek a warranty in respect of them. However, a new regime was introduced whereby close investment-holding companies are not entitled to the small companies' rate of corporation tax, and warranties are now sought in respect of this. Other close company provisions still remain, ie loans to participators and the extended meaning of distribution. These issues are covered in the warranties below.

The company is not close

7.14.1 'The company is not, and never has been, a close company as defined in *ICTA 1988 s 414*.'

It is usual for the purchaser to offer to the seller the opportunity to make a bold statement that the company is not a close company or an alternative set of warranties setting out in detail issues relevant to the company being close. The first warranty is as set out above. To the extent that the seller can give this warranty there is no need for any further close company warranties. In the event that the company is a close company, any damage suffered by the purchaser will flow from, and will be consequential on, the warranty being untrue. However, caution is to be recommended for it is in the nature of disclosure that many facts come to light at the last minute. It is not unknown for the seller to give a warranty that the target company is not a close company and then at the last minute to disclose against the warranty that in fact it is. This obviously totally negates the effect of the warranty. When put in such a position the purchaser has two courses of action: first, the purchaser may refuse to accept the disclosure, in which case any consequence of the company being a close company will be to the seller's account. There is nothing wrong with this approach. Very often the purchaser will give a deadline for the provision of the disclosure material. Second, the purchaser can seek the further warranties that would normally have been sought had not the seller stated that the company was not a close company in the first place. An alternative set of warranties is usually sought where the company is or has been a close company. The number of such warranties has reduced in recent years with the abolition of apportionment.

Close investment-holding company

7.14.2 'The Company is not nor has it been since 31 March 1989 a close investment-holding company as defined in *ICTA 1988 s 13A*.'

ICTA 1988 s 13A defines a close investment-holding company. It does so by exclusion, providing that a company is a close investment- holding company unless it satisfies certain conditions. If it is a close company it will be a close investment-holding company unless throughout the accounting period, it exists wholly or mainly for the purpose of carrying on a trade or trades on a commercial basis, it is a member of a trading group, or a property investment company letting property to completely unconnected persons. The consequence of being a close investment-holding company is that the small companies' rate of corporation tax will not apply. The other effect is that the anti-avoidance provisions in *ICTA 1988 s 231(3A)–(3D)* may apply to prevent the shareholders obtaining repayments of tax credits on distributions.

The seller will have to establish whether the company is within *s 13A*. This will depend upon the company's status at the end of the accounting period (*CHW (Huddersfield) Ltd v IRC* [1963] 2 All ER 952). If it is close then it will be a close investment-holding company unless throughout the period it satisfies the exceptions. Normally, the seller will only warrant the position during its period of ownership or from 1 April 1989 or shorter. Usually, the warranties will only apply to the previous six years in any event.

As far as the purchaser is concerned, the rate of tax applicable should have been reflected in the accounts and provided for at the appropriate rate. This warranty therefore provides information.

The seller will need to take care that the company is not close but carries on activities which, if it were close, would make it a close investment-holding company. If the acquisition by the purchaser makes the company close, it will be treated as a close investment-holding company throughout that accounting period, which may include a period during the seller's ownership.

Distribution within ICTA 1988 s 418

7.14.3 'No distribution within *ICTA 1988 s 418* has been made by the Company within the last seven years and no such distribution will be made before completion.'

ICTA 1988 s 418 treats a wide variety of transactions as distributions including the provision of any facilities to participators which can include the provision of any accommodation, entertainment and domestic or other services. It also extends to facilities provided to associates of a participator. The consequence of *s 418* applying is that until 6 April 1999 there will be liability to advance corporation tax and the participator is liable to income tax on the distribution. After 6 April 1999 the liability to ACT will no longer arise.

The seller will have to review carefully all transactions entered into by the company which may fall within *ICTA 1988 s 418.*

The purchaser will want to know how any liabilities have arisen and whether it is likely that any further liabilities will arise before completion.

Loans to participators

7.14.4 'No loan or advance made by or debt incurred to or assigned to the Company falling within the provisions of *ICTA 1988 s 419* (as extended by *s 422* thereof) is outstanding or has been waived in whole or in part since the accounts date.'

ICTA 1988 s 419 requires a company to pay an amount equal to the advance corporation tax which would have been paid if a loan made to a participator had instead been a distribution. The amount paid is not ACT, it is, in effect, an interest free loan to the Inland Revenue, which, if the loan is repaid is repaid to the company, or, if the loan is waived, is treated as satisfying the lower rate income tax liabilities of the participator. With the abolition of ACT, *s 419* is to be amended and in future the company will have to make a payment of equal to 25% of the amount of the loan or the advance.

The seller, as well as reviewing the transactions which the company has entered into, should also consider the treatment of any payments made under *s 419* in the accounts and whether they have been taken into account in arriving at the purchase consideration.

For the purchaser the warranty is only appropriate where payments under *s 419* have been taken into account in the accounts as the purchaser will not suffer any loss even if the loan is written off and results in the amount paid under *ICTA 1988 s 419* becoming irrecoverable.

Charge for unpaid inheritance tax

7.14.5 'There is no Inland Revenue charge as defined in *s 237* of the *Inheritance Tax Act 1984* outstanding in respect of any asset of the Company or the Shares.'

Under *IHTA 1984 s 237* the Inland Revenue is entitled to charge property which has been the subject of a transfer upon which the inheritance tax liability remains unpaid. The purchaser will therefore wish to ensure that the shares in the target company and the assets owned by the target company cannot be subject to such charge.

Power of sale

7.14.6 'There are not in existence any circumstances whereby the power mentioned in *IHTA 1984 s 212(1)* could be exercised in relation to the Shares or any assets of the Company.'

If a transferor liable to inheritance tax defaults, there is a secondary liability which falls on the transferee. Where the transferee is liable for inheritance tax, the transferor may obtain a power of sale over the relevant property notwithstanding the fact that he does not own it. The purchaser will have a potential defence against both the charge and the power to sell if it is a bona fide purchasers of value without notice.

Tax avoidance

7.15 Both the courts and the legislature have sought to curtail the excesses of the tax avoidance industry. The following warranties seek to identify areas where anti-avoidance provisions might apply.

Statutory anti-avoidance provisions

7.15.1 'The Company has not been a party to or otherwise involved in any transaction to which any of the following provisions could apply:

Sections 29, 30, 31, 32, 33 or *34* of the *Taxation of Chargeable Gains Act 1992*;

Paragraphs 5–10 Sch 12 to the *Finance Act 1984*;

Sections 116–118 of the *Income and Corporation Taxes Act 1988*;

Section 399 of the *Income and Corporation Taxes Act 1988*; or

Sections 729–746 or *ss 774–778* of *Pt XVII* of the *Income and Corporation Taxes Act 1988.*'

The purchaser will usually require to know that the seller has not been involved in any major tax avoidance schemes. It is usual for the purchaser to seek a warranty confirming that the various anti-avoidance provisions of the *Income and Corporation Taxes Act 1988* do not apply. Setting out the sections serves as a check list for the seller.

Clearance applications

7.15.2 'The Company has not been a party to any transaction to which any of the following provisions have been or could be applied other than transactions in respect of which all Inland Revenue clearances have been obtained after disclosure of all material facts:

Section 139 of the *Taxation of Chargeable Gains Act 1992*;

Section 135 or *section 136* of the *Taxation of Chargeable Gains Act 1992*;

Sections 213–218 of the *Income and Corporation Taxes Act 1988* and *Sch 18* to the *Finance Act 1980*;

Section 219 of the *Income and Corporation Taxes Act 1988*;

Section 703 of the *Income and Corporation Taxes Act 1988*;

Section 703 of the *Income and Corporation Taxes Act 1988*; or

Section 776 of the *Income and Corporation Taxes Act 1988*.'

There are a number of provisions in the *Income and Corporation Taxes Act 1988* under which a party to a transaction should or must seek clearance. The purchaser will usually require the seller to inform them of any such circumstances where clearance has been applied for and to warrant that upon such clearance being applied for all material facts were disclosed. Occasionally, where such clearances have been obtained the purchaser will wish to see copies of the relevant correspondence. The seller would normally disclose these documents in any event.

Transactions between persons under common control

7.15.3 'No transactions or arrangements involving the Company have taken place or are in existence which are such that any of the provisions of *ICTA 1988 ss 770–773, 770A* have been or could be applied to them or that a direction has been or could be made under *VATA 1994 Sch 6 para 1*.'

ICTA 1988 s 770 empowers the Board of the Inland Revenue to substitute market value in certain circumstances where it considers trading or other transactions between persons or bodies under common control (normally in cases where one of the persons is non-resident though not exclusively so) have been carried out at an artificially high or low figure eg in order to inflate the profits of a non-UK company at the expense of a UK company. Such transactions are usually referred to as 'transfer pricing'. *ICTA 1998 s 770* was replaced by a new *ICTA 1988 s 770A* introducing a new *Sch 28AA* to *ICTA 1988* applicable to accounting periods ending on or after 1 July 1999.

Value Added Tax Act 1994 Sch 6 para 1, entitles Customs & Excise to make a direction that VAT on supplies or imports for any monetary consideration between connected persons should be charged based on open market value. A direction may apply retrospectively to supplies and imports made in the previous three years and to future supplies and imports. These provisions do not apply to supplies and imports for non-money consideration, since these are in any event subject to VAT on open market value under *VATA 1994 ss 19–21.*

The purchaser will be concerned to know whether such transactions have been entered into.

Depreciatory transactions

7.15.4 'The Company has not been a party to any transaction to which the provisions of *TCGA 1992 s 176* or *s 177* have been or could be applied.'

The seller may resist such a warranty on the basis that no guarantee as to what losses are available (if any) is being given and so the warranty is otiose.

TCGA 1992 ss 176 and *177* enable the Inland Revenue to disallow capital losses arising out of transactions where the value of a subsidiary company has been reduced below its acquisition cost as a result of a depreciatory transaction or dividend stripping operation.

Value shifting

7.15.5 'The Company has not been involved in any transaction whereby the value of any of the Company's assets has been reduced to obtain a tax free benefit if disposed of.'

The value shifting legislation in *TCGA 1992 ss 29–34* provides for the counteraction of schemes where assets or shares have been devalued in order to provide tax free benefits. In general, the value shifting is counteracted by reducing a loss or increasing a gain by an amount that is just and reasonable having regard to the value shifting in question.

Ramsay/Furniss v Dawson

7.15.6 'The Company has not been involved in any transaction or series of transactions which, or any part of which, may for any tax purposes be disregarded or reconstructed by reason of any motive to avoid, reduce or delay a possible liability to tax.'

It is common for the purchasers to seek a warranty to the effect that no schemes within the ambit of the decision in *Furniss v Dawson* HL 1984, 55 TC 324 have been entered into by the company. Such warranties may be extremely wide-ranging.

The seller should scrutinise such warranties very carefully. Occasionally the warranty is limited by the words 'as far as the seller is aware'. This makes very little difference because the whole essence of the typical tax avoidance scheme that *Furniss v Dawson* is meant to catch is that there is a pre-ordained series of transactions. If the seller was not aware that they had entered into such a scheme, it is hardly likely that there was a pre-ordained series of transactions.

Occasionally, the warranty sought is far wider than that given above. It is not unusual to find a warranty which states that the seller has not entered into any transaction which was intended to defer or avoid a liability to taxation. Such warranties should be resisted by the sellers as, for example, the act of rolling over a gain from disposal of one asset into the acquisition of another is in effect a deferral and avoidance of a liability to capital gains tax. There are many other examples of perfectly legitimate tax deferral and avoidance which could be caught by such wording. The seller should ensure that the warranty catches only schemes which are likely to be attacked by the Inland Revenue.

Overseas interests

7.16 The following warranties deal with overseas interests. Where the company has no overseas interests it is sufficient to warrant that fact or to just delete the warranties that deal with overseas interests.

Treasury consent for migration of companies

7.16.1 'The Company has not carried out or caused or permitted to be carried out any of the transactions specified at the relevant time in *ICTA 1988 s 765(1)* otherwise than with the prior consent of HM Treasury and (in the case of a special as opposed to a general consent) full particulars of which are contained in the Disclosure Letter or carried out any transactions to which *ICTA 1988 s 765A* could apply without having duly provided the required information to the Board of Inland Revenue.'

ICTA 1988 s 765 requires that Treasury consent be obtained before certain transactions can be carried out. Failure to obtain all necessary consents can lead to the imposition of severe penalties including criminal sanctions. The importance of *s 765* has reduced in recent years. However, the penalties imposed by *s 765* mean that purchasers will still require that its provisions have been complied with. There is no record of any prosecution ever having been brought under *s 765*. The purchaser will require full details of the *s 765* history of the target company since previous applications for consent under this section can in certain circumstances affect later applications by that company, even though the later application arises out of a separate transaction. The purchaser will therefore seek to confirm that all necessary consents have been received and, in the event that application has in the past been made, full details are required to be given.

In order to give effect to *EC Council Directive No 88/361, Art 1* (25 June 1988), *FA 1990 s 68(2)* inserted *ICTA 1988 s 765A. EC Council Directive No 88/361* requires member states to abolish restrictions on movements of capital between persons resident in member states. *Section 765A* therefore provides that no criminal offence can be committed under *s 765* if a transaction, which would otherwise fall within *s 765*, involves a movement of capital within Art 1 of the Directive. However, regardless of the fact that *s 765A* removes any liability under *s 765*, the Inland Revenue must still be provided with the notice of the transaction not later than six months after it happens. In a Statement of Practice dated 28 February 1992 (SP2/92) the Inland Revenue explained the circumstances when in their view (and in the view of the Treasury) there is a movement of capital to which Art 1 applies.

Company migration without Treasury consent

7.16.2 'The Company has not ceased to be resident in the United Kingdom other than in pursuance of a Treasury consent under *ICTA 1988 s 765* without previously satisfying the requirements of *FA 1988 s 130(2) and (3)* (full particulars of the satisfaction of those requirements being contained in the Disclosure Letter) and there are no circumstances by reason of which any company could be liable to any penalty under *FA 1988 s 131* or be presumed by virtue of *s 131(4)* to be so liable.'

Since 15 March 1988 a company managed and controlled in the UK but not incorporated in the UK has been able to migrate without Treasury consent provided that it provides notice of its intention to migrate, details of how much tax will be payable in respect of periods before that time and in particular of the arrangements it proposes to make for securing the payment of any tax due. The purchaser will therefore require a warranty which ensures that all the necessary conditions have been complied with. In the event that the conditions have not been complied with, severe penalties may be charged under *FA 1988 s 131.*

Secondary liability for tax of migrating company

7.16.3 'No company (not being a Company) has ceased or will cease to be resident in the United Kingdom in circumstances such that a notice might be served on any Company under *FA 1988 s 132* or by virtue of the relationship (as specified in *s 132(3)(a) or (b)*) of any Company with that company on or at any time prior to Completion.'

When a member of a group of companies migrates without paying the tax due, any other company which is a member of the group can be required to pay the tax. This may be so even if that company left the group prior to the migration of the other company. Such an event being a post-completion matter will usually be outside the ambit of the tax deed, although a specific covenant in respect of such matters is often sought by the purchaser. Notwithstanding any specific covenant in the tax deed, the purchaser may still seek a warranty.

A secondary liability for tax of a non-resident company

7.16.4 'The Company is not nor will it become liable to pay any tax under *TCGA 1992 s 191* in respect of a disposal occurring on or before the date of this agreement.'

Where a non-resident company is chargeable to UK corporation tax by virtue of carrying on a business through a branch or agency in the UK, a member of the same group or a controlling director of the non-resident company can be made liable for any unpaid tax on disposals of capital assets made by that non-resident company. The purchaser will require to be satisfied that such a liability will not arise.

Controlled foreign companies and offshore funds

7.16.5 'The Company has not nor has it in the past six years had an interest in a controlled foreign company as defined in *Chapter IV Part XVII of ICTA 1988* nor has it had any material interest in an offshore fund as defined in *ICTA 1988 s 759*.'

ICTA 1988 s 747 requires the Inland Revenue to charge to tax the profits of 'controlled foreign companies' which are corporations resident outside the UK, controlled by persons resident in the UK and which are subject to a low rate of taxation in the territory where they are resident.

ICTA 1988 s 757 applies new rules for the disposal of any material interest in certain offshore funds, charging gains in certain circumstances to income tax rather than capital gains tax.

Unremittable overseas income and/or gains

7.16.6 'The Company has not received or become entitled to any income which is unremittable 'overseas income' within the meaning of *ICTA 1988 s 584* no gain has accrued to the Company to which the provisions of *TCGA 1992 s 279* could apply and the company has not made any transfer to which *ICTA 1988 s 723* could apply.'

Where income or capital gains have arisen or accrued but cannot be remitted to the UK due to, for example, foreign exchange control restrictions *ICTA 1988 s 584* and *TCGA 1992 s 279* apply to such income or capital respectively.

ICTA 1988 s 584 provides that a taxpayer can give written notice to the Board of Inland Revenue and, on satisfying the Board that the overseas income is unremittable and that he will continue to be prevented from remitting that income to the UK, such taxpayer will be assessed to tax only when it is received.

Relief is also given under *TCGA 1992 s 279* where a claim is made by the chargeable person. A similar claim is also allowed under *ICTA 1988 s 723* under the accrued income rules where the claimant is unable to remit to the UK the proceeds of a transfer of foreign securities.

The purchaser will therefore require a warranty in order to seek confirmation that no income or capital gains shown in the accounts is in fact blocked outside the UK and no tax will arise in future in respect of income or capital gains accruing in the accounts which have not yet been remitted.

Agency for non-residents

7.16.7 'The Company has not been nor is it assessable to tax under *TMA 1970 s 78* (including that section as modified and applied for Stamp Duty Reserve Tax).'

TMA 1970 s 78 permits the Inland Revenue to raise assessments on UK residents where they have acted as agents for non-residents. Where such a charge arises the agent will be liable to tax whether or not the income has in fact come into his hands. Further, it may be difficult for the agent to recoup any tax payable by virtue of the fact that the company in whose name he is chargeable is non-resident. The purchaser will therefore require to know whether such an agency or may potentially exist. Such a warranty can be worded as set out below. Although *TMA 1970 s 78* has been repealed it is still relevant to previous years when a liability might have arisen.

Stamp duty

7.17 The date when stamp duty and stamp duty reserve tax are to be abolished on shares and securities continues to be postponed. The abolition of duties on shares and securities was to be effective when the Stock Exchange became a paperless exchange. In the meantime, stamp duty on property other than shares and securities has risen from 1% up to 3%, making it far more of an issue than was the case in the past. It is becoming increasingly unlikely that the abolition will ever take place. In any event, unless further proposals for abolition are introduced, there will still be a residual liability for taxes in respect of documents, agreements and other relevant transactions entered into prior to the abolition date.

All documents duly stamped

7.17.1 'All documents in the enforcement of which the Company may be interested have been duly stamped.'

Although the effect of *Stamp Act 1891 s 117* appears to make an indemnity in respect of stamp duty void what the section is intended to deal with are situations where an asset changes hands a number of times but the contracts are not stamped. Instead each member of the chain indemnifies the next member. A warranty to the effect that stamp duty has been paid by the target company will ensure recovery in the event that the documents that should have been stamped prior to completion have not been stamped. The seller will wish to ensure that the warranty that stamp duty has been paid is not in the form of an absolute statement that all documents potentially liable to stamp duty have been duly stamped. The seller's concern with such a warranty is that following completion, the purchaser may immediately stamp all documents technically liable to duty irrespective of whether the non-payment of duty causes any practical problems or potential problems. For example, if a target company entered into an agreement which may be subject to stamp duty and which was not duly stamped and the agreement has been fully performed, from the seller's viewpoint there would appear to be no need to have the document stamped. To do so would incur penalties and interest. The seller may take the view that, since the contract has been performed, there is little likelihood of the purchaser having to apply to the courts to have it enforced. In theory, the courts will not enforce a document which has not been duly stamped; consequently, the purchaser will suffer no adverse effects by failing to stamp the document if any need to enforce has disappeared.

By giving such a warranty, the seller ensures that only those documents which the purchaser has a bona fide interest in having stamped may be stamped in order to comply with the warranties.

Stamp duty reserve tax

7.17.2 'Since the Accounts Date the Company has not incurred any liability to or been accountable for any Stamp Duty Reserve Tax and there has been no agreement within *s 87(1)* of the *Finance Act 1986* which could lead to the Company incurring such a liability or becoming so accountable.'

Liabilities to stamp duty reserve tax are different to stamp duty liabilities. In the following circumstances a party must pay stamp duty:

(a) to register a document of title at HM Land Registry (or to adduce good title for unregistered land);

(b) to produce documents in evidence before a UK court;

(c) to register a share transfer, registered patent etc.

However, apart from these circumstances the controller of stamps has no sanction against those who fail to pay stamp duty. It is often said that stamp duty is a voluntary tax inasmuch as the taxpayer has to submit the relevant papers to the controller of stamps and there is no power for the controller of stamps to seek out unstamped documents from the taxpayer. However, in the case of stamp duty reserve tax (governed by the *Stamp Duty Reserve Tax Regulations* (*SI 1986/1711*)) the position is different and the controller of stamps may, if it appears that a relevant transaction has taken place, give notice to the taxpayer requiring tax to be paid. For this reason the purchaser will be particularly anxious to obtain an absolute statement that there are no stamp duty reserve tax liabilities. In addition, the purchaser must be aware that if the default continues for more than a year the penalty can be increased to the aggregate of £50 and the amount of the tax that should have been paid together with interest.

Liabilities incurred prior to the accounts date should be reflected in the accounts and consequently, the purchaser, whilst wishing to ensure that no pre-accounts date liability has arisen which has not been included in the accounts, will be most concerned with the period following the accounts date. It is usual for the seller to warrant the accuracy of the accounts and so, to the extent that any liability is not provided for, there will be a claim under that warranty.

Loss of stamp duty relief

7.17.3 'The Company has made no claim for relief under *FA 1930 s 42*.'

FA 1930 s 42 gives relief for transfers within 75% groups. If at the time of the intra-group transfer it was the intention to sell the transferee company then the relief may be forfeited under the provisions of *FA 1967 s 27*. The purchaser will wish to ensure that its purchase of the target company does not follow too soon after an application under

FA 1930 s 42 to assure themselves that there is no risk that the relief will be forfeited.

Value Added Tax

7.18 Value Added Tax is becoming increasingly important. The amount of revenue raised through VAT equals that raised through corporation tax and the law reports now contain as many VAT cases as cases on other taxes.

Further, the penalties for default in filing accurate VAT returns promptly and paying tax when due are severe. Consequently, a purchaser will need confirmation in the warranties that the target company is not liable for penalties, interest or additional VAT in respect of pre-completion periods. The purchaser will also wish to ensure that it has a sufficient understanding of the target company's VAT affairs to assume responsibility for them. As a company's VAT returns are generally made quarterly, the purchaser will have relatively little time to acquaint itself with what is required before a return needs to be prepared. This need has become even more pressing for companies with large turnovers which account monthly for VAT. Consequently, reasonably detailed information must be obtained through the warranties.

Registration

7.18.1 'The Company is a taxable person is registered as such for Value Added Tax purposes and such registration is not subject to any conditions imposed by or agreed with HM Customs & Excise.'

The basic warranties are concerned with obtaining confirmation that the target company is registered for VAT and that there is no peculiarity about such registration.

Membership of group companies

7.18.2 'The Company is not nor has been treated for Value Added Tax purposes as a member of any group within *VATA 1994 s 43* (other than a group comprising only the Companies).'

The wording of an alternate warranty is set out below:

> 'All Value Added Tax returns and payments due in respect of the group of Companies of which the Company is a member for Value Added Tax purposes have been made up to the time when the Company ceases to be liable for Value Added Tax calculated by reference to a supply made by another group company.'

Having obtained confirmation that the target company is registered for VAT purposes, the purchaser will want to confirm that the company is not part of a VAT group or, if it is, that the group only comprises those companies being purchased. The purchaser's concern will be that as VAT liabilities within a VAT group are joint and several, the target company should not be assessed for the VAT on supplies made by a company within the retained seller's group. If the seller is unable to confirm that the target company is not a member of a VAT group, the purchaser will probably seek some comfort that there are no circumstances which could result in the target company being held liable for VAT in respect of supplies made by another company which is a company outside the group being purchased. The purchaser will not be concerned by a group which comprises only the target companies purchased, as within the group being purchased there will be no net diminution in the group's value caused by the payment by one member of another member's VAT liabilities.

Target company exempt from VAT

7.18.3 'The Company is not nor has it in the preceding [six] Value Added Tax years been partially exempt and there are no circumstances by reason of which the Company might not be entitled to credit for full Value Added Tax chargeable on the supplies received and imports made (or agreed or deemed to be received or made).'

Once the purchaser has ascertained that the target company is registered for VAT and whether or not it is registered as part of a group, the purchaser will wish to ascertain whether or not the target company is partially exempt from VAT. If the target company is partially exempt, the purchaser will want to know what arrangements have been agreed with Customs & Excise as this will determine the target company's ability to recover the VAT on its inputs.

If the seller cannot give this warranty or makes disclosure against it, in which case by definition it is not true, the following warranty could be requested:

'The Disclosure Letter sets out full details of the company's partial exemption method, and the method has been agreed with Customs and Excise.'

Compliance

7.18.4 'The Company has complied with all statutory provisions, rules, regulations, orders and directions in respect of Value Added Tax, has promptly submitted accurate returns, and the Company maintains full and accurate Value Added Tax records, has never been subject to any penalty or liability within *VATA 1994 s 64* nor been given any surcharge liability notice within *s 59* of that Act nor been given a warning within *s 76* of that Act nor has the Company at any time been required to give security under *VATA 1994 Sch 11*.'

Having ascertained the current status of the target company with regard to VAT, the purchaser will then be concerned to ensure that in the past the target company has complied with the statutory provisions in respect of VAT. The purpose of this warranty is not only to ensure that there are no potential liabilities but also to alert the purchaser to these difficulties in dealing with Customs & Excise in the future. In general, Customs & Excise recognise that when a company is under new ownership the new owners cannot be held responsible for defaults of the previous owner, although this will not necessarily relieve the target company from previous conditions imposed upon it eg the need to give security. Furthermore, it is sometimes true that it can take some time before Customs & Excise stop treating a company's VAT affairs with some suspicion, notwithstanding a change in ownership, where that company has a history of making inaccurate returns and not accounting for the correct amount of tax.

Secondary liabilities

7.18.5 'No act or transactions have been effected by virtue of which the Company is or may be held liable for Value Added Tax under *VATA 1994 ss 47* and *48*, or *s 29*.'

This warranty seeks information on any potential secondary liabilities of the target company.

Option to tax

7.18.6 'The Company is not bound nor has agreed to become bound by any lease, tenancy or licence under the terms of which the Company is or is likely to become liable to pay an amount in respect of Value Added Tax chargeable as a result of making an election to waive exemption under *VATA 1994 Sch 10*.'

OR

'The disclosure letter contains full particulars of all elections to waive exemption made or agreed to be made under *VATA 1994 Sch 10* made by the Company or any person in relation to which the Company is a relevant associate and in no case has the Company charged Value Added Tax, whether on rents or otherwise, which is not properly chargeable because the Company has not made a valid election to waive exemption having effect in relation to the supply.'

The most common types of VAT warranty which go beyond the core warranties given above are in respect of property. If the target company is a landlord or a tenant, the purchaser will wish to ascertain whether or not the target company, if a tenant, is liable to pay VAT on its rent or, if a landlord, whether or not it has elected to waive its exemption from VAT in order to charge VAT on the rent it charges its tenants.

Notwithstanding the election to waive exemption, certain supplies will remain exempt. The purchaser will want to ascertain whether this is the case.

> 'The Company has never had an option to tax disapplied by virtue of a building being used for exempt purposes.'

Transfer of business as a going concern

7.18.7 'The Company has not acquired any assets to which *Art 5(1), VAT (Special Provisions) Order 1995* applies.'

Article 5(1), VAT Special (Provisions Order) 1995 provides that where a business is transferred as a going concern and the transferee is going to use the assets in carrying on the same type of business as the transferor, the transfer is to be treated as neither a supply of goods nor a supply of services.

The purchaser will be concerned to ensure that any transfers of business either fell within *Art 5* or that VAT was accounted for. Often sale of business agreements provide that in the event that the Article does not apply the price will be deemed to be exclusive of VAT and a VAT invoice will be issued. Under normal circumstances this will not cause a problem; however, if the seller of the business is not financially sound it may be unable to pay the VAT where asked to do so. The purchasing company will still be liable to account.

Bad debt relief

7.18.8 'The Company has not claimed bad debt relief on any debt in excess of the outstanding amount. Any bad debt relief which is repayable to the Company has been repaid.'

VATA 1994 s 36 and *regs 165–172B SI 2518/1995* provide for repayments of VAT where a debt on which VAT has been accounted for becomes bad. A bad debt is one which is unpaid for six months or more and does not have to be proved to be bad for a claim to be made. The purchaser should also ensure that proper procedures are in place for accounting for VAT where a debt on which bad debt relief has been claimed is subsequently paid.

Capital goods scheme

7.18.9 'The Company has not acquired or constructed nor has it disposed of any land, buildings or computer equipment to which *regs 112–116 SI 2518/1995* apply.'

The capital goods scheme is designed to prevent traders which are partially exempt for VAT purposes from recovering all the input tax on the acquisition by putting it to fully taxable use when acquired and then using it for exempt purposes in a later period. This warranty seeks information. It might be thought that if the target is fully taxable that the warranty is irrelevant; however, where a company is fully taxable when the asset is acquired but becomes exempt or partially exempt in a later period the scheme must still be applied. This might be a problem where a building is bought but then later sold by way of exempt supply.

Chapter 8

Disclosure against warranties given on the Sale of Shares in a Private Company

Introduction

8.1 It was stated in Chapter 6 that warranties serve two purposes: first, they afford protection to the purchaser by providing a remedy if they are breached; second, they provide information to the purchaser as a consequence of the disclosures made against them. Because the protection afforded by the warranties is, in most cases, duplicated by the protection afforded under the tax deed, the primary function of the warranties is to provide information. A warranty may do this because of its terms: for example, a warranty which states 'no company in the target group has made any transfers to which *TCGA 1992 s 171* could apply', confirms, in the absence of any disclosure: first that the information regarding the base cost of the target group's assets can be found in the company owning any particular asset; and second, that if a company is sold out of the target group, no liability under *TCGA 1992 s 179* would arise. Often, however, the seller will disclose against such a warranty. This chapter deals with the nature of that disclosure.

The seller's motivation to disclose

8.2 Disclosure against the warranties limits the seller's liability; however, where there is also a tax deed, it is probable that the tax deed will not be limited by disclosure (see para 4.3.9). Consequently, notwithstanding disclosure, the seller's exposure to a liability will remain under the tax deed. What then is the seller's motivation to go through the disclosure exercise as far as tax is concerned? First, there are some warranties which are not duplicated by the tax deed; for example, if the seller warrants the base cost of the target's assets, a subsequent disposal by the target following completion which gives rise to a higher than expected gain because the seller had claimed roll-over relief would not be caught by the tax deed because the actual tax liability will arise after completion. However, the fact that the warranty was incorrect would give rise to a claim for breach of warranty; disclosure of that fact would limit the seller's liability. Second, because of the nature of negotiation, there may be certain exclusions from liability under the tax deed which are not duplicated in the exclusions from the warranties; a failure to disclose would expose the seller to a liability which would otherwise not have arisen. Third, a deliberate failure to disclose a material inaccuracy in the warranties may give rise to a liability under *FSA 1986 s 47* (see [8.5] below). Finally, disclosure does reduce any residual liability under the warranties and the seller will take any opportunity to reduce the risk of claims post completion no matter how remote the risk might be.

What is disclosure in legal terms?

8.3 There is little authority on what the actual legal effect of disclosure is. In *Prentice v Scottish Power plc* [1997] 2 BCLC 264 a decision of the Scottish Court of Session, Outer House, Lord Penrose said: 'As a matter of practice, it appears that, in the ordinary course, disclosure is seen as a means of limiting the scope of what tend to be drafted as wide and unqualified warranties. Whether it achieves that by amendment or variation of the warranty provisions, or by waiver by the purchaser of remedy for what otherwise would be a breach, or by some other principle or rule of contract law must depend upon the terms of the contract in question.' An examination of two typical clauses illustrates this point.

In the case of *New Hearts Ltd v Cosmopolitan Investments Ltd* [1997] 2 BCLC 249 the contract provided:

> 'It is hereby agreed and acknowledged by the parties that the Warranties are given by the Vendor subject to matters fairly disclosed [etc].'

This wording 'subject to' implies that the warranties are qualified by the disclosure letter and, in effect, amended by the disclosure letter. An alternative form of wording is:

> 'The Seller shall not be under any liability under the Warranties in relation to any matter forming the subject matter of a claim thereunder to the extent that such matter or circumstance giving rise thereto are fairly disclosed in the Disclosure Letter [etc].'

This wording would seem to presuppose a liability arising under the warranties which is eliminated to the extent that the matter is covered by the disclosure letter.

The question arises: does this distinction have any practical significance? The answer in the vast majority of cases will be no; the effect either way will be to limit the amount that the seller has to pay for breach of warranty. The issue was raised in the case of *Prentice v Scottish Power plc* [1997] 2 BCLC 264 the facts of which were that S plc entered into an option agreement with P and H under which S plc had an option to buy shares in W Ltd at a price determined by a formula. P and H gave certain warranties to S plc in the option agreement and these warranties were to be repeated if the option was exercised. The option agreement permitted P and H to make disclosure against those warranties and gave S plc 45 days to withdraw the exercise of the option if it objected to any of the later disclosures. P and H's solicitors sent a draft disclosure letter to S plc following the exercise of the option. A dispute arose and P and H withdrew the disclosures. S plc exercised its right to withdraw from the contract. P and H sought a declaration that S plc was not entitled to withdraw.

For P and H it was argued that the disclosures were required to be given in one final disclosure letter and as that was not forthcoming there was no disclosure to which S plc could object. Disclosure to qualify the warranties was permissive not mandatory.

For S plc it was argued that the agreement said that P and H might 'make disclosures' and once that was done in whatever form it was open to S plc to withdraw the exercise of the option. Disclosure was a factual matter not one of form.

Lord Penrose held that on a true construction of the contract, it provided for disclosure to be made at any time during the 45 days. The warranties had been given at the time the option was granted, P and H were given the opportunity to disclose to limit their liability in the event that circumstances had changed since the giving of the warranties; similarly, S plc had to be given the opportunity to withdraw if those changes were not acceptable. Having raised the issue of the nature of disclosure Lord Penrose did not return to it.

What is disclosure in commercial terms?

8.4 During the course of his opinion in the *Scottish Power* case; Lord Penrose described the modern disclosure process in these terms:

> 'It is difficult to avoid the impression that disclosure has become a tactical exercise, with the vendors' representatives seeking to off-load responsibilities by the delivery of indigestible documents in quantity to purchasers' representatives who are put under pressure to investigate the material with inadequate time and facilities, and in turn resort to meaningless qualified acceptances if they are permitted to do so.'

Faced with such comments: what are the tactics used?

The starting point for any discussion on disclosure is the clause in the agreement which limits the seller's liability. Two such clauses were given in 8.3 above, another typical clause would read:

> 'The warranties are given subject to all matters [fully and fairly] disclosed in the Disclosure Letter but no other information relating

to the Target [Group] of which the Purchaser has knowledge shall prejudice any claim by the Purchaser under the Warranties.'

Disclosure falls into two categories: general disclosure and specific disclosure.

General disclosure

8.4.1 General disclosure comprises that information that the purchaser is deemed to know because it is in the public domain; for example, information on share registers or at the land registry. There is little of this type that is generally relevant to tax.

Specific disclosure

8.4.2 Specific disclosure is information provided by the seller that relates to specific warranties. As far as the parties to the contract are concerned, the type of clause described above gives rise to three distinct issues:

(a) how precise does the disclosure need to be to limit liability?

(b) what is full and fair disclosure?; and

(c) to what extent can the purchaser's knowledge be taken into account notwithstanding the exclusion?

How precise does disclosure need to be?

8.4.2.1 Assuming that the disclosure letter is the sole source of all disclosures (and usually the contract will state that this is the case), how precise does a statement have to be before it will limit the warranties? Can a vague disclosure which alludes obliquely to a risk be sufficient to limit the seller's liability? Much will depend upon the circumstances of the particular transaction; however, where there is any doubt as to the ambit of a disclosure, the purchaser should reject it and demand better information. Notwithstanding the ability to reject disclosures, the purchaser may accept a statement without realising its full impact and very often the seller will provide vague information in the hope that it will be accepted. The question then arises as to whether or not such a disclosure is valid.

The matter was addressed in the case of *Levison v Farin* [1978] 2 All ER 1149. The plaintiffs were in the fashion business and in 1972, following the illness of its designer, they offered to sell the business to a competitor. The company was running at a loss and was in a traded down state. The seller warranted that 'Save as disclosed the vendors jointly and severally warrant to and undertake with the purchasers that between the balance sheet date and the completion date . . . there will have been no material adverse change in the overall value of the net assets of the company on the basis of a valuation adopted in the balance sheet allowing for normal trade fluctuations.' Following completion, the purchaser discovered that between the balance sheet date and completion the net assets had reduced by £8,600 (the balance sheet showed net assets of £44,000) and the company had incurred losses of £7,000. The defendants refused to pay instalments of the purchase price and the plaintiffs sued. In their defence, the defendants claimed breach of warranty and counterclaimed for £8,600. In reply the plaintiffs contended that the illness of the designer, the traded down state of the company and the fact that it had been making losses had all been disclosed and that consequently there was no breach of warranty.

Gibson J held that the defendants were entitled to recover under the counter claim for breach of warranty on the following grounds: first, on the facts, there had been a material adverse change in the net assets; and second, the illness and the traded down state of the company were in the nature of a general disclosure as to the probable causes of future loss and were not disclosures of a quantifiable reduction in the net assets.

Gibson J said (at 1157):

> 'I do not say that facts made known by disclosure of the means of knowledge in the cause of negotiation could never constitute disclosure for such a clause as this but I have no doubt that a clause in this form is primarily designed and intended to require a party who wishes by disclosure to avoid a breach of warranty to give specific notice for the purpose of the agreement, and a protection by disclosure will not normally be achieved by merely making known the means of knowledge which may or do enable the other party to work out certain facts and conclusions.'

It is clear from the words quoted above that in order to be an adequate disclosure the seller must quantify the extent of the potential liability or direct the purchaser's mind to the actual factual material by which the seller seeks to limit liability.

Levinson v Farin was cited in the case of *New Hearts Ltd v Cosmopolitan Investments Ltd* [1997] 2 BCLC 249 a case in the Scottish Court of Session, Outer House in which Lord Penrose, having quoted the words of Gibson J set out above, went on to say:

> 'Mere reference to a source of information, which is in itself a complex document, within which the diligent enquirer might find relevant information will not satisfy the requirements of a clause providing for fair disclosure with sufficient details to identify the nature and scope of the matters disclosed.'

8.4.2.1 *Disclosure against warranties given on the Sale of Shares*

The clause in question was:

> 'It is hereby agreed and acknowledged by the parties that the Warranties . . . are given by the Vendor subject to matters fairly disclosed (with sufficient details to identify the nature and scope of the matter disclosed) in the Disclosure Letter in respect of which matters the Vendor shall have no liability to the purchaser.'

Following the *New Hearts* case it would be prudent for a purchaser to include the words '. . . fairly disclosed (with sufficient details to identify the nature and scope of the matter disclosed) . . .'. It would be difficult for the seller to argue against these words without being accused of trying to '. . . confuse rather than enlighten' (per Lord Penrose in *New Hearts Ltd v Cosmopolitan Investments Ltd* at 258).

Full and fair disclosure

8.4.2.2 In order to prevent the seller giving ambiguous information, the purchaser will usually require disclosure to be 'full and fair' or to be 'fully, fairly and clearly disclosed'. This helps to establish a quality level which will enable the purchaser to argue that whilst it may have been possible to identify a risk given a very perceptive reading of the particular disclosure, the disclosure was not 'full and fair' and is therefore insufficient to limit the seller's liability under the warranties.

The ambit of the words 'fairly disclosed' was considered by the Court of Appeal in *Danial Reeds Ltd v EM–Ess Chemists Ltd* [1995] CLC 1405. The defendant bought the entire issued share capital of a company called Glidemay Ltd from the plaintiffs. Glidemay manufactured medicines including paracetamol for which it required a licence. The sale contract was completed in February 1991; however, it transpired that the Glidemay's licence to manufacture paracetamol had expired in December 1990. As a consequence, Glidemay ceased trading in July 1991.

The sale agreement contained a warranty to the effect that:

> 'All necessary licences . . . have been obtained by the company to enable the company to carry on its business . . . and all such licences . . . are valid and subsisting and the vendor knows no reason why any of them should be suspended, cancelled or revoked'.

and:

> 'Without prejudice to the generality of the provisions of [the warranty above] the company has product licences in respect of the products referred to in the disclosure letter and all such product licences are valid and subsisting and the vendor knows of no reason why such product licences should be cancelled, suspended or revoked.'

The warranties were given subject to matters fairly disclosed in the disclosure letter and each warranty was stated to be separate and independent. However, the list of products in the disclosure letter did not include paracetamol. On this basis the seller argued that it had disclosed that there was no paracetamol licence and was not in breach of warranty.

The Court held that the warranties regarding the licences had to be read separately. Consequently, the first warranty meant that the company had all the licences *necessary* to carry on its business and the list of licences in the disclosure letter could not restrict the ambit of this warranty. Further, the list of medicines was specifically disclosed against the second warranty of which Beldon L J said:

> '. . . this suggests to me that fair disclosure requires some positive statement of the true position and not just some fortuitous ommission from which the buyer may be expected to infer matters of significance.'

It was therefore held that the purchaser was in breach of warranty.

Following the four cases cited above, it is probably fair to say that the law in relation to disclosure is tending towards protecting the purchaser and that provided the disclosure clause is properly drafted any attempt by the seller to limit liability by producing a mass of documents with no attempt to identify the issues that go to qualify the warranties in question will be unsuccessful.

Purchaser's knowledge outside the disclosure letter — Eurocopy plc v Teesdale [1992] BCLC 1067

8.4.2.3 It is usual for the agreement to include a clause which states that no other information which the purchaser has shall affect the purchaser's right to claim under the warranties.

Such a clause might include the following wording:

> 'Save as disclosed in the Disclosure Letter information relating to the [Target Group] of which the Purchaser has knowledge either actual or constructive shall not prejudice any claim under the Warranties made by the Purchaser or operate to reduce any amount recoverable by the Purchaser.'

The question therefore arises to what extent, if any, should information which has been given to the purchaser be taken into account when considering disclosure against the warranties. The issue arose in the case of *Eurocopy plc v Teesdale* [1992] BCLC 1067. The exact status of the authority of the case is in some doubt as it was an interlocutory hearing and the case settled before it came to trial so the issues were never fully agreed.

In the *Eurocopy* case, the defendants, who were directors of the target company warranted that there were no material facts or circumstances which had not been disclosed in the disclosure letter and which, if they had been so disclosed, might have affected the decision of the purchaser to purchase the shares. Prior to signing the agreement, the defendants made the purchaser aware of certain facts but these were not included in the disclosure letter. The plaintiff sued for breach of warranty on the grounds that the defendants had failed to disclose material facts and sought to strike out that part of the defence that said that the plaintiff had actual knowledge of the matters. They claimed that the defence was unavailable because the agreement provided that the warranties were given subject to the disclosure letter but that no other information which the plaintiffs had would affect their right to claim.

The plaintiff's application was dismissed on the grounds that the warranties were representations which could not be enforced without reliance and the plaintiffs could not be said to have relied on them if they knew of facts to the contrary.

The plaintiffs' appealed to the Court of Appeal where again the claim was dismissed.

The Court of Appeal's reasoning followed that of the judge at first instance but it was also said that in ascertaining the loss suffered by the plaintiffs, it had to be borne in mind that the knowledge they had which was not disclosed would have affected the amount they offered for the shares.

The issues were never fully argued because the case settled before going to trial.

There are two points to note. First, many commentators have said that the *Eurocopy* decision is unsatisfactory or wrong because it undermines the freedom of the parties to contract as they see fit and goes against the clear words of the contract. However, in recent cases the courts have held that disclosure must identify the matter disclosed and have restricted the ability of the seller to make vague disclosure. Is it right therefore, for the purchaser to say on the one hand that it has a right of action because the disclosure did not pin point the problem, and yet on the other hand to say that notwithstanding that something was made explicit, it does not limit the seller's liability because it was not in the disclosure?

Second, in para [2.5.2.1] it was stated that if there was a legal objection to an indemnity for loss suffered as a result of a pre-completion tax liability this may not be effective because the loss was not as a result of the tax liability but because of an inherent liability of the target at the time the shares were purchased. Following the *Eurocopy* case, this argument would be difficult to sustain in that if knowledge of the tax liability would have affected the price which was offered, no knowledge of the liability should entitle the purchaser to claim if the price was too high.

Disclosure against more than one warranty

8.4.2.4 A frequently contested point is whether a disclosure made against a numbered warranty is a valid disclosure against other warranties. The purchaser will be concerned that it may overlook something disclosed in one area eg details of a property transaction, which has implications in respect of other matters such as tax. The seller's view will be that having put the purchaser on notice of a set of circumstances the seller should not be prejudiced simply because of a failure to disclose those circumstances against all warranties where they could be applicable. Generally, the purchaser will accept that, provided the seller makes a genuine attempt to cross-refer to a particular disclosure in all places where it could be relevant, the disclosure is valid against all warranties. A clause which can be inserted in the disclosure letter may be worded as follows:

> 'For convenience, disclosures have been made against particular paragraphs of the schedules to the Agreement but any matter, whether disclosed generally or by reference to a particular paragraph number is disclosed for the purpose of all the warranties which will be qualified accordingly.'

The general disclosures referred to are matters such as the information in the agreement, in the target company's statutory books and accounts which may otherwise be relevant in places too numerous to mention specifically in the disclosure letter.

The *Scottish Power* case should not cause a problem in this regard. Provided the matter disclosed is identified in sufficient detail, it should not matter that it is disclosed against a number of warranties or indeed all of them. The question is whether the purchaser's mind has been directed towards the issue not whether the issue has been linked to any specific warranty.

Disclosure by reference to documents

8.4.2.5 The Purchaser should reject disclosures which do not attempt to give any explanation of the risk but merely refer to a bundle of documents. The purchaser should insist that the seller gives a detailed explanation of the issues albeit that cross-references are made to bundles of documents. Without a narrative there is an undue onus on the purchaser to evaluate a risk, which may be impossible without a full background of the target company's and the seller's affairs. It is not always easy to determine why a particular scheme works simply by looking at the documents which brought it into effect. In addition, there is the question of whether or not in the light of the *Levison v Farin* case (see para [8.4.2.1] above) it can be said that such documents disclose a quantifiable assessment of the liability or merely provide the means by which the purchaser can work out certain facts and conclusions. Further, to the extent that such documents mislead the purchaser *FSA 1986 s 47* might be in point (see [8.5] below).

Disclosing the accountants due diligence report

8.4.2.6 Occasionally, the seller will seek to disclose the accountants' due diligence report. The purchaser should object to this on a number of grounds. First, the seller will probably not know what the report contains and it is difficult to see how the seller can limit exposure by reference to unknown facts. Second, the accountants will have prepared the report specifically for the purchaser and will have sought to restrict those who can rely on it. Third, the information will have come from the seller and the seller's advisers so in theory the seller has the power to specifically disclose all information given to the purchaser's accountants. Finally, the purchaser's accountants may not have been able to verify all the information given to them. Some of the information may be inaccurate and the absurd position would result whereby the seller was in breach of warranty because of an inaccurate statement of which the seller was unaware but which had been disclosed to the purchaser. If statements in the report are inaccurate the seller may expose themselves to liability under *FSA 1986 s 47* without their knowledge.

One reason often put by the seller's adviser as to why the accountant's report ought to be disclosed is that it would be unfair to sell the shares and then for the purchaser to immediately be able to sue the seller. The fallacy behind this argument is that it supposes that the purchaser would prefer to go through the hassle of making a claim under the warranties and possibly having that claim restricted due to financial limits in the agreement rather than raise the issue and seek a full reduction in the price or back out of the deal altogether.

Requirements of the Financial Services Act 1986

8.5 From the seller's point of view it is important to bear in mind the provisions of *FSA 1986 s 47*. This provides that:

'Any person who:

(a) makes a statement, promise or forecast which he knows to be misleading, false or deceptive or dishonestly conceals any material facts; or

(b) recklessly makes (dishonestly or otherwise) a statement, promise or forecast which is misleading, false or deceptive,

is guilty of an offence if he makes the statement, promise or forecast or conceals the facts for the purpose of inducing, or is reckless as to whether it may induce, another person (whether or not the person to whom the statement, promise or forecast is made or from whom the facts are concealed) to enter or offer to enter into, or refrain from entering or offering to enter into, an investment agreement or to exercise, or refrain from exercising, any rights conferred by an investment.'

Section 47(6) states:

'A person guilty of an offence under this section shall be liable:

(a) on conviction on indictment, to imprisonment for a term not exceeding seven years or a fine or to both;

(b) on summary conviction, to imprisonment for a term not exceeding six months or to a fine not exceeding the statutory maximum or both.'

It seems clear that the wording of the section is wide enough to apply to sales of shares in a private company. The effect of this is that the seller must think hard before giving a warranty which it then fails to disclose against, or makes a disclosure which is misleading or inaccurate. A deliberate failure to disclose may mean that the seller faces not only a claim for damages for breach of warranty but also the threat of criminal action.

Professional advisers should also note that should they be aware of pertinent facts and do not give advice in connection with an inaccurate or misleading disclosure, with the result that a criminal offence is committed, they could be regarded as forming part of a conspiracy to commit such an offence. The extent to which this theoretical risk is a practical consideration is uncertain. However, a well-advised seller must now think much more carefully about disclosure than was thought to be necessary in the past.

The status of the disclosure letter — legal professional privilege

8.6 The disclosure letter is addressed to the solicitor's of the purchaser and is from the seller's solicitors, the reason for this is thought to be so that it attracts legal professional privilege. It is becoming increasingly common for inspectors of taxes to ask for the documentation created during the acquisition of a company. If the Inspector were entitled to the disclosure letter it would provide the

Inspector with knowledge of all the areas which the parties to the transaction considered to be liable to attack by the Inland Revenue. If an Inspector does seek a copy of the disclosure letter it is usual to reply that the information is privileged and this is usually sufficient to halt the enquiry.

Timing of disclosures

8.7 A frequently encountered problem is that disclosures are made late in a transaction. Where disclosures are made late, there is no reason why the purchaser should accept that they limit the seller's liability under the warranties, particularly where the facts and the law applicable to those facts are complex and there is limited time to consider them. In practice, in the case of tax the problem is not as acute as in other areas because generally, irrespective of disclosure, the risk will be covered by the tax deed.

Purchaser's actions in the light of disclosures

8.8 The Purchaser must first consider whether to ask the seller for further and better particulars of the matters disclosed. Having obtained a full disclosure, particularly in respect of tax avoidance schemes where the applicable law may be uncertain, the purchaser should consider what further enquiries should be made on their own account. In particular, if the matters appear to be material, the purchaser may wish to ask their tax advisers to evaluate them, determine the risk of an assessment being raised and the size of the potential tax charge. Having obtained a full evaluation of the disclosure, the purchaser may wish to seek a reduction of the purchase price or in extreme cases withdraw from the transaction altogether. Another course of action may simply be to seek a specific indemnity in the tax deed and exclude such specific indemnity from the usual financial limits on claims.

When evaluating the disclosures the purchaser must be particularly aware of those matters disclosed which may give rise to future problems but which are not capable of being the subject of a claim under the warranties or tax deed. If, for example, the target comprises a group of companies, a warranty may be given that no transfers had been made under *s 171* of the *TCGA 1992* with the result that there will be no tax charge on the disposal of the target group to the purchaser under *s 179* of that Act. However, the purchaser must realise that if details of such *s 171* disposals are disclosed then, although there may be no immediate charge because of the exclusion from *s 179* contained in *s 178(2)*, a charge may arise if the purchaser disposes of members of the group in future. Since a tax charge will arise from post-completion actions of the purchasers outside the ordinary course of business, it would not normally be caught by the tax deed; similarly, a claim under the warranties would be precluded by the disclosure. If the purchaser was intending to break up the group following acquisition, the disclosure of *s 171* transfers would clearly be material to future plans.

Chapter 9

The Conduct of Pre-Completion Tax Affairs and Completion Balance Sheets

Introduction

9.1 Generally, when the shares in the target company are sold, the purchaser assumes full responsibility for all the outstanding tax affairs of the company, subject to the seller's rights under the tax deed to conduct any dispute which could give rise to a claim. However, it is also common, particularly in the case of sales of subsidiaries by large groups of companies, for the seller to take responsibility for the routine tax administration up to the end of the last accounting period prior to completion. It is unusual for the seller to take responsibility for the period from the last accounting date up to completion but sometimes it does happen, particularly where completion takes place close to the end of an accounting period.

The purchaser will have to decide to what extent the introduction of pay and file and in some cases (for larger companies) the quarterly system of accounting for corporation tax will influence its decision on whether it wants conduct of pre-completion tax affairs. Arguably, it should make little difference. Although tax is effectively self-assessed and in some cases paid quarterly on account, the target company will still have to prepare tax computations, calculate its tax liability and make all relevant elections and claims. As in the past, the purchaser will be anxious to ensure that this computation and associated matters are dealt with correctly. Under the quarterly system, interest and penalties can become payable on mainstream corporation tax much earlier than in the past. The period of grace, formerly between the end of the accounting period and the due date for payment of tax nine months later during which the company could sort its tax affairs out, has been eroded. For companies subject to the quarterly pay and file regime with its penalties and interest for under declared tax and for companies accounting for tax, dealing with the tax affairs accurately and quickly will be much more critical. Thus, arguably the purchaser will have a greater need to ensure that the tax affairs of the company are dealt with quickly and efficiently if interest and possible penalties for late payment of tax are to be avoided.

The abolition of advance corporation tax ('ACT') and the introduction of the shadow ACT regime poses some new issues for a purchaser. The seller's need to control the surrender of pre-completion advance corporation tax will disappear to be replaced with a potential ability to allocate surplus shadow ACT in the pre-completion period. A purchaser at arm's length will want to ensure that the conduct of pre-completion tax affairs does not allow the seller to surrender unwanted shadow ACT surplus to the target, which the purchaser will then inherit. Such an inheritance could inhibit the purchaser's group's ability to use its own carry forward ACT surplus.

The clauses dealing with pre-completion tax affairs may be included in the sale and purchase agreement but it is becoming increasingly common to find them included in the tax deed. The reason for this is that as a practical matter it is better to include all the clauses that need to be discussed between the respective parties' tax advisers in the document for which they are primarily responsible.

Circumstances where the seller wishes to retain control

9.2 There are a number of circumstances in which the seller would wish to retain control of the company's tax affairs.

Extracting losses in a target company by a group

9.2.1 In a group situation, the seller may wish to extract losses from the target company either by surrender to the seller or another member of the seller's group. Ideally, a seller will have made the necessary surrenders prior to completion, but in practice this may not be possible, either because the target company's losses or because the remaining group's ability to accept the surrender has not been finally determined. Consequently, the seller will wish to have the ability to extract losses after completion in respect of the pre-completion period for the benefit of the seller's group and will want expressly to reserve power for this to be done.

Surplus losses or ACT surrendered to a target company

9.2.2 The seller's group may have a surplus of losses or for accounting periods ended before 6 April 1999, advance corporation tax which it wishes to surrender to the target company. In doing this the seller would wish to ensure that, to the extent that the target company had made a provision for corporation tax in the accounts, the surrendering group (the seller) is paid for its advance corporation tax or losses which eliminates the tax liabilities for which provision was made in the target company's accounts. The seller is then able to obtain immediately a cash payment for losses or advance corporation tax which would otherwise remain unutilised.

Following the introduction of the shadow ACT regime, the seller may want to allocate shadow ACT to the target. As this will restrict the target's ability to use any surplus ACT carried forward from earlier periods, the purchaser may want to restrict the conduct of tax affairs clause so that when the seller/parent has a discretion over the allocation of surplus shadow ACT, that discretion is not exercised so as to allocate the surplus to the target company.

Subject to the concerns set out later in this chapter and provided the clause is properly drafted, a surrender of losses to the target company should leave the purchaser in no better or worse position than it would have been had such a surrender not been made. To the extent that tax is provided for in the accounts, the purchaser would usually expect to pay the Inland Revenue with no recourse under the tax deed, as the tax deed would normally exclude claims for tax liabilities provided for in the accounts. Thus, the purchaser pays to the seller an amount for the losses (or advance corporation tax), which represents the money which it would otherwise have paid the Inland Revenue, if the seller had not surrendered losses (or advance corporation tax) and a tax liability would arise in the target company. The purchaser must ensure that the seller can only be paid for losses (or ACT) in circumstances where the purchaser would otherwise have to bear the cost, eg where there is a provision in the accounts, and not in the circumstances where the seller would otherwise be subject to a claim under the tax deed.

An incorrectly drafted clause could result in the seller surrendering losses (or advance corporation tax) to avoid a tax liability which would otherwise have given rise to a claim under the tax deed and in doing so becoming entitled to receive a payment from the purchaser.

Tax planning giving rise to problems after acquisition

9.2.3 Often large groups may have been involved in tax planning and in transactions within the group which should not give rise to tax problems provided that the issues are properly explained to the Inland Revenue. The seller may be concerned that the purchaser, without the detailed knowledge of the transactions that took place prior to completion, may present a less than accurate picture to the Inland Revenue. Although the seller has the protection afforded by the conduct clause in the tax deed, the seller will only be able to assume responsibility for a tax matter under such a clause once it has become contentious. A properly drafted conduct clause in the agreement will enable the seller to handle matters before such a stage is reached.

Meddling in pre-completion tax affairs by the purchaser

9.2.4 If valuable surrenders of group relief or advance corporation tax have been made then the seller will wish to ensure that the purchaser does not meddle in the pre-completion tax affairs, eg by disclaiming capital allowances which could reduce the losses available for surrender, in such a way as to adversely affect the pre-completion period.

A seller in administrative receivership after surrendering losses

9.3 The purchaser should be very wary of the terms for payment. In recent years problems have arisen, especially in the case of MBO's, where the purchaser has procured that the target company pays for losses at completion and subsequently the seller has gone into administrative receivership, without the necessary consents for the surrender of these losses having been signed and submitted to the Inland Revenue. The losses, being assets of the seller, will usually be covered by the floating charge under which the administrative receiver was appointed. Administrative receivers are, subject to certain exceptions, able to break pre-receivership contracts which means they can surrender the losses elsewhere or even offer to sell them to the target company again ignoring any suggestion to surrender losses under the sale contract. The purchaser, having paid for something it has not received, is left in the unfortunate position of being an unsecured creditor in any subsequent liquidation. Further, as a surrender of losses is only a matter of set-off in the tax computations of the relevant companies, it would follow that the target company gains no proprietary right in the losses under the contract and therefore it is thought that an action for specific performance would fail. A claim for damages for breach of contract against a company in receivership would just give rise to an unsecured claim and is generally pointless.

In the case of *Charterhouse Investment Trust Ltd and others v Tempest Diesels Ltd* [1986] BCLC 1 specific performance was given for the surrender of losses. However, the case was about financial assistance under what is now *s 151* of the *Companies Act 1985* and the order for specific performance was granted with the consent of both parties. The moral is that the purchaser should only agree to the target company paying for losses as and when a final assessment is issued to the target company showing that the surrender has been effected. The submission of the consents is not enough if there are insufficient losses to cover the profits of the various group subsidiaries unless the target company is guaranteed priority.

The attitude of a seller to conduct clauses

9.4 The seller will usually take the view that as the purchaser is fully indemnified under the tax deed against pre-completion tax liabilities, the purchaser should have no objection to the seller conducting the tax affairs relating to the pre-completion period, in which the purchaser has little vested interest. Apart from the reasons for retaining conduct mentioned above, the seller may be concerned that if the purchaser has control of pre-completion tax affairs, the outcome of which is of little concern to the purchaser, there will be too little time and effort spent by the purchaser ensuring that issues which could result in a liability for the seller are avoided.

The attitude of a purchaser to conduct clauses

9.5 The purchaser's attitude will usually be that, having purchased the company, it does not want the seller and its advisers to have the ability to control pre-completion tax affairs. Such control may interfere with the future relations with the target company's Inspector of Taxes or a tax treatment may be agreed which has an adverse effect in future accounting periods. Further, the target company's staff will have to spend time providing information to the seller although as such time would have to be spent assisting the purchaser's tax advisers if the purchaser has conduct, this argument is a weak one.

The purchaser may be concerned that, if the seller is not up-to-date with tax affairs at completion, matters may become worse once the company has been sold. The purchaser does not wish to find that it is unable to settle the target company's post-completion tax affairs because the seller is slow to agreeing pre-completion tax matters.

A purchaser's attitude to post-completion surrenders by a seller

9.6 Notwithstanding the purchaser's general objections to the seller having conduct of the pre-completion tax affairs of the target company, it may have particular objections to any clause giving the seller the ability to make allocations of surplus shadow advance corporation tax or surrenders of advance corporation tax, or losses by way of group relief, in respect of pre-completion periods after the sale of the target company. The purchaser may reject any such clause altogether or insist that the seller's right to make such surrenders is deferred to the purchaser's prior right to any carry back of the target company's post-completion losses (or surplus advance corporation tax) to the pre-completion period under *ICTA 1988 s 393A* (or *s 239*). The purchaser may adopt this posture for a number of reasons.

Provision for pre-completion tax

9.6.1 To the extent that there is a provision for pre-completion tax in the accounts of the target company, generally the purchaser would prefer to retain the value of such provision in the target company by carrying back losses (or advance corporation tax) than see cash being paid to the seller for surrenders by the seller to the target company.

Tax liability not provided for

9.6.2 To the extent that pre-completion tax is not provided for, a claim would generally arise under the tax deed. In such circumstances one option is simply to allow the seller to avoid a claim under the tax deed by surrendering losses or advance corporation tax (free of cost to the purchaser) so preventing any liability which could give rise to a claim arising. Conversely, the purchaser may wish to insert provisions in the tax deed which enable it to avoid the liability by carrying back losses or advance corporation tax under *ICTA 1988 s 393A* or *s 239*. In such cases the purchaser would expect to be paid the same amount by the seller for the losses or advance corporation tax carried back as would, in the absence of such carry back, have been paid by the seller to satisfy the claim under the tax deed. In other words, it makes little difference to the seller whether it pays the purchaser to settle a claim arising from a pre-completion tax liability or whether it pays an identical amount where no liability arises because the target company carries back losses or advance corporation tax.

Surplus shadow ACT

9.6.3 The purchaser will not want the seller to allocate surplus shadow ACT to the target which may inhibit the future recovery of carry forward surplus ACT.

The seller's objection to clauses preventing carry back of losses etc

9.7 A seller would normally object to any attempt by the purchaser to insert a clause in the tax deed which would prevent losses being carried back where such a carry back has priority over the seller's own surrender of losses or advance corporation tax. The seller's view would be that the purpose of the tax deed is to prevent the value of the target company's shares being diminished by an unforeseen tax liability and that such a purpose is satisfied by the seller making surrenders to avoid a liability that would otherwise arise in the target company. The seller would argue that if the purchaser inserts such a clause, the tax deed would operate to convert the post-completion losses of the target company into cash, which is not its purpose. The seller would normally have no objection to the purchaser carrying back post-completion losses or advance corporation tax and the purchaser being paid for them when the carry back discharges pre-completion liabilities in circumstances where:

(a) the seller is unable to avoid a liability by making use of group relief or surrenders of advance corporation tax; and

(b) a claim under the tax deed would arise in the absence of a carry back by the purchaser.

In such circumstances, a reasonable seller would probably take the view that it makes little difference whether or not it pays the purchaser a fixed sum under the tax deed to discharge a liability for tax or whether it pays the same amount to the purchaser under the tax deed in respect of post-completion losses or advance corporation tax carried back to prevent the liability arising.

Routine pre-completion tax affairs clause

9.8 The extent to which a seller should have control of routine pre-completion tax affairs under the agreement can be as fiercely negotiated as the conduct clause in the indemnity. It is hard to give guidance on the extent to which the purchaser should agree to the seller's request as much depends upon the circumstances of each individual case. The purchaser will clearly wish the seller to demonstrate that there are good reasons for retaining control of the tax affairs of the target company, that the target's tax affairs have been handled efficiently in the past, that tax matters are reasonably up to date and non-contentious and that the seller is likely to obtain good advice through a combination of in-house advisers and outside lawyers and/or accountants.

Conduct clauses

9.9 The types of clauses which might be sought by the seller and purchaser are dealt with below.

PAYE and VAT

9.9.1 PAYE and VAT affairs are frequently dealt with within the target company and the seller has little knowledge of them. In addition, periodic audits may satisfy the seller that there is little tax risk to it in these matters but potentially a cost in the form of administrative time. For these reasons, the conduct of pre-completion VAT and PAYE affairs is frequently passed onto the purchaser even where the seller retains conduct of corporation tax affairs.

Conduct between the last accounts date and completion

9.9.2 As the seller is not generally liable for tax between the last accounting date and completion (other than that on matters outside the ordinary course of business) in the absence of unusual circumstances, such as a pre-sale reorganisation, it will not particularly want the expense and difficulty of retaining conduct for this period. Where the seller wishes to retain conduct in this period it is particularly difficult to negotiate the relevant clauses. The purchaser will be liable for the target's tax on business in the ordinary course prior to completion and for corporation tax generally from completion to the end of the accounting period and it will be reluctant to hand over such conduct to the seller. If it agrees to do so the purchaser will need to impose rigorous safeguards.

Seller's tax conduct clause

9.9.3 The clause below assumes the seller wishes to retain conduct of corporation tax matters up to the last accounts date but reserves the right to surrender group relief from such date to completion.

> 'The Seller and the Purchaser have agreed that subject to the following provisions of this Clause:
>
> (1) As regards all accounting periods ended on or before Completion (the **"relevant accounting periods"**) the Seller shall have a sole conduct of the tax affairs of the Company and the Purchaser shall procure that the Company shall make such claims (including, but not limited to, claiming or disclaiming capital allowances and claiming roll-over relief) and shall execute those documents (including but not limited to returns of profits and losses and amended returns) and do those things in connection therewith as the Seller shall direct in writing and shall provide such information and assistance (including assistance from employees of the Company or the Purchaser) and access to such documents and records of or relating to the Company as the Seller may reasonably require in connection therewith.
>
> (2) The Seller shall have the sole conduct of the PAYE and VAT affairs of the Company in respect of all periods ended prior to Completion in respect of which VAT returns and PAYE returns need to be made; and
>
> (3) The Seller shall (to the extent permitted by law) be free to make claims and obtain consents for the surrender of losses or other amounts eligible for relief ("Group relief") between the Company and [the Remaining Group] or [the Seller] for the period between the Accounting Date and Completion.'

Purchaser's provisos

9.9.3.1 In response to this clause the purchaser may try to add a proviso to the end of the clause worded as set out below:

> 'Provided that the Seller shall first submit all accounts and tax computations before submission to the Inland Revenue, Customs & Excise or other appropriate authority to the Purchaser which may make such representations to the Seller as the Purchaser may think necessary and the Seller shall take account of all such reasonable representations provided always that any reasonable costs incurred by the Company or the Purchaser in connection with the matters specified in this clause shall be paid by the Seller.'

The purchaser may go even further and say that before submitting any papers to the taxing authorities the seller must first obtain its consent which is not to be unreasonably withheld. The seller is likely to resist such a request strongly on the basis that there is no point having the expense and bother of dealing with routine tax affairs if the seller is deprived of the discretion on how to deal with them.

The seller may counter by simply offering the provision set out below:

> 'The seller shall keep the Purchaser informed of the progress of the tax affairs of the Company and shall provide copies of correspondence.'

A seller may take the view that the purchaser's costs for helping to complete tax formalities should be minimal. The seller may expect the purchaser to bear such costs, which are likely to be in-house costs, on the basis that in the absence of the conduct of tax affairs clause in the agreement, the purchaser would not only have to bear considerably greater in-house costs but also the costs of audit fees etc.

Time limits in a conduct clause

9.10 The purchaser may be concerned to ensure that if the seller is to have conduct of routine tax affairs, these activities are brought to a conclusion reasonably swiftly. For this purpose a time limit may be imposed. To this end the purchaser may seek to introduce the provision set out below into any conduct clause:

> 'The seller shall settle the tax affairs of the company as soon as reasonably practical and in any event within the time limits prescribed by the Pay and File Regime [within such time limits as shall enable the company to pay quarterly payments of corporation tax based on a full and accurate calculation of the relevant liabilities].
>
> Notwithstanding anything in this clause [ ] neither the Purchaser nor the Company shall be required to provide any co-operation or execute any document or do anything in connection with the tax affairs of the company after the [ ] anniversary of the date hereof after which time all conduct of the tax affairs of the Company shall become the sole responsibility of the Purchaser.'

The problem that any sort of time limit creates for the seller is that delays may be caused by circumstances beyond its control. For example, it would be particularly unfair if the time limit expired before matters could be concluded due to the company's failure to provide prompt co-operation or due to delay on the part of the Inland Revenue or other taxing authority. The other point the seller should be aware of is that in no circumstances should a time limit imposed in the agreement expire before the statutory time limits for surrendering losses etc. A seller may, however, be prepared to agree a final date provided this is sufficiently far ahead for it to be satisfied that it will be able to conclude matters and extract losses and make surrenders of advance corporation tax. The danger arises where, for example, an Inspector of Taxes makes a 'discovery' in respect of a pre-completion period and allows by concession a late surrender of losses to meet that liability which cannot be taken advantage of due to the time limit imposed in the conduct clause. However, in such situations a discovery of this type may give rise to a liability under the tax deed and in many cases the losses or ACT may be surrendered under the mitigation clause in any event.

Seller's clauses to enable them to make surrenders etc

9.11 The seller should try to insert clauses to ensure that the necessary surrenders can be made in respect of losses and advance corporation tax, that they will not be prevented from so doing by the purchaser after completion and that the requisite provisions are made for payment. Examples of such clauses are as set out below:

> 'The Company shall forthwith upon request from the Seller make such claims and elections and give such consents including such provisional and final claims to accept the surrender of group relief or consents to the surrender of group relief in respect of any of the relevant accounting periods and in respect of the period between the Accounting Date and Completion as the Seller may in its absolute discretion direct in writing including any direction to comply with all the procedural requirements of *chapter IV* of *pt X* and *Sch 17A* of the *ICTA 1988* imposed on a claimant or surrendering company in relation to group relief including the notification of consent to surrender.'

In cases where losses are to be surrendered by way of group relief in the period between the date of the last audited accounts and completion a clause is needed to determine the profits of the target for the period in the absence of audited accounts to completion. A typical clause might be:

> 'Where the seller wishes to make a claim for group relief in respect of the period between the Accounting Date and Completion the losses or profits in respect of which such claim is made shall be based

upon the audited profit and loss account for the period of the company in which Completion takes place on the assumption that profits or losses arose rateably throughout such accounting period.'

This wording merely mirrors the procedure laid down by statute which provides that profits and losses shall be treated as accruing rateably unless it appears that it would give an unjust or unreasonable result. In such circumstances the purchaser may object to the above wording in any event.

The alternative to an apportionment, which theoretically is more desirable but in practice causes accountants and auditors immense problems, is to try and obtain the auditors' agreement to produce a certificate of losses at the specified date which was the date when arrangements came into force. Most auditors would naturally be reluctant to agree to this but if the target has a reasonably sophisticated management accounting system then such a task may be feasible.

Surrender of ACT and surplus shadow ACT

9.12 An example of a set-off or surrender of ACT clause where appropriate would be:

'The Company shall forthwith make such provisional or final claims for set-off or to accept the surrender of advance corporation tax in respect of the accounting periods ending prior to Completion as the Seller may in its absolute discretion direct in writing including any direction to comply with the procedural requirements of *s 240* of *ICTA 1988* imposed upon a subsidiary in relation to advance corporation tax including the notification of a consent under *sub-s (6)* of that section.'

Following the introduction of the shadow ACT regime the seller may wish to insert the following clause:

'The seller or any member of the Remaining Group shall be entitled in its absolute discretion to allocate surplus shadow advance corporation tax to the Company for all periods prior to completion in accordance with the provisions of the *Corporation Tax (Treatment of Unrelieved Surplus Advance Corporation Tax) Regulations 1988*.'

At the very least a purchaser may want to restrict this discretion to allocations which it is aware of by adding the proviso:

'PROVIDED THAT such allocations shall not exceed the surrenders disclosed in paragraph [ ] of the disclosure letter.'

The seller may respond that the precise figures required by such proviso cannot be given until the tax computations for the group are finalised. A possible compromise is to provide that the surrendered shadow ACT 'shall not exceed £[ ]'.

Given that the allocation of surplus shadow ACT is always going to be disadvantageous the purchaser may want to prohibit any further allocations, save where the regulations compel it by adding the clause:

> 'No allocation of surplus shadow advance corporation tax shall be made to the Company at the direction or discretion of the Seller and the Seller shall exercise such discretion to allocate to other members of the Remaining Group in priority to the Company.'

A number of points need to be made in respect of the above clause:

(a) Only the 'parent' (defined in the Regulations as the ultimate parent) of a group can allocate so the clause assumes that the seller is the parent;

(b) if the seller fails to allocate the Inland Revenue will allocate which may involve an allocation of the Company. To avoid this the purchaser will want to put the seller under a contractual obligation to make an allocation (other than to the company); and

(c) under the Regulations, as they stand at the time of writing, to the extent that the seller and other members of the remaining group do not have the capacity to absorb surplus shadow ACT within the group it will have to be allocated to the company for the period when it was a group member.

Pre-sale actions

9.13 An example of a clause preventing actions which prejudice pre-sale allowances or reliefs is:

> 'X.1 save as directed by the seller in writing from time to time, the Company shall not do nor will omit to do any act or thing;
>
> X.1.1 which might affect the ability of the Company to make claims for allowances or reliefs or claims to accept surrenders of group relief or ACT or to set off ACT or to consent to surrenders of group relief or ACT in respect of the relevant periods; or
>
> X.1.2 which would result in any reduction in the amount of group relief or ACT which otherwise could be surrendered by or to the Company or set off by the Company; and

X.2 the Company will not (unless so directed by the amend, withdraw or disclaim any elections or claims previously made including but not limited to elections or claims under *s 247* of the *Taxes Act 1988* (group income), *s 402* of the *Taxes Act 1988* (group relief), *s 240* of the *Taxes Act 1988* (setting of a company's surplus ACT against a subsidiary's liability) nor will the company amend or withdraw any elections or claims pursuant to *ss 152* or *153* of the *TCGA 1992* (roll-over relief) or disclaim first year or writing down allowances nor will the Company carry back ACT or losses from accounting periods ended after Completion in circumstances where such carry back will reduce the Company's ability to make the surrenders, claims and elections previously mentioned.'

Protection for purchaser

9.14 One of the purchaser's objections to the above clause is that it should only extend to claims and elections taken into account when setting the provision for tax in the accounts, by reference to which the Company was purchased. If, for example, capital allowances were disclaimed by the target and this was reflected in the audited accounts, the purchaser will have assumed that those allowances would be available in post-sale accounting periods. The purchaser will not want to find that when an unexpected tax liability crystallises of the type caught by the tax deed the seller simply claims allowances with the result that the liability is extinguished but the purchaser is deprived of the future use of allowances.

The purchaser may also complain that it cannot be expected not to interfere with reliefs and claims unless it knows what they are.

To address both the above concerns the purchaser will seek to restrict the clause only to those matters found in the accounts or in the disclosure letter.

The purchaser may also argue that any action in respect of tax that the target company takes 'might' affect its ability to make claims. To address this concern the purchaser may insist that the wording is changed to read that it shall not do anything 'which on the basis of the information provided by the seller in the disclosure letter makes it reasonably foreseeable that the ability of the company to make claims for allowances or reliefs . . . is likely to be materially adversely affected'.

The purchaser may also wish to add a provision to make it quite clear that it would be unreasonable for the seller to withhold consent to a carry back of advance corporation tax or losses where such carry-back would not deprive the seller of the ability to make its own surrenders of advance corporation tax or losses.

Payments for surrenders

9.15 The seller will wish to provide that to the extent that losses are extracted from the company being sold, it need not make payment for such losses. A suitable clause is set out below:

> 'If group relief is surrendered under sub-clause [ ] to a member of [the Remaining Group] by the Company no member of [the Remaining Group] shall be liable to pay any consideration to the relevant Company or the Purchaser.'

Where losses or advance corporation tax are surrendered by the seller's group to the target company, the seller will want to ensure that the purchaser must pay for such losses or advance corporation tax up to the value of any provisions in the accounts ie the purchaser pays the seller for losses or advance corporation tax rather than paying the taxing authority. The purchaser will want to make it quite clear that in no circumstances can any surrender of losses or advance corporation tax to the company result in a payment to the seller where in the absence of any such surrender the purchaser would have a claim under the tax deed or warranties. If the purchaser fails to do this it may, for example, find itself paying, say, £100,000 for losses where it would otherwise expect to receive £100,000 to settle a claim under the tax deed which would have arisen had losses not been surrendered. Clauses to cover these concerns are set out below:

> 'If the Company accepts a surrender of group relief in respect of any of the relevant accounting periods which can be used against an actual liability to corporation tax, for which provision has been made in the Accounts (and in respect of which no claim could arise under Clause [ ] of the Deed in the absence of such surrender), the Company will make payment to the Company making surrender of such an amount as the Seller may direct in writing but not exceeding the tax which would have been payable but for the surrender, payment to be made on the date or dates on which the tax would otherwise have been payable (assuming no application for postponement of payment of the tax had been made).'

> 'If under sub-clause [ ] ACT has been or is surrendered or set-off against an actual corporation tax liability for which provision was made in the Accounts (and in respect of which no claim could arise under clause [ ] of the Tax Deed in the absence of such surrender) the Purchaser shall procure that the Company shall pay to the surrendering company on the date of surrender or, if later, the date on which the corporation tax against which the ACT has been set would have been payable (assuming no application for postpone-

> ment of payment of the tax had been made) such an amount as the Seller may direct in writing but not exceeding the tax which would have been payable but for such surrender or set-off.'

The purchasers may also wish to insert a provision to ensure that no payment need be made for losses or ACT until the Inland Revenue has irrevocably indicated that it accepts that the surrender is valid to prevent, *inter alia,* the risk mentioned in para [9.3] above of an Administrative Receiver overturning an agreement for a surrender. To the extent that payment has to be made, the seller will normally seek to include a provision charging interest at a punitive rate in the event of late payment. An appropriate clause is:

> 'If any payment due to be made to a member of [the Remaining Group] in respect of a surrender or set-off of group relief or ACT is not made on the date for payment specified above the same shall carry interest from that date until actual payment at the rate of [ ]% above the base rate for the time being of [ ] Bank plc.'

Conduct of tax affairs where the purchaser takes control

9.16 As stated above, traditionally the conduct of tax affairs on the sale of a private company's shares is taken over from the date of completion by the purchaser. However, even where the seller is not sufficiently concerned to wish to retain full control of the pre-completion tax affairs of the target company, it may still wish to have some degree of involvement in the handling of the target company's tax affairs up to the date of completion. The seller will want to ensure it is not exposed to potential claims under the tax deed or tax warranties due to the way in which such tax affairs are conducted by the purchaser after the sale.

It is arguable that in most cases tax liabilities caused by the purchaser's handling of the pre-completion tax affairs cannot be the subject of a claim under the tax deed due to the provisions which exclude liabilities caused by voluntary acts by the purchaser after completion. However, there will still be circumstances where liabilities arise which are not caught by such exclusion. For example, a transaction may have occurred before completion which, if carefully explained the Inland Revenue, would not be regarded as giving rise to a tax liability. The purchaser's handling of the matter could be so poor that the Inland Revenue can raise an assessment, which whilst avoidable, is difficult to appeal against once raised. In such circumstances the purchaser would have strong arguments that the tax liability can only have arisen from the pre-completion transaction and not from their handling or voluntary acts after completion.

Because of the above factors, the purchaser may assume conduct but the seller will try and retain a degree of involvement. A suitable clause is set out below:

> 'As from Completion the Purchaser hereby agrees to take full responsibility for all outstanding tax affairs of the Company and will prepare all outstanding tax computations and returns, shall submit such computations and returns to the appropriate taxing authorities whether in the UK or elsewhere and deal with all negotiations, correspondence and agreements with respect thereto.
>
> The Purchaser agrees and will procure that the Company agrees that they will not submit any tax computations or returns in respect of the pre completion period without affording the Seller a reasonable opportunity to consider such computations, returns and make representations prior to submission to the taxing authority.'

More elaborate clauses can be used but it is generally thought that where the seller is not sufficiently concerned to retain conduct of the target company's pre-completion tax affairs, its level of concern will not justify a clause setting out detailed obligations requiring a greater degree of involvement.

Completion balance sheets and post-completion balance sheets by reference to which the purchase price is adjusted

9.17 Increasingly, transactions take place where accounts are prepared as at the completion date and the sale and purchase agreement provides that there will be an adjustment to the purchase price paid according to the deficit or surplus of the net asset value in such accounts below or above a specified figure. This type of transaction is commonly called a 'completion balance sheet deal'. Furthermore, it is not unusual to see earn-outs where the seller may receive additional consideration where there is a surplus or have part of the consideration clawed back if the profitability of the company shown in the audited accounts for specified post-completion accounting periods of the target company does not reach a pre-determined figure. In these circumstances, it is clearly desirable for both the seller and the purchaser to ensure that the accounts accurately reflect the financial position of the company at the relevant date.

Different accounting policies used by outgoing and incoming accountants

9.18 The fact that the accounts of the target company will be audited by chartered accountants largely eliminates the risk of deliberate manipulation of the figures. However, it is nevertheless possible that the incoming accountants may introduce new accounting policies quite legitimately. For example, the purchaser may alter the target's policies in order to obtain conformity with those adopted within the rest of the purchaser's group. This may result in variation of the figures in those accounts from those figures that would have been produced had pre-completion accounting practices continued to be applied to the target company. Furthermore, because the interests of the seller and purchaser are opposed, the seller will wish to see a high net asset figure in order to increase the purchase price, whereas the purchaser will want a low figure to depress the price. Consequently, this area is a fertile ground for disputes. For this reason it is becoming increasingly common to see clauses specifying the criteria that accountants should use when preparing accounts for a target company. In this way the room for divergence of opinion is reduced. It is also recommended that a clause containing a timetable for the preparation and agreement of such accounts should be included. Such a clause will prevent undue delay and must provide sanctions against a party who proves tardy in producing or commenting on the accounts.

Consistent policies to be adopted

9.18.1 The most important principle is that the accounts should be prepared on a basis which is consistent with that adopted when the accounts were prepared in the past. Clearly, close liaison with both the purchaser's and the seller's accountants is necessary when preparing such a clause. The preamble of such a clause could be worded as follows:

> 'The Completion Accounts will be prepared by the Purchaser under [the historical cost convention (as modified for the revaluation of land and buildings)] and in accordance with generally accepted accounting principles and practices in the United Kingdom and, subject to the foregoing, on a basis consistent with those used in preparing the Accounts in the three accounting periods ended [ ].'

The adviser should also consider how intangibles such as goodwill should be treated (especially after the introduction of FRS 10), the policy on deferred tax etc.

The content of the remainder of the clause will be determined by the particular circumstances of the transaction. However, as stated above it is important to include a provision to enable the seller's accountants to have access to the draft accounts and supporting papers and to afford them the opportunity of making representations. Such a clause will normally provide for a referral to a third firm of accountants for determination of any point that cannot be agreed between the accountants of the purchaser and the seller within a fixed time.

Stock valuation disputes

9.18.2 It is also fairly common where there is any adjustment of consideration by reference to set assets to include a clause which specifies in some detail a method for valuation of stock. It is generally accepted that the agreement of stock values, where such values are material and influence the price of shares, provides fertile grounds for dispute. Strict instructions should be set out in the agreement to avoid difficulties. Such a clause could, for example, specify that stock will be revalued at completion by the company's managing director for inclusion in the completion accounts. The principles upon which such valuation will be conducted will depend upon the shelf life of the stock, the marketability of old stock etc. The type of clause that could be used is set out below:

'(a) All stock more than [ ] months old shall be treated as worthless [unless and to the extent that evidence can be produced of an actual pending sale of such stock].

(b) All stock more than [ ] months but less than [ ] months old will be discounted by 50%.

(c) Subject to (d) below stock less than [ ] months old shall be valued at net cost which is the actual cost taking into account all trade discounts etc.

(d) Stock used for display or samples shall be valued as in (a)–(c) less [%].'

The clause should provide for the seller's accountants to audit the figures with any dispute being subject to referral to independent accountants.

A suitable clause is set out below:

'(1) Once completed the stock valuation shall forthwith be sent in draft to the Purchaser whereupon if the value of the stock is not agreed in writing between the Seller and the Purchaser within 28 days the valuations in dispute shall be determined by:

  (a) such firms of chartered accountants as the parties may agree in writing; or

  (b) failing agreement on the identity of the firm of chartered accountants within a further 14 days from the expiry of the period of 28 days referred to above, such firm of chartered accountants may be appointed for this purpose on the application of either party to this agreement to the President for the time being of the Institute of Chartered Accountants of England and Wales.

(2) the accountant appointed under the above clause [ ] should act on the following basis:

(a) the accountants will act as experts and not as arbitrators;

(b) the terms of reference should be to determine the value of only the items referred to them as being in dispute;

(c) the seller and the purchaser each agree to provide the accountants with all information which they reasonably request;

(d) the determination of the valuation of stock shall, in the absence of a manifest error be conclusive and binding on the parties; and

(e) the fees of the accountants shall [be borne equally by the Seller and the Purchaser] or [shall if the accountants confirm the Seller's accountants' audited figure without any material adjustment (and in this context a material adjustment shall be [£]) be borne by the Purchaser but if there is a material adjustment then such expenses shall be borne by the Seller].'

Chapter 10

Deferred Tax

Introduction

10.1 When negotiating a tax deed and tax warranties on the sale of a company's shares, there are few subjects which cause such genuine difficulty and upon which such a wide spectrum of views are expressed as deferred tax. The key issue is the extent to which a provision for deferred tax in the accounts upon which the sale is based should limit liability in the same way as a specific provision for tax liabilities. Before addressing this practical issue one must first examine the nature of deferred tax and how it is treated in a company's accounts.

From the description that follows it will become clear that the rules laid down by SSAP15 (Accounting for deferred tax) are more in the nature of guidelines than a precise methodology for dealing with deferred tax issues. Consequently, there is a very large subjective element in the analysis involved in determining the correct accounting treatment for deferred tax items. Whilst many areas of accountancy are equally subjective, such as the valuation of stock, deferred tax requires a multiplicity of subjective views to be taken on numerous issues and numerous individual items. The auditor must decide the basis on which the provision will be made (full provision method, partial provision method etc) which tax rates to be applied when looking at numerous individual items, such as unrealised capital gains, and make a subjective judgment on whether such gains will crystallise and when and if so whether relief or roll-over will be available. This myriad of judgment issues inevitably leads to people forming their own legitimate but different views which in turn can lead to practical difficulties when those conflicting views arise on opposite sides in a negotiation. The problem is compounded by the fact that even when the treatment of deferred taxes is agreed, the provision can contain a number of greatly disparate elements. Some, such as an impending crystallisation of a held over gain being very similar to actual crystallised tax liabilities, others, such as uncrystallised capital gains in revalued fixed assets, being much more hypothetical requiring the assumption of a disposal, no roll-over etc. Arguably, such disparate items should be regarded differently in the context of a sale negotiation.

It is widely anticipated following a lengthy debate started by the publication of Accounting Standards Board Bulletin 57 in March 1995 that a new Financial Reporting Exposure Draft on deferred tax will be published in 1999.

What is deferred tax?

10.2 The profits shown in a company's audited accounts are not the profits upon which tax is based. The causes of the discrepancy between accounting profit and taxable profit fall into two main categories:

Fixed, permanent discrepancies ('permanent differences')

10.2.1 Permanent differences are those differences between accounting profits and taxable profits which are fixed and unalterable. If, for example, a company makes sales of £10m which cost £8m and included in that cost is £200,000 of disallowable entertainment expenditure, the accounting profit will be £2m but the taxable profit will be £2.2m. In the tax computation the disallowable element of expenditure will have to be added back. Permanent differences such as these are not the subject of a deferred tax provision but explain why a company's effective rate of tax can be higher or lower than the prevailing mainstream corporation tax rate.

Temporary discrepancies ('timing differences')

10.2.2 Some items are included in a company's accounts before they have any impact upon the tax position of that company. By way of illustration: assume that in the year 2001 company A borrows money from company B which is resident in Holland. Interest is to be paid 14 months following the end of the accounting period in which the loan is made. In the year in which the loan is made, company A makes an accounting profit of £100m, ignoring the interest costs on the loan, which when deducted on an accruals basis leaves a net accounting profit of £99m. However, because the interest is not brought into account for UK tax purposes by company B (because it is based outside the United Kingdom) and because company A will not pay the interest within twelve months of the date upon which it accrued, no tax deduction will be available until the interest is actually paid [*FA 1996 Sch 9 para 2*]. Thus, assuming no permanent difference and a 30% corporation tax rate, on pre-tax accounting profit of £99m there will be a corporation tax charge of £30m as the disallowed interest accrual of £1m will be added back to the accounting profit to give a taxable profit of £100m. However, this discrepancy between the accounting profit and the taxable profit, is temporary. When the interest is subsequently paid, company A will be able to claim the interest payment as a tax deduction. In recognition of this timing difference it is permissible to set up a deferred tax asset of £300,000 (ie 30% of the future interest payment of £1m) in the accounts to reflect the future tax deduction that will be available. This results in an overall tax charge for the year of

£29.7m ie £30m corporation tax charge less the deferred tax credit of £300,000 which equates to a tax charge of 30%.

There are a number of common types of temporary timing differences dealt with in deferred tax adjustments.

Capital allowances v accounting depreciation

10.2.2.1 Typically, assets are depreciated for accounting purposes at different rates than the rate at which capital allowances become available. For example, Company A buys an item of plant and machinery, which for commercial and accounting purposes it depreciates on a straight line basis over four years at 25% pa. Thus, in year one the accounting depreciation and capital allowances match and there is no impact on deferred tax and therefore, assuming no other adjustments, accounting profits and taxable profits will be equal and there are no deferred tax consequences at this stage. However, by the end of year two the accounts show that the asset is depreciated to 50% of its original acquisition cost whereas for capital allowance purposes the asset has only been written down to 56.25%. In year two the accounting profits will be lower than the taxable profits (reflecting the higher accounting depreciation charge compared to capital allowances) and in such circumstances a deferred tax asset can be set up to reflect the additional allowances of 6.25% which will become available. A deferred tax adjustment is calculated in respect of such timing differences by comparing the accounting net book value of an asset to its tax written down value. To the extent that the accounting net book value exceeds the tax written value there will be a deferred tax provision and if vice versa there will be a deferred tax asset.

Pension contributions

10.2.2.2 When a company pays contributions to its employees' pension fund, it obtains a tax deduction on the basis of monies paid. However, the accounting profits reflect the prospective payments on an accruals basis. Thus, at the end of a particular year a company may have reduced its accounting profits by reference to accrued pension contributions and yet it only obtains the tax deduction the following year when the contribution is actually paid. This situation can be reflected by establishing a deferred tax asset to reflect the future tax deduction.

Interest

10.2.2.3 Following the introduction of the loan relationship provisions, loan interest is generally deductible on an accruals basis thus mirroring the accounting treatment. Consequently, this category is not as important as it once was. However, as illustrated above there will be exceptions to the general rule.

Advance Corporation Tax ('ACT')

10.2.2.4 ACT will become considerably less important after 6 April 1999 following its abolition. However, at the time of writing it is not clear how precisely the abolition of ACT where there is surplus ACT carry forward will impact upon the provision for deferred tax.

When advance corporation tax is paid it is first treated as an asset for accounting purposes if it can be used in the period either by set off against mainstream corporation tax or by carry back. However, where it cannot be recovered immediately (either in the year in which it is paid or by carry back) the tax benefit (a carry forward credit) cannot be shown as a deferred tax asset as this requires one to anticipate future profits which is not permissible under UK GAPP. However, it can be offset against deferred tax liabilities to reduce the deferred tax provision. After this, any surplus may be reflected in the balance sheet as an asset if it is regarded as recoverable ACT (as determined in accordance with SSAP8). Broadly, if it is anticipated that the credit cannot be recovered in the next following accounting period the ACT may be treated as irrecoverable for accounting purposes even if for tax purposes it can be carried forward indefinitely. This results in the oddity of ACT credits for irrecoverable ACT being omitted from the accounts then reappearing as an asset, as if by magic, if the credits are subsequently used.

Losses

10.2.2.5 If a company makes a trading loss, that loss has potential value as it may result in a tax saving in a later period. SSAP15 provides that in the case of a trading loss provided that:

(a) such loss results from an identifiable non-recurring source;

(b) the company has been consistently profitable over a considerable period with any past losses being offset and included in later periods; and

(c) it is assured beyond reasonable doubt that the future taxable profits will be sufficient to enable the trading losses to be used;

the losses can be treated as recoverable and a deferred tax asset.

Capital losses can be regarded as recoverable and a deferred tax asset when:

(a) a potential chargeable gain is not expected to be covered by roll-over relief (and assets have not been revalued to reflect inbuilt gains);

(b) the enterprise has decided to dispose of assets and hence unlock gains;

(c) the unrealised gain is sufficient to absorb part of the loss such that it can be assured beyond reasonable doubt that the chargeable gain will be sheltered.

From the above it will be noted that in practice a deferred tax asset for a loss is likely to be hard to establish.

Revaluation of fixed assets

10.2.2.6 For example, a fixed asset is acquired for £100 and is then revalued in the accounts to, say, £200 and there is therefore a potential chargeable gain. Where it is probable that this liability will crystallise a deferred tax provision for the tax payable must be made based on the value at which the fixed asset is carried in the balance sheet compared to the tax base cost of the asset (allowing for indexation and roll-over relief etc). Where sometimes assets are not revalued in the balance sheet but the increased value is referred to in a note to the accounts that a note must also include details of the potential tax payable if the asset were disposed of at the noted value.

Roll-over relief must also be dealt with as this can defer the reversal of a timing difference by carrying forward the potential capital gains charge that would otherwise arise on the disposal of the assets at a future date. Where potential deferred tax following a roll-over is not disclosed SSAP15 requires the accounts to disclose the fact that the revaluation does not constitute a timing difference and tax has not been quantified as otherwise this would not be evidenced on the face of the accounts.

Basis of the deferred tax provision

10.3 SSAP15 requires simply that deferred tax should be accounted for to the extent that it is probable that a liability on an asset will crystallise. This therefore leaves a lot of discretion.

Some companies, particularly those who have a large international business and want to adopt uniform accounting standards throughout the group, adopt the 'full provision' (sometimes known as a comprehensive allocation) method laid down in International Accounting Standard 12 (revised). This is based on the principle that the financial statements for any particular period should recognise all tax effects irrespective of whether they are current or deferred in respect of all transactions occurring during that period. This approach enables a relatively precise mathematical calculation to be made (and, as will be discussed later, lends strength to the argument that a deferred tax provision should be treated no differently from any other tax provision) but this certainty can also be distorting. If, for example, there were large in-built gains in the fixed asset base, is it sensible to provide deferred tax against such gains when it is thought to be improbable either that the assets will be sold, or, if such assets were disposed of and a profit generated, such profits would be not rolled-over into the acquisition of a new replacement asset?

The extreme alternative to the full provision method, which also has the advantage of mathematical certainty, is the 'nil provision' or flow through basis of accounting which is based on the premise that one does not pay tax on accounting profits but on taxable profits and therefore one should restrict provisions to the tax bill that is actually and scientifically established for that accounting period. The argument is that any provision in respect of future events is speculative and therefore best ignored.

The halfway house and one of which is clearly favoured by SSAP15 as drafted but, in practice, is currently rejected by many companies is what is known as the 'partial provision' method. The partial provision method involves making a provision for deferred tax based on the net overall effect of timing differences which will crystallise in the foreseeable future. For example, if one were dealing with revalued fixed assets one may take the view that on a year by year basis only, say, 25% of them are disposed of and of that 25% all but 5% of the overall gain is rolled over or eliminated by reliefs. Therefore, based on this analysis, the probability is that only 5% of such gains will be chargeable to tax and needs to be provided for in the deferred tax provision.

Supporters of the partial provision method argue that it is the method most likely to ensure that the accounts give a true and fair view taking into account everything that has actually happened and is reasonably foreseeable. Its critics, which include the ASB, claim that it is too speculative and subjective and inconsistent with international practice. Those arguing that one should ignore deferred tax provisions when negotiating the disposal of a company find it much easier to do so when such a subjective and speculative approach is adopted in the company's accounts.

The current debate suggests an 'incremental liability' approach may be adopted, which is a watered down full provision method. If this approach is adopted, short-term timing differences such as accrual of a sum in one period which is paid in the next will be fully provided. Items such as revaluations will be provided only if the company is committed to sell the relevant asset in a way which would give rise to tax. Thus, for example, if on any sale the company was committed to roll over the gain, such roll-over would be taken into account.

Having ascertained the provision on this basis there would then be some sort of discounting to allow for the fact that there will be a delay prior to paying the tax.

If this incremental approach is adopted it will be far easier to treat a deferred tax provision and many of the current difficulties that it poses will disappear.

Methods of computation

10.4 Having ascertained that timing differences exist and decided upon a basis upon which the adjustments will be set: whether this means making a full provision, nil provision or partial provision, one then has to decide the tax rate which one will use. In other words, does one simply fix the tax rate at the time the timing difference originally arises and make no subsequent amendment in respect of fluctuations in the tax rate (the 'deferral method'). Alternatively, does one speculate on a scientific basis as to the rate at which tax will actually be paid when the timing difference is reversed? This latter approach is known as the 'liability method'. The liability method is the method required by SSAP15 but this approach again seems to undermine any argument that the deferred tax provision is any more than a speculative, subjective view of the future. However, in the current environment where announcements have been made that tax rates will remain fixed for the life of Parliament this position is not as speculative as it once was.

Practical presentation in the accounts

10.5 The deferred tax provision is shown separately from the transaction to which it relates ie there is no netting off resulting in the accounts just showing the net effect of the transaction. SSAP15 requires that the timing difference should be accounted for to the extent it is probable, based upon reasonable assumptions that a liability or an asset will crystallise.

SSAP15 leaves it open as to whether or not this is dealt with on the face of the profit and loss account or in a note to the profit and loss account. The deferred tax balance and its components should be disclosed either in the balance sheet itself or in the notes and any transfers into or out of deferred tax should also be disclosed in the note.

Should deferred tax be recognised in the tax deed and warranties?

10.6 The tax deed (and warranties) usually contain an exclusion for liabilities to the extent they are provided for in the accounts. The issue is whether or not similar exclusions should be allowed for provisions for deferred tax.

The key to answering the above question is the extent to which the deferred tax liabilities and provisions are taken into account when agreeing a purchase price.

If one accepts that a proportion of deferred tax liability was deducted from the net asset value when agreeing the purchase price it becomes arguable that the deferred tax provision should be recognised to some extent. If the provision is not recognised in the tax deed and warranty limitations it is arguable that the purchaser could benefit twice: once as a reduction in the purchase price and once through a claim under the tax deed.

However, this argument is based on a number of assumptions, notably:

(a) net asset value determined the purchase price;

(b) the deferred tax provision devalued the price on a £1 for £1 basis; and

(c) the purchaser fully evaluated the provision before makings its offer.

The first point to make is that under the current subjective regime in SSAP15 the purchaser would only be in a position to make a reasoned judgement in respect of the deferred tax if it had made a thorough investigation of its composition. For example, if a purchaser found that there were large gains held over into a depreciating asset which were to be unlocked shortly after the end of the tax year for which the accounts were prepared with no shelter, the purchaser would be justified in taking the view that such deferred tax liabilities were close to the equivalent of actual liabilities allowing for some delay until tax is actually paid (which would be limited once the quarterly system of accounting is introduced). In such a case the purchaser would probably reduce the purchase price. In such circumstances if a provision was made against such liabilities it would seem equally reasonable that the provision should be allowed.

One could contrast the above example with the position where the purchaser adopted a full provisioning method of dealing with deferred tax with the result that on the face of the accounts there are huge tax liabilities but in practice there was thought to be little or no prospect of such deferred tax crystallising in the foreseeable future. If a purchaser evaluated on this basis it is unlikely that any significant reduction in price would be made and consequently the provision for deferred tax should equally be ignored. What the above illustrates is that:

(a) depending on the composition of the deferred tax provision and the way in which it is set, the purchaser may take different views;

(b) without a detailed analysis, which would probably require looking at the accountant's working papers when setting the deferred tax provision it would be impossible for the purchaser to make a full scientific analysis of the provision and make a considered view of any discount it should make.

In the light of the way in which sale prices are generally arrived at, in the writers' opinion the general position in the past has been that no material allowance is made for the deferred tax when reaching a valuation. The process of determining the price in most sales is simply not precise enough and the information on deferred tax is generally not available to make a meaningful analysis and evaluation at the time the offer is made. Furthermore, even if such information were available, the likelihood is that on any reasonable basis the purchaser would reach a subjective judgment on the likelihood of deferred tax crystallising and on timing and discount the purchase price accordingly. Consequently, any resulting deduction that it decides to make from net assets will not only be highly subjective but is also unlikely to correspond precisely with the provision for deferred tax set in the accounts. In other words, allowing a full exclusion for deferred tax in the tax deed and warranties implies a corresponding full discount from the purchase price which is highly unlikely. Consequently, one has a potential friction between the seller, who wants a full credit for all deferred tax provisions, and the purchaser, who may have only allowed a small discount in respect of that provision from the net asset value. However, in the event that a more scientific approach, such as the 'incremental method' apparently favoured by the ASB is adopted, a well-advised purchaser should take account of the deferred tax provision and will be in a far better position to accept the provision for deferred tax without a detailed analysis of its composition as required at present as much of the subjective element will have been eliminated. Such a change in practice will greatly strengthen the seller's argument for recognition of the deferred tax position.

Market practice

10.7 The market practice is increasingly towards allowing a provision for deferred tax to limit liability. In the writer's opinion the position is far from clear cut although an allowance for a deferred tax provision should be made for items which are relatively clear and certain to limit liability in respect of those items. If SSAP15 is replaced with an incremental method or something comparable it seems likely that the market will move towards allowing for the full deferred tax provision when limiting a seller's liability.

Chapter 11

Indemnities and Warranties on a Flotation

Introduction

11.1 In order to bring its shares to the market, whether for a full listing on the Stock Exchange or for a listing on the Alternative Investment Market ('AIM') of the London Stock Exchange, a company will need to appoint sponsors. The sponsors to the issue will be members of the International Stock Exchange. The sponsors are responsible for guiding the company through the formalities that are necessary in order for a listing to be made.

The sponsors and their advisers will prepare the necessary documentation including the following:

(a) listing particulars;

(b) application forms on offers for sale;

(c) placing letters;

(d) letters of acceptance; and

(e) renounceable allotment letters in favour of selling shareholders together with nil paid provisional allotment letters in favour of the sponsors to such others as the sponsors may direct.

Depending on the size of the issue and the value of shares being sold, the shares may be marketed either by way of an offer for sale, which is broadly an open offer to members of the public, or by a placing whereby the sponsors, often acting together with a syndicate of other underwriters, will contact potential investors prior to the listing with a view to obtaining an agreement to purchase a specified number of shares at a pre-determined fixed price and allocating the shares before they come on to the market. The tax issues, unlike the regulatory position, are similar whether the listing is on the AIM or is a full listing and irrespective of whether the shares are marketed by way of an offer for sale or by way of a placing.

The seller, the sponsors, the directors of the company and sometimes the company itself will enter into an agreement, the offer for sale agreement or placing agreement, depending upon the method by which the company is to be brought to the market, which sets out the terms and conditions upon which the sponsors will back the issue. It will be necessary to determine the extent to which the sponsors should seek an indemnity and/or warranties from the seller of a shares issue in this agreement. The sponsors have an interest in ensuring that as much protection as possible is given in respect of tax liabilities arising prior to listing of the shares. Generally, the sponsors are also the underwriters and as such wish to ensure that there is no tax problem which may result in the shares being difficult to market. Alternatively, if the sponsors have to take some of the shares under the underwriting agreement, they will wish to ensure that they do not find themselves holding shares which are devalued due to tax liabilities not provided for in the last set of audited accounts.

In addition to commercial considerations the sponsors will wish to ensure that statutory obligations are met.

11.2 The legal, statutory and regulatory framework affecting tax

The Financial Services Act 1986

11.2.1 *Financial Services Act 1986 s 146* imposes upon the person responsible for listing particulars an obligation to ensure that in addition to information specified by listing rules, or required by the competent authority as a condition of admission of securities to the Official List, they contain all information that a prospective investor and professional advisers would need in order to make an informed assessment of the 'assets and liabilities, financial position, profits and losses, and prospects of the issuer of securities'.

FSA 1986 s 146(2) states that the information specified in *s 146(1)* shall be the information 'which is within the knowledge of any person responsible for the listing particulars or which it would be reasonable for him to obtain by making enquiries'. A person responsible, in addition to the company and its directors, can include the sponsors being a person under *s 152(1)* of the *Financial Services Act 1986* who has 'authorised the contents of, or any part of, the particulars'. The requirements of *FSA 1986 s 146* which apply to a full listing are mirrored by the *Public Offers of Securities Regulations 1995 (SI 1995/1537)* (*POS Regulations*) which apply to offers on AIM (see para 16.10 of the AIM admission rules). The wording in *reg 9* of the *POS Regulations* effectively mirrors the wording of *s 146*.

Sponsors who fail to provide the necessary information to a purchaser of the shares must pay compensation to those shareholders who can show that they have suffered loss as a result of any misleading or untrue statement. (*FSA 1986 s 151*).

From the above it will be seen that the sponsor and others responsible for listing particulars will want to ensure that they have made proper enquiry to satisfy their statutory obligations and that they have some protection if, having done so, there is still a claim by shareholders who feel they have been misled. Hence, the sponsors will use warranties as part of their enquiry process and will look to those existing owners benefiting from the flotation to indemnify them.

Common law remedies

11.2.2 If the sponsors can be shown to have been negligent they may be liable for the tort of negligence under the rule in *Hedley Byrne & Co Ltd v Heller & Partners Ltd* [1964] AC 465. Although establishing a breach of a duty of care would be difficult, there appears to be no technical reason preventing an investor pursuing the sponsors for a remedy under this doctrine if the sponsors failed to ensure that the investor was informed of a material tax liability of the target company.

The AIM admission, rules and the *Yellow Book*

11.2.3 Apart from a prospectus and/or listing particulars containing the information an investor needs (which will include tax information) pursuant to *FSA 1986 s 146* or para 16.10 of the AIM admission rules and *reg 9* of the *POS regulations,* the AIM admission rules and the *Yellow Book* require listing particulars to contain details of tax on income withheld at source from the listed securities including tax credits. The *Yellow Book* goes further and requires a statement whether the issuer assumes responsibility for any withholding of tax at source.

OFEX

11.2.4 The OFEX code of best practice states that companies and their advisers must be scrupulous in bringing out 'information which they consider is material to an analysis of the investment potential of the applicant'.

Apart from the need for indemnities and warranties to ensure compliance with the legal requirements mentioned above, the sponsors will require indemnities and warranties to ensure that they are protected commercially against unforeseen tax liabilities as well as to reduce the risk of their reputation being tarnished by bringing a company to the market which has undisclosed tax liabilities. The combined effect of the tax indemnity and warranties should reduce the risk of any material inaccuracy in the listing particulars. Furthermore, whilst the sponsors may remain primarily liable to the investors, they should be able to recover any sums awarded against them from the warrantors or parties to the tax deed.

Indemnification

11.3 Whether the sponsors obtain indemnification and if so how wide-ranging it is, depends upon the circumstances of each individual case. For example, sponsors acting for a few shareholders who control substantially all of a company's shares are more likely to obtain a tax indemnity than sponsors acting for a company with numerous small shareholders, where practical considerations may make it impossible to obtain any indemnity at all.

A full tax indemnity

11.3.1 Traditionally, sponsors would seek a comprehensive tax indemnity. Such an indemnity would broadly follow the type of indemnity given on a purchase of a private company's shares with some essential differences such as those listed below. It is now extremely rare, not to say unheard of, to encounter an indemnity against general tax liabilities. The increasingly competitive nature of the market has led to the market practice of seeking indemnities only against a narrow range of liabilities, if at all.

The effective date of the indemnity

11.3.2 On a sale of a private company's shares a tax deed will usually cover all liabilities of the company up to and including completion. On a flotation the tax deed will have to be entered into prior to listing, which is the date of admission of the shares of the company on to the official list of the International Stock Exchange or the AIM. Thus, the tax indemnity will usually cover the liabilities up to and including the first day of dealing on the exchange, which becomes the equivalent of completion in a private company sale. In addition, the tax deed is normally expressed to be conditional upon listing taking place so that the deed does not come into force in the event that the shares are not brought to the market eg if there is a market collapse and the seller decides to defer listing until market conditions are more favourable.

Parties

11.3.3 On a private company sale, the seller generally indemnifies the purchaser and more rarely the company. In the case of a flotation there will usually be too many purchasers of the shares for it to be practical for them to be adequately indemnified in the tax deed or to enable such shareholders to bring claims. It is common to find that on a flotation the seller indemnifies the sponsors and the company with the provision that the sponsors will pay any sums they receive to the company. Thus, although the sponsors can enforce the covenant they will effectively be doing so on behalf of the shareholders, as monies must always be paid over to the target company to increase the target company's net asset value, which would otherwise be diminished by the tax liability. One effect of this is that the risk of an indemnity payment being taxable in the hands of the company is greatly increased and sponsors usually insist on a gross-up clause being included in the tax deed.

Conduct of disputes

11.3.4 It is difficult to allow a seller to have the same degree of control over the conduct of any dispute with taxing authorities as is permitted in the case of a private company. A company in public ownership, where directors are answerable to shareholders and whose affairs may be publicised, is likely to find it undesirable to allow former controlling shareholders to interfere with the running of its tax affairs. Conversely, it is difficult to insist on the seller giving an indemnity if it has no say in the manner in which any dispute is dealt with. One often finds that whilst the tax deed may give the seller conduct of a tax dispute, there are severe limitations imposed upon it eg the company need not contest any claim where it may suffer a material disadvantage. The seller will find that many of the restraints which the purchaser seeks unsuccessfully to impose in the context of a private company acquisition prove difficult to resist in the context of an indemnity given on a share flotation.

Limitations

11.3.5 Most tax deeds given on the sale of a private company's shares contain time limits and maximum and minimum financial limits. It is usual in tax indemnities given in flotations to have no such limits. However, sometimes the indemnities are limited to the value of shares taken up at their value on the first day of listing.

A limited tax indemnity

11.3.6 The seller of shares will often argue that it should not be liable for tax to the extent to which it arises in the course of the company's trading activities. The seller can argue, with some justification, that investors in the open market must accept the adverse effects of such trading activities just as they expect to reap the rewards of the profits generated by such activities. The seller may accept that where it has manipulated the company's affairs for its own advantage it should indemnify the company but not otherwise. It is becoming increasingly common to see indemnities limited to such actions as an alternative to full indemnities.

In such tax deeds, in place of the usual clause giving blanket protection against all tax liabilities arising from transactions before a certain date, there are a series of specific indemnities.

An operative clause in a limited flotation indemnity may cover liabilities arising in the following circumstances:

'(a) in consequence of a seller or a person connected with the seller either having failed or failing to discharge when due any tax liability of his [in respect of any period ending on or before the Commencement of Dealings]; or

(b) in consequence of or in connection with a transaction or arrangement which the Company has entered into or enters into on or before the Commencement of Dealings with any person otherwise than by way of a bargain made at arm's length; or

(c) in consequence of or in connection with a transaction or arrangement which the Company has entered into or enters into on or before the Commencement of Dealings the main purpose (or one of the main purposes) of which is to provide any form of benefit to the seller or a person connected with the seller, including a benefit by avoiding, reducing or deferring any loss or liability (whether to tax or otherwise); or

(d) in respect of PAYE or National Insurance contributions which relate to a seller or a person connected with the seller and are referable to payments made, services rendered or any agreement or arrangement entered into on or before the Commencement of Dealings.'

Clause (a) above is designed to catch circumstances where the company may have a secondary liability to tax and where the primary liability is that of the seller. Sections such as *ICTA 1988 s 767A, s 767AA* and *TCGA 1992 s 190* means that this indemnity should not be restricted to matters occurring on or before the commencement of dealing.

An example of clause (b) above would be where a controlling shareholder procured the transfer of the company's assets to him at a value considerably less than open market value. This could give rise to a number of issues: open market value could be substituted under *TCGA 1992 ss 17* or *18* and the company could be taxed on a capital gain the proceeds of which it never receives. Alternatively, there could be a distribution to the extent of the difference between the market value of the asset and the sum received on its sale, on which the company has to pay advance corporation tax under *ICTA 1988 s 209(4)* (prior to 6 April 1999). If the shareholder is an employee there could be PAYE implications. Other examples of where clause (b) above may be applicable are the situations described in *TCGA 1992 s 282* which provides for the recovery of taxes from the beneficial owner and donee of a gift.

Clause (c) above is designed to catch schemes of tax avoidance by the seller whereby the company is used as part of a scheme to secure a tax benefit for the shareholders. For example, the company may have paid for living accommodation, servants etc for participators in a close company and as a result *ICTA 1988 s 418* could apply to deem a distribution to have been made. Another example, is the type of tax avoidance envisaged in *ICTA 1988 s 703.*

Probably the most common example of the risk covered by clause (d) above is where shareholders provide services to the company purporting to be self-employed consultants whereas in fact they are employees. The result of any such ruling by the Inland Revenue or Department of Social Security could be a liability on the company for employers' National Insurance contributions and, if the employee failed to discharge its own tax, income tax and national insurance for these liabilities, which should have been deducted under the PAYE system.

Warranties

11.4 In addition to obtaining a tax indemnity, the sponsors will generally seek some basic tax warranties. The purpose of the warranties is to elicit any information which may be material to the sponsors' obligations. The warranties also provide a mechanism for recovery in place of the indemnity. The warranties are usually general in scope and limited in number and may run as follows:

'1 The Accounts of the Company were prepared in accordance with generally accepted accounting principles and provide fully for all tax liabilities at the Accounts Date.

2 Since the Accounts Date, the Company has not incurred any material tax liability otherwise than as a result of carrying out its trade in the ordinary course.

3 The Company has paid all tax which it has become obliged to pay.

4 The Company has not been involved in any material dispute with any tax authority nor so far as the Directors and the Seller are aware is there any material risk that such a dispute will arise.'

Apart from warranties on the standing of the company, when shares are placed the sponsor will also seek a warranty from the placees confirming that they are only liable to stamp duty reserve tax at 0.5%.

When shares are placed they will generally fall into two principal categories: first those shares allotted direct to the placees and second those allotted to the existing owners and renounced in favour of placees. As regards the first category of shareholding, no stamp duty or stamp duty reserve tax ramifications arise as there is no transfer of securities. As regards the second category, although shares will be issued direct to the renouncee, there will be stamp duty reserve tax to pay on the renouncement by the original owner/allottee in favour of such renouncee. In effect there is a transfer of a chargeable security. Clearly the shares must be fungible. For example, A and B each successfully apply for £600,000 £1 shares for which they each pay £1m. It would be unacceptable for A to receive an allotment direct from the company and have no liability to stamp duties and for B, who would expect to be in the same position, to receive shares following a renouncement and to be liable for duty of £5,000 (0.5% × £1m). To ensure equality of treatment the owner of the company agrees as part of his contractual arrangements with the sponsor to fund the stamp duty and SDRT costs of persons in B's position. The sponsor then pays the duty on behalf of B. However, the owner will generally limit the amount paid to duty at 0.5% per £100 or part thereof and will not agree to pay the duty of any renouncee/placee liable to duty at the higher rate of 1.5% per £100 or part thereof applicable to certain categories of placees, such as those providing clearance services.

The sponsor will then seek a promise from all selling shareholders to pay all stamp duties and will seek a warranty from placees confirming that they are not persons subject to the higher rate of charge. These principles are broadly applicable for dealings within CREST.

The sponsor (and/or underwriter) will also seek a covenant to pay any other incidental costs of placing the shares. This covenant often includes a phrase to the effect that the shareholders/company whose shares are placed will covenant to pay the sponsor such costs and VAT in respect of such costs. Whilst many supplies made will be exempt or, if standard rated, will be made in respect of an exempt supply (thus rendering the VAT irrecoverable and an absolute cost) in some cases the VAT may be recovered. Therefore the covenantor will want to ensure that the indemnity/covenant only applies to 'irrecoverable VAT'.

Chapter 12

Indemnities and Warranties in Special Situations

Introduction

12.1 Although the most usual indemnity met in practice is that given on the sale and purchase of a private company, there are numerous other situations where an indemnity or an undertaking to make good a loss is given. This chapter deals with some of the more common situations.

Banking — loan documents

12.2 Most bank loans are based on the premise that a lending bank will receive interest (or other return, such as a premium on redemption) free from any withholding or deduction of tax at source or any other taxation (other than tax on its overall profits). To ensure that this is the case, it is usual for the lender to insert a clause in the loan documentation, known as a gross-up clause, which provides that payments of interest on a loan will be made by the borrower free and clear of any deductions or withholding in respect of taxation. In the event that such a withholding or deduction is imposed by law or otherwise, the lender will expect to be paid such additional amounts as will result in it receiving an amount (net of all deductions) equal to the amount it would have received had the original payments been made gross.

In order to get the funds, the borrower will have to agree to include a gross-up clause in the loan agreement, as its inclusion is generally accepted market practice and it would be very unusual for a lending bank to proceed without one. However, the borrower can reasonably expect to impose certain limitations.

Borrower's position

12.2.1 The borrower's position should be that a gross-up clause is intended to protect the lending bank against the unexpected, for example, the imposition of a deduction of tax as a result of a change in law. It is not expected to operate immediately to cover withholding tax issues current at the date of the draw-down of the loan. Thus, the borrower will want to ensure that the status of the lending bank is such that at the outset it can be paid free from deduction or withholding.

The borrower will expect the lending banks to confirm that they can be paid gross either because they can benefit from the exemptions for certain banks and financial institutions in *s 349, ICTA 1988,* or, alternatively, because the obligation to deduct tax is eliminated by the terms of an applicable double tax treaty. If a lending bank cannot give such confirmations it should not benefit from a gross-up.

The borrower will also wish to ensure that if an obligation to deduct or withhold arises following the loan advance as a result of voluntary actions of a lending bank, for example, switching the facility office from a London branch to a branch based in a tax haven (with no double tax treaty relief) the consequences of such actions should be borne by the lender and not passed on to the borrower.

Loan covenants

12.2.2 Another aspect of the loan documentation relevant to the tax adviser is the loan covenants. This aspect is frequently overlooked as (beyond a representation from the lending banks confirming their status) the covenants rarely contain provisions which deal directly with tax matters and in consequence tend to be dealt with exclusively by those advising on the commercial banking aspects of the transaction. Generally, this does not cause any issues but the tax adviser should review the covenants to ensure that they will not restrict routine tax planning. For example, it is common for large groups to routinely route the sale of capital assets through a capital loss company within the group. However, it is not uncommon to find blanket restrictive covenants which inhibit the free movement of charged assets, notwithstanding that the companies which are party to the intra group transfer are subject to the lending banks' charge.

The tax adviser should also check any provisions dealing with assignment (or novation) of the loan to ensure that if the assignee is able to step into the shoes of the assignor, it can only rely on the gross-up provisions to the extent that at the date of the assignment no deduction or withholding arises. For example, X plc borrows money from USA Bank to which payments can be paid gross under the terms of the US/UK double tax treaty. USA Bank assigns to Tax Haven Bank Ltd with the result that no treaty relief is available and X Plc must deduct tax. In such circumstances X Plc would expect no gross-up to apply as the problem arose immediately as a result of the assignment. If however, USA Bank assigned to another bank based in a jurisdiction with a double tax treaty which eliminated the need to deduct, one would expect the assignee to benefit from the gross-up clause.

In summary, whilst the tax advisers reviewing the loan documentation should review the entire loan, he or she should concentrate particularly on three key areas:

(a) the gross-up clause;

(b) the clauses dealing with assignment and novation; and

(c) the loan covenants, particularly those imposing restrictions on the movement of assets.

Example of gross-up clause

12.2.3 An example of a typical gross-up clause is set out below:

> 'All payments to be made by a Borrower to any person under the [Finance Documents] shall be made free and clear of and without deduction or withholding from or on account of Tax unless the Borrower concerned is required by law to make payment subject to the deduction or withholding of tax (or if any Agent is required by law to make payment to a Bank subject to the deduction or withholding of Tax) in which case the Borrower concerned shall promptly upon becoming aware thereof notify the [Agent] thereof and the Borrower shall pay at the same time as the payment in respect of which the deduction or withholding is required to be made is due such additional amounts as may be necessary to ensure that the person concerned receives and retains (free from any liability in respect of any deduction or withholding including withholding or deduction in respect of additional amounts and from any other liability other than Tax on its overall net income) a net amount equal to the full amount it would have received and retained had no such deduction or withholding been made.'

Tax on overall net income is usually defined as tax on normal trading profits. The reference to an 'Agent' is to catch those situations where a person, usually a lending bank, acts on behalf of other lenders in collecting interest. Alternatively, it can catch paying agents acting on behalf of the borrower. It is necessary to ensure that the status of the agent is such that no deduction issues arise ie generally that it is a recognised UK Bank.

Indemnity

12.2.4 The basic gross-up clause above will cover only the position where the person making the payment is obliged to deduct or withhold tax at source with the result that the recipient receives the payment net of taxes. A bank will generally look for an indemnity to cover the possibility that a payment may be received free of deduction or withholding at source but in respect of which a liability to tax arises (other than tax on trading profits). Under current UK law, whilst there may be an obligation upon any UK borrower to deduct tax when making a payment, no secondary or other liability can arise on the lending bank and the indemnity is regarded very much as a safety net.

However, it may be that borrowers or recipients are resident in jurisdictions other than the UK, or due to some other unforeseeable circumstance, a charge arises and therefore an indemnity is required. Such an indemnity is set out below:

> 'Without prejudice to the provisions of the clause at [ ] if a Bank or Agent on its behalf is required by law to make any payment on account of tax (other than tax on its overall net income) on or in relation to any sum received or receivable under the [Finance Documents] by such Bank or Agent on its behalf (including any sum received or receivable under this clause), or any liability in respect of such payment is asserted, imposed, levied or assessed against such person or the Agent on its behalf, the Borrower will upon demand by the Bank or Agent, promptly indemnify the Bank or Agent (as appropriate) against any such payment or liability, together with any interest, penalties and expenses payable or incurred in connection therewith.'

Tax receipt

12.2.5 Most banks will expect a borrower, when deducting tax, to provide a tax receipt confirming that tax has been deducted and paid to the appropriate Tax Authority. One reason for this is the concern that a bank has a potential secondary liability for tax not deducted or paid to any appropriate Tax Authority (under current UK law this is not relevant). However, the main reason for giving a tax receipt is to enable a recipient bank to claim a tax credit in respect of the tax deducted from the payment made to it. A borrower might question why a bank which has received the full amount due should, in addition, be able to claim the benefit of a tax credit. The effect of this could leave the bank in a better position than it would have been in had no deduction or withholding been made from the payment. However, the banks will often hold out the prospect of some repayment to the borrower in the event that they receive a tax credit. In addition, market practice will usually dictate that such a clause is required to be given.

It should be noted that there may be practical difficulties in obtaining a credit if, notwithstanding the issue of a certificate of tax deduction, tax has not been paid to the Inland Revenue. However, on the authority of *Stokes v Bennett (Inspector of Taxes)* 34 TC 337 no such difficulties should, in law, arise.

The form such a clause relating to a tax receipt can take is usually similar to that set out below:

> 'If any Borrower makes any payment under a [Finance Document] in respect of which it is required to make any deduction or withholding, it shall pay the full amount to the relevant taxation or other

authority within the time allowed for payment under applicable law and shall deliver to the Agent for each of the persons with whose account such payment was made, [within 30 days] [as soon as reasonably practical] after it was made, an original tax receipt or certified copy thereof) issued by that authority evidencing receipt by that authority of all amounts required to be deducted or withheld in respect of that person's share of the payment.'

Two points should be noted in respect of the tax receipt clause. First, a 30 day time limit may not be appropriate. If, for example, the loan is made to a group of companies, some may be resident in jurisdictions outside the UK where tax authorities do not have any time limits for providing receipts. In such cases the alternative wording in parenthesis should be used. Further, the borrower's adviser should ensure that receipts are issued in the relevant jurisdiction. If they are not, the best that can be offered is a confirmation that the payment was made, possibly backed up with a copy of the relevant return. Secondly, if there is more than one lender, it is clearly impossible to supply an original receipt for each lender hence the words in parenthesis restricting the obligation to the supply of a certified copy of the receipt.

Limitations

12.2.6 The gross-up clause and tax receipts clause are inserted for the benefit of the bank. Having inserted these clauses, the borrower will normally insist on a number of limitations being imposed. The main limitation agreed between a borrower and a bank is what is commonly known as the 'qualifying bank' limitation.

The obligation to deduct tax at the basic rate from annual interest under *ICTA 1988 s 349* is excluded under *s 349(3)(a)* where the Borrower makes a payment of interest in the UK to a UK bank which brings such payment into account for corporation tax purposes. Where the loan agreement is entered into on this basis, the borrower will seek a clause which provides that the gross-up will not apply where it is required to make a deduction simply because the bank is not, or ceases to be recognised as, a qualifying institution for the purposes of *s 349* or because it does not bring payments into account for the purposes of UK corporation tax.

A typical form of qualifying bank limitation is:

'If any Bank is not or ceased to be a Qualifying Bank then it shall promptly notify the relevant Borrower upon becoming aware of the same and the relevant Borrower shall not be liable to pay to such bank under clause [gross-up clause number] any amount in excess of the amount it would have been obliged to pay if such Bank was or had not ceased to be a Qualifying Bank Provided that this clause

[ ] shall not apply (and the relevant Borrower shall be obliged to comply with its obligation under clause [gross-up clause number]) if after the date hereof there shall have been any change in, or in the interpretation or application of, any relevant law, directive, treaty (including without limitation, any applicable double tax treaty) or regulation or practice of the United Kingdom or any other applicable taxation authority and as a result thereof the relevant Bank ceases to be a Qualifying Bank or the relevant Borrower would be required to make a deduction or withholding on account of tax irrespective of whether the recipient of the relevant payment is or is not a Qualifying Bank.'

A Qualifying Bank is broadly any bank to which, under current law, interest can be paid free from deduction or withholding. In the case of a loan between a UK resident bank and a UK resident borrower, a 'Qualifying Bank' can be restricted to those banks whose status eliminates the need to deduct tax by virtue of *ICTA 1988 s 349*. In some cases the banking syndicate will include non-resident banks which do not lend out of a UK Branch but which, nevertheless, can avoid any deduction or withholding under the terms of a double tax treaty. In such cases the definition of a Qualifying Bank can be extended to catch such banks. The borrower should only agree to this extension if the relevant treaty fairly eliminates entirely the obligation to deduct eg Art 11 of the US/UK double tax treaty.

The definition of a 'Qualifying Bank' and other relevant definitions are as follows:

' "Qualifying Bank" means an institution which for the time being is:

(a) A *s 349* Bank and satisfies the *s 349* Interest Requirement with respect to interest which is (or which, if it were a Bank, would be) payable to it hereunder; or

(b) a Double Tax Treaty Bank.

"Section 349 Bank" means a bank defined for the purposes of *ICTA 1988 s 349*.

"Section 349 Interest Requirements" means in relation to any Bank the requirement that such Bank is within the charge to United Kingdom corporation tax as respects interest payable hereunder at the time when such interest is paid.

"Double Tax Treaty Bank" means a bank or financial institution whose Facility Office is outside the United Kingdom and resident (as such term is defined in the appropriate double tax treaty) in a jurisdiction which has a double tax treaty with the United Kingdom under which the payment of interest by the Borrower to that Facility Office may be made without deduction or withholding of United Kingdom income tax.'

Two clear criteria must be met by the Bank to qualify for the relief given by *s 349(3)(a)*: first it must be an institution of a designated type and second, it must bring the interest into account for the purpose of UK corporation tax.

Section 349(3AA) defines a bank by reference to *ICTA 1988 s 840A* which specifies that a bank means:

'(a) the bank of England;

(b) an institution authorised under the *Banking Act 1987*;

(c) a relevant European Institution; or

(d) a relevant international organisation which is designated as a bank for the purposes of the provision by an order made by the Treasury.'

In practice, practitioners are only likely to encounter (b) or (c) the latter being defined in *s 840A(2)* as an institution authorised under the *Banking Co-ordination (Second Council Directive) Regulations 1992* which has complied with *Sch 2 para 1* in relation to establishing a branch. As the interest must also be brought into account for corporation tax, it means in effect the London branch of a European bank.

The significant aspect of the changes introduced in *s 349(3)(a)* by the *Finance Act 1996* is that it is no longer necessary when making payments to a bank to establish that the loan was made in the ordinary course of business, nor that the bank is recognised as a bank by the Inland Revenue as was formerly the case.

A UK bank will usually have no difficulty in accepting such a limitation where it is applicable, subject to the proviso (included in the above clause) that the gross-up shall not be excluded if such a bank ceases to be within the *s 349* exemption because of a change of law. In practice most banks will be aware of their status for the purposes of *s 349* and will be confident that nothing in their activities is likely to result in their ceasing to be such a bank during the currency of the loan.

Limitations — formalities

12.2.7 Although the gross-up clause does not entitle a non-UK resident bank to the gross-up unless it is entitled to full relief under a double tax treaty, the borrower will still require the bank to complete the necessary formalities. The borrower can quite reasonably take the view that if deduction or withholding can be avoided under a treaty but relief is not given because the bank neglects or refuses to complete any necessary formalities, such bank should be excluded from the gross-up. It is difficult for the banks to resist such a request provided that the administrative burden is, as far as possible, borne by the borrower. It would be manifestly unfair if a bank wilfully failed to claim relief under an appropriate double taxation clause and as a result the borrower had to deduct tax and gross up its payment. The borrower will not unreasonably take the view that the bank must suffer the consequences of its failure. An example of a double tax formalities clause is:

> 'Upon being reasonably requested to do so by a relevant Borrower a relevant Bank shall complete any administrative formalities and documents necessary to enable the Borrower to apply under any relevant double tax treaty authority in accordance with such treaty not to deduct or withhold from any sum payable to the Bank [provided that if the Bank fails to comply with the reasonable request of the Borrower with the result that a deduction or withholding is required then Clause [ ] (gross-up) shall not apply to the extent that a deduction or withholding would not have been required had the Bank complied with such formalities and a successful application made under an appropriate double tax treaty].'

The borrower may seek to extend the drafting of the above clause to impose time limits on the bank for complying with any requests made by the borrower and giving greater emphasis on the need for the bank to co-operate.

Limitation — tax credits

12.2.8 In return for agreeing to provide the bank with the evidence it needs to claim a credit for the tax deducted (see para [12.2.5] above), a borrower will often insist that if the banks obtain the benefit of a tax credit, the value of that tax credit will be refunded to the borrower. In principle it is hard for the bank to resist this. For example, a bank expecting to receive gross interest of £100 receives that amount plus a certificate of deduction resulting from the fact that there has been a withholding and an additional payment under the gross-up clause. Upon reclaiming the benefit of the tax credit the bank is in a better position than that in which it would have been had the original payment not been subject to any withholding or deduction and been paid gross.

Care needs to be taken where the bank promises to repay the amount of any credit reclaimed. Arguably the amount of the credit and the amount of any gross-up is taxable income in the hands of the bank. An obligation to repay the amount of the credit should therefore be net of any tax accounted for by the bank as otherwise the bank will be out of pocket.

In practice, banks are very reluctant to agree to a request for such a clause, unless the clause has a very limited format. Potentially a bank could have many tax credits during the course of an accounting period and it would be totally impractical for it to have strict duties to a large number of borrowers to show them what has happened to a particular tax credit in respect of the payment made by them. In addition, if a bank is put under any obligation to prove to a borrower that the credit had not been used it would require it to divulge potentially sensitive information about its financial affairs, which no bank would permit.

In practice the type of clause that the borrower is able to agree with the bank is very limited indeed and can be worded as set out below:

> 'If any Borrower makes a payment under clause [ ] (gross-up) for the account of a relevant Bank and such Bank, in its sole opinion, determines that it has actually received a credit against or relief or remission for, or repayment of, any tax paid or payable by it in respect of or calculated with reference to the deduction or withholding giving rise to such payment, such Bank shall (to the extent that it can do so without prejudice to the retention of such relief, credit, remission or repayment and such Bank is not in its determination otherwise prejudiced) pay to the Borrower such amount as such person shall, in its sole opinion have determined to be attributable to such deduction or withholding. Nothing herein contained shall (i) interfere with the right of a Bank to arrange its tax affairs in whatever manner it thinks fit and, in particular without limitation, no Bank shall be under any obligation to claim credit, relief, remission or repayment from or against its corporate profits or similar tax liability in respect of the amounts of such deduction or withholding in priority to other claims, reliefs, credits or deductions available to it, or (ii) oblige any Bank to disclose any information relating to its tax affairs or computations in respect thereof.'

Whilst the above clause is not particularly satisfactory from the borrowers' point of view, it is likely to be the best that they will be able to secure. In effect, a clause of this type is little more than a 'moral obligation' on the bank to make a payment to a borrower in the event that it obtains use of a tax credit. It is difficult to imagine circumstances where a borrower may be in a position to enforce such a clause.

Often it is agreed that a double tax treaty will apply and that the bank will make application for the interest to be paid without any deduction or withholding under *s 349*. However, such an application may take a considerable time to be processed, during which time the first interest payment may have become due under the loan document. In order to cover this eventuality it may be agreed that, instead of a gross-up on such interest payments, the borrower will make an interest-free loan of the amount to be withheld, repayable as and when the bank receives a credit for it. Once permission is received payment will be made without any withholding. A more common solution is to defer payment of the first interest payment to a date when it is likely that the UK Financial

Intermediaries and Claims Office (International) (formerly the Inspector of Foreign Dividends) will have given permission to pay interest without deduction under a relevant double tax treaty.

Assignment

12.2.9 Banks generally require the loan documentation to give them the ability to assign their interests. From the tax standpoint, it is essential to ensure when acting for the borrower that the borrower cannot be prejudiced. If, for example, a clearing bank assigns to a bank based in a tax haven (where no *ICTA 1988 s 349* or double tax treaty relief is available), it is important to ensure that the assignee is excluded from the gross up. This can be achieved by defining a bank as not just the original lender but any lender from time to time and then ensuring that the gross-up applies only to Qualifying Banks (ie lenders entitled to be paid interest gross under a double tax treaty or under *s 349*). It is preferable to avoid any ambiguity by also including words in the assignment clause which make this absolutely clear.

Tax indemnities where there is a foreign resident target company

12.3 When the target company is resident outside the UK, the purchaser should, and generally will, seek tax advice in the jurisdiction in which the target company is resident. However, in some cases where a foreign company is a subsidiary of the target company which is resident in the UK, the UK tax adviser will be asked to include any tax liability of the foreign company in the tax indemnities and warranties prepared for the sale and purchase of the group as a whole. This is particularly likely when both the seller and the purchaser are UK-resident. Subject to sending the tax documents to tax advisers in the relevant jurisdiction, there is no reason in principle why the foreign company should not be dealt with by using a slightly modified tax deed and tax warranties.

The tax deed for a foreign company

12.3.1 The usual modern form of tax deed gives indemnification against tax arising from pre-completion events. Consequently, subject to some modification of the tax deed, eg to ensure the definition of taxation is not restricted to UK tax, the tax deed can be used both for UK and foreign companies. Tax warranties can be written in general form although it is especially important to take local tax advice in this area to ensure that risks peculiar to the jurisdiction are covered.

Definition of taxation

12.3.2 The first problem for the UK tax adviser wishing to adapt a standard UK tax deed to cover a foreign company is to ensure that the definition of tax is drafted widely enough to catch tax in the foreign jurisdiction. A usual definition of taxation defines taxation as:

> 'All forms of taxation, duties, imposts and levies whether of the United Kingdom or elsewhere including . . . corporation tax . . . .'

This is probably sufficient to cover foreign taxes. However, it is clearly desirable to ensure that the definition is more specific where possible. This can be done by adding names of particular foreign taxes to the list in the usual definition. Alternatively, particularly where there are companies in a group in a number of jurisdictions and references to taxes in those jurisdictions will make the list unmanageable, a more generalised section to deal with foreign taxes can be added to the definitions clause. For example, taxation can be defined as set out below:

> 'All forms of taxation, duties, imposts and levies of the United Kingdom, [France], [Japan], [Australia], or elsewhere including (but not limited to) income tax, corporation tax, advance corporation tax, capital gains tax, value added tax, customs and other import or export duties, stamp duty, stamp duty reserve tax, national insurance, social security or other similar contributions and trade taxes, franchise taxes, tax on gross income, profits or gains, taxes on sales, net worth, property, receipts, use, occupation, value added, capital gains, social security dues and any interest surcharge, penalty or fine in connection with any such tax.'

Currency problems

12.3.3 Financial limits where the main group company is UK resident would normally be expressed in sterling in the documentation, yet claims in respect of the foreign companies will arise from liabilities in a currency other than sterling. This could cause potential problems in determining whether the *de minimis* limits have been exceeded. For example, does a claim for a tax liability of 100,000 French Francs exceed a *de minimis* limit, for claims of £10,000? Due to the vagaries of the exchange rate it may be that if one took the exchange rate on the date of the deed such claim would exceed the *de minimis* limit, yet at the exchange rate prevailing at the time the claim is made it does not but then does at the date the claim is settled. The validity of a claim in such circumstances would be difficult to determine. To avoid dispute and uncertainty it is better to provide for a method of translating claims in foreign currencies into sterling. Thus, the tax deed could contain a clause as set out below:

> 'Where any amount in this deed is expressed in a particular currency and in a particular context another currency would be applicable the reference to such amount shall be deemed to be the amount translated into that other currency using the mid buy/sell spot price

in the London Market for that currency against sterling at the close of business on the date of the Agreement published in the relevant issue of the *Financial Times.*'

In the event that the United Kingdom becomes party to the Economic Monetary Union this issue will be eliminated in many cases.

Time limits

12.3.4 Time limits may also have to be revised to take into account limits in a foreign jurisdiction. For example, certain jurisdictions operate a system similar to the UK pay-and-file system. Under this system a company submits its tax computations together with a cheque for the tax due and is then subject to periodic audits which can either result in a clearance for the years since the last audit, or alternatively a demand for payment of additional tax together with interest and penalties. In such cases it may be appropriate to put in a time limit for claims for foreign companies linked to a periodic audit. Such a clause can be worded as set out below:

> 'No claim shall be made under this deed against the Seller for any tax liability arising in respect of an accounting period more than one year after the final (uncontested) assessment based on a tax audit covering such a period and for the purposes of this clause "final (uncontested) assessment" shall mean the final decision of the relevant authority either by agreement of the relevant tax or social security liability with the company or after all available appeals have been exhausted.'

The other question that sometimes arises is the extent to which provisions for taxation in different jurisdictions should be aggregated to determine whether or not there is an over-provision or a right to claim. There is an argument that where there is an over-provision in French Francs in a French company and a corresponding under-provision in sterling in a UK company the net value of the group is not diminished and no claim should be possible under the tax deed. The problems of deciding whether or not there are over- or under-provisions in various jurisdictions and their value against the base currency for the purposes of set-off against liabilities in other jurisdictions are immense and for purely practical reasons this approach for seeking set-offs is not to be recommended.

Tax warranties for a foreign company

12.4 The usual format for tax warranties is to ask specific questions related to sections in *TCGA 1992* and *ICTA 1988* or to tax case law. If UK warranties are adapted to cover a foreign company they must be more general and aimed at uncovering serious tax anomalies. The sort of warranties which can be used are set out in Appendix 3.

Indemnities in contracts for services

12.5 Often a party, which for convenience shall be called, 'an employer' may be uncertain whether or not the contract it offers a 'consultant' is a 'contract of service' or a 'contract for services'. If having proceeded on the basis that the contract offered is a 'contract for services', the employer may find that the arrangement is categorised by the Inland Revenue or Department of Social Security (soon to be a single agency in this respect) as an 'employment' with the result that the employer will have failed to have deducted income tax and national insurance under the pay-as-you-earn (PAYE) system and failed to account for the secondary (employer's) liability to national insurance. The purpose of the indemnity is therefore to ensure that the employer is as far as possible protected against such potential liabilities by a person who represented himself or herself as a self-employed consultant.

What is employment?

12.5.1 Even with the full knowledge of the facts and the relevant law, it can be difficult to determine whether an arrangement amounts to an employment or not. The fact that the contract describes itself as a contract for services and uses the appropriate language, eg a consultant, is paid a fee rather than a salary that the person does not affect the proper categorisation of the arrangement for tax purposes. The categorisation is based on the underlying facts. How those facts are labelled is irrelevant (*Massey v Crown Life Insurance Co* [1978] 1 WLR 590).

The courts have laid down a number of criteria which should be applied to any set of given facts to determine whether or not the arrangement amounts to an employment. A full examination of these criteria is beyond the scope of this book but in general the more important tests are set out below:

(a) A control test which looks at the degree of control exercised by the employer over the task performed by the consultant.

(b) The integration test which looks at the degree to which the consultant's tasks form an integral part of the employer's business.

(c) The economic reality test which looks at the extent to which the consultant bears the risks and the economic consequences of his work.

(d) The mutual obligations test which looks at the cross-obligations between the employer and the consultant.

The position was examined in some detail in the cases of *Hall v Lorimar* [1992] STC 599 and *McManus v Griffiths* [1997] BTC 412.

A more detailed examination of these tests is contained in *Tolley's Employment Handbook.*

When to give an indemnity

12.5.2 In a case where the employer examines the facts and applies the relevant criteria but is still unsure he may approach his PAYE or Department of Social Security office for guidance. Inland Revenue leaflet IR56/N139 provides, *inter alia,* that officers will always be available to give a written determination of the position. In some cases, however, an employer may feel such an approach cannot be made either because there is insufficient time or because it is reasonably confident that the arrangement is a *bona fide* contract for services. In such cases the employer would be well advised to include an indemnity in the consultancy arrangement.

It is difficult for the consultant to resist the inclusion of an indemnity as in most cases he would have represented himself as being self-employed and it would only be if such representation proved to be inaccurate that the indemnity would be called upon by the employer. Furthermore, the bulk of what the employer would be seeking to recover under the indemnity will be the income tax and national insurance that they should have been deducted from the payments to the consultant and which are therefore primarily the liability of the consultant and not the employer. Often the argument is raised that an indemnity merely highlights the uncertainty of the arrangement and should be avoided. Whilst there is some truth in this, the question of whether a consultant is self-employed or not is a matter depending on the facts of each case and which should not be influenced by the inclusion of an indemnity. On balance, the employer may prefer to include an indemnity as set out below:

> 'The Consultant will be paid a fee of £[ ] plus value added tax to be payable in arrears on the last Friday in every calendar month. The Consultant will pay to the Company on demand an amount equal to any Tax including in particular Income Tax (PAYE) and National Insurance to which the Company is liable in respect of the payment of the fee.'

Where the consultant is employed by a consultancy company, the indemnity will be modified to ensure that it is the consultancy company which has the liability for PAYE and national insurance. Such an indemnity may be worded as follows:

> 'The Consultant shall at all times be an employee of [XCo].
>
> [XCo] shall be responsible for the payment of any National Insurance (including employer's National Insurance) and income tax (PAYE) and other Taxes required by law to be paid by an employer in relation to the Consultant and shall make all appropriate deductions in respect of such National Insurance and income tax from the Consultant's salary.'

There is some doubt as to how effective the indemnity is if the employer is regarded as employing the consultant as an employee. However, clauses of this type are often inserted in consultancy agreements.

National insurance

12.5.3 The main doubt concerning the efficacy of indemnities is whether or not they are effective for the purposes of recovering national insurance. As regards primary Class 1 contributions, which the employer would normally deduct from the employee's pay, the employer's first line of defence is to recover under-deductions for previous payments from future payments to the employee. *Social Security (Contributions) Regulations* (*SI 1979/591*), *Sch 1 para 13(2A)* states the following:

> 'If the employer on making any payment of emoluments to an employee does not deduct therefrom the full amount of earnings-related contributions which by virtue of these Regulations he is entitled to deduct, he may, subject to the provisions of the next succeeding paragraph of this Regulation, recover the amounts so undeducted by deduction from any subsequent payment of emoluments to that employee during the same year:
>
> (b) this paragraph applies only where—
>
> (i) the underdeduction occurs by reason of an error made by the employer in good faith . . .'

There is a limitation on the employer's ability to recover underpayments by future deductions as this ability is limited to underpayments in the same year. The employer must show that the underdeduction was made in good faith. In most circumstances this should not be a problem. However, there may be circumstances where the employee is no longer employed and so deductions from future payments is not possible or the under-payments were made in previous years, in either case the employer would look to the indemnity.

The problem of seeking to recover under-deductions of primary Class 1 contributions under the indemnity from *Social Security (Contributions) Regulations* (*SI 1979/591*) *Sch 1 para 6(2)* which states the following:

> 'An employer shall not be entitled to recover any earnings-related contributions paid or to be paid by him on behalf of an employee otherwise than by deduction in accordance with these regulations.'

It can therefore be argued by the 'consultant' that if the employer sought to recover under-deductions under the indemnity it will be contrary to law, as by recovering under the indemnity the employer would not be recovering the contributions by deduction from subsequent payments to him. The position is not clear but most employers take the view that an indemnity can only be helpful.

As regards recovery of secondary Class 1 contributions, it is even more difficult for the employer to seek recovery under the indemnity as the *Social Security Contributions and Benefits Act 1975 Sch 1 para 3(3)* states the following:

> 'A secondary contributor shall be entitled, subject to and in accordance with regulations, to recover from an earner the amount of any primary Class 1 contribution paid or to be paid by him on behalf of the earner; and . . . notwithstanding any other provision in any enactment, regulations under this sub-paragraph shall provide for recovery to be made by deduction from the earner's earnings, and for it not to be made in any other way.'

Income tax and the PAYE system

12.5.4 Where an employer has failed to deduct income tax under the PAYE system from the employee, its first protection against a potential claim from the Inland Revenue for the under-deduction would be if the Inland Revenue sought to recover the under-deductions from the employee. Under *Income Tax (Employment) Regulations* (*SI 1993/744*), *reg 42(2)* the Inland Revenue may direct that the under-deduction of tax is recovered directly from the employee when satisfied that the employer took reasonable care to comply with the regulations and that the under-deduction was due to an error on the part of the employer made in good faith. However, the risk for the Inland Revenue, should it choose to pursue this course, is that once a direction is made the employer cannot subsequently be made liable to pay the amount of the excess. Consequently, one would normally expect the Inland Revenue to choose to seek recovery from the employer which is far more likely to result in the tax being collected. *Regulation 42(3)* also enables the Inland Revenue to direct the employee to pay the under-deduction where such employee has received emoluments knowing that the employer has wilfully failed to deduct PAYE. In practice it is rare for the Inland Revenue to pursue the employee since it is much easier to collect the money from the employer and in practice employers will have to look to their indemnity in such circumstances.

There is nothing in the tax legislation which enables an employer to recover under-deducted tax from the employee. There is no firm case law which gives such a right although in the case of *Bernard & Shaw Ltd v Shaw* [1951] ATC 187 Lynskey J said, at page 190:

> 'It is next suggested, that because there is a legal liability to pay the tax to the Inland Revenue, the plaintiff is entitled to recover it from the defendant. I know of no such form of action. If the money had in fact been paid by the plaintiff in discharge of the tax liability, it might well be that there would be a cause of action for money paid by the plaintiff to the use of the defendant, on the basis that the company was compelled by process of law to pay the money, which was due in respect of his remuneration, as to which he would ultimately be responsible for taxation. In those circumstances, the money might be recovered, but in the present case the money has not been paid, and until the money is paid, it seems to me that there can be no action for money paid to the use of the defendant.'

This would seem to imply that there might be a right of recovery by an employer against an employee although it is clear that it would be far safer to have a specific contractual obligation in the form of the indemnity.

Management buy-outs

12.6 Where the management of a company purchases its shares, the usual tax deed and warranties given on the sale of shares between unconnected third parties are modified. The modifications take into account the fact that management buy-outs are often preceded by a reorganisation and the fact that the managers have a greater knowledge of, and responsibility for, the tax problems of the target company.

Seller's concerns

12.6.1 The seller will generally refuse to give warranties in respect of any tax matter which was dealt with by the management of the target company. The seller will normally only agree to give warranties in respect of matters which were primarily under the seller's control and direction and where the seller's knowledge is greater than that of the management. In large groups, for example, it is not unusual to find that whilst the corporation tax affairs of the target company are dealt with centrally within the group, each individual company within the group retains responsibility for value added tax (VAT) and pay-as-you-earn (PAYE). In such circumstances one would expect to find that at the very least the seller would refuse to give warranties in respect of these two liabilities.

If the seller did not seek to limit the warranties to those areas which the managers did not control, the seller would find itself in the position where the managers seeking the warranties are the only people in a position to provide a comprehensive disclosure against them. This would make a nonsense of the idea that the purpose of inserting warranties is to elicit information. The effect would be to make the warranties primarily a means of recovery in respect of tax liabilities, which may have arisen due to default on the part of the managers and about which the seller has no knowledge. To allow the warranties to be available as a means of redress to the managers in such circumstances would be inequitable.

In areas controlled by the seller the position is more difficult. In the example cited, whilst the seller would be most reluctant to give any warranties on PAYE and VAT, there may also be a reluctance to give warranties and indemnities in respect of corporation tax. The seller may argue that the returns made by the target company were prepared by the group's head office and tax advisers on the basis of information supplied by the managers and if the returns are defective it is as a result of defective information provided by the managers. The seller may insist that if indemnities and warranties are given, there should be an exclusion for liabilities which arise due to the default of the managers in question.

The seller may also seek to exclude liability under the tax deed and warranties which arises from particular transactions of which the managers were the direct beneficiaries eg transfers of assets to managers are potentially liable to attack on the basis that the transfers were at an under-value.

The position of the managers

12.6.2 The managers will have two particular concerns when considering what indemnities and warranties they should seek on a management buy-out. The managers' first concern is to cover particular risks which arise because of the way in which the management buy-out has been structured. Their second concern is to ensure that they satisfy the requirements of their financiers.

Particular concerns for the purchasers arising from the structuring of the management buy-out

12.6.3 A management buy-out can be structured in a number of ways the examination of which is beyond the scope of this book. Generally, the managers will seek to define the type of reorganisation that is to take place in respect of the target company and seek a specific indemnity in respect of all tax liabilities arising from it. However, where there are definite anticipated liabilities, the management may wish to have more specific indemnities. Some of the more common types of risk that may arise are as follows.

It is quite common for the selling group in a management buy-out to establish a new company and hive down into it the business which the management wish to purchase. The transfer of the business in this way being intra-group should not give rise to any tax liabilities. Any capital gains tax that would otherwise arise from the disposal of the assets comprising the business would be subject to the relief in *TCGA 1992 s 171*. In these circumstances, the purchaser will be anxious to ensure that upon purchasing the target company and causing it to leave the group a liability will not arise under *TCGA 1992 s 179*. The managers will seek to include warranties which will give them details of the potential *s 179* charge. In addition, one would expect the managers to seek to cover the *s 179* risk in the tax deed under a specific indemnity, claims under which are excluded from any *de minimis* limits. An alternative is for those assets upon which it is anticipated there will be a gain to be left out of the hive-down and to be transferred to the new company once the buy-out is complete. In this way the gain will crystallise in the selling company and no liability under *s 179* will arise.

Where a hive-down has taken place, the supply of assets from the selling group to the target company would normally be free of VAT under the exemption given in *Value Added Tax (Special Provisions) Order 1995* (*SI 1995/1268*), *Art 5* of which exempts the transfer of a business as a going concern from VAT. The managers will be particularly concerned to ensure that such relief was applied for and obtained and will include a warranty to elicit this information. Alternatively, it may be possible to include the new company in the selling company's VAT group (if it has one). This will ensure that there is no VAT on the transfer. However, the new company will become jointly and severally liable for the VAT of the representative member during the period for which it was a member of the VAT group registration. If this route is followed then the managers will require an indemnity to cover any such liability.

On a hive-down the managers would normally expect that the transfer of assets will be exempt from stamp duty by virtue of *FA 1930 s 42*. The managers will wish to include a warranty to ensure that such an application was made and the relief given.

Where there is no hive-down, it is quite usual for the seller to procure that the target company distributes all available distributable reserves prior to the sale to the management team. Such dividend strips have two potential advantages. First, by extracting all free cash the seller is able to reduce the price that would otherwise have to be charged to the management for the target which makes the target company more affordable. It will be noted that there is an exclusion for dividends from the prohibition from giving financial assistance for the purpose of acquiring shares in *CA 1985 s 153*. Second, the seller will also hope that by reducing the purchase price its potential capital gains tax liability on the sale of the target company will be reduced. The aim (prior to 6 April 1999, after which time it will not be necessary) is to pay the dividend to the selling parent company under a group income election under *ICTA 1988 s 247*. However, the seller should give careful thought to the possible application of the value shifting provisions contained in the *TCGA 1992 ss 29–34* and also whether the group relationship has been broken because of 'arrangements' for the purposes of *ICTA 1988 Sch 18* in which case there is a potential liability to advance corporation tax.

The obligation of the managers to the financiers

12.6.4 The managers will be aware that whatever warranties and indemnities may be agreed between them and the seller, their financiers will still be looking for a minimum level of protection against tax liabilities. Often the financiers take an active part in negotiations of the indemnities and warranties. If the managers do not obtain warranties or indemnities from the seller, for example on VAT or PAYE liabilities, the financiers may ask the managers to provide them with warranties themselves. The managers are always therefore conscious that every point they concede to the seller on the tax indemnities and warranties is likely to increase their exposure to their financiers.

Sales by insolvency practitioners

12.7 With the increasing number of business failures it is not uncommon for the seller to be an administrator, administrative receiver or liquidator (referred to in the following paragraphs as 'Insolvency Practitioners'). However, in order to minimise the risk of tax liabilities passing to the purchaser, the seller is more likely to sell the assets of a business than shares, unless the business assets have been hived down into a new company in an attempt to preserve tax losses, although such schemes were severely restricted by provisions introduced by the *Finance Act 1986* and now incorporated in *ICTA 1988 s 344*. Hive downs for the purpose of preserving tax losses cannot, of course, be effected once the company has gone into liquidation. This is because the three-fourths ownership test required by *ICTA 1988 s 343*, will not be satisfied. A company loses beneficial ownership of its assets when it goes into liquidation (see *Ayerst v C & K (Construction) Ltd* [1976] AC 167).

Sale of business assets

12.7.1 A sale of assets will generally be more advantageous to a prospective purchaser than a sale of shares because Insolvency Practitioners will not normally give warranties and the seller, ie the company, for whom the Insolvency Practitioner will act as agent, will be insolvent. The purchaser may, in the absence of warranties and indemnities seek a reduction in the price or a retention from the sale proceeds. This is likely to be met with the argument that the purchaser is already getting a bargain and that the Insolvency Practitioner wishes to wind up the affairs of the insolvent company as soon as possible so that a retention would only serve to prolong the process. Although this may, to some extent, be true, the Insolvency Practitioner may be prepared to accept an adjustment clause whereby the price is adjusted in certain circumstances. The extent to which such adjustments are made is a matter for negotiation.

Effect of VAT legislation on sale of assets

12.7.2 The principal taxation question to be addressed in an assets sale is that of VAT. In the light of what has been said in previous paragraphs about Insolvency Practitioners not giving indemnities or warranties, it will probably come as no surprise to find that the Insolvency Practitioner may require an indemnity from the purchaser to cover any VAT that may arise on the sale. This is because many sales of assets will amount to the sale of a business or part of a business as a going concern for the purposes of the *VAT (Special Provisions) Order 1995*. The effect of this is to put the sale of assets outside the scope of VAT. However, although the purchaser may be convinced that the sale is that of a going concern the Insolvency Practitioner may not be and in the event of an adverse determination by Customs & Excise, unless the contract provides otherwise, the sale price will be deemed to be inclusive of VAT. This will need to be accounted for to Customs & Excise thus reducing the Insolvency Practitioner's recovery. It is therefore common to find a clause in the sale agreement which provides for the price to be VAT-exclusive in the event that VAT is payable. However, the Insolvency Practitioner may not wish to take the risk of the purchaser becoming insolvent and will therefore require an amount equal to the VAT to be paid into an escrow account pending a determination by Customs & Excise. The purchaser may resist this: indeed the purchaser may not have the money. Once again it is a matter for negotiation. The requirement of the Insolvency Practitioner to have the VAT in an account may be tempered by their requirement to complete the transaction. A typical clause found in such agreements is set out below:

> 'The Consideration is exclusive of VAT (if any) but the parties envisage the sale of the Assets being free of VAT as the transfer of a going concern. If, however, for any reason HM Customs & Excise indicate that VAT should be accounted for by the Sellers and/or the Administrators in respect of the whole or any part of the Consideration, or otherwise on any supply pursuant to this agreement, then the Purchaser shall forthwith pay the VAT, and any applicable penalties and interest, in addition to the amount paid or payable already. Where VAT is payable, the Revised Consideration shall be the original Consideration plus the VAT and any penalties and interest. Upon payment of VAT the Purchaser shall be entitled to

and the Sellers shall deliver to the Purchaser a VAT invoice'. This clause does not cover retentions.

Further problems may arise if the assets include properties. The Insolvency Practitioner may not know whether the option to tax has been exercised. If it has and the purchaser does not opt then, by virtue of *VAT (Special Provisions) Order 1995 Art 5(2)*, the transfer will not be that of a going concern. The purchaser may therefore require that any VAT which is payable as a result of the option having been exercised but of which the purchaser was unaware is to be for the account of the Insolvency Practitioner.

A simple solution to this problem is for seller and purchaser to opt immediately before the sale. However, although an Insolvency Practitioner is usually an agent of the company an administrative receiver is an agent unless and until the company goes into liquidation *(s 44(1)(a), Insolvency Act 1986)* therefore, where the sale is by an administrative receiver, and the company is in liquidation, the administrative receiver cannot elect on behalf of the company and any purported election would be void.

Value Added Tax Act 1994 s 49 provides for the business records to be transferred to the purchaser where the transfer is that of a business as a going concern. Usually the Insolvency Practitioner will seek to retain the records to fulfil any obligations under the *Insolvency Act 1986.*

Sales of shares

12.7.3 There is little to be said about share sales. An Insolvency Practitioner will not normally give indemnities or warranties for taxation. Where there has been a hive-down in order to preserve tax losses, the purchaser may try to make payment conditional upon the losses being available. However, the Insolvency Practitioner will usually require payment in the event that the losses become unavailable as a result of the application of *ICTA 1988 s 768* through the fault of the purchaser. Often losses are not paid for but are included as a 'sweetener' to persuade a purchaser to take shares rather than assets. In such an event the Insolvency Practitioner will not be concerned if the losses are unavailable.

Business sales

12.8 When a company (or other entity) sells a bundle of assets comprising a business, most tax liabilities arising from the conduct and disposal of that business remain with the seller. However, there are some exceptions and it has become market practice to include warranties in the Business Sale Agreement in respect of such exceptions. The most common of these are set out below.

Inheritance tax

12.8.1 In certain cases an Inland Revenue charge in respect of IHT can attach to property under *IHTA 1984 s 237*. The charge can attach to property if transfer gave rise to the IHT liability (in whole or in part) and to property held in a settlement where the liability relates to making the settlement, or to a chargeable transfer of the settled property treated as made under *IHTA 1984 Pt III*. The charge applies not only to the original property subject to the charge but also other property which represents it. For example, if an asset is sold and the proceeds are used to acquire a new asset, the new asset could be subject to the charge.

The concern for the purchaser of a business is that it may acquire business assets which are subject to an undisclosed charge.

In practice, commercial business assets will rarely be caught by IHT. Further, the issue is likely to be avoided as a *bona fide* purchaser of UK personal property and all non-UK property, who has no notice of the facts giving rise to the charge, will not acquire the assets subject to it. In the case of UK real property, the existence of the charge will be revealed by a land charges search or by a search of the charges register in the case of registered land. If the charge is not registered, the purchaser can acquire the land free from incumbrances. It should also be noted that the charge lapses even, if the purchaser has notice of the existence of the charge, six years from the date when tax becomes due or a proper account is provided under *IHTA 1984 s 238(2)*. However, a purchaser will be concerned to avoid any question on the level of its knowledge. Thus, if the purchaser asks whether such a charge exists through a warranty and receives a negative reply it is prima facie proof that the purchaser had no knowledge of the incumbrance. Further, the breach of warranty, if the charge crystallises, should provide redress for the purchaser. Consequently, it is not unusual to find a warranty to the effect that:

> 'There is no Inland Revenue charge under *IHTA 1984 s 237* over or in respect of any of the Assets.'

Furthermore, in the case of settled property, trustees and certain beneficiaries who pay IHT can have recourse to trust assets, which may include the business assets being sold under *IHTA 1984 s 212*. To protect against this a warranty is sometimes included in a Business Sale Agreement as follows:

> 'No circumstances exist which enables the powers within *IHTA 1984 s 212* to be exercised in relation to any Asset.'

PAYE and national insurance

12.8.2 The purchaser has a number of concerns.

The first is that the seller has failed to deduct tax as required by the PAYE rules with the result that the Inland Revenue could seek to collect tax from the employee. The purchaser does not want to find members of the workforce are being pursued for tax with the resulting adverse effect on morale. In practice, this is unlikely but is possible under *IT (Employments) Regulations SI 1993/774, reg 42(2)* and *(3)*.

Although *reg 80* means that a purchaser of a business is not liable for the seller's failures, it will wish to ensure that it does not perpetuate mistakes through the operation of the PAYE system it inherits, and that the records are sufficient to ensure that it can comply with its obligations. To this end a warranty such as the one set out below is often used:

> 'The Seller has operated the PAYE system in accordance with all relevant rules and regulations and in particular has made all deductions required to be made in respect of income tax and national insurance in respect of the employees and has accounted for all such deductions to the Inland Revenue or the Department of Social Security on the due dates.'

Once PAYE and national insurance contributions are administered by a single agency the reference to the Department of Social Security will have to be changed.

Stamp duty

12.8.3 The purchaser will want to ensure that its title to all property is not adversely affected due to the non-payment of stamp duty. To this end a warranty such as that included in a share sale can be included:

> 'All documents in the possession or under the control of the Seller which establish or are necessary to establish the title of the Seller to the Assets have been duly stamped and any applicable stamp duties or charges in respect of such documents have been duly accounted for and paid, and no such documents which are outside the United Kingdom would attract stamp duty if they were brought in to the United Kingdom.'

Capital allowances

12.8.4 The purchaser will want to ensure that the price apportioned to assets which, prima facie, qualify for capital allowances qualify on the anticipated basis. For example, the purchaser will want to ensure that it has not previously been agreed that the assets are non-qualifying or long life assets qualifying only for restricted allowances (because normal 25% writing down allowances have not been claimed). A warranty such as the one set out below is often used to address such concerns:

'There is no reason why any part of the Consideration payable by the Purchaser that is apportioned under this Agreement to those of the Assets which are plant or machinery for the purposes of *Capital Allowances Act 1990 Pt II* should not, assuming such apportioned Consideration represents capital expenditure incurred for the purposes of the Purchaser's trade, qualify in full for writing down allowances at [25%] [40%] on a reducing balance basis and none of such Assets are leased (as in the meaning of *s 50* of such Act); and the Seller accepts that no election may be made in respect of any of such Assets pursuant to *s 77* of such Act.'

Disputed and agreed treatments

12.8.5 Most disputes will be of relevance only to the seller's tax position but it is conceivable that such dispute could affect the purchaser. If, for example, the Inland Revenue were contesting the tax status of a category of asset, some of which are acquired by the purchaser, the outcome is likely to affect the purchaser. Similarly, a special treatment agreed could follow the asset into the purchaser's hands. An appropriate warranty could be:

'[The Seller is not involved in any] [So far as the Seller is aware there is no] dispute with the Inland Revenue, Customs & Excise or other appropriate fiscal authority concerning which will affect the Business or any of the Assets.'

VAT

12.8.6 Much discussion on VAT will revolve around clauses which deal with the transfer of a business as a going concern. However, a number of other issues arise.

If leasehold premises are transferred the purchaser will want to establish whether an option to tax has been made and will ask for a warranty:

'Neither the Seller (nor any relevant associate) has elected to waive exemption (or applied for written permission to elect) in accordance with *VATA 1994 Sch 10* in relation to the Premises (or any of the Assets which constitute an interest in or right over land).'

HM Customs & Excise take the view that liabilities arising in respect of goods covered by the capital goods scheme passed as part of a transfer of a business as a going concern pass to a purchaser who is obliged to operate the scheme (Customs & Excise Leaflet 702/6/90). A warranty is thus sometimes sought that:

'None of the Assets are or could be subject to the Value Added Tax Capital Goods Scheme provided for in *Value Added Tax Regulation 1995 Pt XV (SI 1995/2518)*.'

Chapter 13

Statutory Indemnities

Introduction

13.1 Increasingly, legislation provides for the Inland Revenue to recover tax from someone other than the taxpayer who is principally liable; for example, when one company in a group fails to pay a tax liability, the legislation might provide for recovery from a company which was a member of the same group (see for example *TCGA 1992 s 190*). When this happens, the legislation will often provide for the company with the secondary liability to recover the amount from the company which is principally liable. These statutory indemnities raise a number of issues. First, are they of any value? If the Inland Revenue have been unable to recover the tax due, why should someone else with perhaps fewer resources be able to do so? In a recent Tax Bulletin, the Inland Revenue have stated that where there is a statutory right to recovery, the person with the secondary liability should consider seeking contractual indemnities as well. Second, what mechanism is to be used to enforce such indemnities? Presumably, the person with the secondary liability would have a right of action under a statute. One of the most common cases where the Inland Revenue are likely to use such provisions is where the actual taxpayer is abroad. If the person with the secondary liability seeks to enforce judgment abroad will the foreign courts enforce it? It is a principle of private international law that one state will not enforce another state's revenue laws. Under this principle, the Inland Revenue would not be able to enforce judgment in a foreign court. So it is difficult to see how, in circumstances allowing the person with the secondary liability to enforce judgment would have any value. Finally, what is the tax position of the various parties to the statutory indemnity? This chapter examines briefly the tax aspects of the statutory indemnities and some of the more commonly encountered provisions.

Statutory indemnities

13.2 A statutory indemnity will typically provide for recovery from another party eg *TCGA 1992 s 82(4)* which provides: 'Any amount which a person is required to pay by notice under this section may be recovered from him as if it were tax due and duly demanded of him; and he may recover any such amount paid by him from the migrating trustees.' It is thought the notice, if valid, crystallises the amount due and the amount recoverable is recoverable as a debt due from the other person: ie there is a certain sum due. Presumably, once the debt arises, it is amenable to summary judgement under RSC Order 14 as the taxpayer would have no defence other than the tax was not due, in which case the matter would be determined by appeal by the taxpayer. However, notwithstanding the ability to obtain summary judgement, it is difficult to see how the judgment can be enforced unless the taxpayer has assets in the UK. Frequently, the reason why the Inland Revenue can seek to make another person liable is because the taxpayer is outside the jurisdiction. As mentioned above, it is a principle of private international law that one state will not enforce another state's revenue laws. Whether the person with the secondary liability can enforce abroad may depend upon whether the statutory provision creates a separate debt or whether it subrogates the person with secondary liability to the rights of the Inland Revenue. It is thought that the latter is the case. Taking again the example of *TCGA 1992 s 82(4),* the notice which is served on the person with secondary liability requires them to pay 'the amount of the unpaid tax or the aggregate of the unpaid tax and the unpaid interest.' It does not require payment of 'an amount equal to the unpaid tax'. Furthermore, *TCGA 1992 s 82(4)* provides that any amount payable under a notice is to be recovered 'as if it were tax due and duly demanded of him'. Consequently, the amount paid is tax and the right to recover is a right to recover tax; therefore any attempt to enforce judgment in a foreign jurisdiction would be met with the argument that it was the enforcement of a revenue judgment. If this conclusion is correct, it would appear that whenever the legislature gives a right to recover against a person outside the jurisdiction, that right is, from the outset, unenforceable.

Taxation of statutory indemnities

13.3 Where a person has to pay an amount of tax as a result of a secondary liability imposed by statute, the statutory provision normally provides that no deduction shall be allowed for the payment. Again, taking *TCGA 1992 s 84,* subsection (5) provides: 'A payment on pursuance of a notice under this section shall not be allowed as a deduction in computing any income, profits or losses for any tax purposes.' Although not normally stated, the corollary of no deduction would be that any amount recovered under a statutory indemnity would not be taxable. The Inland Revenue have confirmed as much in respect of recoveries made under *ICTA 1988 s 767B(2)* in item 7 of their Bulletin No 16 dated 21 April 1995. There is no reason why this should not be the case under other sections. The Inland Revenue also confirmed that where a contractual indemnity is given to supplement a statutory indemnity, any payments made under such an indemnity will not be taxed. Although some practitioners had expressed concern over whether such payments are taxable, the Inland Revenue's view based upon their own concession is clearly correct. The statute gives rise to a cause of action which when settled is disposed of for a capital sum;

similarly, a sum received under an indemnity would be capital for the same reason. Under the principle in *Zim Properties Ltd v Proctor* [1985] STC 90, the disposal of a right of action would be a disposal for CGT purposes; under ESC D33 there is no underlying asset which disposed of which has given rise to the cause of action. Consequently, under the concession, no chargeable gains should arise. However, it is unsatisfactory that a concession needs to be relied upon to relieve a potential tax charge in a situation where a deduction for the sum which has been reimbursed is specifically denied by statute.

13.4 Examples of statutory indemnities

Finance Act 1973 Sch 15 para 4

13.4.1 Where tax is assessed under *TCGA 1992 s 276* or *ICTA 1988 s 830* on a person who is not resident in the UK in respect of profits and gains arising from activities authorised by a licence granted pursuant to the *Petroleum (Production) Act 1934* and that tax remains unpaid, the Board of the Inland Revenue may serve a notice on the holder of the licence requiring that holder to pay the tax. Paragraph 4(2) provides that the amount to be paid may be recovered as if it is tax due and that the licence holder may recover such an amount from the person on whom the assessment was made. Paragraph 4(3) provides that any payment made pursuant to a notice under para 4 is not to be allowed as a deduction in computing any income, profits or losses for any tax purposes.

Income and Corporation Taxes Act 1988 s 465A

13.4.2 *Financial Services Act 1992 s 6(5)* provides that a registered Friendly Society which is being incorporated may identify property, rights and liabilities of any of its branches which are not to be transferred to the Society on incorporation. Where assets are identified, *ICTA 1988 s 465A* provides that for tax purposes the assets are to be treated as assets of the Society. Consequently, any tax liability arising in respect of those assets will fall on the Society and *s 456A(3)* allows the Society to recover such tax from the trustees in whom the assets are vested.

Income and Corporation Taxes Act 1988 ss 551 and 551A

13.4.3 Under these two sections individuals and companies respectively are entitled to recover amounts from trustees where that amount has been included in their income by virtue of *ICTA 1988 s 547(1)(a)* and *(b)*.

Income and Corporation Taxes Act 1988 s 660D

13.4.4 This section provides that where income tax has become chargeable on and is paid by a settlor by virtue of the provisions in *ICTA 1988 Chapter 1A Part 15* the settlor is entitled to recover from the trustee, or any other person to whom income is payable by virtue of or in consequence of the settlement, the amount of the tax which the settlor has paid.

Income and Corporation Taxes Act 1988 s 767B(2)

13.4.5 This section provides that 'a payment in pursuance of an assessment under *s 767A* or *s 767AA* shall not be allowed as a deduction in computing any income, profits or losses for any tax purposes; but any person making such a payment shall be entitled to recover an amount equal to the payment from the taxpayer company or the transferred company or an associated company (as the case may be)'.

A person assessed under *ICTA 1988 s 767A* is '. . . assessed by the Board and charged (in the name of the taxpayer company) to an amount of corporation tax in accordance [s 767A]'. This differs from other sections in that the taxpayer is charged in the name of the company and the amount that is recovered is an amount equal to the tax payable.

Income and Corporation Taxes Act 1988 s 777

13.4.6 This section provides that where a person is assessed to tax under on *ICTA 1998 ss 775–778* in respect of consideration which has been received by another person, that person is entitled to recover from the other person any part of the tax he has paid. Furthermore, where any such tax remains unpaid at the expiration of a period of six months from the date when it became due and payable, it is recoverable from that other person as though that other person were the person assessed. However, that person is still able to recover from the person actually assessed. *Income and Corporation Taxes Act 1998 s 777* does not contain a provision prohibiting the amount assessed as deductible. However, it is doubtful whether any such deduction would be allowed under general principles.

Income and Corporation Taxes Act 1988 s 821

13.4.7 *Section 821* of *ICTA 1988* provides that where any half-yearly or quarterly payments have been made on account of any interest, dividends or other annual profits or gains and, subsequent to the making of such payments an act is passed imposing a rate of tax different to that at which deduction was made, the under deduction can be recovered by an assessment under *Schedule D Case III.* Any person who is assessed in this way can, under *s 821(2)*, make a deduction out of the next payment.

Where there is no next payment, the amount is recoverable as a debt due from the person against whom the original deduction could have been made.

Finance Act 1988 s 132

13.4.8 Under *FA 1988 ss 130* and *131* a company which migrates has to make arrangements to pay its outstanding tax. Where a migrating company fails to pay such tax, *FA 1988 s 132* allows the Board to recover that amount of tax from a company which was in the same group as the migrating company within the twelve months before it migrated or from any person who was a director of the migrating company in that twelve-month period. The amount recovered is recovered as if it were tax due and that person may recover any such amount from the migrating company. No deduction is allowed in computing any income, profits or losses of the person so assessed.

Finance Act 1990 s 96

13.4.9 Under *FA 1990 s 96* an adjustment can be made where the amount of losses surrendered by way of relief is excessive. The company which has surrendered the group relief is principally liable. However, any other company which had obtained group relief through the surrender can be assessed and charged in the name of the surrendering company. That company is then entitled to recover from the surrendering company a sum equal to that amount together with any interest which has been paid.

Taxation of Chargeable Gains Act 1992 s 78

13.4.10 *Section 78* of *TCGA 1992* provides that where tax becomes chargeable on, and is paid by, a person in respect of gains treated as accruing to that person under *TCGA 1992 s 77* (charge on settlor with interest in settlement) that person is entitled to recover the amount of the tax from any trustee of the settlement.

Taxation of Chargeable Gains Act 1992 s 82

13.4.11 *Section 82* of *TCGA 1992* provides that where any capital gains tax payable (by trustees who have become neither resident nor ordinarily resident in the UK) by virtue of *TCGA 1992 s 80(2)* is not paid within six months from the time when it became payable, the Board may require any person who was a trustee within the twelve months before the trustees migrated to pay the unpaid tax and any unpaid interest. By *TCGA 1992 s 80(4)* any amount which a person is required to pay under such a notice may be recovered by them from the migrating trustees.

Taxation of Chargeable Gains Act 1992 s 137(4)

13.4.12 *Section 137(4)* of *TCGA 1992* provides that where there has been an exchange, reconstruction or amalgamation within *ss 135* or *136* of *TCGA 1992* and that exchange, reconstruction or amalgamation was not affected for bona fide commercial reasons, and any tax assessed on a person is not paid within six months of either the later of the date when the tax became due and payable or the date when the assessment was made, any other person who holds any shares or debentures which were acquired through a tax free intra-group transfer, or an inter-spouse transfer, can be assessed for the unpaid tax or a corresponding part of it. That person is then entitled to recover from the taxpayer a sum equal to the amount together with any interest.

Taxation of Chargeable Gains Act 1992 s 139

13.4.13 Under *s 139(7)* of *TCGA 1992* where there has been a reconstruction or amalgamation involving a transfer of business and that reconstruction or amalgamation was not affected for bona fide commercial reasons, any tax due which is not paid can be collected from any person who holds the assets, being a transferee of those assets. Such a person is then entitled to recover from the taxpayer a sum equal to that amount together with any interest paid.

Taxation of Chargeable Gains Act 1992 s 168

13.4.14 Under *s 168(9)* of *TCGA 1992* where the donee of an asset under either *s 165* or *s 260* of *TCGA 1992* emigrates and the tax payable is not paid within a period of twelve months, the transferor can be assessed and charged, in the name of the transferee, to all or any part of the tax. Where the transferor pays the tax, the transferor is entitled to recover a corresponding sum from the transferee.

Taxation of Chargeable Gains Act 1992 s 179

13.4.15 Under *s 179(11)* of *TCGA 1992* where a charge made under *TCGA 1992 s 179* is not paid, the principal company of the group of which the chargeable company was a member can be assessed and charged the tax. That company is then entitled to recover from the chargeable company a sum of that amount together with any interest paid.

Taxation of Chargeable Gains Act 1992 s 189

13.4.16 Under *s 189* of *TCGA 1992* where a company makes a capital distribution to a connected shareholder otherwise than on a reduction of capital, any corporation tax chargeable on the company's capital gain may be recovered from the shareholder, if not paid by the company, together with any interest.

Taxation of Chargeable Gains Act 1992 s 190

13.4.17 Under *TCGA 1992 s 190(3)* if corporation tax on a chargeable gain is not paid, the principal company in the group, or any other company which has been a member of the group within the previous two years and held the asset on which the gain arose, can be charged corporation tax in the name of the company to whom the chargeable gain accrued. Any company so assessed is entitled to recover a sum of that amount from either the company to which the chargeable gain accrued or from the principal member of the group. Where the amount is recovered from the principal member of the group, the principal member can then recover from the chargeable company.

Taxation of Chargeable Gains Act 1992 s 191

13.4.18 Under *TCGA 1992 s 191(5)* where corporation tax due on chargeable gains is not paid by a non-resident company, the tax due can be charged on a resident company or a controlling director. Any amount so paid can be recovered from the taxpayer company. Any payment is not to be allowed as a deduction in computing any income, profits or losses for any tax purposes.

Taxation of Chargeable Gains Act s 282

13.4.19 Under *TCGA 1992 s 282* where a chargeable gain accrues to a person on the disposal of an asset by way of gift and the amount of the tax is unpaid, the donee can be assessed to the tax. Any donee so assessed is entitled to recover that amount from the donor.

Chapter 14

Tax Clauses and Tax Assumptions in Finance Leases

Introduction

14.1 A business wishing to finance the acquisition of plant and machinery can use one of two basic methods: a bank loan or a finance lease. Under the latter, the finance lessor effectively acquires the equipment for its client and then leases it to the client, receiving in return periodic payments comprising an element of capital (to repay the finance lessor's cost of acquisition) and an interest element, to compensate the finance lessor for the cost of funds. Generally, the finance lessor can offer a cheaper alternative to a bank loan because of the tax treatment it receives, particularly in respect of capital allowances. Some of this benefit is passed on to its client resulting in a cheaper funding cost.

Tax assumptions

14.2 The transaction is based on the premise that a set return will be produced for the finance lessor based upon a number of assumptions, such as a finance lessor's cost of funds, its obligations to comply with regulatory regimes and, most notably, assumptions regarding the tax treatment of the transaction. The finance lessor's attitude will be that should any of these assumptions prove to be ill founded, there will have to be an adjustment to the rentals to ensure that the net yield of the transaction remains constant.

The tax assumptions are normally based on the consequences of entering into the transaction, its termination, the tax treatment of cash received and paid in the transaction and the tax treatment of the finance lessor's own funding costs. Although a bank also makes certain assumptions regarding its tax treatment in a normal bank funding transaction, with the exception of gross-up clauses, the market practice is that no assumptions are made in bank loan documentation because a bank loan is not tax dependent in the same way as a finance lease.

When drafting the assumptions in the lease documentation, the finance lessor will be concerned to ensure that they are drafted as widely as possible so that any conceivable change in the circumstances assumed to prevail when making the cashflow projections at the outset of the transaction will be caught by the necessary rental adjustments. The lessee, whilst accepting the basic structure will have to look at the assumptions carefully. Notably to ensure that:

(a) the finance lease is not being made artificially attractive. It is not unknown for finance lessors to make unreasonable assumptions in order to enhance the competitiveness of their quote to the customer. For example, if a finance lessor assumed writing down allowances at 40% when clearly it is only entitled to 25%, the financial profile of the lease will be artificially enhanced. The customer will be given a funding cost which ultimately will prove to be illusory as there would have to be an immediate adjustment of rentals to compensate for the shortfall in allowances;

(b) the finance lessor does not try and put risks associated with its own voluntary acts onto the lessee. For example, if the benefit of capital allowances is delayed because the finance lessor fails to submit its tax return and accounts on time, the cost of delay should not be passed on to the lessee;

(c) certain key facts within a finance lessor's knowledge and control are set out at the outset and, if incorrect or varied, should not effect the lessee. For example, the lessee is entitled to assume that the finance lessor is tax resident and, if this is not the case and the transaction proceeded on a mistaken basis, the finance lessor should not be entitled to pass on that cost to the lessee;

(d) that the lessee benefits from any tax benefit arising from variations in the assumptions as well as suffering any burden arising from such change. Many finance lessors draft their finance leases on the basis that if there is a variation which is disadvantageous there is a rental adjustment but this does not operate the other way round. If for example, the rate of corporation tax goes up then the deal is worth more to the finance lessor which can set off capital allowances and save more tax than originally anticipated. Generally, few drafts prepared by finance lessors give all appropriate benefits back to the lessees.

The assumptions are divided between two basic categories: variable assumptions and fixed assumptions or principles. A change in variable assumptions leads to an adjustment of rental, for example, when there is a change in the rate of writing down allowances. Fixed assumptions, sometimes called principles, are the fundamental basis upon which the transaction is based, such as the residence of the finance lessor which, if incorrect or varied, should not result in a change in the rentals.

14.3 Variable assumptions

Assumed capital costs

14.3.1 The lease should make an assumption of the capital cost incurred by the finance lessor upon which allowances and the rental payments are based. Apart from the cost of supply, there may be incidental costs which are capitalised, such as fitting costs. The clause normally sets out the amortisation/payment schedule as well. A typical clause reads as follows:

> 'The Total Capital Cost will be [£] and will be payable in the following instalments:'.

Capital allowances

14.3.2 Sometimes the clauses dealing with the capital allowance treatment are relatively short and all embracing such as:

> 'The rates and times at which Capital Allowances are obtainable under the Tax System at the date hereof will not change and Capital Allowances given to the Lessor in respect of its expenditure on the Assets will not be withdrawn in whole or in part.'

The alternative approach is to go into a little more detail such as:

> 'The Lessor will be and will remain entitled to and will receive writing down allowances (on a reducing balance basis) on the whole of its expenditure on the Assets at the rate of 25% in respect of the accounting period of the Lessor in which the total Capital Cost was incurred and in respect of its subsequent accounting periods falling partly or wholly within the Primary Period and the full benefit of such allowances will not be refused, disputed, withdrawn or effectively postponed in whole or in part except where occasioned by some act or default of the Lessor.'

From the finance lessor's point of view these clauses are both reasonably acceptable as they provide the lessor with protection not only against changes in law but also against other potential problems which could result in allowances being denied.

The lessee will be concerned to ensure that non-availability of allowances due to a voluntary disclaimer or postponement by the finance lessor, or because the finance lessor fails to submit its tax returns properly, should not affect the lessee. These concerns are largely addressed in the second clause above but not the first clause. However, the second clause does not cover the position where the finance lessor has inadequate profits to absorb the allowances. Before condemning either assumption as inadequate, one should ensure that there are no carve-outs in the fixed assumptions or elsewhere which, for example, may make a non-variable assumption that the finance lessor will always have adequate profits and put in its tax returns on time.

Corporation tax

14.3.3

> 'The rate of corporation tax for the financial year (as defined in *ICTA 1988)* ended [28 February 2001] and each financial year thereafter will be thirty per cent (30%).'

In producing cashflow statements, the finance lessor will assume that the capital allowances will be worth a certain amount, based on the tax charges that would have otherwise have resulted in the absence of such allowances. Clearly if the tax rate changes, the financial profile of the lease changes. An increase in the rate of corporation tax, which is normally greeted with dismay by taxpayers, will benefit the finance lessee as regards the finance lease as, provided the lease adjustment mechanism ensures that the benefits as well as the burdens are passed on to the lessee, there will be a rental reduction. It is often the case, particularly in the smaller transactions, that the finance lessor's documentation will adjust only in the finance lessor's favour. Given that the stability in the rate of corporation tax at the current time and Gordon Brown's pronouncements that it will remain the same for the life of the parliament current at the time of writing, this is not the pressing issue that it once was but, nevertheless, where the transaction is of sufficient size the lessee should insist that the clause works both ways.

Lessor's status

14.3.4

> 'The Lessor's taxable income receipts and outgoings in respect of the Transaction will fall to be assessed and dealt with under *Case I Sch D* (in the case of rental payments or Termination Payment) or *Case III Sch D* (in the case of interest income).'

The finance lessor will wish to insert such a clause to ensure that the transaction is regarded as a trading transaction and therefore that the finance lessor will be entitled to capital allowances etc. The lessee may quite justifiably object to this on the basis that the status of the finance lessor is something that only the finance lessor can have real knowledge of and the finance lessor should not enter into the transaction if there is doubt about its trading status. In fact, the lessee will try to make the assumption that the finance lessor is a trader and the transaction will be brought into account for trading purposes a fixed assumption. The finance lessor will try to resist this, at least to the extent of saying that whilst it is happy to take the risk that it is not regarded as trading generally, the lessee should bear the risk if anything in the particular transaction under contemplation causes it to be regarded as a non-trading transaction.

Deductibility of finance costs

14.3.5 The finance lessor will want to make sure that any interest on the loans it takes out to fund the acquisition of the plant and machinery is deductible for tax purposes. Whilst this is reasonable, the lessee will want to make sure that there is nothing peculiar about the nature of the funding which could prevent the deduction of interest. For example, if monies were borrowed from a parent company offshore at rates higher than market rates, part of the interest element is likely to be regarded as an attribution of profit and non-deductible. Consequently, there is usually something in the fixed, non-variable assumptions confirming that the transaction is funded by way of an advance from an independent bank carrying on a bona fide banking business. Sometimes the transaction will be funded from the finance lessor's own funds and so a notional rate of interest is assumed on a notional borrowing, the logic of this being that the finance lessor should be compensated in the same way as it would have been had it borrowed outside the group. An appropriate clause may be as follows:

> 'Any interest paid in respect of funds borrowed by the Lessor for the purposes of the Transaction will be allowable as a trading expense.'

Accounting period and the date on which tax is paid

14.3.6 In producing its cashflows the finance lessor would have assumed the tax benefit from the transaction would arise upon claiming the allowances against tax, nine months after the end of the accounting period, or (if a large company) following the introduction of the quarterly system of accounting for corporation tax on the usual quarterly payment dates. Thus, the finance lessor will be concerned that if its accounting period changes or tax becomes payable later than 9 months following the accounting period (or upon the normal quarterly payment dates), the benefit of the allowances will be deferred and its cashflow adversely affected. Consequently, the finance lessor will want to ensure that in such circumstances it is able to secure a rental variation.

The lessee will be concerned to ensure that if payment of corporation tax is accelerated it gets the benefit. Further, if the finance lessor voluntarily changes its accounting period such that there is a cashflow disadvantage, the lessee will be concerned to ensure that it does not suffer the consequences. For this reason the following variable assumptions will normally be inserted:

> 'Neither the Lessor [nor a Group Relief Recipient] will be required by law or standard accounting practice in the United Kingdom to draw up accounts at any date other than [28 February] and/or for any other period other than twelve months.

> Neither the Lessor [nor any Group Relief Recipient] will be required by law to have Accounting Periods which are other than twelve months in duration nor will any of them be required to draw up accounts for periods which do not coincide with the relevant accounting period.'

The question of paying corporation tax will, before the quarterly system of accounting is introduced (provided the lease does not extend beyond it), be dealt with as follows:

> 'The provisions of *ICTA 1988 s 10* will not be amended with a result that the Lessor [or any Group Relief Recipient] becomes liable to pay corporation tax for any accounting period on a date other than the date which is nine months and one day after the end of that accounting period.'

For leases extending beyond or starting after the *Finance Act 1998* where the lessor is a large company, the clause will have to be varied so that it reads something along the lines of:

> 'The provision of *FA 1998 s 30* and *The Corporation Tax (Installment Payments) (Large Companies) Regulations 1998* will not be amended so as to result in [any Group Relief Recipient or] the Lessor first becoming liable to pay corporation tax for any accounting period on a date other than the normal quarterly accounting dates as provided for in that Section and in the cashflow statement.'

The above clauses make it clear that the assumption in respect of the accounting date only applies to statutory or accounting standard changes, rather than voluntary changes by the finance lessor and therefore meet the lessee's requirements. However, the clauses dealing with the date for payment of tax should give the lessee any credit for any benefits arising from any changes to the due date for payment of tax. Thus, for example, the adviser must ensure that in the first clause referred to above, which requires payment nine months after the end of the accounting period, if the finance lessor benefits as the payment of corporation tax is accelerated, thus accelerating the availability of the capital allowances, this produces a corresponding rental adjustment for the lessee.

Accruals basis of account

14.3.7 The finance lessor will assume that its profits on the transaction will be calculated on an accruals basis and therefore will put in an assumption to this effect. This should be relatively non-contentious as a trading finance lessor is unlikely to be taxed on any other basis. The only area that could cause some discussion is the question of how a termination payment should be treated. In view of the position on negative depreciation (see *Gallagher v Jones, Threfall v Jones* [1993] STC 537, CA and *Finance Act 1997 Sch 12*) the lessee should be concerned to ensure that if there is a balloon payment it is spread evenly throughout the lease and that the cashflow reflects this and does not simply bring in the whole of the payment on the date of its receipt. The type of clause that may be appropriate is as follows:

> 'The Lessor will be entitled to prepare its tax computations (and the Inland Revenue will accept such computations as a basis for charging tax) on the basis so far as they relate to interest received or paid or rental on a daily accruals basis for the period in respect of which the interest is received or paid or the rentals are paid and in so far as they relate to a receipt of Termination Sum on the basis of the accrual as shown in the cashflow statement.'

In the light of the above clause it would be incumbent upon the lessee to check the accruals in the cashflow statement.

Group relief

14.3.8 The finance lessor may have assumed that it will always be able to use any losses generated by the transaction by surrendering them by way of group relief to other members of its group. It will therefore include an assumption that group relief will be available for such losses. The lessee will be concerned to ensure that it is in no way providing an assumption that the finance lessor's group will always have sufficient profits to offset the losses, which it will regard as an internal matter for the finance lessor. The lessee can quite reasonably take the view that if the finance lessor does not have sufficient tax capacity it should not be entering into the transaction. Further the lessee will want to ensure that if the failure to obtain group relief is not due to a failure on the part of the finance lessor or a member of its group, to make a proper claim, or because the group relationship is severed. A reasonable, balanced clause might be as follows:

> 'There will be no change in the Tax System as it relates to set off of losses against other profits under *ICTA 1988 s 393A* and/or group relief under the provisions relating to Group Relief contained in *ICTA 1988 Ch IV Pt X* which in either case would affect or in any way restrict the Lessor's ability to set tax losses against other profits of the Lessor and/or the ability of any Group Relief Recipient (assuming it to have available taxable profits) to claim and enjoy relief in respect of tax losses surrendered by the Lessor to the relevant Group Relief Recipient in an amount equal to such losses surrendered.'

Qualifying purpose

14.3.9 In order to secure the desired tax treatment, the finance lessor must enter into the transaction in the ordinary course of its trade as a finance lessor and the lessee must use the leased equipment for the purpose of its trade so that it is fulfilling the 'qualifying purpose' test required by the capital allowances regime. In some cases, the transaction documents do not include any assumption in respect of the finance lessor because it is felt by the lessee that a large lessor dominant in the market is clearly entering into the lease as a trading transaction. Similarly, if the lessee is, say, a ball bearing manufacturer and is buying a ball bearing making machine it may be felt unnecessary to state that the equipment will be used for the purpose of the trade. However, it is prudent to include such assumptions. Finance lessors are often part of a large financial organisation and it is dangerous to assume, however likely, that the transaction will automatically be part of the leasing trade. Similarly, a lessee may, for example, change its trade with the result that the equipment ceases to be used. Thus, the lessee will often insist that the finance lessor agrees to a non-variable assumption confirming that it is engaged in the trade of leasing and the transaction is in the ordinary course of that trade (see below). In the variable assumptions the lessee may be required to agree to the following:

> 'The Lessee will use the Asset for the purpose of its trade of [ ] and for no other purpose and shall continue to use the Asset for such purpose during the currency of the Lease.'

The sweeper provision

14.3.10 A finance lessor, particularly in a long lease, will want to ensure that it is protected against any unforeseen change in the tax system which could have a detrimental effect on the cashflow. By definition it is impossible to be specific about these concerns because they are concerns which at the time the lease is entered into are not identifiable. Consequently, the finance lessor will try and put in a clause along the following lines of an assumption saying that:

> 'There will be no other change in the Tax System affecting the Cashflow.'

Although the lessee sometimes claims that this is too vague, it is difficult to be more specific and as a matter of market practice the lessee may have difficulty resisting such a sweeper.

Value Added Tax

14.3.11 The treatment of value added tax rather depends upon the way in which it has been shown in the cashflow. Often VAT is ignored altogether in cashflows in which case there should be an assumption that the payments do not cover value added tax which will not be taken into account. Alternatively, if for whatever reason, VAT and its recovery is reflected in the cashflow the assumption should dovetail into the cashflow statement.

Termination payments

14.3.12 The assumptions will have to deal with the mechanisms for terminating the lease. There are a number of types of termination but generally it is assumed that at the end of the lease on early termination or expiry, the assets will be sold for net proceeds equal to their tax written down value, which therefore does not result in a clawback of allowances. Consequently, it is usual to include an assumption that on termination the assets will be disposed of for the value shown in the cashflow.

Non-variable assumptions (principles)

14.4 As discussed above, there will be fixed assumptions which are so fundamental to the transaction that whether they are varied or not should make no difference to the cashflow. Often such matters are within the control of the parties and are of such a type that the other party should be entitled to make an unvariable assumption in respect of these: for example, assuming that the other party is UK resident. The principal debate and negotiation that occurs in this area is not so much on the wording of the assumptions themselves but on whether such assumptions should be included in the non-variable or variable list. The usual non-variable assumptions are as follows:

Residence

14.4.1 Because the finance lessor is claiming capital allowances, it is essential that it is resident for United Kingdom tax purposes and a fixed assumption is normally put in for this purpose. Somewhat surprisingly, as it can affect the availability of allowances, there is not always a similar fixed assumption for the lessee. Consequently, the assumption is normally as follows:

> 'The Lessor is and will remain resident in the United Kingdom for tax purposes.'

Claiming capital allowances

14.4.2 As mentioned above, the variable assumption on the availability of capital allowances will sometimes contain an exclusion if the failure to obtain them is due to default on the part of the finance lessor. Alternatively, in some leases the non-variable and variable assumptions must be read together so that having given a variable assumption that allowances will be available the non-variable assumption states:

'The Lessor will claim all capital allowances to which it is entitled on a due and timely basis and will not voluntarily postpone or disclaim its rights to such allowances.'

Change in accounting period

14.4.3 Similar to the point made above, the lessee will be looking to ensure there is no voluntary change in the finance lessor's accounting period, which is sometimes included in the variable assumptions but sometimes by way of a fixed assumption, as follows:

'Neither the Lessor nor any Group Relief Recipient will voluntarily change its accounting period.'

Adequacy of profit

14.4.4 A transaction is undertaken on the basis that capital allowances can be utilised by the finance lessor. If the finance lessor is unable to utilise such allowances because it does not have adequate profits then the lessee is entitled to take the view that it is a problem solely for the finance lessor. This leads to the following non-variable assumption:

'The Lessor and Group Relief Recipient will have available taxable profit of an aggregate amount in relation to each accounting period equal to or in excess of the amount required to utilise the Tax Loss shown in the Cashflow Statement for such accounting period.'

Adjustment to rentals

14.5 Having established that the assumptions are as stated above, there must then be a mechanism included in the lease for an adjustment to the rentals in the event that the assumptions prove to be incorrect, in which case a clause similar to those set out below may be inserted. The mechanism for effecting a change in rent following a change in an assumption normally starts by requiring the finance lessor to provide a revised cashflow showing the effects of the change. Such a provision may be as follows:

'(a) Change in Assumptions

'On or as soon as reasonably practicable and, in any event, within thirty (30) Business Days after any date on which the Lessor becomes aware of the fact that there has been a change in the Variable Assumptions (but not, for the avoidance of doubt, a change in the Non-Variable Assumptions) on the basis of which the Cashflow or (as revised) any Applicable Cashflow has been prepared and the occurrence of such an event would, if a new Cashflow were then prepared, produce different figures in respect of the Capital Outstanding and, therefore, Rentals payable hereunder the Lessor shall provide to the Lessee a new Applicable Cashflow, calculated so as to take effect from the next Rental Payment Date (or, where that is impracticable because the Lessor becomes so aware shortly before a Rental Payment Date, the second Rental Payment Date to occur), which shall:

(i) subject to sub-paragraph (ii), (iii) and (iv) below, be prepared on the same basis as the Cashflow was prepared and by reference to the Assumptions in order to ensure that the Percentage Return is maintained on the Notional Capital Outstanding from time to time;

(ii) take into account any changes in any of the Variable Assumptions which have occurred (and are known to the Lessor) between the date of this Agreement and the date of preparation of such new Applicable Cashflow and be on the basis of such varied Assumptions (which shall thereafter become replacement Variable Assumptions);

(iii) take into account the Rentals previously payable hereunder; and

(iv) procure that, subject to the payment by the Lessee of Rentals on each subsequent Rental Payment Date, the Notional Capital Outstanding on the Final Date will be zero or as near thereto as may be. Each such subsequent Rental shown in such Cashflow shall bear the same ratio to the other such subsequent Rental shown therein as the corresponding Rentals bear to each other in the Initial Cashflow.

(b) Effect of Substitution of New Applicable Cashflow

As from the date any New Applicable Cashflow is to take effect in accordance with paragraph (A) above, the same shall be deemed to be incorporated herein in substitution for the previous Applicable Cashflow and payments to be made hereunder shall be determined by reference thereto.'

Having provided a revised cashflow, there needs to be a provision which deals with the actual payments that result. The lease term is usually divided into fixed periods of, say, three months and any adjustment is made in respect of the rent in the three month period ('Adjustment Period') in which the change occurs and for subsequent periods. Although future rentals for future periods can be adjusted to take into account the change there must also be a payment to compensate for the shortfall (or overpayment) of rent between the date of the change and the end of the Adjustment Period in which the change occurs which will be included in the revised rent. The clause implementing the revised rental is:

'(c) Adjustments in respect of Applicable Rate

On the Adjustment Date for each Adjustment Period the Lessor shall pay to the Lessee by way of rebate of Rental or the Lessee shall pay to the Lessor by way of further Rental (as appropriate) the difference between:

(i) the amount of interest which has been debited or credited to the relevant Cashflow for such Adjustment Period calculated by reference to the Reference Rate; and

(ii) what would have been debited or credited thereto if the amount of the debit or credit to be made had been calculated by reference to the Applicable Rate for such Adjustment Period including, where appropriate, interest at the relevant Applicable Rate.'

It will be noted that the adjustment mechanism works in favour of both the lessee and finance lessor depending on the effect of the change in assumption. Having provided that a change in assumption gives rise to a new cashflow and revised rental, one then has to address how one determines whether a change of assumption has really taken place:

'(d) Occurrence of Change

For the purposes of this Financial Schedule:

(i) a change shall be regarded as having occurred if the Lessor reasonably determines [or if it is determined pursuant to paragraph] that any Variable Assumption is incorrect;

(ii) a change shall be regarded as having occurred in any of the Variable Assumptions when any statute or statutory instrument embodying such change becomes law even though such change will only take effect in the future and a Cashflow prepared, in such a case and at that time, shall immediately take into account all changes so embodied but only from the date on which such change is to take effect; and

(iii) on or after the occurrence of a Termination Event, the Lessor shall be entitled to deem a change in any of the Variable Assumptions to have occurred, at any time when it has reasonable grounds for believing that such a change will occur and, in such case, if the change does not in fact occur and take effect when anticipated a further change shall then be regarded as having occurred.

The Applicable Cashflow prepared as a consequence of the occurrence of any such change or deemed change shall take into account the date from which such change or deemed change becomes effective.

The Lessor shall not be obliged, for the purpose of demonstrating to the Lessee that any change has occurred or that a particular payment or transaction has been treated for tax purposes in a particular way and without prejudice to the Lessee's right to challenge such determination in a court of competent jurisdiction, to allow the Lessee to inspect any of the books or other records or correspondence of the Lessor or to make any disclosure in relation thereto. The Lessor shall act in good faith but, subject thereto, shall be entitled to arrange its tax and commercial affairs in whatever manner it thinks fit having regard to its own interest and those of its various customers (including the Lessee).'

Reference to an expert

14.6 Many leases contain an arbitration clause so that in the event of a dispute on the breach of assumptions the matter can be referred to an independent expert. Often as a precursor to referring the matter to an expert there is a provision requiring the parties to consult and co-operate, with the aim of resolving the issue. If this fails the clause for reference to the expert might be as follows:

'(a) Disputed calculations

If the Lessee does not accept that any calculation or cashflow prepared pursuant to this Schedule has been made or prepared in accordance with the terms and provisions of this Agreement, the Lessee may (without prejudice to its obligations to make payment hereunder in accordance with such Cashflow and/or calculation pending determination of the matter as hereinafter provided) give notice to the Lessor within thirty (30) Business Days of receiving a copy of such Cashflow and/or calculation from the Lessor together with the Lessee's reasons for such non-acceptance and the notice. The Lessee's reasons together with the Lessor's calculation and/or Cashflow and/or any adjustment thereto and reasons therefor, together with a statement of the amount disputed by the parties together with such information relevant to the dispute as the [Accountants] shall reasonably require, shall then be referred to the [Accountants] who shall act as experts and not as arbitrators and whose decision as to the correctness of such calculations and/or Cashflow and/or any adjustment thereto in accordance with the terms of this Schedule, as the case may be, shall, except in the case of manifest error until the same has been corrected, be conclusive and binding on the Lessor and the Lessee unless an until overruled by a court of competent jurisdiction. The [Accountants'] costs in so acting shall be borne by the Lessee unless they determine that the Cashflow and/or figures were erroneous by an amount equal to or greater than the higher of

[£10,000 or 0.1 per cent] of the amount in dispute, in which case the [Accountants'] costs shall be borne by the Lessor.

(b) Adjustments

Should the [Accountants'] decision require variation of an amount previously paid hereunder, such variation shall apply retrospectively from the date on which the relevant amount was paid and the amount of any deficiency or excess in or of such amount previously paid by or received by the Lessor shall, within ten (10) Business Days after receipt by the Lessor and the Lessee of written notice of the decision and of a revised Cashflow (which the Lessor shall produce forthwith after, and in accordance with, the decision of the [Accountants]), be remedied by a payment by or to the Lessor by way of adjustment to Rentals or to Termination Sum or any adjustment thereto (as appropriate), together with interest at overnight LIBOR compounded quarterly on the amount of the deficiency or on the amount of any excess from the date or dates on which such amount or amounts were required to be paid or received by the Lessor to the date on which such adjustment is made.

(c) Detail of calculations

All calculations provided by the Lessor to the Lessee under this Schedule shall be in reasonably sufficient detail to enable the Lessee to substantiate the same.'

14.7 General tax indemnity and other tax provisions

General tax indemnity and payment of certain outgoings

14.7.1 As well as the more sophisticated tax considerations involved in making the assumptions and arriving at the cashflow, a lease will normally contain a more general indemnity. A finance lessor takes the view that the lease is a transaction for the provision of finance. Thus, any tax liabilities associated with the ownership or use of the machinery should be borne by the lessee, for whom the machinery was purchased and for whose benefit the transaction was structured. If, for example, the machine concerned is subject to any annual tax or licence fee, levied on the finance lessor as the registered owner, the finance lessor would expect to pass this onto the lessee. To cover this, a general indemnity such as the type described below is entered into. In the case of aircraft which move between jurisdictions, increasing the likelihood of local taxes and duties, a more sophisticated and detailed clause may be required. The sort of indemnity that may be given is:

'The Lessee shall pay and discharge or cause to be paid and discharged, as soon as the same arise or become payable (and shall, if requested by the Lessors produce to the Lessor evidence of the payment and discharge thereof) and indemnify the Lessor and each and every other member of the Lessor's Group and keep the Lessor and each such member fully indemnified against:

(i) any Tax Liabilities; and

(ii) any licence duties, registration, recording, titling, filing or other fees, charges or levies and any interest or penalties payable in connection with any of the same;

which arise or become payable at any time in respect of:

(iii) the Asset or any interest therein; or

(iv) any document, payment, matter, circumstances or transaction contemplated by this Agreement or by any of the other Operative Documents including (without limitation) the agreement to purchase, purchase, ownership, delivery, leasing, use, possession, operation, import, export, return, storage, maintenance, protection, sale, attempted sale or other disposition of the Asset or any interest therein;

or which arise or become payable as a result (whether alone or in connection with any other matter or circumstance) of anything done in response to any request in writing by the Lessee.'

Restriction on general tax indemnity

14.7.2 The most important restriction on the indemnity from the lessee's point of view is that it should be limited to taxes associated with the use or ownership of the leased asset and that it should not extend to cover corporation tax on profits from the transaction. Hence, the following exclusion is generally included, which provides that the indemnity will not protect the lessor against:

> 'Corporation Tax attributable to any Rental or Termination Sum (including any adjustment to or amount treated for the purposes of the Lease as any Rental or Termination Sum) actually receivable hereunder or to any other amounts payable to and retained by the Lessor under any of the [Operative Documents] [or to any net Disposal Proceeds or Net Total Loss Proceeds] actually received and retained by the Lessor in respect of the Asset (regardless of the Accounting Period of the Lessor in which such amounts accrue or arise).'

The lessee will also restrict the protection of the finance lessor to matters other than those caused by the finance lessors, voluntary acts or defaults, thus excluding:

> 'any Tax Liability to the extent it would not have arisen but for the reasonably avoidable delay or failure by the Lessor or any member of the Lessor's Group in the filing of Tax returns or the payment of

Taxes assessed on the Lessor or any member of the Lessor's Group which delay or failure has not been requested or consented to or in any of the [Operative Documents] or consented to in writing by the Lessee or unless such failure or delay by the Lessor or any member of the Lessor's Group arises from a failure by the Lessee promptly to provide the Lessor or any member of the Lessor's Group with correct, suitable and adequate information which is or should be reasonably available to the Lessee to enable the Lessor or any member of the Lessor's Group to file the relevant Tax return to pay such Taxes.'

The lessee will want to ensure that the finance lessor does not receive compensation for the indemnified matters twice: once under the cashflow or an adjustment to the cashflow and once under the indemnity. To avoid this the following exclusion may be included:

> 'this paragraph [indemnity paragraph] shall not apply to any Tax Liability to the extent that it is taken into account in accordance with the provisions of the Financial Schedule in computing the amount of any Rental or Termination Sum of any adjustment thereto.'

Withholding and gross-up

14.7.3 As with any indemnity, the finance lessor will expect to receive payment free from deduction or withholding of tax and with the benefit of a gross-up. The clauses and the logic behind them are similar to those in a tax deed given on the sale of shares or in a banking document. A typical clause dealing with deduction may be:

'(a) All the sums payable to the Lessor pursuant to or in connection with this Agreement or any of the other Operative Documents, or any document contemplated by or entered into pursuant hereto or thereto, shall be paid in full without any set-off or counterclaim whatsoever and free and clear of all deductions or withholdings whatsoever save only as may be required by law.

(b) If any deduction or withholding is required by law in respect of any payment due to the Lessor pursuant to or in connection with this Agreement or any of the other Operative Documents or any document contemplated by or entered into pursuant hereto or thereto, the Lessee shall:

(i) ensure or procured that the deduction or withholding is made and that it does not exceed the minimum legal requirement therefor;

(ii) pay, or procure the payment of, the full amount deducted or withheld to the relevant Taxation or other authority in accordance with the applicable law;

(iii)

(a) if the payment is to be made by the Lessee, increase the payment in respect of which the deduction or withholding is required so that the net amount received by the Lessor after the deduction or withholding (and after taking account of any further deduction or withholding which is required to be made which arises as a consequence of the increase) shall be equal to the amount which the Lessor would have been entitled to receive in the absence of any requirement to make a deduction or withholding; or (as the case may be)

(b) if and to the extent that the payment is to be made by any person other than the Lessee, pay directly to the Lessor such sum (a 'compensating sum') as will, after taking into account any deduction or withholding which is required to be made in respect of the compensating sum enable the Lessor to receive, on the due date for payment, a net sum equal to the sum which the Lessor would have received in the absence of any obligation to make a deduction or withholding; and

(iv) promptly deliver or procure the delivery to the Lessor of appropriate receipts evidencing the deduction or withholding which has been made.

(c) If the Lessor determines in its absolute discretion that it has received, realised, utilised and retained a Tax benefit by reason of any deduction or withholding, in respect of which the lessee has made an increased payment or paid a compensating sum under this Clause the Lessor shall, provided it has received all amounts which are then due and payable by the Lessee under any of the provisions of this Agreement and the other Operative Documents, pay to the Lessee (to the extent that the Lessor can do so without prejudicing the amount of that benefit and the right of the Lessor to obtain any other benefit relief or allowance which may be available to it) such amount, if any, as the Lessor shall determine will leave the Lessor in no better and no worse position than the Lessor would have been in if the deduction or withholding had not been required.

Provided that:

(i) the Lessor shall have an absolute discretion as to the time at which and the order and manner in which it realises or utilises any Tax benefit and, in particular, the Lessor shall not be under any obligation to claim any Tax credit, Tax deduction or similar benefit in respect of the amount of such withholding or deduction in priority to any other claim, relief, credit or deduction available to it;

(ii) the Lessor shall not be obliged to disclose any information regarding its business, Tax affairs or Tax computations to the Lessee or to any other person;

(iii) if the Lessor has made a payment to the Lessee pursuant to this Clause (c) on account of any Tax benefit and it subsequently transpires that the lessor did not receive that Tax benefit, or received a lesser Tax benefit, the Lessee shall pay on demand to the Lessor such sum as the Lessor may determine as being necessary to restore the after-tax position of the Lessor to that which it would have been had no adjustment under this proviso (iii) been necessary. Any sums payable by the Lessee to the lessor under this proviso (iii) shall be subject to the provisions of [the gross-up clause];

(iv) the Lessor shall not be obliged to make any payment under this Clause, if, by doing so, it would contravene the terms of any applicable law or any notice, direction or requirements of any governmental or regulatory authority (whether or not having the force of law) compliance with which is customary.'

A typical clause dealing with gross-up could be:

'If the Lessor makes a payment or suffers a loss in respect of which it is entitled to be indemnified or reimbursed or otherwise kept harmless pursuant to any provision of this Agreement or any of the other Operative Documents and the Lessor determines that:

(a) (i) the loss or payment is not or is unlikely to be wholly deductible in computing the profits of the Lessor for the purposes of Tax whilst the payment to be made by way of indemnity or reimbursement (for the purpose of this Clause, the "Payment") will or is likely to give rise to a Tax Liability for the Lessor; or

(ii) the Payment will or is likely to give rise to a Tax Liability for the Lessor in any Accounting Period of the Lessor earlier than the Accounting Period in which the loss or payment is or is likely to be deductible;

then, at the time of the Payment the Lessee shall pay such an amount (the "Additional Payment") as will, after taking into account any Tax Liability likely to be suffered or incurred by the Lessor in respect of the Payment or the Additional Payment, leave the Lessor in the same after-Tax position as it would have been in had the Payment not given rise to any such Tax Liability and the loss or payment had not been so deductible PRO-

VIDED THAT if at the time of the Payment the Lessor considers that no Additional Payment is necessary but subsequently determines that an Additional Payment is necessary so to indemnify the Lessor, the Additional Payment shall be paid by the Lessee to the Lessor following a demand by the Lessor;

(b) the loss or payment has proved to be wholly or partly deductible in computing the profits of the Lessor for the purposes of Tax whilst the Payment by the Lessee has proved not to give rise to any Tax Liability for the Lessor, (or to have given rise to a Tax Liability which is less than the value of the deduction attributable to the relevant loss or payment) then the Lessor shall pay to the Lessee a rebate of Rental (for the purposes of this Clause the "Rebate") of such amount as will leave the Lessor in no better and no worse position than it would have been if the Payment had not given rise to a Tax Liability for the Lessor and the loss or payment had not been so deductible,

provided that:

if the Lessor subsequently determines that any payment by the Lessee to the Lessor under this Clause by way of an Additional Payment or, as the case may be, any Rebate was calculated on an incorrect basis, such adjustment shall be made between the Lessor and the Lessee determines necessary to restore the after-Tax position of the Lessor to that which it would have been if no adjustment had been necessary.'

Lessee tax warranties/undertakings

14.7.4 Apart from ensuring that it is protected against unforeseen tax liabilities, the finance lessor will want to place positive obligations on the lessee to act in the way anticipated by the lessor when the lease was entered into. In particular, the finance lessor will want the lessee to confirm that it will pay taxes associated with the Asset and co-operate in making the necessary returns. The type of obligations sometimes inserted, which need no further explanation, are as follows:

'The Lessee hereby undertakes to the Lessor from the date hereof and thereafter until the sale (if any) of the Asset that it will:

(a) Pay taxes

Duly pay and discharge or cause to be paid and discharge all Taxes, assessments and governmental charges levied upon it or its property in respect of or on the Asset not later than the due date of payment;'

(b) Capital allowances

Not claim any capital allowances or analogous tax allowances in respect of the Asset in the United Kingdom;

(c) Tax authorities

Furnish promptly to any tax authority or to the Lessor for the Lessor to furnish to such an authority such information as may be required to be furnished about the Asset, the use to which the same is being or has been put or any other matter or circumstance contemplated by this Agreement and the other Operative Documents and furnish to the Lessor promptly upon request such information, books, records or documents concerning the Asset or any of the transactions contemplated by the Operative Documents which is or should be reasonably available to the Lessee or any other member of the Guarantor's Group as may be necessary in order to enable the Lessor to respond to such a request of the Lessor from any tax authority.'

Appendix 1

Illustration of a Tax Deed of Covenant to be used when acting for the Vendor

THIS DEED is made on [date] BETWEEN:

[(1) THE SEVERAL PERSONS whose names and addresses appear in the First Schedule (together called the 'Covenantors');] [or]

[(1) [VENDOR] incorporated in [England and Wales] [Scotland] with number* [ ] (the 'Covenantor');] and

(2) [PURCHASER] incorporated in [England and Wales] [Scotland] with number* [ ] (the 'Purchaser').

WHEREAS: by an agreement (the 'Agreement') dated [appropriate date] the Purchaser has agreed to purchase [the whole] [part] of the issued share capital of the Company from the Covenantor[s] in reliance *inter alia* on the covenants contained in this Deed.

THIS DEED WITNESSETH as follows:

1. INTERPRETATION

In this deed unless the context otherwise requires:

1.1 save as herein otherwise provided words and expressions defined in the Agreement shall bear the same meanings in this Deed and any provisions in the Agreement concerning matters of interpretation or construction shall apply equally to this Deed;

1.2 '*Accounting Date*' means [appropriate date];

1.3 '*Accounts*' means the audited balance sheet of the Company as at the Accounting Date and the audited profit and loss account of the Company for the financial year of the Company ended on the Accounting Date;

1.4 '*ACT*' means advance corporation tax as defined in section 14 of the Income and Corporation Taxes Act 1988 (the '*Taxes Act 1988*');

1.5 '*Business Day*' means a day which is not a Saturday or Sunday or a bank or other public holiday in England;

1.6 '*Claim*' means:

1.6.1 any assessment, notice, letter, determination, demand or other document issued by or on behalf of any taxing or other competent authority (whether within or outside the United Kingdom and whether issued or taken before or after the date hereof and whether satisfied or not at the date hereof);

1.6.2 any return, amended return, computation, accounts or any other documents required for the purposes of taxation (whether within or outside the United Kingdom)

from which it appears that a Tax Liability has been or may be imposed on the Company or increased or further payment to such authority or body required to be made;

1.7 '*Company*' means [ ]

1.8 '*Relief* means any loss, allowance, credit, deduction or set off;

1.9 '*Remaining Group'* means the Covenantor[s] and all companies (other than the Company) which at or within four years of Completion were 51% subsidiaries (as defined in section 838 of the Taxes Act 1988) of the Covenantor;

1.10 '*Tax*' or '*Taxation*' means all taxes, levies, imposts, duties, charges and withholdings of whatsoever nature whenever and wherever imposed and without prejudice to the generality of the foregoing includes:

1.10.1 within the United Kingdom, income tax (including income tax required to be deducted or withheld or accounted for in respect of any payment), corporation tax, advance corporation tax, capital gains tax, the charge under section 601(2) of the Taxes Act 1988, value added tax, Customs and Excise duties, amounts corresponding to any of corporation tax or income tax or advance corporation tax, inheritance tax, national insurance contributions, stamp duty, stamp duty reserve tax, landfill tax and insurance premium tax;

1.10.2 outside the United Kingdom, identical or substantially similar taxes to those United Kingdom taxes referred to at Clause 1.10.1 together with all other taxes on gross and net income profits or gains, receipts, sales, use, occupation, franchise, added value, net or gross value or worth or personal property; and

1.10.3 all penalties, charges, costs and interest included in or relating to any Tax regardless of whether such taxes, penalties, charges, costs and interest are directly or primarily chargeable against or attributable to the Company or any other person and regardless of whether the Company has or may have any right of reimbursement against any other person;

1.11 references to any '*Tax Liability*' of the Company shall include not only liabilities of the Company to make payments of or in respect of tax but also the loss of a right to repayment of tax which has been treated as an asset in the Accounts;

1.12 in the cases described in Clause 1.11 the amount of the Tax Liability shall be the amount of the repayment which would otherwise have been obtained;

1.13 references to:

1.13.1 '*Income, Profits or Gains*' means revenue profits, chargeable gains, and any other similar measure by reference to which tax is chargeable or assessed;

1.13.2 Income, Profits or Gains earned, accrued or received on or before a particular date or in respect of a particular period shall include Income, Profits or Gains which have been deemed to have been earned, accrued or received at or before the date or in respect of that period for the purposes of any tax assessment;

1.13.3 any '*Dividend*' shall include anything which has been deemed to be a dividend or distribution to shareholders or others for the purposes of any Claim for Taxation and shall also include any other event which gives rise to an obligation to account for advance corporation tax or amounts corresponding to or similar to advance corporation tax including any events generating or taken into account for calculating shadow advance corporation tax;

1.14 '*Event*' includes (without limitation) the death of any person, any transaction (including the execution of the Agreement), event, action or omission;

1.15 references to Clauses and sub-Clauses are references to clauses and sub-clauses of this Deed; and

1.16 headings are included in this Deed for ease of reference only and shall not affect its interpretation.

2. COVENANT

The Covenantor[s] hereby [jointly and severally] covenant[s] to pay to the Purchaser an amount equal to:

2.1 any Tax Liability of the Company arising as a result of any Event which occurred on or before Completion or arising in respect of any Income, Profits or Gains which were earned, accrued or received on or before Completion; and

2.2 any costs and expenses reasonably and properly incurred by the Purchaser and/or the Company in connection with any such Tax Liability (or claim therefor) or in taking or defending any action under this Deed.

3. EXCLUSIONS

The covenants given in this Deed shall not cover any Tax Liability of the Company:

3.1 to the extent that provision or reserve in respect of such Tax Liability was made or reflected in the Accounts (including any provision or reserve made in respect of deferred Tax) or referred to in the notes thereto or to the extent that payment or discharge of such claim has been taken into account in the Accounts;

3.2 to the extent that such Tax Liability arises or is increased as a result of a change or changes in tax rates or in legislation made after the date of this Deed (whether relating to taxation or otherwise) or the change or withdrawal after the date of this Deed of any previously published practice or concession of any tax authority with retrospective effect;

3.3 to the extent that such Tax Liability would not have arisen but for a voluntary act or transaction carried out [(other than in fulfilment of a legally binding commitment entered into by the Company on or before Completion)] by the Purchaser or the Company after Completion otherwise than in the ordinary course of business of such company as such business is conducted at Completion;

3.4 to the extent that such Tax Liability arises as a result of transactions in the ordinary course of business of the Company after the Accounting Date but on or before Completion PROVIDED THAT (without prejudice to the generality of the foregoing) any Claim for Taxation arising from any of the following shall not be regarded for the purposes of this sub-Clause 3.4 as arising 'in the ordinary course of business of the Company':

3.4.1 any event which results in a Tax Liability arising in the Company where such liability is chargeable or attributable primarily to a person other than the Company (including any liability under Part VIII of the Taxes Management Act 1970 (charges on non-residents));

3.4.2 any liability under Part XVII of the Taxes Act 1988 (tax avoidance);

3.4.3 any liability in respect of any distribution (as defined in section 209 of the Taxes Act 1988) or deemed distribution for tax purposes;

3.4.4 the disposal of any asset (including trading stock) where the consideration actually received (if any) for such disposal or supply is less than the consideration deemed to have been received for the purpose of any tax but only to the extent the tax liability is attributable to the difference between the consideration actually received and the consideration deemed to have been received for the purpose of any tax;

3.4.5 any liability arising as a result of the Company ceasing for tax purposes to be a member of any group or associated with any other company;

[*Note: Clause 3.4 is likely to be inappropriate where there are completion accounts*]

3.5 to the extent that recovery of such Tax Liability is made under the Warranties;

3.6 which would not have arisen but for a cessation of trade, or a change in the nature or conduct of the trade, by the Company on or after the date hereof;

3.7 to the extent that such Tax Liability arises by virtue of any disclaimer or disallowance of industrial building or other capital allowances or other transaction by the Company after Completion which has the effect of increasing the Tax Liability of the Company in respect of any period ending on or before the Accounting Date;

3.8 to the extent that such Tax Liability would not have arisen or would have been reduced or eliminated but for a failure on the part of the company to make any claims, election, surrender or disclaimer or give any notice or consent or do anything after completion the making, giving, or doing of which was taken into account in the Accounts;

[*Note: Clauses 3.7 and 3.8 are not appropriate where clause 9 is included*]

3.9 to the extent that the Tax Liability arises or is increased in consequence of any failure by the Purchaser to comply with, or failure to procure the compliance of the Company with, any of their respective obligations under this Deed;

3.10 to the extent that such Tax Liability arises in respect of Valued Added Tax ('*VAT*') and duties relating to supplies made and imports received, the liability for which has been incurred in the ordinary course of the business of the Company;

3.11 to the extent that such Tax Liability results from or is increased or extended by the change of the accounting reference date of the Company on Completion or any subsequent change thereafter or by any change in the accounting policies of the Company or the basis upon which the company values its assets after Completion or the payment of any unusual or abnormal dividend;

3.12 to the extent that the Covenantor[s] [or a member of the Remaining Group] [has] [have] satisfied such Tax Liability by reason of being liable for such Taxation under section 767(A), 767AA or other statutory provision.

4. LIMITATIONS

4.1 [Subject to Clauses 4.3 and 4.4 the liability of the Covenantor[s] under this Deed shall not (when aggregated with any liability under the Warranties) exceed £[ ]*.

4.2 The liability of the Covenantor[s] under this Deed shall terminate on the [third] anniversary of Completion except in respect of any claim under this Deed of which notice in writing is given to the Covenantor[s] before that date containing in reasonable detail a description of the Claim and the estimated total amount of the Claim.]

4.3 The Covenantor[s] shall [only be liable under this Deed to the extent that] [not be liable under this Deed unless] the amount of any Tax Liability subject to the covenants contained in this Deed (when aggregated with any liability under the Warranties) exceeds in aggregate £[ ].

4.4 The Purchaser shall not be entitled to recover any sums whatsoever in respect of any particular Claim under this Deed in respect of which the amount claimed does not exceed £[ ] and such claims shall be be disregarded for the purposes of sub-Clauses 4.1 and 4.3.

[*Note: ensure that the above clauses conform with Agreement*]

5. OVERPROVISIONS AND CORRESPONDING SAVINGS

5.1 If the Purchaser or the Company become aware that any provision for Tax contained in the Accounts is likely to be an overprovision (the '*Overprovision*') or that any Tax Liability which has resulted in a payment being made by or becoming due from the Covenantor[s] under this Deed has given rise to a corresponding saving for the Company, the Purchaser shall forthwith give details thereof to the Covenantor[s] and the Covenantor[s] may request that the Company's auditors for the time being certify the extent of such overprovision or corresponding saving in which event an amount equal to the value (as certified by the Company's auditors for the time being) of such Overprovision or corresponding saving shall be paid forthwith to the Covenantor[s] to the extent that the Covenantor[s] have already made any payment[s] under this Deed and to the extent that there is any excess such excess shall be carried forward and set against any future payment or payments which become due from the Covenantor[s] under this Deed in chronological order until exhausted.

5.2 The amount of the Overprovision shall be calculated on the basis that no Overprovision will arise or be increased by:

5.2.1 a retrospective change in the law of Taxation after Completion; or

5.2.2 any Relief arising after Completion.

6. RECOVERY FROM OTHER PERSONS

Without prejudice to the Covenantor[']s['] obligation to make any payment hereunder, where the Company is entitled to recover from some other person (other than the Purchaser but including any taxing or other competent authorities) any sum in respect of any such Tax Liability as is mentioned in Clause 2, the Purchaser shall procure that the Company shall as soon as reasonably practicable following it becoming aware of its entitlement notify the Covenantor[s] and if so required by the Covenantor[s] and at [its] [their] expense, take all appropriate steps to enforce such recovery (keeping the Covenantor[s] fully informed of the progress of any action taken) and shall account to the Covenantor[s] for any amount so recovered together with any interest or repayment supplement received in respect of the sum so recovered forthwith *provided that* the amount so repaid less any interest and repayment supplement shall not exceed the amount paid by the Covenantor[s] hereunder in respect of that Tax Liability and so far as not repaid or paid, the amount of the sum recovered (including any interest or repayment supplement) shall be set against the liability of the Covenantor[s] in respect of any future claims under this Deed.

7. MITIGATION

7.1 The Purchaser shall at the Covenantor[']s['] request procure that the Company:

7.1.1 uses such Reliefs (other than Reliefs arising in the Company by reference to an accounting period commencing or expenditure incurred after Completion) available to them (including by way of surrender from one Subsidiary to another or between [the name of the company] and any Subsidiary and vice versa) such Reliefs to be used in priority to Reliefs arising after Completion;

7.1.2 make all elections, save in respect of matters after the date of this Deed, so as to reduce or eliminate the Covenantor[']s['] liability under this Deed;

7.1.3 at the Covenantor[']s['] request and expense deliver to the Covenantor[s] a certificate from the Company's auditors for the time being confirming that all such Reliefs have been so used and elections made.

7.2 The Covenantor[s] may by notice in writing to the Purchaser elect to mitigate or eliminate any liability under this Deed by surrendering or procuring the surrender to the Company of group relief (as defined in section 402 of the Taxes Act 1988) [or ACT] to the extent permitted by law but without any payment being made in consideration of the surrender and the Covenantor[s] shall be absolved from liability under this Deed to the extent of the amount of Taxation relieved by such surrender. The Purchaser shall procure that the Company takes all such steps as the Covenantor[s] may reasonably require to permit and effect any surrender and claim of such Relief including (but not limited to) making a claim in a corporation tax return.

[*Note: Clause 7 should be included only if the covenantor does not retain conduct of pre-completion tax affairs*]

8. VAT

8.1 The Purchaser hereby covenants with the Covenantor[s] to pay the Covenantor[s] and each company in the Covenantor[']s['] group (other than the Company) an amount equal to:

8.1.1 any VAT recoverable from the Covenantor[s] or any of such other group companies under section 43 of the Value Added Tax Act 1994 where such Value Added Tax is attributable to imports or acquisitions or supplies actually made by the Company (whether or not such imports or acquisitions or supplies are treated as made by the Covenantor[s] or any of such other group companies under that section); and

8.1.2 any Tax assessed on the Covenantor[s] under section 767A, 767AA and 767B of the Taxes Act 1988 to the extent that such Tax is not of a type which would allow it to be claimed from the Covenantor[s] under Clause 2 of this Deed.

8.2 Clause 17 (Notices), 10, 11, 12 (Conduct of Claims and Disputes) shall apply to the covenants in this Clause 8 as they apply to the covenants in Clause 2 *mutatis mutandis.*

[Note: Only insert above clause 8 where company is a member of VAT group which includes Covenantor[s] or members of retained group.]

9. CONDUCT OF PRE-COMPLETION TAX AFFAIRS

[*Note: This clause is appropriate only where the Covenantor[s] wish[es] to retain conduct of pre-completion Tax Affairs*]

9.1 The Covenantor[s] and the Purchaser have agreed that subject to the following provisions of this Clause:

9.1.1 as regards all accounting periods ended on or before Completion (the '*relevant accounting periods*') the Covenantor[s] shall at its expense (subject to Clause 9.1.2) have the sole conduct of the tax affairs of the Company (including, but not limited to, the preparation of returns and all correspondence and negotiation in relation to the agreement of Tax Liabilities) and the Purchaser shall procure that the Company shall make such claims (including, but not limited to, claims for group relief or surrenders of advance corporation tax claiming or disclaiming capital allowances and claiming roll-over relief) and shall execute those documents (including but not limited to returns of profits and losses and amended returns) and do those things in connection therewith as the Covenantor[s] shall direct in writing and the Covenantor[s] (and its advisers) shall be provided with such information and assistance (including assistance from employees of the Purchaser or the Company) and access to such documents and records of or relating to the Company as it may reasonably require in connection therewith

[9.1.2 the [Covenantor[s]] [or] [the Purchaser] shall have the sole conduct of the PAYE and VAT affairs of the Company in respect of all periods ended prior to Completion in respect of which VAT returns and PAYE returns need to be made;] and

9.1.3 the Covenantor[s] shall (to the extent permitted by law) be free to make claims and obtain consents for the surrender of losses or other amounts eligible for relief (*'Group Relief'*) between the Company and [the Remaining Group] or [the Covenantor[s]] for the period between the Accounting Date and Completion.

[9.2 The Covenantor[s] shall keep the Purchaser informed of the progress of the Tax Affairs of the Company and shall provide copies of correspondence and shall use [its] [their] best endeavours to settle the Tax Affairs of the Company as soon as reasonably practicable and within the time limits prescribed by the Pay and File regime.] or

[9.2 The Covenantor[s] shall first submit all accounts, tax computations [and correspondence] before submission to the Inland Revenue or other tax authority to the Purchaser which may make such representation as it thinks fit and provided such representations are made reasonably, promptly and in any event within [14] days the Covenantor[s] shall take account of any reasonable representations.]

9.3 Without limitation to the generality of the foregoing the Purchaser shall procure that:

9.3.1 the Company shall forthwith upon receiving a written direction from the Covenantor[s] make such claims and elections and give such consents including such provisional or final claims to accept the surrender of Group Relief or consents to surrender Group Relief in respect of any of the relevant accounting periods and in respect of the period between the Accounting Date and Completion as the Covenantor[s] may in [its] [their] absolute discretion direct including any direction to comply with all the procedural requirements of Chapter IV of Part X and Schedule 17A of the Taxes Act 1988 imposed on a claimant or surrendering company in relation to Group Relief including the notification of consent to a surrender;

9.3.2 the Company shall forthwith upon receiving a written direction from the Covenantor[s] make such provisional, conditional or final claims for set off or surrender or acceptance of a surrender of ACT in respect of any of the relevant accounting periods as the Covenantor[s] may in [its] [their] absolute discretion direct including any direction to comply with all the procedural requirements of section 240 of the Taxes Act 1988 imposed on a subsidiary in relation to ACT including the notification of consent under section 240(6) of the Taxes Act 1988;

9.3.3 save as directed by the Covenantor[s] in writing from time to time, the Company shall not do nor will omit to do any act or thing:

9.3.3.1 which might affect the ability of the Company to make claims for allowances or reliefs or claims to accept surrenders of Group relief or ACT or to set off ACT or to consent to surrenders of Group relief or ACT in respect of the relevant periods; or

9.3.3.2 which would result in any reduction in the amount of Group Relief or ACT which otherwise could be surrendered by or to the Company or set off by the Company;

9.3.4 the Company will not (unless so directed by the Covenantor[s]) amend, withdraw or disclaim any elections or claims previously made including but not limited to elections or claims under section 247 of the Taxes Act 1988 (group income), section 402 of the Taxes Act 1988 (group relief), section 240 of the Taxes Act 1988 (setting of a company's surplus ACT against a subsidiary's liability) nor will the Company amend or withdraw any elections or claims pursuant to section 152 or 153 of the TCGA 1992 (roll-over relief) or disclaim first year or writing down allowances nor will the Company carry back ACT or losses from accounting periods ending after Completion in circumstances where such carry back will reduce the Company's ability to make the surrenders, claims and elections previously mentioned.

9.4 If Group Relief is surrendered under sub-Clause 9.3.1 to [a member of the Remaining Group] [the Covenantor[s]] by the Company [no member of the Remaining Group shall be liable] [the Covenantor[s] shall not be liable] to pay any consideration to the Company or the Purchaser.

9.5 If the Company accepts a surrender of Group Relief in respect of any of the relevant accounting periods which can be offset against profits, the liability to corporation tax on which has been provided for in the Accounts (and in respect of which no claim would arise under Clause 2.1 in the absence of such surrender), the Company shall make payment to the surrendering company of an amount equal to the Tax which would have been payable but for the surrender, payment to be made on the date or dates on which the Tax would otherwise have been payable (assuming no application for postponement of payment of the Tax had been made).

9.6 If under sub-Clause 9.3.2 ACT has been or is surrendered or set off against an actual corporation tax liability for which provision was made in the Accounts (and in respect of which no claim would arise under Clause 2.1 in the absence of such surrender) the Purchaser shall procure that the Company to which the ACT has been or is surrendered shall pay to the surrendering company on the date of surrender or, if later, the date on which the corporation tax against which the ACT has been set off would have been payable (assuming no application for postponement of payment of the Tax had been made) an amount equal to the Tax which would have been payable but for such surrender or set off.

[9.7 The Covenantor[s] shall in its absolute discretion be free to allocate surplus shadow advance corporation tax to the company for all periods prior to completion in accordance with the provisions of the Corporation Tax (Treatment of Unrelieved Surplus Advance Corporation Tax) Regulations 1988.]

[9.8 Where the Covenantor[s] wish[es] to make a claim for Group Relief in respect of the period between the Accounting Date and Completion the losses or profits in respect of which such claim is made shall be based upon the audited profit and loss account for the accounting period of the Company in which Completion takes place on the assumption that profits or losses arose rateably throughout such accounting period.]

10. NOTIFICATION OF CLAIMS AND CONDUCT OF DISPUTE

10.1 If the Company or the Purchaser (as the case may be) shall become aware of a claim in respect of a Tax Liability relevant for the purposes of this Deed or of any determination or direction in respect of losses which could increase such Tax Liability [of which the Covenantor[s] [is] [are] not then aware] written notice thereof shall be given to the Covenantor[s] as soon as reasonably practicable and in any event within [14] days.

10.2 [Without prejudice to the Covenantor[']s['] right to full conduct of the tax affairs of the Company for all relevant periods in accordance with Clause 9] the Covenantor[s] shall at [its] [their] expense be entitled to resist any Claim in respect of a Tax Liability (including a determination or direction in respect of losses) and the Purchaser shall, or shall procure that the Company shall, take such action as the Covenantor[s] may reasonably request in writing to avoid, dispute, defend, resist, appeal or compromise any Claim (such a Claim where action is so requested being hereinafter referred to as a '*Dispute*').

10.3 The Purchaser shall and shall procure that the Company shall make available to the Covenantor[s] such persons as the Covenantor[s] may reasonably require and all such information as may be available to it or them for avoiding, disputing, resisting, appealing, compromising or contesting any such Claim and neither the Purchaser nor the Company shall accept or pay or compromise any such Claim without the Covenantor[s] having had a reasonable opportunity to resist the same.

10.4 If the Covenantor[s] do[es] not request the Purchaser or the Company to take any action under sub-Clause 10.2 within [30] Business Days of written notice having been given to the Covenantor[s], the Purchaser or the Company shall (without prejudice to their rights under this Deed) be free to pay or settle the Claim on such terms as they may reasonably consider fit.

10.5 Notwithstanding that the Dispute may be managed by the Covenantor[s] and dealt with in accordance with [its] [their] wishes pursuant to Clause 7 the Company and/or the Purchaser shall be kept fully informed of all matters pertaining thereto and shall be entitled to see copies of all correspondence pertaining thereto.

11. PAYMENT OF CLAIMS IN THE CASE OF A DISPUTE

Where there is or has been a Dispute and that Dispute relates to a Claim where the tax the subject matter of the Claim has to be paid before the action requested by the Covenantor[s] in respect of such Claim can be taken, the Covenantor[s] shall make payment of such amount of Tax which must be paid as aforesaid forthwith upon service of a notice containing a written demand for the same from the Purchaser and in any other case, the Covenantor[s] shall make payment within [10] Business Days of the settlement, compromise or abandonment of such Dispute.

12. PAYMENT OF CLAIMS WHERE THERE IS NO DISPUTE

12.1 Subject to the provisions of Clause 9 the Covenantor[s] shall be liable to make payment (the '*due date for payment*'):

12.1.1 in respect of a Claim under Clause 2.1 in respect of an actual payment of Taxation on the date [5] Business Days before the date on which the Company has become finally liable to pay the Tax the subject of the Claim in question;

12.1.2 in respect of a Claim under Clause 2.2 on the date [5] Business Days following the date on which notice setting out the amount due has been served by the Purchaser [or the Company] on the Covenantor[s]; and

[12.1.3 in the case of a Claim under Clause 2 in respect of any of the matters referred to in sub-Clause 1.11 which do not involve an actual payment of Tax, the Purchaser [and/or the Company] shall request the Company's auditors for the time being to certify (at the expense of the Covenantor[s]) the amount of the liability under this Deed and the Covenantor[s] shall be liable to make any payment under Clause 2 on the later of:

12.1.3.1 [5] Business Days after the date when notice of such certificate is given to the Covenantor[s]; and

12.1.3.2 in the case of a loss of a repayment of Tax where the amount due for repayment has been offset against a Tax Liability which in the absence of such offset would have given rise to a claim under Clause 2.1, the date when the Tax would have been payable in the absence of such offset;

13. INTEREST ON LATE PAYMENT

If any payment due to be made by the Purchaser or the Covenantor[s] under this Deed is not made on the due date for payment thereof the same shall (in addition to any interest or penalties payable in respect of such liability) carry interest from such due date of payment until actual payment at the rate of [ ] per cent above the base rate for the time being of [Bank] calculated and compounded on a daily basis (whether before or after any judgment).

14. DEDUCTIONS FROM PAYMENTS

14.1 All sums payable by the Covenantor[s] to the Purchaser [or the Company] under this Deed shall be paid free and clear of all deductions or withholdings whatsoever save only as may be required by law.

14.2 If any such deductions or withholdings as are referred to in sub-Clause 14.1 are required by law the Covenantor[s] shall be obliged to pay to the Purchaser [or the Company] such sum as will after such deduction or withholding has been made leave the Purchaser [or the Company] with the same amount as it would have been entitled to receive in the absence of any such requirement to make a deduction or withholding.

14.3 If, following any deduction or withholding from any payment, the Covenantor[s] make an increased payment pursuant to Clause 14.2 the Purchaser shall reimburse the Covenantor[s] such amount as the Purchaser shall (acting in good faith) determine so as to leave the Purchaser in the same position it would have been in had no such deduction or withholding been made, but only to the extent that the Purchaser can do so without prejudicing the retention of any credit or relief obtained as a result of the deduction or withholding.

[*The following clauses to conform with agreement.*]

15. ASSIGNMENT

The Purchaser shall not be entitled to assign the benefit of this Deed or any part of it to any other person.

16. GOVERNING LAW AND JURISDICTION

This Deed shall be governed by English law and for the benefit of [ ] the other parties hereto hereby submit to the jurisdiction of the English Courts.

17. NOTICES

17.1 Any notice or other document to be served under this deed may be delivered personally or sent by pre-paid first class recorded delivery post or facsimile process to the party to be served at his address appearing in this deed or at such other address as he may have notified to the other parties in accordance with this clause.

17.2 Any notice or document shall be deemed to have been served:

17.2.1 if delivered personally, at the time of delivery; or

17.2.2 if posted, at 10 a.m. on the second Business Day after it was put in the post; or

17.2.3 if sent by facsimile process at the expiration of two hours after the time of despatch if despatched.

17.3 In proving service of a notice or document it shall be sufficient to prove that delivery was made or that the envelope containing the notice or document was properly addressed and posted as pre-paid first class recorded delivery letter or that the facsimile message was properly addressed and despatched as the case may be.

17.4 If a notice which is delivered personally or by fax is given:

17.4.1 on a day that is not a Business Day the relevant notice still be deemed to be given by the Business Day next following that day;

17.4.2 after 5.30 p.m. on a Business Day the relevant notice shall be deemed to be given at 9.30 a.m. on the Business Day next following such Business Day.

18. COUNTERPARTS

This Deed may be entered into in any number of counterparts and by the parties to it on separate counterparts, each of which when so executed and delivered shall be an original but all the counterparts together shall constitute one and the same Deed.

IN WITNESS whereof this Deed has been duly executed the day and year first before written.

[SIGNED as a deed

by

in the presence of:

[THE COMMON SEAL of

[SELLER]

was hereunto affixed in the

presence of:

Director

Secretary]

Appendix 2

Illustration of a Tax Deed of Covenant to be used when acting for the Purchaser

THIS DEED is made BETWEEN:

[(1) THE SEVERAL PERSONS whose names and addresses appear in the First Schedule (together called the '*Covenantors*');] [or]

[(1) [SELLER] incorporated in [England and Wales] [Scotland] with number [ ] (the 'Covenantor');]

(2) [PURCHASER] incorporated in [England and Wales] [Scotland] with number [ ] (the 'Purchaser'); and

(3) [COMPANY] incorporated in [England and Wales] [Scotland] with number [ ] [and THE SEVERAL COMPANIES whose names and registered numbers appear in the Second Schedule (the 'Subsidiaries')] ([together called] the 'Company').

WHEREAS by an agreement (the 'Agreement') dated [appropriate date] the Purchaser has agreed to purchase [the whole] [part] of the issued share capital of the Company from the Covenantor[s] in reliance inter alia on the covenants contained in this Deed.

THIS DEED WITNESSETH as follows:

1. INTERPRETATION

In this Deed unless the context otherwise requires:

1.1 save as herein otherwise provided words and expressions defined in the Agreement shall bear the same meanings in this Deed and any provisions in the Agreement concerning matters of interpretation or construction shall apply equally to this Deed;

1.2 '*Accounting Date*' means [appropriate date];

1.3 '*Accounts*' means the audited balance sheet of the Company as at the Accounting Date and the audited profit and loss account of the Company for the financial year of the Company ended on the Accounting Date;

1.4 '*Business Day*' means a day which is not a Saturday or Sunday or a bank or other public holiday in [England];

1.5 '*Claim*' includes:

1.5.1 any assessment, notice, letter, determination, demand or other document issued or action taken by or on behalf of any taxing or other competent authority (whether within or outside the United Kingdom and whether issued or taken before or after the date hereof and whether satisfied or not at the date hereof); and

1.5.2 any return, amended return, computation, accounts or any other documents required for the purposes of Taxation (whether within or outside the United Kingdom) from which it appears that a Tax Liability has been or may be imposed on the Company or increased or further payment to such authority or body required to be made;

[1.6 '*Covenantor[s]*' includes the [respective] estate[s] and personal representatives of [any of] the Covenantor[s];]

1.7 '*Relief*' means any loss, allowance, credit, deduction or set off;

1.8 '*Tax*' or '*Taxation*' means all taxes, levies, imposts, duties, charges and withholdings of whatsoever nature whenever and wherever imposed and without prejudice to the generality of the foregoing includes:

1.8.1 within the United Kingdom, income tax (including income tax required to be deducted or withheld or accounted for in respect of any payment), corporation tax, advance corporation tax, capital gains tax, the charge under section 601(2) of the Taxes Act 1988, value added tax, Customs and Excise duties, amounts corresponding to any of corporation tax or income tax or advance corporation tax, inheritance tax, National Insurance contributions, stamp duty, stamp duty reserve tax, landfill tax and insurance premium tax;

1.8.2 outside the United Kingdom, identical or substantially similar taxes to those United Kingdom taxes referred to at Clause 1.8.1 above together with all other taxes on gross and net income, profits or gains, receipts, sales, use, occupation, franchise, added value, net or gross value of worth and personal property; and

1.8.3 all penalties, charges, costs and interest included in or relating to any tax regardless of whether such taxes, penalties, charges, costs and interest are directly or primarily chargeable against or attributable to the Company or any other person, firm or company and regardless of whether the Company has or may have any right of reimbursement against any other person;

1.9 references to any *'Tax Liability'* of the Company shall include not only liabilities of the Company to make payments of or in respect of Tax but also:

1.9.1 the loss, for whatsoever reason, whether by set off against Income, Profits or Gains (whether present, past or future) or by set off against Tax Liabilities or otherwise of any Relief, which would (were it not for the loss or set off) have been available to the Company [and has been taken into account in computing (and so reducing) any provision for deferred taxation which appears (or which but for such Relief would have appeared) in the Accounts or has been treated as an asset therein];

1.9.2 the loss of a right to repayment of Tax which has been treated as an asset in the Accounts or the setting off of any such right to repayment of Tax against any actual liability in respect of which the Purchaser would, but for that setting off, have been able to make a claim against the Covenantor[s] under this Deed; and

1.9.3 the setting off against Tax Liabilities, Income, Profits or Gains earned, accrued, incurred or received on or before Completion of any Relief, which was not available before Completion but arose in respect of any event occurring after Completion in circumstances where, but for such setting off, the Company would have had an actual Tax Liability in respect of which it or the Purchaser would have been able to make a claim against the Covenantor[s] under this Deed;

1.10 in the cases described in Clause 1.9 above the amount of the Tax Liability shall be:

1.10.1 in any case falling within Clause 1.9.1, the amount of Tax which could thereby have been saved (on the assumption (whether or not it is the case) that there are sufficient Income, Profits or Gains against which to set off the Reliefs lost)

on the basis of the tax rates current at the Accounting Date;

1.10.2 in any case falling within Clause 1.9.2, the amount of the repayment which would otherwise have been obtained; and

1.10.3 in any case falling within Clause 1.9.3, the amount of Tax which has been saved in consequence of such set off;

1.11 references to:

1.11.1 *'Income, Profits or Gains'* include (without limitation) revenue profits, chargeable gains, and any other similar measure by reference to which Tax is chargeable or assessed;

1.11.2 Income, Profits or Gains earned, accrued or received on or before a particular date or in respect of a particular period shall include Income, Profits or Gains which have been deemed to have been earned, accrued or received at or before the date or in respect of that period for the purposes of any Tax assessment;

1.11.3 any payment or distribution made on or before a particular date shall include:

1.11.3.1 any payment or distribution which on or before that date has fallen due to be made; and

1.11.3.2 any act or transaction which has occurred on or before that date and is or has been deemed to be a payment or distribution for the purposes of any Tax assessment; and

1.11.4 any *'Dividend'* shall include anything which has been deemed to be a dividend or distribution to shareholders or others for the purposes of any Claim to Taxation and shall also include any other event which gives rise to an obligation to account for advance corporation tax or amounts corresponding to or similar to advance corporation tax;

1.12 *'Event'* includes (without limitation) the death of any person, any transaction (including the execution of and completion of all the provisions of the Agreement), action or omission (including omitting to comply with its obligations under the Pay and File regime) and a failure to make sufficient Dividend payments to avoid an apportionment or deemed distribution of income whether alone or in conjunction with any other transaction, action, omission or failure and includes further (without limitation) becoming, being or ceasing to be a member of a group of companies (howsoever defined) for the purposes of any Tax, the combined result of two or more events, the first of which shall have taken place (or be deemed to have taken place) or the commencement of which shall have occurred (or be deemed to have occurred) on or before Completion;

1.13 a company is a 75 per cent subsidiary of the Purchaser if it is a 75 per cent subsidiary of the Purchaser for the purpose of section 838(1) and section 413(7) of the Taxes Act 1988;

1.14 references to Clauses and sub-Clauses are references to clauses and sub-clauses of this Deed; and

1.15 headings are included in this Deed for ease of reference only and shall not affect its interpretation.

2. COVENANT

The Covenantor[s] hereby [jointly and severally] covenant[s] with the Purchaser and (as [a] separate covenant[s]) with the Company that subject to the following provisions of this Deed the Covenantor[s] will, as directed by the Purchaser, pay to the Purchaser or the Company (but so that the Covenantor[s] shall not be liable to pay both the Purchaser and the Company in respect of the same claim) an amount equal to:

2.1 any Tax Liability of the Company arising:

2.1.1 as a consequence of any Event which occurred or was deemed to occur on or before Completion or arising in respect of or with reference to any Income, Profits or Gains which were earned, accrued or received on or before Completion or arising as a consequence of a Dividend declared on or before Completion; or

2.1.2 under section 132 of the Finance Act 1988 by virtue of the relationship on or at any time before Completion of the Company with the migrating company (referred to in that section) where such migrating company is not the Company [or any of the Subsidiaries];

2.1.3 as a result of the disposal by the Covenantor or any member of the Covenantor's group of any asset or of any interest or right over any asset;

2.2 any liability of the Company arising from an obligation to repay the whole or any part of any payment received for group relief pursuant to an arrangement entered into by the Company on or before Completion;

2.3 any amount paid (or payable to the extent it is actually paid) by the Company for a surrender to it of group relief or advance corporation tax in respect of any periods or accounting periods ended on or prior to Completion to the extent that such group relief or advance corporation tax is lost, cancelled or disallowed or otherwise proves to be unavailable to set off against Income, Profits or Gains or Tax for the period in respect of which the surrender is made together with interest calculated in accordance with Clause 12 from the date of payment for such surrenders by the Company until the later of the due date for payment laid down in Clause 10.1.2 and the date when the claim under this Clause is satisfied *provided that* any claim under this Clause 2.3 shall arise only to the extent that the amount paid for group relief or advance corporation tax exceeds any satisfied claim made under Clause 2.1 in respect of taxation assumed to have been discharged by the group relief or surrendered advance corporation tax which is lost, cancelled, disallowed or otherwise unavailable; and

2.4 any costs and expenses [reasonably and properly] incurred by the Purchaser and/or the Company in connection with any such Tax Liability (or claim therefor) or in taking or defending any action under this Deed (such costs and expenses to include reasonable compensation for time spent in connection with such matters as aforesaid by employees of the Purchaser and/or the Company):

provided always if any Tax Liability in respect of which a claim could have been made against the Covenantor[s] under this Deed has been discharged or satisfied by payment by the Company or the Purchaser (whether before or after the date hereof) the covenants given under this Deed shall take effect as a covenant by the Covenantor[s] to reimburse the Company or the Purchaser (as the case may be) for any amount so paid.

3. EXCLUSIONS

The covenants given by Clause 2 shall not cover any Tax Liability of the Company:

3.1 to the extent that specific provision or reserve in respect of such Tax Liability was made in the Accounts excluding the notes thereto and excluding any provision or reserve made in respect of deferred Tax;

3.2 to the extent that such Tax Liability arises or is increased as a result only by reason of any increase in rates of Tax made after the date of the Agreement with retrospective effect;

3.3 which would not have arisen but for a voluntary act or transaction carried out (other than pursuant to a legally binding commitment created on or before Completion) by the Company after Completion and otherwise than in the ordinary course of business and which the Company was aware [or ought reasonably to have been aware] would give rise to such a liability;

3.4 to the extent that such Tax Liability (other than a liability which has become due and payable but has not been settled on or before Completion) arises solely as a result of transactions in the ordinary course of business of the Company after the Accounting Date but on or before Completion *provided that* (without prejudice to the generality of the foregoing) any Claim for Taxation arising from any of the following shall not be regarded for the purposes of this sub-Clause 3.4 as arising 'in the ordinary course of business of the Company':

3.4.1 any event which results in a Tax Liability arising in the Company where such liability is chargeable or attributable primarily to a person other than the Company (including any liability under Part VIII of the Taxes Management Act 1970 (charges on non-residents));

3.4.2 any liability under Part XVII of the Taxes Act 1988 (tax avoidance);

3.4.3 any liability in respect of any distribution (as defined in section 209 of the Taxes Act 1988) or deemed distribution for tax purposes;

3.4.4 any liability arising from the disposal acquisition or deemed disposal or acquisition of any asset other than trading stock; and

3.4.5 any liability arising as a result of the Company ceasing for tax purposes to be a member of any group or associated with any other company;

3.6 to the extent that recovery of such Tax Liability is (at the Purchaser's discretion) made under the Warranties.

4. LIMITATIONS

4.1 The liability of the Covenantor[s] under this Deed:

4.1.1 [subject to Clauses 4.2 and 4.3 shall not (when aggregated with any liability under the Warranties) exceed £ ; and

4.1.2 shall terminate on:

4.1.2.1 the twenty second anniversary of Completion in any case attributable to fraud or negligent conduct of the Company or person acting on its behalf except in respect of any claim under this Deed of which notice in writing is given to the Covenantor[s] before that date containing to the extent reasonably practicable a description of the Claim and the estimated total amount of the Claim;

4.1.2.2 the tenth anniversary of Completion in the case of consequential group relief adjustments mentioned in section 96 Finance Act 1990; and

4.1.2.3 the seventh anniversary of Completion in any other case.]

4.2 The amount in Clause 4.1.1 shall be increased by any amount received by the Covenantor[s] by way of payment or set off under Clauses 5 or 6.

4.3 The amount in Clause 4.1.1 shall be increased by the amount of any liability of the Covenantor[s] arising (or which would have arisen but for Clause 4.1.1) in respect of Taxation which is primarily the liability of or is attributable to a person other than the Company.

[*Note: Ensure that these clauses conform with Agreement*]

5. OVERPROVISIONS

5.1 If the Company's auditors for the time being shall (at the Covenantor[']s['] request and expense) certify at a time when the Company is a 75 per cent subsidiary of the Purchaser that:

5.1.1 any provision for Tax contained in the Accounts (other than a provision for deferred Tax) is an overprovision otherwise than by reason of:

5.1.1.1 a reduction in the rates of Tax or other change in legislation made after Completion with retrospective effect; or

5.1.1.2 any Relief arising after the Accounting Date; or

5.1.1.3 any act of the Purchaser or the Company carried out after the Accounting Date or;

5.1.2 any Tax Liability which has resulted in a payment being made by or becoming due from the Covenantor[s] under this Deed has given rise to a corresponding saving for the Company;

then an amount equal to the value (as certified by the Company's auditors for the time being) of such over-provision or corresponding saving shall be set off first against any payment then due from the Covenantor[s] under this Deed and secondly (to the extent there is any excess) against any payment(s) already made or subsequently due under this Deed in chronological order until exhausted *provided that* to the extent that such over-provision or corresponding saving is set off against any payment already made by the Covenantor[s] that payment shall forthwith be repaid to the Covenantor[s].

6. RECOVERY FROM OTHER PERSONS

Without prejudice to the Covenantor[']s['] obligation to make any payment hereunder, where the Company is entitled to recover from some other person (other than the Purchaser but including any taxing or other competent authorities) any sum in respect of any such Tax Liability as is mentioned in Clause 2, the Company shall as soon as reasonably practicable following it becoming aware of its entitlement notify the Covenantor[s] and if so required by the Covenantor[s] and at [its][their] expense, take all appropriate steps to enforce such recovery (keeping the Covenantor[s] fully informed of the progress of any action taken) and shall account to the Covenantor[s] for any amount so recovered not exceeding the amount paid by the Covenantor[s] hereunder in respect of that Tax Liability.

7. NOTIFICATION OF CLAIMS

7.1 If the Company or the Purchaser (as the case may be) shall become aware of a claim in respect of a Tax Liability relevant for the purposes of this Deed (including any determination or direction in respect of losses which could increase such tax liability) of which the Covenantor[s] [is][are] not then aware it shall as soon as reasonably practicable give written notice thereof to the Covenantor[s].

7.2 If the Covenantor[s] shall indemnify and secure the Company and/or the Purchaser (as the case may be) to its or their (as the case may be) reasonable satisfaction against all liabilities, costs, damages or expenses which may be incurred thereby including any additional claim in respect of a Tax Liability the Company and/or the Purchaser shall take such action as the Covenantor[s] may reasonably request in writing to avoid, dispute, defend, resist, appeal or compromise any claim (such a claim where action is so requested being hereinafter referred to as a *'Dispute'*) *provided that*:

7.2.1 the Company shall not be obliged to appeal against any assessment to Tax or determination raised on it if having given the Covenantor[s] written notice of the receipt of such assessment or determination the Purchaser or the Company (as the case may be) has not within [15]days thereafter received instructions in writing from the Covenantor[s] in accordance with the preceding provisions of this sub-Clause to do so; and

7.2.2 the Company shall not be obliged to take any action under this sub-Clause which would mean contesting any Tax assessment or determination before any court or other appellate body (excluding the authority or body demanding the Tax in question) unless the Covenantor[s] provide[s] the Company with the written opinion of Tax Counsel (of at least 10 years call) that an appeal against the Tax assessment in question will, on the balance of probabilities, be won.

7.3 If the Covenantor[s] do[es] not request the Purchaser or the Company to take any action under sub-Clause 7.2 or fail[s] to indemnify and secure the Purchaser and the Company to their reasonable satisfaction within [10] Business Days of written notice having been given to the Covenantor[s], the Purchaser or the Company shall (without prejudice to their rights under this Deed) be free to pay or settle the Claim on such terms as they may in their absolute discretion consider fit.

7.4 The Covenantor[s] shall not have any rights under this Clause 7 where a claim derives from or arises out of any dishonest or fraudulent act or omission by the Covenantor[s] or by the Company prior to Completion and the Covenantor[s] shall cease to have any such rights if the Purchaser has reasonable grounds to believe that in connection with a claim the conduct of the Covenantor[s] or of the Company amounts to fraud.

8. CONDUCT OF DISPUTE

Notwithstanding that the conduct of a Dispute may be delegated to the Covenantor[s] and dealt with in accordance with [its][their] wishes pursuant to Clause 7:

8.1 the Company and/or the Purchaser shall be kept fully informed of all matters pertaining thereto and shall be entitled to see copies of all correspondence pertaining thereto;

8.2 the appointment of solicitors or other professional advisers shall be subject to the prior approval of the Purchaser, such approval not to be unreasonably withheld or delayed;

8.3 all communications written or otherwise pertaining to the Dispute which are to be transmitted to the Inland Revenue, HM Customs and Excise or other statutory or governmental authority or body whatsoever shall first be submitted to the Purchaser and/or the Company for approval and shall only be finally transmitted if such approval is given, such approval not to be unreasonably withheld or delayed; and

8.4 the Covenantor[s] shall make no settlement or compromise of the Dispute or agree any matter in the conduct of the Dispute which is likely to affect the amount thereof or the future Tax Liability of the Company and/or the Purchaser without the prior approval of the Company or the Purchaser (as may be appropriate), such approval not to be unreasonably withheld or delayed.

9. PAYMENT OF CLAIMS IN THE CASE OF A DISPUTE

Where there is or has been a Dispute and that Dispute relates to a Claim where the Tax the subject matter of the Claim has to be paid before the action requested by the Covenantor[s] in respect of such Claim can be taken, the Covenantor[s] shall make payment of such amount of Tax which must be paid aforesaid forthwith upon service of a notice containing a written demand for the same from the Purchaser and in any other case, the Covenantor[s] shall make payment forthwith on settlement, compromise or abandonment of such Dispute.

10. PAYMENT OF CLAIMS WHERE THERE IS NO DISPUTE

10.1 Subject to the provisions of Clause 9 the Covenantor[s] shall be liable to make payment (the *'due date for payment'*):

10.1.1 in respect of a claim under Clause 2.1 on the date [5] Business Days before the date on which the Company has (or would but for the availability of some other Relief have) become finally liable to pay the Tax the subject of the Claim in question;

10.1.2 in respect of a claim under any of Clauses 2.2, 2.3 and 2.4 on the date [5] Business Days following the date on which notice setting out the amount due (or, in the case of a claim under Clause 2.3, the amount due at the date of the notice) has been served by the Purchaser or the Company on the Covenantor[s]; and

10.1.3 in the case of a claim under Clause 2 in respect of any of the matters referred to in sub-Clause 1.9 which do not involve an actual payment of Tax, the Purchaser and/or the Company shall request the Company's auditors for the time being to certify (at the expense of the Covenantor[s]) the amount of the liability under this Deed and the Covenantor[s] shall be liable to make any payment under Clause 2 [5] Business Days after the date when notice of such certificate is given to the Covenantor[s] in the case of a loss of a repayment of Tax or in a case within sub-Clause 1.9.1 or 1.9.3 on the earlier of such date and the normal due date for payment of United Kingdom corporation tax for the accounting period in which the Company is deprived of the Relief.

11. CONDUCT OF PRE COMPLETION TAX AFFAIRS

The Covenantor[s] agree[s] to provide the Purchaser and the Company with all such reasonable assistance, co-operation and information as they request in respect of pre Completion tax affairs of the Company at the Covenantor['][s]['] expense including (but not limited to) information and co-operation requested in connection with tax computations and returns outstanding at

Completion and in connection with all negotiations, correspondence and agreements in respect of the Company's Tax Liabilities.

12. INTEREST ON LATE PAYMENT

If any payment due to be made by the Covenantor[s] under this Deed is not made on the due date for payment thereof the same shall (in addition to any interest or penalties payable in respect of such liability) carry interest from such due date of payment until actual payment at the rate of [%] above the base rate for the time being of [Bank] calculated and compounded on a daily basis (whether before or after any judgment).

13. DEDUCTIONS FROM PAYMENTS

13.1 All sums payable by the Covenantor[s] to the Purchaser or the Company under this Deed shall be paid free and clear of all deductions or withholdings whatsoever save only as may be required by law.

13.2 If any such deductions or withholdings as are referred to in sub-Clause 13.1 are required by law the Covenantor[s] shall be obliged to pay to the Purchaser or the Company such sum as will after such deduction or withholding has been made leave the Purchaser or the Company with the same amount as it would have been entitled to receive in the absence of any such requirement to make a deduction or withholding.

13.3 If any sum payable by the Covenantor[s] to the Purchaser or the Company under this Deed (including interest under Clause 12 but only to the extent it is paid in respect of sums due under Clause 2.3) shall otherwise be subject to Tax in the hands of the recipient the same obligation to make an increased payment as is referred to in sub-Clause 13.2 shall apply in relation to such Tax liability as if it were a deduction or withholding required by law.

[The following clauses to conform with Agreement]

14. ASSIGNMENT

The Purchaser shall be entitled to assign the benefit of this Deed or any part of it to any other person but [none of] the Covenantor[s] shall [not] be entitled to assign the benefit of this Deed or any part of it save with the prior consent in writing of the Purchaser. [The benefit of this Deed or any part of it may (save as otherwise expressly provided in this Deed) be assigned to any company which is a subsidiary of the relevant party or which is a holding company of that party or which is a subsidiary of that holding company save that any assignment so permitted shall provide that, immediately prior to such company ceasing to be a subsidiary or holding company of the relevant party or a subsidiary of that holding company, such company shall re-assign such assigned benefit to the relevant party.]

15. GOVERNING LAW AND JURISDICTION

This Deed shall be governed by English law and for the benefit of the other parties hereto hereby submit to the jurisdiction of the English Courts.

16. NOTICES

16.1 Any notice or other document to be served under this deed may be delivered personally or sent by pre-paid first class recorded delivery post or facsimile process to the party to be served at his address appearing in this deed or at such other address as he may have notified to the other parties in accordance with this clause.

16.2 Any notice or document shall be deemed to have been served:

16.2.1 if delivered personally, at the time of delivery; or

16.2.2 if posted, at 10 am on the second Business Day after it was put in the post; or

16.2.3 if sent by facsimile process at the expiration of two hours after the time of despatch if despatched.

16.3 In proving service of a notice or document it shall be sufficient to prove that delivery was made or that the envelope containing the notice or document was properly addressed and posted as pre-paid first class recorded delivery letter or that the facsimile message was properly addressed and despatched as the case may be.

16.4 If a notice which is delivered personally or by fax is given:

16.4.1 on a day that is not a Business Day the relevant notice still be deemed to be given by the Business Day next following that day;

16.4.2 after 5.30 pm on a Business Day the relevant notice shall be deemed to be given at 9.30 am on the Business Day next following such Business Day.

17. GENERAL

The Purchaser may release or compromise in whole or in part the liability of [any of] the Covenantor[s] under this Deed or grant any time extension or other concession without affecting [the liability of any other Covenantor or] any other liability of that Covenantor.

18. COUNTERPARTS

This Deed may be entered into in any number of counterparts and by the parties to it on separate counterparts, each of which when so executed and delivered shall be an original but all the counterparts together shall constitute one and the same Deed.

IN WITNESS whereof this Deed has been duly executed the day and year first before written.

SIGNED as a DEED)
by)
in the presence of:)

SIGNED as a DEED)
by)
in the presence of:)

THE COMMON SEAL of)
[VENDOR])
was hereunto affixed in the)
presence of:)

Director

Secretary

THE COMMON SEAL of)
[PURCHASER])
was hereunto affixed in the
presence of:)

Director

Secretary

THE COMMON SEAL of)
[COMPANY])
was hereunto affixed in the)
presence of:)

Director

Secretary

[THE COMMON SEAL of)
[SUBSIDIARY])
was hereunto affixed in the)
presence of:)

Director

Secretary]

[THE COMMON SEAL of)
[SUBSIDIARY])
was hereunto affixed in the)
presence of:)

Director

Secretary]

Appendix 3

Short Form Warranty Clauses

[These warranties may be used where full warranties are inappropriate. When used for a non-UK company they should be reviewed by local tax advisers.]

(a) General

(i) Tax returns

All necessary information, notices, accounts, statements, reports, computations and returns which ought to have been made have been properly and duly submitted by the Company to the relevant taxation or excise authorities and all information, notices, computations and returns submitted to such authorities are true and accurate and are not the subject of any material dispute nor are likely to become the subject of any material dispute.

(ii) Taxation liabilities

All taxation of any nature whatsoever the liability for which arises or arose in respect of the Company has been paid (insofar as such taxation ought to have been paid) and without prejudice to the generality of the foregoing each Company has made all such deductions withholdings and/or retentions as it was obliged or entitled to make and all such payments as should have been made.

(iii) Penalties and interest

No liability to pay any penalty, fine, surcharge or interest in connection with taxation which has not been paid has been incurred by the Company.

(iv) Audits and investigations

The Company has not been nor is likely to become the subject of any investigation audit or visit by any taxation or excise authority.

(b) Payments

All rents, and interest and other sums of an income nature paid or payable by the Company in respect of the Company are or will be wholly allowable as deductions in computing the taxable income of the Company.

(c) Depreciation of tangible assets

(i) No tax would have arisen on the disposal by the Company of any asset if that asset had been disposed of on the Accounts Date for a consideration equal to the book value of that asset shown in or adopted for the purpose of the Accounts.

(ii) No claim has been made by the Companies for the depreciation of any asset for tax purposes in circumstances in which the claim is likely to be disallowed.

(d) Capital gains

(i) The company has only disposed of or acquired any asset in circumstances such that the disposal or acquisition would be treated for tax purposes as an arm's length transaction.

(ii) Execution and completion of this Agreement will not result in a capital gain being realised in the company.

(e) Tax grouping

(i) The tax affairs of the Company have not at any time within the last six years been dealt with on a consolidated basis nor has any tax sharing arrangement (including, without limitation, any arrangement under which tax losses or tax reliefs are surrendered or claimed or agreed to be surrendered or claimed) been entered into in respect of the profits gains or losses of the Company.

(ii) The Disclosure Letter gives details of every written arrangement referred to in paragraph [ ] above.

(iii) Except as provided in the Accounts there exists no obligation on the Company to make any payment in respect of any period ending in or before the Accounts Date under the arrangements referred to in paragraph [ ] above nor do any circumstances exist which may give rise to such an obligation.

(f) Deemed income and gains

Except as provided in the Accounts, there is in relation to the Company no liability to taxation on income or gains except in respect of and to the extent of income and profits accruing to the Company nor do any arrangements exist in relation to the Company which may give rise to any such liability.

(g) Tax avoidance

The company has not been a party to or otherwise been involved in any transaction which is or forms part of a scheme of tax avoidance.

(h) Stamp tax

All stamp tax and similar taxes or duties have been paid in respect of all transactions carried out by the Company.

Appendix 4

Gross up Clauses: Proof

S owes P an amount of money, *A*, on which tax is due at a rate of *R*%. If P makes the payment of tax and recovers it from *X*, then they may proceed in two ways:

I – S may make a single grossed up payment to P, which will be:

$$\text{Total due by grossed-up payment} = A \times \frac{100}{100 - R}$$

II – S may make repeated payments to P. First to cover the amount, *A*, and then subsequent payments to cover the tax which P has had to pay on the previous payments. This proceeds as follows:

An initial payment of *A*,

followed by a 2nd payment of $A \times \frac{R}{100}$,

followed by a 3rd payment of $A \times \left(\frac{R}{100}\right)^2$,

followed by an nth payment of $A \times \left(\frac{R}{100}\right)^{n-1}$.

The total after *N* payments is thus:

Total after *N* payments =

$$A + A \times \left(\frac{R}{100}\right) + A \times \left(\frac{R}{100}\right)^2 + \ldots + A \times \left(\frac{R}{100}\right)^{N-1}$$

which is equal to:

$$A \times \frac{\left(1 - \left(\frac{R}{100}\right)^N\right)}{1 - \left(\frac{R}{100}\right)}$$

Eventually these payments will be of a negligible amount. If the amount *A* is £100,000 and the tax is at 50% then this will be when

$$A \times \left(\frac{R}{100}\right)^{N-1} < 1 \text{ penny}$$

Which will be when $N = 25$ i.e. after 25 payments. Thus the total payment by this method will be:

$$\text{Total by repeated payment} = \frac{A}{1 - \frac{R}{100}}$$

$$= A \times \frac{100}{100 - R}$$

= Total by a single grossed up payment.

The two methods of payment result in the same total payment. However, the second method will take some time with 25 payments being a typical number of payments needed.

Index

Note. The following abbreviations have been used (entered as if set out in full): ACT — Advance Corporation Tax; AIM — Alternative Investment Market; NI — National Insurance; PAYE — Pay as you earn; VAT — Value Added Tax

D

E